Statistics and Experimental Design for Psychologists

A model comparison approach

Statistics and Experimental Design for Psychologists

A model comparison approach

Rory Allen

Goldsmiths, University of London, UK

World Scientific

NEW JERSEY · LONDON · SINGAPORE · BEIJING · SHANGHAI · HONG KONG · TAIPEI · CHENNAI · TOKYO

Published by

World Scientific Publishing Europe Ltd.

57 Shelton Street, Covent Garden, London WC2H 9HE

Head office: 5 Toh Tuck Link, Singapore 596224

USA office: 27 Warren Street, Suite 401-402, Hackensack, NJ 07601

Library of Congress Cataloging-in-Publication Data

Names: Allen, Rory (Rory James), author.
Title: Statistics and experimental design for psychologists : a model comparison approach /
Rory Allen (Goldsmiths, University of London, UK).
Description: New Jersey : World Scientific, [2017]
Identifiers: LCCN 2017007724| ISBN 9781786340641 (hc : alk. paper) |
ISBN 9781786340658 (pbk : alk. paper)
Subjects: LCSH: Psychology--Statistical methods. | Psychology--Experiments. |
Psychometrics. | Experimental design.
Classification: LCC BF39 .A448 2017 | DDC 150.72/7--dc23
LC record available at https://lccn.loc.gov/2017007724

British Library Cataloguing-in-Publication Data
A catalogue record for this book is available from the British Library.

Desk Editors: V. Vishnu Mohan/Mary Simpson/Jennifer Brough/Koe Shi Ying

Typeset by Stallion Press
Email: enquiries@stallionpress.com

Printed in Singapore

Preface

Given the many excellent statistics texts already in the market, why write a new one? The main reason is that there is currently no textbook for psychologists at this elementary level which uses the model comparison viewpoint,[1] and I think this approach is worthy of a wider audience. One reason why students seem to find orthodox statistics so baffling is that affirming the research hypothesis by rejecting the null hypothesis is such a back-handed way of doing things. By contrast, the model comparison viewpoint brings the research hypothesis to prominence from the outset. The present treatment is also closer in spirit to Bayesian statistics, in case students later need to turn to Bayesian methods, which are likely to become more popular.

Another factor that led me to take the model comparison approach was the discovery that using it, one could display a key concept underlying orthodox statistics — the F-ratio — very simply in graphical terms, as the ratio of the slopes of two straight lines on a model comparison plot. This seems to me a more vivid illustration of what is really going on, and more easily understood at an intuitive level, than the usual definition of the F-ratio in terms of algebra. The model comparisons are based on partitioning of sums of squared differences, which is equivalent to the more usual

---

[1] Though there are excellent texts at a more advanced level, cited in the Further Reading section.

partitioning of variance but seems marginally simpler to understand. I have added a short technical note after this preface setting out very briefly what the graphical method involves, to justify this rather sweeping claim to those who are already familiar with the formal properties of the F-ratio but who may well hesitate before investing in this book simply to learn an approach which could amount to little more than rearranging the living-room furniture.

I further believe that model comparison can yield a deep understanding of the basic processes in orthodox statistics, and that depth over a narrow range is preferable to a comprehensive coverage of methods that is explained at a more superficial level. Model comparison provides a mental roadmap that once acquired, can be used to give insight into practically any method in statistics.

The chapters in the book are divided into two sections, Need to Know and Going Deeper. Anyone who studies teaching theory will come across the concepts of deep learning and surface learning, the former being held out as the ideal, and the latter regarded as somewhat disreputable. However, in my experience, students appreciate having a summary of the basic ideas available in "need to know" format. While it may seem regrettable, it is better to have some ability to apply statistical methods without necessarily understanding them in depth, than to have no knowledge at all. And a relatively painless introduction to practical applications may lead to a more fundamental understanding in the fullness of time. Many research psychologists have told me that they did not fully grasp statistics until they had gathered their own data and analysed them. The "need to know" sections at least enable the student to embark on this process of discovery.

I should explain why I have used SPSS to illustrate the statistical methods in this book, and mention some of the alternatives. I used SPSS first because I am familiar with it and its quirks, and second because it is likely to be the package that most psychology students encounter in their own institutions. However, it would be misleading to give the impression that this is the only, or even necessarily the best option available. SPSS requires a licence to operate it. Many students will be able to use their college licence at no extra cost to them personally, and for those students it will be an adequate package for all the applications in this book (and on the website).

For anyone wanting to use SPSS on their own account as a single user, the standard package (as of 2016) costs $2600 a year. They can, on the other hand, download a package called JASP which does much the same as SPSS, but is free. There are some respects in which JASP is not quite as flexible as SPSS, but it is constantly being improved. Moreover, it works much faster (at least on my desktop) than SPSS edition 22 that I am currently using. Anyone using JASP should not find it too difficult to follow the procedures demonstrated in this book using SPSS. There is also a package called rather cheekily, PSPP, which is also free to download, again faster than SPSS, but with a much restricted capability compared with SPSS or JASP.

I should mention R, a very powerful programming tool that does, however, require some familiarity with writing code. It too is free, and with the development of R Studio and R Commander, makes fewer demands on users in terms of syntax writing. I am not personally familiar with it, but it is the package of choice for many.

The text contains references to datasets, on which students can apply the analyses illustrated in this book. These can be downloaded from the book's website, where they are available in three formats: .sav, .xlsx, and .csv. Those with SPSS should be able to download .sav files and open them directly in SPSS. .csv files can be opened in JASP, and will retain the variable names used in the files. I will also give instructions on the website for importing .xlsx and .csv files into SPSS, in case anyone has difficulties with downloading the .sav files. Files in any of these formats can be imported into R. One disadvantage of not using SPSS is that the "labels" for levels of variables are lost when a non-SPSS program is used to open any of these files. So, for each dataset, I will include a guide to what the numerical values for the nominal variables correspond to: for example, 1 = autism group, 2 = Williams syndrome group etc.

So much for what this book contains: now for what it doesn't. Traditionally, books on research methods tend to concentrate on either statistics or experimental design. This has always seemed to me an unnatural division: design and analysis are part of a single process within the research cycle. In the first drafts of this book, I tried to include an adequate treatment of both areas up to the level expected for students taking an MSc course in psychology. I then discovered that a book dealing fully with both areas would be far too long for a single volume. As a result, I decided to restrict the print version of the book to a basic treatment of statistics and research design up to multifactorial and repeated measures ANOVA and their related experimental designs.

The website associated with this book contains extensive further material, not only extending the coverage in the earlier chapters, but also dealing with multiple regression, ANCOVA and exploratory factor analysis. It also contains sets of examples with solutions, besides the datasets illustrating the methods explained in the book. In addition, it provides a basic coverage of the vital area of power analysis.

The website also contains a treatment of meta-analysis, which is an area that will at some stage probably be of interest to every researcher, as well as a chapter on signal detection theory. Current treatments of meta-analysis and SDT seem to me to make the topic appear harder than it needs to be: the fundamental ideas can be quite simply understood, and at least a passing familiarity with the underlying concepts will help to remove the mystique that seems to surround these two areas.

The website also goes in more detail into the ideas contained in the so-called *new experimentalism*. This is mentioned briefly in the book, but I believe that its value as a philosophical basis for psychology is under-appreciated. Classical approaches such as logical positivism, and neo-classicists such as Popper, assume that the aim of science is to find universal "covering laws", whereas NE emphasises the importance of reliable accounts which are specific and local, and the replicability of experimental procedures as a whole. In studying the human brain, the most complex system we know, specific and local questions seem already ambitious enough. Moreover, NE's concerns with replicability tie in well with the approach to internal, external and other validities developed by Campbell and Stanley and their successors, which is now an established pillar of experimental design in psychology. The website describes validity using these ideas.

I would like to express my thanks to Windy Dryden for his generous advice, vital help and ongoing encouragement to write this book, to my publishers and editor for their patience, to Alan Pickering for teaching me nearly all I know about statistics and to my students from whom I learned the rest, to Geoff Bird, whose lab meetings were a masterclass in the art of experimental design, to Mary Claire Halvorson, who taught me how to teach, to Alwyn Taylor for suggesting the King Solomon example, to Jet Hilborne for helpful discussions about causality, and above all to my wife Pam Heaton for her continual support, encouragement and persistent belief that this book would eventually be finished.

Online supplementary material is hosted on http://www.worldscientific.com/worldscibooks/ 10.1142/q0019#t=suppl.

Technical Note

The aim of this note is to explain, for those who already understand the formulae for the F-ratio, how to derive its geometric counterpart. Mathematically, my version is identical to the usual one: its purpose is to show visually what the F-ratio is doing, as in the diagram at the end of this note. Take the example of a one-way ANOVA, with the independent variable comprising k different groups and a sample size of N, used to analyse the results of an experiment. The data assigns a value of the dependent variable for each point in the sample. A model attempts to reproduce the data by assigning each to sample point a value determined by that model. The measure of how far a model departs from the data, is given by the lack-of-fit sum of squares (lofsos): the sum of the squares of the differences between the actual value of the DV and the model predicted value, for each sample point.

The null model assigns to each sample point the overall sample mean, the causal model[1] assigns to each sample point the mean of the group to which that sample point belongs, and the saturated model assigns to the sample point the exact value of the DV for that

---

[1] I am assuming here that the experimental design is such that a significant result *does* allow us to assert a causal relation between the IV and the DV. The method is applicable, of course, more generally, but in that case one has to use some alternative name such as "full model" or "IV-determined model" which requires further explanation.

sample point. The lofsos for the null model is by definition the total sum of squares, SS_{total}, the lofsos for the causal model is the within group or error sum of squares, SS_{error}, and the lofsos for the saturated model is zero. The causal model is the best fit to the (usual) research hypothesis that the DV is causally linked to the IV.

Model parameters are those numbers needed to specify that model, that must be estimated from the data.[2] The null model has one parameter (the overall mean), the causal model has k parameters (group means), and the saturated model, N parameters (namely, the actual values of the DV for the dataset). If the null model is used as a baseline, the "degrees of freedom" for the other two models can be naturally defined as the difference in parameter numbers between the null model and the other two models. So the df for the causal model is $df_{between} = k - 1$ and the df for the saturated model is $df_{total} = N - 1$. The "error" or "within groups" df can be defined as the difference between the number of parameters for the saturated model and the causal model, so that $df_{error} = N - k$.

Plot the three models on a diagram with parameter number as the horizontal axis, and lofsos value as the vertical axis (it will be helpful to refer to Fig. A at this point). The causal model point must fall below the line joining the null and saturated models (the "null line") if it is to provide useful information about the data. The causal model plot falls below the null line if and only if the line joining it to the null model point has a steeper slope than the line joining it to the saturated model point: put another way, the "elbow" on the bent line connecting the causal model to the null and saturated models must point downwards. (As explained in Appendix C, the null line has a real significance: it can be interpreted in a certain sense as a plot line of the expected value of the lofsos of any model if the null hypothesis is true.)

The vertical distance from the null to the causal model plots is $SS_{between}$, and the horizontal distance is $df_{between}$, so the slope of the first line, joining the null and causal models, is $MS_{between}$: this can

---

[2]Strictly speaking, it is not the model but the hypothesis that has well defined parameters. The model is the result of substituting actual numbers for the parameters, which in the hypothesis are unspecified.

also be regarded as the "signal". The vertical distance from the causal to the saturated model is SS_{error}, the horizontal distance is df_{error}, and therefore the slope of the second line, joining the causal and saturated models, is MS_{error}, which can be seen as the "noise" component. The ratio of the two slopes is $\frac{MS_{between}}{MS_{error}} = F(df_{between}, df_{error})$, or the signal-to-noise ratio. Therefore, the condition that the causal model plot should fall below the null line is that $F(df_{between}, df_{error})$ should be greater than one, or allowing for random variation, that it should be *significantly* greater than one, the criterion for rejecting the null hypothesis.

It is an immediate consequence of the definitions that if the null hypothesis is true, the slope of the null line is an unbiased estimator of the variance of the DV in the population from which the sample is randomly drawn. It is not hard to see that the slopes of the lines joining the causal model plot to the null and saturated models (slope 1 and slope 2, say) are also unbiased estimators of the population variance. If the null hypothesis prevails, the expected values of the slopes of the null line, and of the other two lines, will all be equal to one another. In that case, the expected position of the plot of the causal model will lie on the null line.

This observation leads to the usual justification for calculating the *F*-ratio, that if the null hypothesis is true, the numerator and denominator are two separate estimates of population variance, so both should be approximately equal. So conversely, if the *F*-ratio is sufficiently large, it can be concluded that the null hypothesis can be rejected. However, this does not explain why the test is one-tailed, that is, why we are only interested in excessively large values of *F*, not excessively small values. The model plot shows that only group models plotting *below* the null line are of interest, and so only *large F* values need be considered in deciding whether to reject the null in favour of the group model. Incidentally, the fact that if the null hypothesis is true, then the causal model will on average plot on the null line, does not imply that the expected value of the *F*-ratio is one; it is in fact $df_{error}/(df_{error} - 2)$. This does not invalidate the analysis; it is due to the nonlinear relationship between slope 1, slope 2 and slope 1/slope 2.

This diagram can be extended to multifactorial ANOVA, but in this case several model points need to be plotted, one for each main effect, and one each for the interactions; there are also issues about which convention to adopt on sums of squares (types I, II or III). The diagram can also be used to illustrate the value of a popular effect size measure in ANOVA, namely η^2. More interestingly, it can also be used to show the key disadvantage of η^2, the fact that it is biased in favour of overestimating the true effect size; and the obvious correction suggested by the diagram yields in a very natural way one of the recommended alternatives, namely ε^2, as I demonstrate in Appendix A.

Purely for illustrative purposes, the diagram for a one-way ANOVA on a "baby" dataset with $N = 20$, $k = 5$ is plotted below. The dataset, TechNoteDataset, is also available online. For this example, the total sum of squares is 33.002 and the error sum of squares is 16.43. $F(4, 15) = 3.782$, and this is the ratio of the slopes of the lines connecting the null and group models, and the group and saturated models. This F-value is significant at the 0.05 level, so the group model is established as lying below the dashed line of minimal models, and the null model can be rejected in favour of the group model.

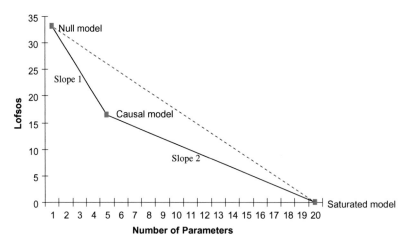

Fig. A.   The F-ratio is *Slope* 1/*Slope* 2.

About the Author

After completing an undergraduate degree in mathematics, I worked in the Diplomatic Service from 1972 to 2004. In 2004, I began a one-year MSc in Research Methods at Goldsmiths and subsequently studied for a PhD in psychology, focusing on the impact of music on autism, which was awarded in 2010. In 2011–2012, I conducted a grant-funded study continuing my PhD research. In addition to this research, from 2008 to the present I taught courses in research methods at MSc level in Goldsmiths, and in 2012–2013 carried out a study, funded by a Goldsmiths learning and teaching fellowship, into the effectiveness of screencasts as a teaching aid. This led to the award of the PG Cert in 2013, and in 2014 I became a Fellow of the Higher Education Academy. I have authored or co-authored 14 papers in peer-reviewed journals relating to psychology and statistical methods.

Contents

Chapter 1
What is Science?

The master said: "Yu, do you want me to teach you what knowledge is? If you know something, you must state what you know. If you do not know something, you must confess that you do not know. That is knowledge."

Analects of Confucius, II, 17

SUMMARY

The experimental method as a test of rival hypotheses, involving the creation of conditions in which the hypotheses would give different results. Causality and causal hypotheses. The relationship between hypotheses and models. Model comparison as a basic procedure in science. Effect sizes and causal models. The role of variables, and their types. Populations and samples. Occam's razor and goodness of fit to data as the twin criteria behind model comparison. An analogy with animal behaviour.

NEED TO KNOW

A story told of Solomon, King of Israel, who was famous for his wisdom, concerns two women who appeared before him both disputing that they were the true mother of a baby boy. Each woman appeared to have an equal claim, but one of them obviously had to be lying. The king was asked to resolve the dispute, but without clear evidence either way, what could he do?

In an episode of "House, M.D." called "Moving the Chains", the medical team are faced with a patient with a mysterious condition. They finally narrow it down to just two possibilities: lymphoma, and Takayasu's arteritis. The problem is that the two conditions cannot be treated in the same way. If the patient has lymphoma, then the recommended treatment is to remove his spleen, but if the correct diagnosis is Takayasu's, then he needs to be put on a course of steroids. Giving him the wrong treatment may kill him. What can they do?

Solomon resolved the problem by asking for a sword to be brought, saying that as both women appeared to have an equal right to the baby, he would divide the baby and give half of it to each. One of the two announced herself content with this decision, whereas the other asked for the entire baby to be handed over to her rival. Solomon concluded that the second woman was the true mother and awarded the child to her.

In the second story, House told his team to put the patient on an ethanol drip. In the event that the patient had lymphoma, then the drip would make him itchy. If the disease was Takayasu's, then he would lose his radial pulse. The outcome would make clear what disease the patient was suffering from and therefore which treatment was appropriate, without endangering his life.

These two stories have something in common. There were two possibilities (the baby's true mother was the first, or the second woman; the patient had lymphoma, or Takayasu's), but not enough information to determine which was true. It was important to know which of the possibilities was correct, because a decision had to be made (giving the baby to one of the women; treating the patient in a certain way), and making the best decision depended on knowing which possibility was correct. The problem was resolved in each case by taking some action — doing an experiment, if you will — and observing the outcome. The two possibilities would give different outcomes, and therefore observing the outcomes would enable the correct possibility to be inferred by a sort of reverse logic. Knowing the correct possibility enabled the best decision to be taken in terms of giving the baby to its real mother, or giving the correct treatment to the patient.

It is a bit clumsy to refer all the time to the "two possibilities" in these stories. It is better to refer to them as "hypotheses": things which might be true about the world. In both cases, there are two hypotheses, and one of them must be right, but not both. The logic of how Solomon and House both dealt with the problem can be illustrated using something called an $X - O$ diagram,[1] introduced by Campbell and Stanley:

$$H_1 \Rightarrow X - O_1$$

$$H_2 \Rightarrow X - O_2$$

The H's represent the two possibilities, X is the "intervention", and the O's represent certain features of the outcomes.

The symbol "$\Rightarrow$", the mathematical sign for "implies", means that if the hypothesis to the left of it is true, then if the intervention X is applied, it will produce the outcome (or observation) O. In the Solomon example, H_1 could represent the possibility that the baby belongs to the first women, H_2 that the second woman is the mother. X represents the king's threat to cut the baby in half. O_1 is the response where the first woman offers to give up the baby, and the second woman agrees to its being divided, and O_2, to the response where the second woman gives up the baby and the first one wants it cut in half. In the House instance, the hypotheses represent lymphoma and Takayasu's respectively, X is the ethanol drip, and the two outcomes are the patient feeling itchy, and the loss of a radial pulse. The point is that it is known *in advance* that if H_1 is true, than the intervention X will be followed by O_1, and similarly with the other possibility.

---

[1] In fact, Campbell and Stanley's version applies to different groups of individuals on the left side of the diagram, rather than different hypotheses. I have adapted it to the present use since it expresses the situation economically. For details of the book, see the Further Reading section.

The situation described above, where we have two or more hypotheses and an experiment which will give distinct outcomes depending on which of them is true, was first described in this general form by the philosopher Francis Bacon. He called this type of procedure an *instantia crucis*, usually translated as "instance of the fingerpost". If the two outcomes are different, they provide a signpost telling us which of the two hypotheses must be true. This idea might be regarded as the core of the experimental method in science.[2] For short, I will refer to this as the Bacon paradigm.

When Bacon introduced the idea of the *instantia crucis*, he wrote that one might meet one accidentally, but that "for the most part they are new, and are expressedly and designedly sought for and applied" (Aphorism 36 of The New Organon). In other words, he envisaged that hypotheses should be distinguished not through mere passive observation, but by creating experiments that were designed to distinguish between the alternatives. The "creating experiments" part consists in finding the right intervention, X, which will produce distinguishable outcomes for the two hypotheses.

There are several reasons why the method works in the cases considered above. The first feature of this experimental design is perhaps an obvious or even trivial point, though worth making. It is that the intervention, X, is the same in both cases. Clearly, this must be so if the experiment is to be carried out in ignorance of which hypothesis is true.

The second feature is that we must be able to predict in advance what the outcome O would be for each of the two possible hypotheses. We must be able to *deduce* that if H_1 is true, then after applying X, we would observe O_1, and that if H_2 is the case, then after X, we would observe O_2. This combination of stating hypotheses with deducing their consequences explains why this approach is

---

[2] This method is referred to by some writers as "induction by elimination", though this could be misleading as induction is really something quite different. The strength of the present design is that it is based on deduction, not induction. Induction has had a bad press since the work of Karl Popper.

sometimes called the **hypothetico-deductive method** (it is also the core of what the medical profession refers to as "differential diagnosis"). Solomon's grasp of psychology told him that *if* the first woman was the mother, she would rather give up the baby than see it killed, but that the second woman would not care: outcome O_1. Similarly, if the second woman was the mother, she would offer to give it up: outcome O_2. He could predict this in advance, even without knowing which alternative was true.

The third feature is that the observations O_1 and O_2 should *differ*. Ideally, there is no ambiguity or overlap between the two outcomes. In that case, if we know that O_1 has happened then we know that O_2 has *not* happened, and so the only possible conclusion we can draw from this is that H_2 is false.[3] Since one of the hypotheses must be true, it has to be H_1. We know in advance in this no-overlap case that the outcome of the experiment will show *decisively* one way or the other which hypothesis is correct. In the opposite extreme, when the observations are predicted to be identical for the two hypotheses, then it would be foolish to bother with that intervention: no useful information could be obtained which would help distinguish the hypotheses, and the whole exercise would be a waste of effort. It may happen, in realistic cases, that the situation lies somewhere between these two extremes as we will see below.

I have of course simplified the situation in the simple, two alternatives diagram given above. It may be that there might be three, four or even more possible hypotheses in any particular case. It might also be that there are other potential hypotheses that we have not considered, but should have done. In the Solomon case, this problem did not arise because it could be assumed that one of the women was the true mother. But in the second case, where the only options considered by the medical team were lymphoma and Takayasu's arteritis, it eventually turned out that the true cause of the illness was neither of these. This illustrates a valuable lesson: an

---

[3] This deduction uses a principle known as *modus tollens* or "the way of denying". Though it sounds rather Zen, the idea apparently originated with the Stoics.

experimental design is only as good as the assumptions that go into it, and the conclusions are only dependable if the true hypothesis has actually been included in the initial set of hypotheses.

Of course, if we are lucky enough to generate experimental data that single out one hypothesis, say H_3, from the whole set as the true one, that is not the end of the matter. No hypothesis is either complete or totally accurate, and in practice the problem remains, of improving its precision and range. The next stage might be to elaborate H_3 to a set of possible more detailed refinements, H_{31}, H_{32}, H_{33}, and to discover which one is most correct; and so on.

Note that the sort of application of the hypothetico-deductive method described above might be described as using the method *in parallel*: different hypotheses are being compared at the same time. The more traditional view (as for example in Medawar's book, see Further Reading) uses the method applied *in series*: a particular hypothesis is tested under a sequence of different conditions, to discover at what point it breaks down; a modified hypothesis is then created to take account of this, which is in turn tested to destruction and a second modification is made, and so on. I would suggest that in practice, the parallel method is more difficult to use well, but more productive when it does work.

I also have not discussed what a set of possible hypotheses might look like in the case of psychology research. Both examples given above referred to very specific instances involving certain individuals, whereas research usually deals with hypotheses that are expected to apply across a whole range of instances and to have a degree of generality. Science is sometimes said to have the making of general statements as one of its central aims. To illustrate an example of a more general situation as provided in an actual published paper, consider the experiment described in Kirkby *et al.* (2011),[4] in which the "magnocellular theory" of dyslexia is put to the test.

---

[4] The paper is freely available online at https://www.ncbi.nlm.nih.gov/pmc/articles/PMC3208567/pdf/pone.0027105.pdf.

This hypothesis claims that developmental dyslexia is caused by a general visual impairment, specifically by deficient binocular coordination. It is known that children with dyslexia show poor binocular coordination when reading, and the magnocellular hypothesis maintains that this is the underlying condition that causes the reading difficulties in dyslexia. This is the first hypothesis. The second hypothesis is that on the contrary, the underlying cause of dyslexia is not a simple visual impairment, but a higher level cognitive impairment in the processing of actual words compared with non-verbal stimuli.

The researchers reasoned that if the first hypothesis were true, then children with dyslexia would show similar impairments compared with typical children in both a reading task, and in a dot-scanning task which did not involve processing words, but which required eye movements similar to those involved in reading and therefore was a measure of binocular coordination. If the second hypothesis were true, however, the performance of the dyslexic children on the dot-processing task would be normal compared with typical children, but they would be impaired on the reading task.

Since the two outcomes are predicted to be different on the basis of the two hypotheses, this study evidently used the Bacon paradigm. The study in fact discovered that the binocular coordination deficit in the dyslexic children tested *was* specific to the reading task, and was not apparent in the dot-fixation task. The authors concluded that the first hypothesis could be rejected in favour of the second one.

In my experience, this kind of example is quite rare. Few research papers in psychology directly compare two (or more) alternative causal hypotheses as in the Kirkby *et al.* paper. The majority of papers in psychology involve a simpler idea, explained below. However, even these papers often include a causal hypothesis comparison at some point, as a subsidiary argument. This involves what are known as "construct confounds". Put simply, if I apply an experimental treatment to a group of people, and observe an effect, the effect may not be due to the treatment itself but to something different that is inseparable from the treatment but distinct from it.

For example, if a sample of autistic children is given regular music therapy and show an improvement in social skills, a critic may claim that the improvement is due not to the music, but to the regular interaction with the therapist. The two hypotheses would then be "the musical experience causes the improvement" and "interaction with the therapist causes the improvement". To forestall this criticism, the experiment can then incorporate a subsidiary condition in which another group of children has a similar level of interaction with a therapist as the music group, but doing something non-musical such as art practice. If the results show no effect in the art group, then it was likely the music itself that was responsible for the effect in the music therapy group. This also uses the Bacon paradigm.

I claimed above "The majority of papers in psychology involve a simpler idea": on the face of it, many papers consider only *one* hypothesis. Many research programmes begin with a speculative idea of the form "A causes B", and the aim of the research is to discover whether this is true or false.[5]

An example of a simple research hypothesis might be that listening to music changes a person's heart rate. The challenge may appear simply to prove the hypothesis true or false. There seems to be only one hypothesis on offer. But the problem can be posed in a different way, which makes it similar to the $X - O$ pattern shown above. The first hypothesis is that listening to music alters heart rate, but the second hypothesis is that listening to music does *not* alter the heart rate. In terms of the Bacon paradigm:

$$\text{Music alters heart rate} \quad \Rightarrow \quad \text{Music} - \text{altered heart rate,}$$

$$\text{Music does not alter heart rate} \quad \Rightarrow \quad \text{Music} - \text{unaltered heart rate.}$$

---

[5] Incidentally, any research effort must include such a **research hypothesis** at the outset. One of the commonest problems students face when they come to write up the results of a research project is they do not know how to begin the report, because they never had a clear research hypothesis to begin with.

This may appear to be a very trivial statement. However, it is important to bear the second hypothesis in mind. It is known as the **null hypothesis**: null, because it states that there is *no* causal connection between music and heart rate. It is important because in most statistical analyses, it is the null hypothesis which occupies centre stage. The way it works is that the outcome of the experiment is examined, and if it is found that it is inconsistent with the null hypothesis, then the null hypothesis is rejected, and the experimental hypothesis is confirmed. "Inconsistent with the null hypothesis" has a very specific and technical meaning here, which will be explained later.

There is one point worth making at this stage. You will often read that the aim of any scientific study or experiment is to "test a hypothesis". In one sense this is wrong, or at least, it is easy to interpret the claim in a misleading sense. I am not aware of any experiment which tests just a single hypothesis. Experiments do not *test*, they *compare* hypotheses, and for any comparison there clearly must be two or more things to be compared. This pedantic insistence on comparing rather than testing hypotheses is important, because it is the basis for the claim that statistical analysis is mainly about model comparison. It turns out that models are a way of making hypotheses concrete and specific; comparing models then stands as a proxy for comparing hypotheses. The hypothesis that is left standing at the end of this process, is the one that we claim to be true.

But this is to anticipate. I will close this section by attempting to summarise the ideas. A research challenge usually involves finding out which of two or more possible hypotheses is true, where the hypotheses cover the possible statements about some facet of the world that we are interested in. The art of experimental design is to plan some intervention that will give rise to a range of possible outcomes, one for each hypothesis, such that the outcomes are *as distinct as possible*.

This can be put in a slightly different way. At the outset of a research project, there will always be a degree of uncertainty about which of a series of possible hypotheses is the true one. The best design will be that which is expected to reduce the uncertainty by as much as possible, consistent of course with the resources available to carry out the study.[6]

Choices need to be made over not only the alternative hypotheses that need to be considered, but also the type of intervention X to be applied, and the precise aspects of the outcome O that are of interest. There may of course be no "intervention" as such: the experiment may be purely observational. But even then decisions have to be made about how to do the observation. *The act of observation is itself an intervention,* and describing O as the "outcome" to be observed is not enough: the researcher must specify in advance which aspects of the outcome are significant. Usually this requires a list of measurements which need to be made, that represent the important features of the outcome. The choice of measurements is a key part of any experiment.

Models and hypotheses

I will be referring to both hypotheses and models in this book. I define a hypothesis as a statement which contributes to the explanation of a phenomenon of interest. An example might be "Guinness is good for you": this hypothesis claims that consumption of a particular brand of Irish stout helps to explain some of the variability in human wellbeing. A model is a mathematical formula (sometimes a very simple one) that gives precision to a hypothesis: for example, "drinking a pint of Guinness increases a person's score on the PANAS[7] scale by five units on average".

It is a curious fact that although hypotheses are the rock stars of science, we can often only determine whether they are true or

---

[6] If you are a fan of information theory and Bayesian statistics, you might want to express this as: "the task of experimental design is to maximize the expected posterior reduction in the entropy of the set of hypotheses within given resource constraints". For the purposes of this book, experimental design will be treated in a much more practical and limited way than this.

[7] The positive and negative affect score, a common questionnaire-based measure of wellbeing.

not by digging down to the level of models, which are like the sound engineers and stage-builders which enable the stars to perform. Hypotheses take all the glory, but it is the models that do the heavy lifting.

In understanding the model-based approach to science, one needs to be able to develop a facility for switching back and forth between the language of hypotheses and that of models. In formulating causal relations, it usually makes sense to state them broadly, using the language of hypotheses. If we attempt to make a causal statement precise, it becomes a model. The next section goes further into models, and the following one into cause–effect relations, where both hypotheses and models come into play.

Models in general

The word "science" derives from the Latin word for knowledge, "scientia". This book is based on the approach that knowledge involves not merely the accumulation of facts, but the construction and improvement of models of the world. Here, models are basically things that exist in the mind (or on computers), and that we can control. But no model exists in isolation: it needs to refer to some "thing" in the world. An example might be a mathematical model of how the world's climate will change over the next 50 years. We can run this on computers to our hearts' content. The "thing" it refers to, is the world's climate. We cannot control the climate, at least not directly. The climate model will, however, enable us to predict, more or less accurately, what the real climate will do. So a model involves **something independent** of the world — an idea, a computer program, a physical model, a mathematical equation — and a specification of how the idea and its parts **correspond** to things in the real world.

It is this dual nature, involving the linkage between something mental and something physical, which gives the concept of models their power. We can play around with models, and use them to tell us something practical about the world, without taking the risks that playing with the real world might entail. We can use a climate model to see what happens if we fail to restrict carbon dioxide emissions, for example. If the result shows a runaway greenhouse effect which would be a disaster for humanity, the disaster is (at that stage) merely hypothetical. We can afford to make many mistakes with the model, in the sense that we can try out the effects of different policy decisions and see which work and which do not; if we make a mistake in managing the real world, by contrast, we may have no second chance.

Models are usually mathematical. An example is Kepler's first law: the orbit of a planet is an ellipse with the Sun at one of the foci. Here the ideas are "ellipse" and "foci"; the correspondences are "orbit", and "Sun". Non-mathematical explanations are probably better classified as hypotheses, but these have, in common with models, the requirement that an idea is linked with reality via some correspondence. "Smoking causes lung cancer" is a hypothesis; the idea is the "causes" part, and the correspondences are the definitions of "smoking" and "lung cancer".

Why do we need models? Models enable us to **explain, predict** and **control** our environment. If a model is unsuccessful at predicting the world, we may wish to change the model, so that it fits reality better. The process of changing and improving models is a sophisticated form of learning. Nearly all animals have the capacity to modify their basic behaviour through some kind of learning; in a crude sense, a rat that learns to find food in a maze is probably using an internal model of the maze to predict the presence of food. Models which predict how the environment will behave enable animals to survive, and better models enable them to survive better, which explains why learning is important. The process of improving models is equally important in science, indeed in a certain sense it *is* science.

Prediction often implies the ability to *control*. A climate model which shows that increasing CO_2 concentration by 50 parts per million will result in a sea-level rise of one meter, may make it possible to limit sea-level rise to below that figure by controlling the emission of CO_2 into the atmosphere. Prediction of an outcome and control of that outcome are, as far as the model is concerned, the same thing, though in practical terms they may of course be very different.

Models are therefore involved in two processes. One is the improvement of models, and the other is the exploitation of models. The world cannot always wait for scientists to build perfect models, so there may be tension between improving the model, and putting it to use. The debate about climate change illustrates the problem. Some advise that we need to develop fully reliable models before taking action. Others consider that we need to take action now on the predictions of admittedly inaccurate models, as otherwise it may be too late. This debate lies outside science, but should be informed by an understanding of it.

Science is a dynamic process. The **aim** of this process is to construct accurate models of natural phenomena. The **process itself** involves taking existing models, comparing them, and improving them by creating better models, until our models reach an acceptable level of accuracy. This claim raises two questions. Firstly, where does the process of model development begin? This is an important issue, but I will not attempt to answer this question right here. There is a long history of attempts to justify generating models from scratch, and some philosophers of science[8] claim that this is impossible. It is a chicken and egg problem. For our immediate purposes, it is not necessary to answer it.

Secondly, as part of the process of improving models, it is obvious that some means must exist to **compare** models. Otherwise, how can one tell whether a newly developed model is better than the existing one? The notion of comparison involves a willingness to admit that an existing model is inferior to a new one, which may bring with it the need for a degree of professional humility (hence the relevance of the quote from Confucius). The mechanics of how to do the comparison, forms the backbone of this book. But first we need to be more specific.

Causality

Causality seems to be closely connected to the concept of explanation. This is a complicated idea, and there are still philosophical

---

[8] Most famously, Karl Popper.

difficulties with it. The simplest definition of explanation is that it seeks to answer the question "**why** does a phenomenon happen?", and the answer attempts to show the existence of a cause for the phenomenon. Any complete account of explanation, and of causality, seems to require different *levels* of explanation. The issue has a long history, going back at least as far as Aristotle and his four causes. There is more on this in the website for those interested.

For present purposes, the term "explanation" will be taken to refer to the process of **establishing cause–effect relationships between two phenomena**. This usually starts with the observed effect, and tries to work backwards to the cause. A criminal investigator, an archaeologist and a geologist may all be in the situation of observing an effect (a body, a ruin, or a rock stratum) and may be interested in finding the cause that was responsible for it (a criminal, a culture, or a geological process). Models in psychology research are often causal in this sense.

In the physical sciences causality is seldom made explicit, with some exceptions such as geology where it appears to be important. However, the social sciences and of course the medical sciences[9] use the concept extensively. We all understand intuitively what causality is about. An event happens — the cause — and is followed by another event — the effect. The causal claim consists in the statement that the cause is always followed by the effect, and that the link between cause and effect is necessary in some sense. The claim is justified by showing that when the cause is present, the effect always follows.

If you are convinced by this argument, beware. In the supplementary material, I show that if causality is limited to this condition *on its own*, we have a thought process characteristic not of science, but of magical beliefs. The simplest correct formulation of causality involves a second claim. We need to show not just that the cause is always followed by the effect, but that the **absence** of cause is always followed by the **absence** of the effect. This is usually

---

[9] With symptoms being the effect, the challenge is to diagnose the disease, which is the cause.

supplemented by the statement that the cause must always occur **before** the effect in time. A deeper justification involves showing the mechanism by which the cause leads to the effect — that is, the chain of intermediate causal links leading from original cause to effect — but this raises issues which I do not want to open up here.[10]

To summarise: the simplest causal claim involves a relationship between two things in the world, a cause C and an effect E, satisfying the following criteria:

(1) • C precedes E in time
 • When C is present, E is always present.
 • When C is absent, E is always absent.

An example is if C is the presence of the malaria parasite in the blood, and E is the symptoms of malaria.[11]
Note that this link between C and E can also run the opposite way, and there is *still* a causal link. Suppose we have the situation where:

(2) • C precedes E in time
 • When C is present, E is always absent.
 • When C is absent, E is always present.

In a region where everyone has malaria, C might be the administration of an anti-malarial drug. Evidently there is still a link between C and E, and in this case it is of great practical importance.

Criteria (1) and (2) both express causal links. In the first case we might say C **causes** E, and in the second case, that C **suppresses** E.

---

[10] The intermediate causal links are usually ones which are already understood and often very general. Explaining a causal relation in terms of intermediate links of this kind is satisfying because it endorses the value of our existing understanding of basic processes. Simply stating a cause–effect relation is sometimes referred to slightingly as "black box causality". It could be argued that all explanations, however deep, must at least *begin* with black box causality.
[11] I am ignoring complications, such as some individuals not showing symptoms even though the infectious agent is present, which happens with most diseases.

The presence of two different causal links, (1) and (2), is really an unnecessary complication. Both can be summarised in the following form:

(3) • *C* precedes *E* in time
 • The presence of *C* causes a subsequent **change** in *E*.
 • If *C* is not present, there is no change in *E*.

For the benefit of those who are interested in Aristotle's pioneering work on causality, this is closer to his original definition of an effect as a "change or movement" in something.

One great benefit of definition (3) is that it enables us to consider effects which are not just "there" or "not there" like black and white, but those with shades of grey involving more subtle effects, such as an improvement in life expectation caused by better health services, or a change in blood pressure caused by taking a particular drug. In other words, it enables us to consider effects which are **changes in some variable**. This is will be fundamental in the rest of the book.

In fact it will be better still to take a slightly different formulation of causality, extending the key idea of change, to include not only the effect but the cause as well. So finally there is a causal link between *C* and *E* if:

(4) • A **change** in *C* is always followed by a subsequent **change** in *E*.
 • If *C* does not change, neither does *E*.

What is the opposite of a causal link? It must be some statement to the effect that: A change in phenomenon *C has no effect on E*, or *E* is **independent** of *C*. When *C* changes, there is no subsequent change in *E*.

Causal hypotheses and models

I will refer to a "causal hypothesis" as a statement involving the *presence or absence of a causal relationship*. In other words, a hypothesis may take the form "*C* causes *E*" or "*C* suppresses *E*", in which case it is a **causal hypothesis**, or it may take the opposite form "*E* is independent of *C*", which will be called a **null hypothesis**. However, a causal hypothesis is not generally a model: it is not specific enough. A causal hypothesis states that there *is* a causal link; it does not state *how strong* the causal link is.

Take as an example, someone studying the need for imposing legal limits on drinking, who is interested in the causal hypothesis: "drinking alcohol causes longer reaction times in drivers". There are already practical complications. For example, to answer the question "does drinking alcohol cause longer reaction times?" we need to know who is doing the drinking, since people differ in their tolerance of alcohol. This raises the issue of how far individual variability affects the causal link. Setting this aside for the moment, the obvious question is, *how badly* are reaction times affected? How much alcohol needs to be consumed to delay reaction times by, say, 100 ms? Policy makers will not be impressed by a scientist who claims the presence of a causal link, unless there is some evidence not only that an effect exists, but that the *size* of the effect is sufficiently large to be of practical concern.

If there is one clear trend in orthodox statistical thinking in recent years, it is that **effect sizes** are essential in any useful statement involving causal relationships.

Causal models

To begin with, I will define a **causal model** as a causal hypothesis *together with a specified effect size*. Later on, causal models will need to be developed that are more complex than this, but it will do for present purposes. A particular causal hypothesis is consistent with a large number of causal models — usually with infinitely many — each with different effect sizes. You can look on a causal hypothesis as like a kind of sack, containing a whole bundle of causal models. In the driving and alcohol example, a causal model might be:

> "an increase in blood alcohol level of 0.01 g per decilitre causes an increase in reaction times of 100 ms".

Another causal model would be:

"an increase in blood alcohol level of 0.01 g per decilitre causes an increase in reaction times of 200 ms".

Yet another causal model would be:

"an increase in blood alcohol level of 0.01 g per decilitre causes a *reduction* in reaction times of 200 ms".

It is important to get the sign right when considering models: there is usually the possibility that the effect might be in one of two possible directions.

If a causal hypothesis contains a whole set of causal models, is there a similar statement that we can make about a null hypothesis? I will defer the answer to this question as it introduces complications, but essentially the answer is "yes".

The process of model building used in orthodox statistics normally starts with attempting to show that a set of data provides evidence to enable us to claim that a particular causal hypothesis is true. This is done using something known as a "significance test", introduced in Chapter 6. The next step is to find the size of the effect.

So the first step establishes that *some* causal model is true,[12] and the next one settles on *which* causal model best describes reality. We might deduce that yes, alcohol consumption does influence reaction times (the causal hypothesis is true), and the best causal model is that an increase in blood alcohol level of 0.01 g per decilitre causes an increase in reaction times of 150 ms. This is a very simplified version of what happens, but it gives a rough idea of how the system works.

Having found a causal model, this can then be used to make predictions, or to exercise control in some way by manipulating the cause and producing a desirable change as an effect.

Variables

Science is famous for the tendency to measure everything. The important notion of a **variable** is tied up with the idea of defining

---

[12] Strictly, we can only conclude that there is evidence to favour the causal hypothesis. At this stage I will blur the technical details in favour of clarity.

a concept and then measuring it, often, but not always, numerically. In experimental psychology, variables are the basic language in which hypotheses, models and results are expressed. A variable can be defined as denoting **a well-defined property or characteristic of the objects of the population of people or things in which we are interested, a property which can exist at different values or levels**. Measurement involves the recording for a specific person or object of the particular value or level of that property that they have. Gender comes in (mostly) the values male and female, though other non-binary alternatives also exist; age in a range of numbers from zero to upwards of 100 years, and so on.

Variables come in different types, but the most common ones used in this book are **nominal** and **scale** variables. Essentially, a nominal variable can only take one of a finite number of values. Scale variables have values which are numbers, which can vary continuously between certain limits. Put crudely, scale variables can vary smoothly, whereas nominal variables vary in a "jumpy" way, like a light switch which can only be either on or off.

In psychology, the individual items of the universe in which we are interested are usually people in a particular group or population. Variables are then going to be characteristics of people in that population. Nominal variables are sometimes referred to as categorical variables, since they have the effect of classifying people in a population into categories. Gender, for example, divides the population into the categories of male, female, and some non-binary alternatives. Scale variables are also known as continuous variables, interval variables, covariates or parametric variables. This multiplicity of terms can be confusing. In this book, I will attempt to standardise by referring to nominal and scale variables, if for no better reason than that these are the terms which SPSS uses, so it helps avoid confusion.

There is not much to be said about nominal variables: they must divide a population into a number of clearly defined, non-overlapping categories which cover the whole population.[13] Scale

---

[13] The division of the population into levels is in mathematical terms, exclusive and exhaustive.

variables are somewhat more complicated. Those with a mathematical background may object that, for example, height in centimetres is not a scale variable because it is not really continuous: it can only have whole number values (if we only record height to the nearest centimetre). This is true, but for most purposes we can treat such variables as continuous or scale variables without running into difficulties. The key thing about scale variables is that they are measured on some directional scale in which the individual scale units (kg, cm, years, points of IQ) are comparable with each other. For the purposes of using SPSS, categorical variables also have to be entered into the program with numerical values, but here the units are meaningless: they are simply a way of encoding the data to enable the program to operate on them.

Scale variables can be subdivided into those measured on an *interval scale*, and those using a *ratio scale*. A ratio scale has a meaningful point which is an "absolute zero". Most measurements in physics involve ratio scales; examples are mass, energy and electric charge. Most scale measurements in psychology involve interval scales, in which there is no natural zero point. Models in psychology do not usually require the use of ratio scales, and they are mentioned only because you will come across the term in books and papers on research methods.

There is an intermediate class of variables known as *ordinal* variables. These will seldom be used in this book, but you should be aware of their existence. They share with continuous variables the property of having a "sense of direction": a typical example is that of ranks in the army, where there is an upwards trajectory between private soldier and field marshal. However, unlike continuous variables, there is no natural unit of measurement; one cannot say that the difference between a lance-corporal and a corporal is equal in some sense to that between a brigadier and a major general. Ordinal variables pose some problems when it comes to statistical analysis, but I will deal with those as and when we come to them. For the time being, they can be ignored.

The language of science

Every area of expertise has its own language, or jargon, and science is no exception. Within science, psychology has its own particular dialect of this language. The claims in psychology usually amount to causal statements, which function rather like verbs, and the "nouns" in this language consist of variables. Instead of sentences like "Caesar crossed the Rubicon" with the structure noun–verb–noun, we have statements such as "increased levels of oxytocin cause changes in emotional face processing in women", with the structure variable-causal link-variable.

Many psychology papers have titles of the form "the effect of X on Y", which are essentially claiming that changing variable X leads to corresponding changes in variable Y. When such a claim is made, the variable X, which is acting as the cause, is referred to as the *independent variable*, abbreviated "IV". Y, which is the one affected by X, is referred to as the *dependent variable* or "DV". The reason for these names is buried in history but it is probably because the changes in the DV are dependent on changes in the IV, whereas the IV (in some cases, at least) can be changed independently of anything else, certainly independently of the DV.[14] In this book, the IV will always be categorical, though the supplementary material will include cases where it can be a scale variable. The DV will always be a scale variable, though again with an exception in the supplementary material (Pearson's chi-square).

It is possible to have more than one IV involved in a given causal claim. For example, age and state of health may both have an effect on short term memory. Humans are not generally very good at coping intuitively with multiple causes, and dealing with two or more IVs requires a special approach, that will be covered in a later chapter. It is possible also to deal with the case of multiple DVs, and this is sometimes useful, but in this book I will only treat the case of a single DV.

---

[14] In the sense that we can change the IV without first changing the DV. Obviously, the DV may then change as a result of the change in IV.

Science and evidence

In history, statements like "Caesar crossed the Rubicon" require proof. Most psychology research starts with a causal hypothesis of the form "Changes in variable X cause changes in variable Y". In psychology, this is usually referred to as the *causal hypothesis* or the *experimental hypothesis*. Such a claim also requires supporting evidence, and much of the work of researchers in psychology involves providing evidence in support of claims of this form.

This is where both physics and history have certain advantages over psychology. A statement about the properties of the electron can be made on the basis of measuring variables relating to any electrons anywhere, at any time, and can then be confidently generalised to all electrons at all places and times. Claiming that Caesar crossed the Rubicon is at the other end of the spectrum of generality from the statement that the mass of the electron is 9.1×10^{-31} kg, but it can also be made with confidence, because it does not claim anything other than a single fact.

Psychology on the other hand attempts to make statements which are at least to some degree general, but which refer to a very specific part of the universe, namely the population of human beings. Despite being restricted to a tiny speck within a vast universe, humans are so diverse that it is much less safe to make precise statements on the basis of testing a few of them, compared with electrons. Different cultures, age groups, professions and genders may behave very differently in response to different circumstances. The only way we can hope to get any traction on the question of finding regularities in the link between cause and effect here is to agree to limit our search at least to begin with to specific subgroups of the human race, although the ultimate aim might be a theory that applies to everyone. This involves defining a group, or *population of interest*, and then seeking evidence from members of that group. Gaining such evidence involves finding group members and persuading them to take part in the study: these two steps are *sampling* and *recruitment*.

GOING DEEPER

I wrote above about hypotheses and models. How do they fit into this picture of experimental hypotheses? In particular, how does model comparison help us in the aim to find statements of the form "Changes in variable X cause changes in variable Y"?

For the moment, let us set aside the difficulty caused by human diversity. Consider for example carrying out an experiment on some pure substance, such as copper, where consistent results are to be expected. We wish to examine the causal hypothesis that **a change in temperature will cause a copper bar to change in length**. The null hypothesis is that **changing the temperature will lead to no change in the length of the bar**. The causal hypothesis can also be seen as comprising a whole collection of possible causal models. Each of these gives some specific value for the effect size. One of them might be "increasing the temperature by 1 degree Celsius will lead to an expansion in length of 0.01%".

If the experiment is done and after increasing the temperature by 1 degree C we find that the length has expanded by 0.02%, then two things can be said. One is that the causal hypothesis is confirmed. But we can go further than this. The data allow us to pick one particular causal model out of all the original ones and give this one a special status. Out of all possible causal models, it is the one that best fits the data. That causal model states that "increasing the temperature by 1 degree Celsius will lead to an expansion in length of 0.02%".

It is evident that this causal model has more useful information in it than merely supporting the causal hypothesis that "heat makes copper change in length". But this value, which is the result of its making a quite precise claim, is achieved at the cost of some lack of complete certainty. We may be very confident that heat causes expansion, but the exact amount of expansion cannot be estimated precisely. The figure of 0.02% is a useful number to know, as long as we do not treat it as gospel truth. In physics, such numbers are usually given with some kind of health warning, such as that the true figure lies between 0.019% and 0.021%.

The model which states that the bar will expand by 0.02% is the one which fits the experimental result best. An engineer designing some system using copper bars who wishes to predict how a piece of copper will behave under temperature changes will choose that one to do her calculations. However, if accuracy is important, she had better take into account that it may expand anywhere between 0.019% and 0.021%, and had better design the system so that it will still work well if the real expansion is anywhere between these limits.

Suppose, however, that the measurements possible in this experiment are not very precise, and that all we can tell is that the change in length of the bar is somewhere between an expansion of 0.04% and no change in length at all. Then one could argue that the best estimate for what happened is still that the bar expanded by 0.02%, on the basis that one should average the two readings. But how far are we justified in claiming that the bar expanded at all? The lack of precision of the readings allow for the possibility that the figure at the lower end of the range, 0%, is the true one.

Here we seem to be in a dilemma. The null model which states that "the bar does not change in length in response to a change in temperature" seems to fit the facts just as well as the model which claims that "the bar expands by 0.02% in response to a 1 degree rise in temperature". How do we choose?

At this point we need to appeal to another idea, the principle of Occam's razor. This states that if we have two possible explanations for something, we always prefer the simpler explanation, or the one which makes the fewest assumptions. Applying this to the case of two models which fit the facts equally well, then *we prefer the simpler model.* In this case the null model is simpler, because it does not assume the presence of any causal link between temperature and the length of the bar.

In this case, one might argue that the causal model does actually fit the facts *better* than the null model. 0.02% is bang in the middle of the possible range from zero to 0.04%, whereas the null model just scrapes in since its prediction of zero expansion is on the edge of the range. Archer 1 who places an arrow in the bullseye has made a better shot than archer 2 who just hits the outer ring of the target. But if we knew that archer 2 had used a replica mediaeval bow and arrow, whereas archer 1 had used an ultra-modern high-tech bow and arrow, we might still judge archer 2 as the better athlete. Occam's razor as it were imposes a handicap on more complex models. They not only have to do at least as well as simpler models, they have to do *significantly* better than simpler ones, otherwise the comparison is unfair.

To sum up, in testing a causal hypothesis we are in effect putting two models in head to head competition with one another, the null model (no change) and the best fitting causal model (a change equal to the change that is actually observed). In comparing the two models we need to balance two virtues which a model can have: fitting the facts well, which is obviously a good thing, and simplicity, which by Occam's principle is to be preferred to complexity.

Whenever there are two "measures of goodness" such as we have here, there is a need for some systematic way to combine them to find an overall "goodness" figure which will enable us to decide which is best on an overall merit rating. Otherwise we have no means of deciding whether a really complicated model which fits the facts really well, is any better than a simple one which fits the facts much less well. An archery competition to find who is the better archer between two people shooting with different bows will be hard to judge. This is why there are regulations in sport to ensure similar standards of equipment. But in experimental science, we cannot get around the issue: it is built into the whole process, as it were.

It looks as though there is one situation at least where the decision is easy. Suppose in the comparison between a simple and a complex model, the simple model (the null model, as it might be) is actually a *better* fit to the data than a more complex model (the causal model, for example). Then, surely, there is no contest: the simple model wins on both counts. It is as though an archer with a rubbish bow still outshot her competitor who was using the latest thing in high tech wizardry. However, in the situations we will be dealing with, this actually never happens. Going into this would take us too far afield at this stage, but the online material will contain an explanation. Meanwhile, just accept that things are never made this simple for us. More complex models, at least if well chosen, *always* fit the data better than simpler models. There is always a conflict between goodness of fit to the data (the more complex model always fits the data better) and complexity (we tend to prefer the simpler model).

The answer is effectively that in comparing one model with another, we apply a handicap to the more complex model. The details will be explained when we come to significance tests. The default approach is to prefer the simplest possible explanation, in accordance with the Occam principle, and only to prefer a more complex model if it still wins out, even after applying the handicap. Each additional layer of complexity has to justify itself. If at any point the justification for adopting a yet more complex model fails, we stop adding new layers of complexity and stick with that model. Another analogy is that a model is like a ship that carries no passengers. If a variable wants to get on board, it has to pull its weight in terms of doing a basic minimum of extra work as a member of the crew.

One criticism that could be made at this point is that by preferring simple models in this rather dogmatic way, we are running into the danger of over-simplifying. Surely the world is in reality highly complex, and a complete explanation of even the most basic thing such as a hydrogen atom is not only elaborate, but tends to become more elaborate over time as our understanding of it grows. So, are we not in the dilemma that either science stays simple and fails to account for the facts, or it becomes increasingly complicated over time and violates the principle of simplicity?

One answer is suggested by the saying attributed to Einstein, that everything in science should be made as simple as possible, but no simpler. We do not reject a complex model, provided it justifies its complexity by doing a sufficiently better job of describing nature than the simple alternatives. Assuming that there is an explanation for anything if we could only find it, this implies that a perfect model does exist, though we may not ever gain complete knowledge of it. This perfect model, despite its complexity, would account for 100% of reality. If we call this hypothetical perfect-fit model Omega, it turns out that Occam's razor no longer applies. However complex Omega may be, if it is a perfect fit then Omega is superior to any other model that fits reality with less than total perfection.

There are in fact no perfect explanations known to us, but science appears to be slowly inching towards a complete account of various areas of research. Models tend to grow through time by accumulating new layers of explanatory complexity, with each new layer being justified by a substantial increase in the ability of the model to account for reality. There is some similarity with the effect of Darwinian selection on the evolution of plants and animals, though this should not be taken as more than a very rough analogy. The notion of "progress" in evolution is no longer fashionable, but there is some justification for thinking about progress in science, in that new theories, explanations and models really do explain the world better than their predecessors.

Models and life

Finally, here are some ideas which put the notion of models in a more general context. The French scientist Claude Bernard famously said that the stability of the internal environment is the condition for free and independent life. This has been taken to mean that an organism is engaged in a continual struggle to maintain some kind of internal constancy in the face of changes and challenges in the external world, which is the condition of its continued survival. For example, the blood which bathes the human brain must lie within a very narrow range of temperature, pressure and chemical composition, or the brain will either lose consciousness or begin to function erratically.

Life can be described as a highly improbable condition, whose natural tendency is always to degrade into a state of chaos, like a teenager's bedroom; but if it succumbs too completely to this tendency, it dies. How does an organism maintain, at least for a while, this improbable state of being alive? Partly it does this automatically, as when a person shivers when they are too cold. But very largely, at least with humans, it does so by its behaviour. Most behaviour is an attempt to maintain internal stability.

Automatic behaviour is rather like a simple room thermostat. When the temperature falls, the thermostat switches on the heating. This is useful, but can never be entirely successful in keeping the temperature constant: the temperature must fall before the heating comes on, and must rise to some extent before the heating is switched off, so the temperature will swing up and down within some range. An intelligent system would anticipate the fall in temperature and prevent it by turning the heating on at just the right time.

Models can be viewed as functioning in effect as a kind of intelligent thermostat. They simulate external changes so that life can anticipate them and take countermeasures in advance to prevent internal changes. That is the predictive use of models. And they simulate the consequences when an organism interacts with the environment, and enables it to maximise the benefits of such interactions: that illustrates the use of models to control and manipulate the environment.

Of course humans and animals will use "models" very differently. I do not mean to imply that nest-building in birds, for example, is intentional, goal-seeking behaviour. But I would suggest that there is a conceptual link between animal behaviour which is driven by some kind of internal template, and the most subtle use of models in driving human scientific endeavour.

These ideas were further developed by a pioneer in the field of cybernetics, W. Ross Ashby. Following Bernard, Ashby believed that if an organism was to survive possible changes in the environment, it needed to behave in such a way as to prevent these changes from impacting on the organism's internal environment, which must remain stable. He drew the analogy of a fencer who skilfully parries the thrusts of some adversary. The environment is, as it were, attempting to transmit information to the organism, and the organism is acting so as to block the transmission. "Information" here implies "change", and internal change is just what the living organism must strive to counter.

Ashby showed[15] that to survive, an organism must have a repertoire of behaviours at least as complex as the threats it will face from the environment — for every thrust, the organism must have a specific counter-thrust — a conclusion he calls the "law of requisite variety". Complex behaviour requires a complex system to drive it, and this means that an organism needs to have a "model" of reality which is at least as elaborate as the changes in the environment which may threaten its internal stability. The model does not have to be perfect, but it needs to be good enough to keep the organism's internal state within certain limits. From this point of view, the formulation and testing of scientific models is merely the continuation by other means of a survival strategy which is to be found throughout the animal kingdom. Science is, in fact, the most natural thing in the world.

---

[15] In "An introduction to cybernetics", chapter 11; the book is downloadable free at: https://archive.org/details/introductiontocy00ashb/pdf.

Chapter 2
Comparing Different
Models of a Set of Data

SUMMARY

A model based on a dataset should reproduce the data and generalise to future datasets. Models likened to digital photographs: the tradeoff between accuracy and complexity. Measuring accuracy: the postman's distance versus sums of squares. Measuring complexity: the number of model parameters. Null and saturated models of a dataset. The distance–parameter diagram, and the Occam line as a measure of model adequacy in comparison with the null model. The F-ratio defined in terms of the slopes on the distance–parameter diagram.

NEED TO KNOW

Since model comparison is the focus of this book, it seems a good idea to outline the idea in principle even before dealing with the actual collection of data. This may seem the wrong way round. One could compare running an experiment and collecting data to growing and harvesting oranges, and data analysis to making juice out of the product. In that case it seems paradoxical to begin with the process of juicing, which is the end of the process.

However, there is a logic to this: if getting the juice is the end product, then the whole business of growing and harvesting the oranges will be determined by it. What are the best trees to plant, in order to produce a good yield? How does one prevent the oranges drying out or being infected, and the juice tainted, before harvest? It all depends on the final process, and in the same way, the demands of the analysis stage should always be borne in mind right from the planning stage of any research program.

Value for money versus mud polishing

The process to be described is designed to help answer a specific problem that arises when an experiment has already been run, and the data collected. It is assumed that when the experiment was planned, a number of possible models were envisaged that might underlie whatever it is that you were investigating. This chapter is not about designing the experiment, and it is not particularly about creating the possible alternative models to be compared. This will be developed in more detail later. It is about developing analytical tools, which will help you to decide which of a number of possible alternative models should be preferred as a description of the data. Which model is best? And how do we reconcile maximising accuracy and simplicity?

First, I should try to describe in more detail what is meant by a model. We already have a set of data. There are several characteristics of a model but the one I want to consider here is the one specifically relevant to that data. A model for a set of data can be defined as a **simplified version** of the data, that **reproduces certain important features** of the data. But there is another requirement. We not only want the model to be a close fit to the existing data, but we also want it to *fit any similar data that may be collected in the future*. In other words, the model should **generalise**.

This connects with the notion of a model introduced above, as something which has validity in terms of explaining and predicting reality. If the model is to accomplish this successfully, it must be moulded by our experience of reality, and in practice this means that any model should be a good fit to the data that we already have. I am assuming that an experiment has been conducted and data gathered, and will attempt to show how we can choose the model that not only fits the data well, but does so without sacrificing too much in terms of being over-complex. Such a model will be our best bet for use in predicting the future behaviour of the population that we are studying.

To illustrate the idea of models as a means of reproducing data, consider a physical model of the solar system such as an orrery.[1] This is something which reproduces the known movements of the planets, on a small and manageable scale. The details may not be totally accurate, but there is enough similarity between the model and the actual solar system for the model to be useful. And the model can be used to predict the planets' future positions, by setting it up to correspond with the current positions of the planets, turning a handle and running the machine forwards to represent future times.

Another analogy for a model based on data, is a photograph of a particular scene. The photograph reproduces key features of the scene, if it is a good photograph. Even an early digital camera with 130 thousand pixels would give reasonable if somewhat impressionistic images, certainly less good than a 35-mm film camera, though a modern SLR camera with upwards of ten million pixels outperforms its film based predecessor. In fact useful information can be conveyed by much less information than that. A famous experiment in facial recognition showed that one iconic image can reliably be identified with as few as 256 pixels.[2]

In deciding how to model a scene in this way with a photograph, it might seem sensible to go for the highest resolution option, that is, the one with the largest number of pixels, or in model language, the model with the maximum degree of complexity. That is because a high resolution photograph, and a highly complex model, is likely to reproduce the data (the landscape) more accurately than a low resolution picture or a simple model.

---

[1]There is a nice one illustrated at http://zeamon.com/wordpress/?p=670.
[2]To identify the image for yourself, and find out how it influenced an artwork by Dalí, go to http://blogs.scientificamerican.com/illusion-chasers/dali-master pieces-inspired-by-scientific-american/.

However, there is a price to be paid for this. Complex photos, or models, are both more accurate and more expensive. Anyone with experience of trying to transmit complex images as attachments to underpowered email networks knows that complexity comes at the price of slower transmission speeds. It may be better to model reality with a larger number of low pixel photos than with a small number of high pixel ones. This advantage of low resolution images is analogous to the preference for simple models enshrined in Occam's principle.

One should always prefer the simpler explanation, or the simpler model, to the complex one, other things being equal. "Other things being equal" means that the benefit from the complex model is not sufficient to justify its cost. Of course, sometimes other things are *not* equal, and the complex model is so much better than the simpler one, that you override Occam and go for the better and pricier alternative. The rather banal motto of people developing models might be summed up in the phrase "choose the model which provides the best value for money". "Value" here refers to the closeness with which the model reproduces the data — the closer, the more valuable — and "money" refers to the complexity of the model — the more complex it is, the more expensive it is.

Another example of the principle at stake is provided by someone instructing an architect about building a house. An architect tells me that the first instinct of someone commissioning a house is to make a list of all the things they want included, regardless of cost. There will be a large number of bedrooms including spare rooms to accommodate the maximum number of visitors they might ever conceivably have, plus a games room, studies for everyone, a library, utility room, a basement to store things, an attic, a larder, a pantry and so on. The thinking seems to be, they want the best possible house. But each additional room comes at a cost, and the additional benefit it provides diminishes as the size of the house increases. A value for money calculation would show that there is a sweet spot at which the benefits are maximised relative to cost, beyond which things go downhill. And it is the same with models.

Another way of looking at models is in terms of what models are intended to achieve. The motivation for constructing models is that we wish to summarise some aspect of truth about the real world: this is what will give it predictive power. The data available to us represent information sampled from the real world, and so to some extent will convey truth about the world. But given that the data are only a sample of all possible data, they will be incomplete, and therefore not fully representative of the real world. If the aim of a model is to reproduce the data, as I have suggested above, then you might object that when a model is based on a sample, the model aims to reproduce something incomplete, and therefore inaccurate. What is the point of developing a model that is bound to be wrong?

This turns out to be another argument in favour of finding the sweet spot between over-simple and over-complex models, and locating the best balance between value and cost. Finding a model which fits a set of data perfectly will usually involve a complicated, and therefore expensive model. Fitting data perfectly when the data themselves only represent the real world imperfectly, is not a useful aim.

It seems better to go for a cheaper model which fits the data with about as much error as the likely error between the data and the real world. If the data are a relatively poor sample of reality then finding a model which fits them perfectly is an exercise in polishing mud. The perfect model has incurred a cost, with little or no corresponding benefit. This is, at a very basic level, the justification for Occam's principle. I include in the online material a more specific illustration of the idea based on performance tests for cars, which you may find more convincing.

Modelling rainfall data in Sri Lanka

Fitting models to data is best illustrated by means of a very simple example. Suppose you are attempting to provide a website which will tell holiday makers when would be a good time to visit, say, the resort of Negombo in Sri Lanka. They may be interested in whether the rainy season is likely to have started, and therefore be concerned about rainfall at different months of the year, and days of the month. If you have the data for daily totals for rainfall in millimetres in Negombo between 2000 and 2012, and wish to provide information on the likely rainfall in the various months in future years, the task is to provide a number for each month which models the likely rainfall for future years.

One option is to take the average rainfall for each month, January through December, over the period and to provide those figures. It will turn out that rainfall peaks in October and November, with slightly lower peaks in April and May.[3] That would be one model, with twelve numbers, one for each month. The conclusion for travellers who want to avoid rainy days could be to travel outside these months.

Another option would be to provide average rainfall for each day of the year. So for 1 January, you could find the average rainfall on 1 January between 2000 and 2012, and provide this, doing the same calculation for each of the days. That would be another model, with 365 numbers, one for each day. This second model is a lot more complex. It would fit the existing data better, but there is little reason to suppose that the daily averages would have much validity in future years; the added complexity of having 365 rather than 12 numbers would probably not be very helpful. The model would be better at fitting past data, but not, probably, future data, which is what a traveller would be interested in.

To make the example more specific, let us just focus now on one month, June. How do you model the rainfall for this month? Suppose you wanted to provide a **single figure** to summarise rainfall in Negombo in June, and you had the daily totals in millimetres given below, based on averages for these days over the years 2000 to 2012.[4] The numbers are given in order of the days of the month from the 1st to the 30th:

99 106 100 110 114 108 90 96   78 92 86 102 112 108 106
97   83   94   93 103 105 92 81 101 90 97   92   88   98   83

---

[3] As shown, for example, at http://www.worldweatheronline.com/negombo-weather-averages/western/lk.aspx.
[4] These actual numbers are entirely fictitious. Negombo is not really that rainy.

The single figure should in some sense be as close as possible to the whole set of numbers. What number can satisfy this criterion of being "closest" to the set? Or, to put it another way, which number has the smallest "distance" from the set? How would one even set about measuring such a distance? The distance from one geographical location to another is a simple idea, but the notion of distance from one number to a set of other numbers is something outside our experience.

The postman's distance

But let us try to develop such a notion. Suppose you are a postman located at a small village at A, and that you have to visit another village at B. If B is 5 miles distant from A, you will need to travel 10 miles to do the round trip. Writing (AB) for the distance from A to B, your daily round will involve a distance of 2(AB). Now suppose that your workload is increased by the addition of villages at C and D, at distances of 3 miles and 6 miles respectively from A. Suppose also that the only roads are those connecting A with B, A with C and A with D: A is a hub for these three places, in other words. So each time you go from B to C, say, you will need to return to A first. How far will you need to travel to do your rounds now, beginning and ending at A?

The distance will evidently be twice the distance from A to B, plus twice that from A to C, plus twice that from A to D, which works out as 10 + 6 + 12 or 28 miles. Written in symbols, this is 2(AB) + 2(AC) + 2(AD). Those familiar with basic algebra will see that this is equal to 2[(AB) + (AC) + (AD)]. What would be a sensible way to define the "distance" from A to the set of villages {B, C, D}?

Well, there is no controversy about the distance from A to B: it is 5 miles. And the travel involved in servicing that route is 10 miles. So the travel is twice the distance. Apply the same idea in reverse to the travel involved in servicing {B, C, D}, which we know is 28 miles. This suggests a "distance" of half that, or 14 miles, which seems a reasonable definition. But this seems a complicated way to define it. We can find the same answer more quickly by just adding the separate distances from A to B, C and D, which is 5 + 3 + 6 miles, also equal to 14 miles. Symbolically, we need to find half of 2[(AB) + (AC) + (AD)], and even without much mathematics you should be able to see that this is just [(AB) + (AC) + (AD)], which gives the same result. This could be called the "postman's distance" from A to the set {B, C, D}.

This suggests that a reasonable first attempt at defining a distance from one single place A to a whole set of other places, would be to simply *add all the distances from A to the other places*. Let us now apply this idea to the rainfall data. Suppose our first, very basic forecasting model was that the rainfall on every day in June would be just 100 mm. We wish to know the distance of this model from the actual data. The analogue of "distance between two villages" would be "difference between two numbers". For example, the difference between a predicted rainfall of 100 mm for every day in June and an actual rainfall of 90 mm on, say, 15 June would be 10 mm.

But the difference between a predicted value of 100 mm and an actual value of 110 mm would be −10 mm (negative ten millimetres), yet by any sensible criterion an estimate of 100 should be as far from 90 as it is from 110. These numbers should therefore be equal, whereas one is the negative of the other. A simple-minded attempt to add distances would end up with 10 − 10 or zero, suggesting that the estimate of 100 gives a precise estimate for both days, which is hardly reasonable. And certainly the postman's distance from A to B should be the same as that from B to A.

The answer clearly is to take the *absolute value* of the difference and not allow negative values. The absolute value of a real number is found by taking the number itself if it is positive, and eliminating the negative sign if it is negative. So the absolute value of 23 is 23, and the absolute value of −14 is 14. So if the rainfall for 15 June turned out to be 90 mm and that for 16 June was 110 mm, the total distance of the estimate of 100 mm from the data for these two days would then be not zero, but 10 mm plus 10 mm, or 20 mm.

So, it seems that one candidate for the "distance" between our rainfall prediction would be the sum of the absolute values of the differences between our prediction for each day and the actual values of rainfall for each day in June. Going back to the data, apply this idea to the model that each day the rainfall will be exactly 100 mm. The differences between this and the individual items of data would be:

−1	6	0	10	14	8	−10	−4	−22	−8	−14	2	12	8	6
−3	−17	−6	−7	3	5	−8	−19	1	−10	−3	−8	−12	−2	−17

Taking absolute values, the differences — we could now call them "distances" — become:

1	6	0	10	14	8	10	4	22	8	14	2	12	8	6
3	17	6	7	3	5	8	19	1	10	3	8	12	2	17

If you add all these numbers together you will find the "distance" to be 246.

Can we do better with our simple model? If I take 97 rather than 100 as the single number to model these data, the total distance can be calculated as 234, an improvement. There is a reason for this. 97 is the median of the set of data (the median is the middle value in a set of data arranged in order of size: for the full definition see page 85). It turns out that using this distance measure, where we add absolute values of differences, the median always gives the smallest total distance, so is in a sense the single best estimate of the whole set of data. In some cases, the median is not unique in this: with the small set {1, 3, 4, 6} for example, any number between 3 and 4 will be at the same smallest distance (of 6) from the data; the median value of 3.5 gives just one possible "best fit".

The sum of squares distance

Having reached this stage, I am now going to suggest an alternative measure of distance. It is not that the arguments so far have been a waste of time. In fact there is really not a right or wrong answer for measuring distance, and the absolute value definition given above is a good one, for many purposes. Taking this measure of distance has the virtue of being an obvious and natural measurement. But it is not ideal mathematically. If we do use this distance measure, the single number which fits the data best is the median. The median has a number of benefits as a "best fit" number. However, there are alternatives, and one in particular has the great advantage that not only does it provide something that is close to the intuitive notion of distance, but also has certain "nice" mathematical properties that make it easier to work with when doing the abstract maths that lies behind most statistical calculations.

This is not so much an issue today, when computers can carry out heavy calculations in fractions of a second, but historically it was important. It dictated the way the subject developed, and therefore helped determine its present form. Everything we do is influenced by context, which is shaped by history. So at this point I need to take account of this historical context, and define a different version of distance. This is somewhat analogous to defining distances in terms of kilometres instead of miles. In fact the difference is a bit deeper than this. But in order to tackle traditional, orthodox statistics, it is the correct one to use.

So, going back to the rainfall data, and faced with the challenge of finding the distance between the model of 100 mm daily rainfall and the given amounts, the first step is the same: find the discrepancy between the model and each daily amount, by subtracting one from the other, giving as before:

−1	6	0	10	14	8	−10	−4	−22	−8	−14	2	12	8	6
−3	−17	−6	−7	3	5	−8	−19	1	−10	−3	−8	−12	−2	−17

We are faced with the same problem as before, of negative as well as positive numbers, which cannot be taken immediately as distances, because all distances have to be positive. One way to make a negative number into a positive one is simply to replace the minus sign with a plus, as we did above. This is simple but effective, yet mathematically it is a bit brutal.

Another way, which turns out to be mathematically nicer, is to first take the **square** of every number, and *then* add the results.

Squaring a negative number makes it a positive one, so this achieves the aim of making everything positive. The result is the **lack of fit sum of squares** distance. Sum of squares is obvious, and lack of fit refers to the fact that the larger the number, the worse the fit. I will refer to this as the **lofsos** measure.

When we do this, the model of 100 mm rainfall every day turns out to have a lofsos distance of 2958 from the actual data. Do not be put off by the fact that this total is much larger than the former distance, which used absolute values. We are using different units. A person may have a height of 182 if the units are centimetres or 6 if the units are feet; it is still a measure of the same actual height. What really matters is the *relative* distance of different models to the data.

It turns out that in this case, too, we can fit the data better than with this model. Previously, the best fit of a single number to the data was found by taking the median of the original set of numbers; it turns out that with this measure of distance, the best single number to take is the *mean* of the actual rainfall data. This is just another reason why the mean is so important in statistics. A proof of this well-known result can be found in, for example, Judd and McClelland (see Further Reading).

The simplest model

Here, the mean can be calculated to be 96.8 mm per day. And running through the calculation, using the lofsos distance measure, shows that this model has a distance of just 2650.8, less than with the 100 mm model. If you were wondering how the median (97) performs under this new criterion, it gives a distance from the data of 2652, which very slightly worse than the mean, in that it is more "distant" from the data. The difference is small, but the median in this case is very close to the mean, so this is what we would expect. It hardly matters in this case which model we take. But we know from the mathematics, that the mean will always perform better than any other single number. This model is the simplest one we can construct if the only thing we have to go on is the set of data presented above.

The most complex model

This is a very simple model, with just one number to be specified. I suggested above that one could also take a model which predicted, on a daily basis, the precise number given above in the sequence:

99	106	100	110	114	108	90	96	78	92	86	102	112	108	106
97	83	94	93	103	105	92	81	101	90	97	92	88	98	83

In other words, the model states that on 1 June, the rainfall will be 99 mm, on the second day, it will be 106 mm, and so on. If we calculate the distance between *this* model and the data, it can be seen that it will be the square of $(99 - 99)$ plus the square of $(106 - 106)$ plus the square of... etc. And since each of these individual numbers is zero, the total distance of our model from the data will also be zero.

The model is a perfect fit! But unlike Cinderella and the glass slipper, this perfect fit is not a good thing. Or rather, it is to be expected, and neither good nor bad. Of course, if we use the data themselves to reproduce the data we will be successful in one sense, but it tells us nothing about how good the model is. Or rather, it tells us nothing about the value of the model in predicting *future* data: fitting the data with the data is simply the ultimate in mud polishing.

Nevertheless, the model which fits the data with the data themselves, does serve one purpose: it provides one element of a standard of comparison by which we can judge the relative worth of models. This ultimate model which does nothing but use the data to predict themselves, is therefore worthy of a name. The literature tends to use the term "saturated model" to describe this situation, and I will adopt this term. I am not sure of the origin of the name, but possibly it has is so named because it is a model that has absorbed as much of the data as it can, and is therefore saturated with data.

So we now have two possible models to reproduce the rainfall data. One is about the simplest one possible: it calculates the mean of the data and uses that number as the prediction of rainfall for every single day: in this case, it predicts 96.8 mm every day. I will call this, for reasons that will appear later, the null model.

The other model, at the opposite extreme, uses the rainfall for each day to predict the rainfall for any future June day: so for 1 June it predicts 99 mm, for 2 June, 106 mm, and so on. This is the saturated model. These two models lie at opposite ends of a spectrum of complexity, from the simplest to the most complicated.

However, neither of them is really very interesting. Any fool can take a set of data and find the mean, and then predict that all future measurements will equal that mean. And any fool can use the data themselves to predict future data on the basis of the past data. Neither of these seems to involve much intelligent thought. As "models" they seem pretty hopeless. We will see below, however, that between them they define a certain standard of comparison which can be used to assess other, potentially more powerful models. Therefore they do serve a purpose, if only as setting a baseline which needs to be improved upon by any possible alternative model if it is to have a chance of being either interesting or useful.

GOING DEEPER

Model parameters

At this point, it is worth introducing the concept of model parameters. The parameters in a model represent the numbers which need to be specified in order to make the model definite, rather than generic. For example, when modelling daily rainfall during the month of June with a single number, such as the mean of past rainfall for that whole month, the model has just one parameter, the single number in question. If we attempt to model the rainfall for each day separately, the model will have 30 parameters, because we can give a separate expected rainfall total for each day.

The number of parameters is a measure of a model's complexity. So we are now almost in a position to answer the question about a model's value for money. If "money", i.e., complexity, is measured by the number of parameters, and if "value" is measured by lofsos distance,[5] we have the tools to be able to compare the worth of different models, and choose the one which gives the best value for money.

There are some further refinements before we get to that point, however. Firstly, the correct definition of the "parameters" of a model based on data is not quite the same as the "numbers which can be varied" in the model. The very first model above, which took a number of 100 mm for the daily rainfall, may appear to be a one parameter model. However, it used a number drawn not from the data, but from — let us suppose — some other source of information. This does not count as a parameter as far as Occam's principle is concerned, because the information does not use the data. It is a complexity cost that has already been incurred, if you will. So the 100 mm model is really a zero-parameter model. The parameters we are concerned about are only those that have been *estimated from the data themselves.*

An example of a parameter which really is a parameter, is the null model based on the mean of the data, namely 96.8 mm, because this is found from the data. It is therefore a one parameter model. The saturated model is a 30-parameter model, because there are 30 numbers, one for each day, each of which is taken from the data. This can in fact be taken as the definition of a saturated model: there are as many parameters as data points.[6] Another way of describing saturated models is that they fit the data perfectly: their distance from the data is zero.

There are models with parameter numbers ranging all the way between 1 and 30. I will shortly introduce one with two parameters. A model with fewer than 30 parameters has, as it were, a number of parameters "left over": the null model has 29 parameters left over. These remaining parameters represent information in the data points that are not used to create the model itself. It turns out

---

[5]Strictly speaking, of course, distance represents a sort of negative value, in that we want to *minimise* the distance in order to *maximise* the value.
[6]The literature claims that there are exceptions to this general rule, but for practical purposes it applies nearly everywhere.

that they can be used for another purpose: to estimate the reliability of the model in terms of future predictive accuracy. The saturated model has no such leftover parameters: this seems to imply that there is no way of estimating its reliability in terms of future prediction. The saturated model is indeed something of an oddity, lying at an extreme position in every respect. It fits the data perfectly, and yet is valueless in terms of guaranteeing that it will have any ability at all in terms of fitting future data.

Comparing the null and saturated models

So at this point we have two models describing the rainfall data. One is very simple, and has one parameter estimated from the data: it predicts the daily rainfall as being that mean value. The actual daily values differ more or less widely from the model, and the lofsos distance between model and data is 2650.8. The other is very complex, and has 30 parameters estimated from the data, and the distance between it and the model is zero.

I will put this in Table 2.1.

As we are in the business of model comparison, let us compare the null and saturated models. The saturated model achieves a reduction in distance of 2650.8, compared with the null model, at the cost of an additional 29 parameters.

Suppose we are trying in a simple-minded way to work out the "value for money" of this improvement. Well, the value, i.e., the improvement in fit, is 2650.8, and the money, or number of parameters, is 29. So one way of trying to estimate value for money is just to divide the improvement by the number of parameters, to get a number representing the *improvement per parameter*, provided by the saturated model when compared with the null model using just

Table 2.1.   The null and saturated models.

Model	Distance from data	Number of parameters
Null	2650.8	1
Saturated	0	30

the overall mean. This improvement per parameter is just 2650.8/29, or 91.4. But to be frank, the saturated model is really not very good: it is the lazy person's model, if you like. No insight or thought has gone into constructing the saturated model.

Suppose then that we are going to try to improve on the null model, based on the data. Clearly we are going to move in the direction of greater complexity, i.e., more parameters. How do we measure how effective the new model is going to be? A measure of value for money will be reduction in distance divided by the number of new parameters needed.

But how do we know whether this value for money is sufficiently good to prefer the new model over the old, null model? Well, we already have one value for money figure: that for the saturated model. We know that the saturated model is not really achieving much, and so we will certainly require our new model to do better than the saturated model in this respect. In other words, if we are to accept a new model, we will need it to achieve a figure of *greater than* 91.4 in terms of improvement per parameter, compared with the null model.

So here at last we have a plausible, measurable definition of what it takes to choose a model to supplant the null model in this situation. Calculate the distance of the null model from the data, compare it with the saturated model, work out the improvement-per-parameter figure for the saturated compared with the null model, and set this figure as the threshold such that *any new proposed model must do better than this, compared with the null model, to be accepted.*

It will be useful to have a concrete example at this point. Suppose that someone proposes for the rainfall example that there may be a trend during the month of June for the rainfall to vary over the month, with rainfall during the first half being different from the second half. What model might be suitable to describe this situation?

The obvious model to take will be one with just two parameters, one predicting the daily rainfall from 1 to 15 June, and the second one predicting a different daily figure for 16 to 30 June.

If these parameters are based on the data, the numbers required will be the actual average of the data for the first 15 days, and the actual average for the second 15 days, which turn out to be 100.47 mm and 93.13 mm respectively.

What is the distance of this model from the data, using the usual sum of squared deviations measure? It is the sum of the figures $(99 - 100.47)^2 + \cdots$ etc. for the first 15 days, plus $(97 - 93.13)^2 + \cdots$ etc. for the second 15 days. This distance turns out to be 2247.5. This is an improvement on 2650.8, and the amount of this improvement is $(2650.8 - 2247.5)$ or 403.3. It has achieved this result at the cost of just one additional parameter, since the new model has two parameters.

All this can be summarised in Table 2.2.

The column "extra parameters" compares the parameters in each model to those in the null model. This has one parameter, so the extra parameters are found by subtracting 1 from the "number of parameters" column. The column "improvement" refers to how much closer to the data each model is, compared with the null model. The numbers in this column are therefore found by subtracting the "distance from data" for that model from the distance for the null model, which is 2650.8.

The final column, "improvement per extra parameter", is found by dividing the improvement for a model by the number of extra parameters for that model. We cannot divide 0 by 0 so the first entry is not applicable, but the second and third entries are simply 403.3/1, or 403.3, and 2650.8/29, or 91.4.

This final column provides the key figure for assessing the new proposed model. Its improvement per new parameter of 403.3

Table 2.2. Null, saturated and proposed models.

Model	Lofsos distance from data	Number of parameters	Extra parameters	Improvement	Improvement per extra parameter
Null	2650.8	1	0	0	NA
Proposed	2247.5	2	1	403.3	403.3
Saturated	0	30	29	2650.8	91.4

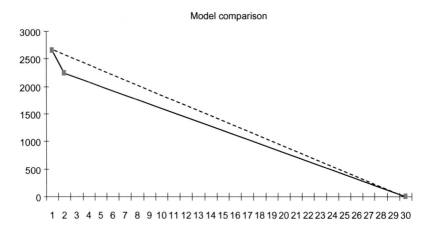

Fig. 2.1. Graph comparing the null, proposed and saturated models.

looks promising when measured up against the saturated model, which manages only 91.4 per extra parameter. It seems as though the proposed new model is in with a chance. 403.3 is impressively more than 91.4.

Another way of visualising these results is with a graph of distances and parameters that shown in Fig. 2.1.

The vertical axis represents the lofsos distance of a model from the data, and the horizontal axis measures the number of parameters for that model. The first plotted point to the left of the figure refers to the null model, the second point refers to the proposed new model and the one at the far right, is the plot of the saturated model.

What about the dotted line joining the basic model to the saturated model? By elementary geometry its slope is the vertical drop divided by horizontal length, which is 2650.8/29, or 91.4. This is equal to the figure found earlier for the improvement-per-parameter for the saturated model compared with the null model. This is no coincidence of course: the slope is just the geometric counterpart of the "value for money" or improvement-per-parameter concept defined earlier, applied to the comparison between the null and saturated models.

We can look on the dotted line as plotting those models which do no better than the saturated model, when compared with the null model. One can look on it as a sort of line representing the rubbish models. The null is not intelligent, because it is a simple-minded attempt to predict everything as the data average. Nor is the saturated model, because it is simply dictated by the data: it is an example of mud polishing.

So, any model which lies on the dotted line, when plotted in terms of its distance from the data and the number of parameters that it requires, should also not be preferred to the null model. It is a combination of two rubbish models. It is doing no better, in terms of improvement-per-parameter, than the saturated model. The dotted line, in other words, plots the possible rubbish models which might be proposed to supplant the basic model, and which we would immediately reject, or at least, find unattractive. Anything plotting above the line would of course be rejected as well, as being worse than rubbish. This gives a useful criterion for finding good models: *such a model must plot below the dotted line*, and the further below the line, the better.

Just in case you are wondering whether rubbish models really exist that plot on the dotted line, they do. There is, however, a slight tweak that needs to be applied to demonstrate this. Briefly, a rubbish model with, say, ten parameters can be found by randomly choosing nine dates in June, fitting the model exactly to those nine dates, then taking the average of the rainfall on the remaining dates and using that to predict rainfall on those remaining dates. It turns out that *on average*, a model put together in this way will indeed plot precisely on the dotted line. A mathematical proof of this claim is in Appendix C.

Therefore, we have a simple visual method of detecting models which are candidates for supplanting the null model. If you accept the criterion that to be accepted, a new model must do better than 91.4 in terms of improvement-per-parameter over the null model, then such models are very easy to spot: they are precisely *those which plot below the dotted line*. And the proposed new model does just this. We have already discovered this fact from the calculation that the improvement-per-parameter for that model is 403.3, well greater than 91.4. But the line plot confirms it. Since the downward slope of the dotted line represents the improvement in goodness of fit that any model with more parameters must achieve compared with one with fewer parameters, if it is to pass the test of Occam's principle, I will call this line the **Occam line**.

To summarise: firstly, we are agreed that a model which does no better than the saturated model in terms of improvement-per-parameter, compared with the basic model, is not to be preferred to the null model. This is the form which Occam's principle takes in this case: it has now been given a definite form, with a numerical criterion. If the new model does no better than this, its value (in terms of being closer to the data) is not sufficient to offset its cost (in terms of the extra parameters required to specify it). Secondly, a model which fails this criterion lies on, or above the Occam line joining the null and saturated models in the figure given above. In order to be considered at all as an alternative to the basic model, a proposed new model must plot *below* the Occam line.

Now let us look at the issue of plotting below the line, from another point of view. The proposed model found above, where we use two parameters and predict rainfall separately for the two halves of the month of June, had an improvement-per-parameter value of 403.3, which is impressively greater than a rubbish model. It plots below the line, and the line joining it to the null model has a slope of greater than 91.4, in fact of 403.3. These are just two ways of saying the same thing.

But another fact about the proposed new model that you will notice is that the slope of the line joining it to the saturated model, is *less than* the slope of the Occam line. This too is implied by the new model's location below the Occam line, as a moment's thought will show. Furthermore, the slope of the line joining the new model to the null model is *greater than* the slope of the Occam line. This suggests a slightly different way of deciding whether a proposed new model lies below the line or not. What follows may seem unnecessary and somewhat weird, but the compensation is that at the end of it, we will have discovered something that will be of immediate relevance to the most important number in the whole of orthodox statistics, namely Fisher's F.

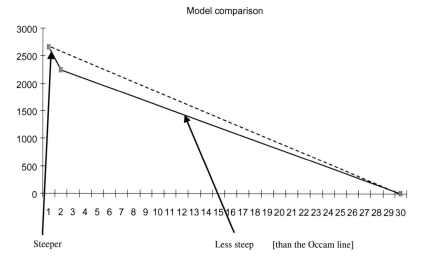

Fig. 2.2.   Model comparison with connecting lines.

To repeat: the hopeful looking new model has a steeper line joining it to the null model, and a less steep line joining it to the saturated model, compared with the Occam line (Fig. 2.2).

If this is so, *can we find another way of detecting models which are below the line*, and which will give a measure of how far below they are, i.e., how good they are?

One way would be to find a number which measures *how much steeper* the left-hand solid line is, for that model, than the right-hand solid line. The obvious single number to take, is the *ratio* of the two slopes, i.e., the *left-hand slope divided by the right-hand slope*. **This is Fisher's famous F-ratio.**[7]

In this case, the slope of the left-hand line is 403.3 divided by 1, or just 403.3, since the new and null models differ in distance by 403.3, and in parameters by one (two parameters versus one parameter).

The right-hand slope is the vertical drop divided by the horizontal distance, which is 2247.5 divided by 28. The horizontal

---

[7]A key step in the argument, is that as is clear from the figure, the model plots below the Occam line if, and only if, this ratio is greater than one. Note that this remains true even if, as here, the horizontal and vertical scales are different. Having different scales does not affect the **ratio** of the slopes.

distance is 28 because the new model has two parameters and the saturated model has 30, and the difference is 28. The right-hand line therefore has a slope of 2247.5/28, or 80.3. The ratio of these two numbers is 403.3/80.3, which is 5.02.

We can say, therefore, that Fisher's F number for this model is 5.02.

Given that a rubbish model would lie on the Occam line, this value of F, which is greater than one, is alone sufficient to show that the proposed model lies below the line. However, there is a complication to consider at this point. In order to be useful, the model needs to predict future outcomes, as well as reproduce past outcomes reasonably accurately. Rainfall on any given month will vary from year to year. If we have no way of calculating in advance how it varies, then this variability is not something we can get a handle on: it is "random error".

So any model based on past data will itself be tainted to some extent by error. This is a reason for not trying too hard to find a model which fits the data with maximum precision: there is no point fitting data more precisely than the error term in the data. Further precision incurs a cost, with little or no corresponding benefit.

What we are aiming for with a model, such as the proposed model based on separate rainfall totals for the first and second halves of June, is to find one which will do better than the rubbish models not just for the present set of data, *but for any future month of June*. Only then will the model have any real validity or usefulness.

If a racing tipster claimed to be able to calculate the outcomes of horse races with a better result than a rubbish model such as always betting on the favourite, we would not be convinced by a demonstration, however accurate, that the model worked well for the last ten races run at Doncaster, say, or Saratoga. It might be that the model had been devised retrospectively, precisely in order to fit the data, i.e., the list of winners already known to the tipster. Such a model, derived from the data themselves, would have much in common with the saturated model based on the rainfall data: it would have no better status than a rubbish model. We would require some guarantee that the model would work for future races in Doncaster, and possibly at Catterick, Uttoxeter and Kempton Park for that matter. Even with an honest tipster who really had come up with a winning formula, we would want some demonstration that it had validity.

For the tipster, one demonstration that would carry conviction would be for him to forecast for us in advance the results of the next five races, for example, and to record his picks. If he turned out to be accurate every time, we would probably begin to believe him. In the case of the rainfall model, we could monitor the June rainfall in Negombo for the next five years, and check whether the average rainfall in the first half was close to 100 mm, and the average in the second half, close to 93 mm. There would certainly be some random variation, but if the averages were, say, 98 mm and 92 mm respectively, we might be convinced: the trend is at least in the same direction, of greater rainfall in the first half of the month. But this would involve a considerable delay before verifying the model. Is there any means by which we can estimate the predictive reliability of the model from the data themselves?

The remarkable answer, provided as always by the ubiquitous Fisher, is yes. The mathematics behind the method is complex, but the basic idea is simple enough. *If the Fisher's F ratio is large enough*, this provides some guarantee that the result is not down to random error.

To motivate the idea, we know that an *F*-ratio of 1 means that the model is rubbish: it lies exactly on the Occam line, in this case. What if the ratio is 1.01? It is greater than 1, but even a rubbish model will sometimes produce slightly better results from time to time, if the noise term happens to work in its favour, just as a stopped clock is right twice a day. We will want the *F*-ratio to be large enough that it would be very unlikely to happen by chance, if the model were really not a good one, in fact no better than a rubbish one.

What about an *F* of 1.5? This could also be due to chance. Values of 2, or even 3, might sometimes be purely down to chance. The exact cutoff point varies with the parameters involved, but it turns out that for two parameter models an *F*-value of more than 4 is a fairly good indicator that the model really is worth keeping.[8] This may seem a high value, but that's what the mathematics is telling us. In the present case, the proposed model turns out to be good enough to pass the test, so we can decide that it really does do better than the simple-minded alternative of taking the month's average and predicting on the basis of that.[9]

All we can claim is that the new model is better than the old one, not that it is "correct" in any absolute sense. Models are essentially in the business of prediction, and prediction will always involve some error,[10] so no model is ever perfect. The new model — we might call it the two-halves model — has two parameters and is slightly more complex than the one-size-fits-all model based on the monthly average, but its better fit to the data more than makes up for the handicap[11] imposed by Occam's principle. So we prefer it to the old model, but we don't fall in love with it.

It may be that someone may come up with a better proposed model, for example one suggesting that rainfall drops off gradually over the month of June, and it may be that this new model fits the data better than the two-halves model, and that when any considerations of parameters are taken into account, we decide the gradual model is even better than the two-halves model. In that case we won't hesitate to dump the two-halves model, and the new model may in turn be subject to challenge and displacement by a still better model, perhaps when more rainfall data become available.

Incidentally, there is one important point that should be stressed here. If someone comes up with a model such as the two-halves model or the gradual model, they should do so in advance of seeing the data. What ought to happen is that the model is put forward, new data is gathered, and the model is tested against the

---

[8] The crucial *F*-ratio varies with the number of parameters in the new model: the crucial value tends to reduce as the number of parameters goes up.

[9] This is not a formal piece of statistics: I am taking liberties with the calculation to simplify things.

[10] "It's tough to make predictions, especially about the future" — *Yogi Berra*.

[11] In the racing sense of the word "handicap".

data. This removes any chance of cheating by sneaking a look at the data and putting up a model which is in fact designed to fit the data retrospectively, like our dishonest racing tipster. The model should be put forward before the data are gathered, or at least, before the data are analysed. Sneaking a peek at the data and then coming up with a model is known as "data fishing" or "data dredging" and amounts to a form of scientific fraud.

The reason is that data fishing involves, in effect, basing a model on more parameters than one is declaring. For example, if one looks for the days in the June record that have numbers less than the average, and the days that have rainfall greater than average, it is easy to find a model that suggests that the rainfall for the low rainfall days will be say 88 mm (or whatever it turns out to be) and for the high rainfall days, it will be 106 mm or whatever. A model suggesting that days 2 through 6, 12 through 15, 20, 21 and 24 will have high rainfall and the remainder lower rainfall will fit this dataset very well, and will appear to have a high F number, when plotted on the lofsos distance/parameter diagram.

On the surface, this model has just two parameters, just as for the two-halves model. But in fact it has a lot more than two, because it has been created by looking at all 30 data points, and singling out the days where rainfall was more than 100 mm to fall into one group, and the remaining days into the other group. This model ought really to have been plotted somewhere vertically above the 30-parameter point on the horizontal axis, not above the two-parameter point. An honest plotting of the model would certainly take it above the Occam line, meaning it is in fact a rubbish model, indeed rubbish plus as it is above the line. Claiming that it has only two-parameters is simply a lie. With the earlier two-halves model, this was acceptable, because in our scenario this was not based on peeking at the data but on a plausible hypothesis, stated in advance, that the rainfall might change over the course of the month, making the two halves different.

Being honest about making models in advance, and refraining from data-fishing, is a virtue in science not for some abstract ethical reason but because data-fishing leads to input of a knowingly wrong number for the parameter complexity of a model, and gives rise to an incorrect calculation of its F number, and mistaken conclusions about its validity. We all make mistakes, but knowingly leading others to make them is the fundamental sin in science.

Models and hypotheses

I should mention that in psychology, models are usually somewhat in the background, but models and hypotheses are intimately connected. Nearly all statistics books begin with the concept of hypotheses. In the present case, we have essentially been comparing the null model with the two-parameter model, and deciding in favour of the latter. Usually, however, we are not so much interested in modelling how the rainfall varies systematically over the month, but in asking the question *does* the rainfall vary systematically over the month? Proposing that it does, is to put forward a hypothesis.

Hypotheses can be couched in the language of models, and in what follows this is an approach that I will take, but you should be aware that in conventional analysis the conclusion of the comparison would probably be put as follows: "The rainfall in Negombo in the first half of June differs significantly from that in the second half, with the average for the first half exceeding that for the second half." The model comparison process is just one essential step towards reaching this conclusion. This will be explained in detail subsequently.

Signal-to-noise ratio

Most statistics can be viewed as calculating what experts in communication theory call a "signal-to-noise ratio". If the data are trying to tell us something interesting, such as a systematic variation in rainfall over the month, this message is the signal. But it is like a signal being transmitted over a crackly telephone line, in which some of the message consists of pops, hisses and whistles.

To discover the nature of the message — or indeed to find whether there is a message at all — it is helpful to have some way of measuring the strength of the underlying random variation, or noise. If we can measure both signal and noise we can calculate the signal/noise ratio. A high value of this ratio means that any signal we perceive is likely to be genuine, and not the accidental outcome of a series of hisses and pops which may by chance come together to sound like a meaningful message. If you find it implausible that pure noise could be mistaken for a signal, recall that the so-called *Satanic backmasking* controversy almost certainly included satanic "messages", allegedly heard when certain records were played backwards, which were the result of listeners reading meaningful words into what was simply gibberish.

In the present instance, if the signal is represented by the slope of the left-hand solid line in the diagram, and the noise is measured by the slope of the right-hand solid line, then the *F*-ratio is indeed a signal-to-noise ratio.

But if one uses this approach, one should draw a distinction between "error" and "noise". The "error" term in the model calculation refers to the error component of the two parameter model, and is the lofsos distance of the model from the data. The "noise" term is found by dividing the error term by the number of "unused" parameters of the model, in this case 28. The literature is not always clear about this, but the point is worth making.

Data, models and error: the basic equation

The general relation between data and models can be written symbolically as follows:

$$\text{Data} = \text{model} + \text{error.}$$

In one sense, this is a trivial observation. It merely states that the data consists of whatever can be accounted for by the model, plus whatever is left over. In the case where for example the numbers 1, 2, 3, 4, 5 are modelled by the constant number 3, the equation can be written as a series of numerical equalities:

$$1 = 3 - 2$$
$$2 = 3 - 1$$

$$3 = 3 + 0$$
$$4 = 3 + 1$$
$$5 = 3 + 2.$$

For each one, the data value is equal to the model predicted value (constant, at 3) plus the difference between the actual data and what the model predicts it to be. So in this case, the error terms are $-2, -1, 0, 1$ and 2 for the data points.

However, it can be helpful to look at it this way, because of the fact that the error term is very much dependent on the model being analysed. A more complex model will be expected to give smaller values for the error terms. To take an extreme case, the saturated model will give zero values for the error terms, because in that case the equation becomes:

$$Data = Data + error.$$

However, this is not an interesting case. Of more value is the type of model which is built up using a number of sub-models, each of which accounts for some of the variability in the data in a way which does not overlap with the other sub-models.

The way this works can be seen as follows. Suppose model 1 accounts for some of the variability in the data, so that

$$Data = model\ 1 + error\ 1.$$

But now suppose there is another model, model 2, which is a model for the error term, so that

$$error\ 1 = model\ 2 + error\ 2.$$

In general, error 2 will be smaller than error 1, so we can now write

$$Data = model\ 1 + model\ 2 + error\ 2.$$

If error 2 can in turn be approximated by model 3 we will have

$$Data = model\ 1 + model\ 2 + model\ 3 + error\ 3.$$

And at each step the error term has been reduced.

This only works in this simple way if the models are genuinely non-overlapping. In the language of statistics, this arises if the models are "orthogonal". In this case, the most accurate possible model is built up by adding the maximal number of orthogonal models, each accounting for some well-defined effect. This is, to antici-pate, the way ANOVA works: by approximating the data by using main effects and interactions, each of which accounts for a chunk of the error term left over by the previous accumulated models.

The mathematics of calculating models and their sums of squares is particularly simple in the case of orthogonal designs. One way to ensure this is to insist that the number of data points in each of the subgroups (or "cells") of the experimental setup are all equal to one another. It is possible to create models and to calculate *F*-ratios when these numbers are not all equal (such cases are known, logically enough, as non-orthogonal designs), but this introduces complications, though I will cover the mathematics in the online material. SPSS uses a particular approach which covers the non-orthogonal situation adequately. Alternatives are available, but the pros and cons of using them would take us too far afield.

LOOKING AHEAD

This, though a useful beginning, is still far from a complete account of how scientific research is carried out, and it may be helpful to state the remaining steps which are needed, and which will be pro-vided in later chapters. The questions that arise are as follows.

(1) How does one select experimental participants, and having done that, how does one set about testing any particular causal hypothesis or model with this sample, in practical terms: how does one run the experiment, in other words?

(2) Having carried out the testing and gathered in the data, how does one translate the causal hypothesis into the mathematical model which best fits the data, by some procedure such as that outlined above?

(3) Having done that, how does one determine whether the *F*-ratio for that model is large enough to be able with some confidence to prefer it to the null model?

(4) For that matter, how confident can one be that the causal model which happens to be the best fit to the data, is actually a good fit in reality? We can be fairly sure that our sample will not be precisely representative of the whole population, even with a large sample: this is one of the reasons why the results of opinion polls of voting intentions are often in error. This suggests that rather than give just one causal model we should give a *range* of possible models, within which we can be reasonably confident that the true causal model will lie. How does one calculate such a range of probable models?

Question 1 raises issues about sampling and experimental design, including those of **validity** in its various forms.

Question 2 is relatively straightforward. A typical causal hypothesis will generally claim that the value of the DV is influenced by the value of the IV. In practice, this means that if the set of data is divided into a number of separate subsets, such as the two groups comprising the first 15 days of June and the second 15 days in the rainfall example, then the means of the DV in the subsets will differ systematically between these subsets. The best fitting model is generally that which allots to each point, the mean of the subset to which it belongs.

Question 3 deals with the statistical issue of significance testing, and estimating the probability that in claiming that a particular causal model is preferable to the null model, we may be making a so-called **type I error**: that is, rejecting the null model when it is in fact true.

Question 4 raises the idea that rather than simply rejecting the null model, it will be more useful to provide a **confidence interval** to describe a range of causal models, within which we can state that the true model lies.

Unfortunately, these issues require a fairly lengthy diversion into what is known as **descriptive statistics**, as well as considering in some detail techniques of experimental design. We will need to touch on at least a minimum of mathematics, though this will be discussed, as far as possible, in descriptive rather than technical language. However, to proceed further we have to go in some detail into two ideas, that of means or averages, and standard deviations. These are the basic concepts on which everything else is built, and are the subject of the following chapter.

In order to bring some concreteness to these concepts, the chapter will also explain how to enter data into SPSS, and how to use SPSS to calculate these basic descriptive statistics.

Chapter 3

Testing Hypotheses and Recording the Result: Types of Validity

SUMMARY

An analogy between the formation and refinement of hypotheses and models, and trial and error learning in animals. Three stages in science: testing, evaluation and claim-making. Testing as passive (observational) or active (experimental) styles. Details given of basic data entry procedures in SPSS which represent the first step in the evaluation phase. A brief account is given of the new experimentalism, and of the concepts of operational definitions and construct validity, important in expressing scientific claims.

NEED TO KNOW

How models arise

Models are clearly both necessary and useful, but I have not clearly stated how they arise in the first place. There is a double aspect to models: they need to be created and validated, and then they need to be used. Broadly speaking, scientific research is concerned with the first aspect, whereas the second, the application and use of models, is the province of clinical medicine, engineering and technology. Without the applications, science would arguably have little social value, but without the research, the applications might not exist.[1] In this book, I focus on the first aspect.

If the *use* of models in science corresponds to the *implementation* of patterns of behaviour by living creatures which ensure their survival, then the *formation* of models presumably corresponds to the *learning* of such behaviour. An animal may find by trial and error that a certain model is invalid, in the sense that following that model results in poor outcomes. For example, a bird may find that eating a monarch butterfly makes it sick. The bird will modify its model of what is good to eat, and will in future avoid prey with the monarch's distinctive orange and black warning coloration. It will also learn that other creatures are wholesome, and will add this fact to its feeding model and will be rewarded accordingly. What is the scientific equivalent of this?

Chapter 1 brought in the notion of a research hypothesis, which typically states that there is a link between a specified cause C and a specified effect E. This hypothesis can be satisfied by a whole family of models, with different effect sizes (and maybe differing in other ways as well). The connection will be developed below. A research hypothesis is the indispensable starting point of any research programme.[2]

The bird learns not to eat a toxic butterfly by trying the effect of assuming the opposite, and getting a bad result. The original hypothesis "all butterflies are good to eat" is compared with the results of experience, and is found wanting. The bird learns accordingly. Science works similarly in testing the experimental hypothesis that C and E are causally linked. The bird's education involves three components: eating the butterfly, getting sick and learning that association between eating the butterfly and sickness. The

---

[1] Francis Bacon called the first process "experiments of light" because they illuminated the way nature worked, and the second process "experiments of fruit" because they were fruitful to humankind.

[2] That is for "hypothesis driven" research, which is the great majority. In exploratory research the research hypothesis may take the form of a research question, typically "what is the nature of phenomenon X?" or "what are the links, if any between X and Y?"

scientific process also requires three stages: **testing** the hypothesis by applying the casual variable, **evaluating** the results and **claiming** an outcome in terms of the validity of a new or more specific hypothesis.

In the case in the previous chapter concerning rainfall in Negombo, the original hypothesis might have been: there is a difference in rainfall between the first and second halves of June. The causal variable here has two values, say 1 and 2: 1 refers to the first half of June, and 2 to the second half. So every day in June will be given the number 1 or 2 accordingly: that is the value of this variable for that day. The testing phase consists of gathering the rainfall data for each day, and the evaluation consists of measuring the fit of the causal model to the data. The causal model here states: "if the value of the causal variable is 1, predict the rainfall for that day to be 100.47 mm; if the value is 2, predict the rainfall to be 93.13 mm". We know that the evaluation yields the claim that this model is to be preferred to the null model.

From here on, I will change the terminology from C and E language to the language of variables. The causal variable will be referred to as the "IV": it is the independent variable. The effect will be referred to as the "DV", the dependent variable. A typical causal hypothesis states that a change in the IV is followed by a change in the DV. So it is evident that the "testing" part of the process must consist in arranging somehow for a change in the IV, and then measuring the values of the DV. The "evaluating" part consists in looking at those values, and comparing them to see whether there was any change, in response to the change in the IV.

The "testing" part can happen in one of two ways. Either we can wait around until the IV changes of its own accord and observe what happens to the DV, or we can in some way compel the IV to change, and then observe what happens to the DV. These are termed the **observational** and **experimental** approaches. In many cases, the second alternative is the better one for reasons which will be explained later, though sometimes it is not possible for practical or ethical reasons (if the IV is gender, for example, or if the IV refers to smoking: we cannot compel non-smoking humans to smoke in order to see whether they develop lung cancer, though similar experiments were carried out on beagles in the 1970s).

It might seem that the "evaluating" part involves observing whether there is, or is not, a change in the DV in response to a change in the IV. But things are not quite that easy. The null hypothesis of no change in the DV is simpler than the causal hypothesis, so by Occam's principle should be preferred to it unless there is good reason to override the principle. "Good reason" here means that the causal hypothesis should fit the data much better than the null hypothesis. Deciding whether or not this is true, is the task of the evaluation phase of the study.

The details of designing experiments and evaluating the data will be covered in subsequent chapters. The methods of evaluation are common to most statistical analysis packages, but the particular program used for illustration in this book will be taken from SPSS. Before describing how data are evaluated, it seems logical to begin with explaining how the data are entered into SPSS, and so this will be the next topic of the present, very practical chapter.

In this section you will learn how to open a new blank dataset in SPSS, to manually enter numerical data, to name and describe variables and to save your dataset with a new name. The situation I am describing refers to some notional observational study, set up to evaluate the hypothesis that gender (the IV) has a causal link with scores on some computer-based test of performance: in other words, that test score is affected by gender. This is an example of a very common situation, where there is a nominal IV and a scale DV.

Let us assume that you have already run the data collection phase in which you have tested a sample of people (incidentally, the individuals who have been evaluated as part of some study are always known as **participants**; this replaces the older term, "subjects"). So you have the data from your participants and you are now in the evaluation phase. Determining the truth of the research hypothesis involves operating on the data with certain programs in SPSS, but first of course the data have to be entered into SPSS in a form in which the program can process them.

The most basic operations with SPSS (or any other statistical package) involve opening a blank dataset and entering some numbers, together with the names for variables. I will give instructions for those using a PC; Mac users will need to translate the mouse operations "left click" into "click" and "right click" into "Ctrl-click". I will assume you have already installed SPSS onto the PC or Mac.

1. To open a new blank dataset

Go to Start >> All Programs. One of the list of programs will be called "IBM SPSS Statistics", and to the right, a Greek capital sigma, or Σ, with the number of the edition that you have (at time of writing, it is up to the 22nd). **Left click on this**.

A window will appear, giving access to recent datasets if any, looking as in Fig. 3.1.

Click on "new dataset" within the "new files" window at top left, then **OK**.

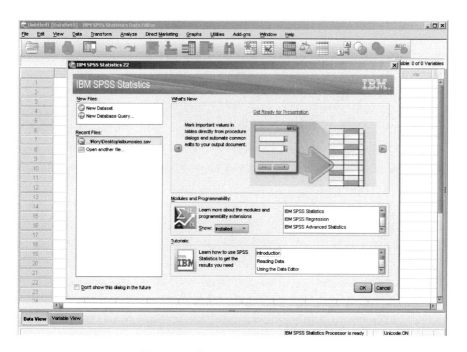

Fig. 3.1.   Opening a new dataset.

This takes you to an empty array of cells. If you move your mouse and left click on any cell, it turns orange and is now active. This view is called the Data View, and the data you enter next will form the dataset.

2.   To manually enter numerical data

Click on the cell in column 1, row 1, and type in a number from your keyboard. (You need to use the row of numbers *above* the QWERTY keys; the numbers on the right-hand end of the keyboard, if you have them, operate the arrow functions).

Press the enter button. Three things happen. Cell 2 in that column becomes the active cell, the number you typed in appears to two decimal places (so for example, 12 becomes 12.00 and 3.456 becomes 3.46), and the column acquires a name, which in SPSS defaults to VAR00001. If you had started entering numbers in the fourth column, the first four columns would have been automatically named as VAR00001 through VAR00004. You can manually enter any number in any cell of the data view array.

The columns in SPSS correspond, as the default names suggest, to your variables. The rows, in nearly every case (there are two exceptions that will be covered later), correspond to individual experimental units, which in psychology generally means individual participants.

3.   To name and describe variables

In order to give a realistic example, I suggest you create two variables. One is called "gender" and the other is "score". Gender is a nominal variable: here we give it just two values. Score is a scale variable. Gender will be treated as the IV, and score as the DV, in a causal model. Before doing this clear the dataset of any numbers you may have randomly typed in: you can do this by holding down the left click, sweeping along the row of variable name buttons and releasing. All the cells in the columns will be active and coloured orange. If you now right click and "clear", the cells will empty.

At the bottom of the SPSS screen you will find two tabs. At present you are in "Data view". **Click on the other tab named "Variable view"**.

That will take you into another screen where all the information on your variables is stored.

Before entering the gender and score variables, I recommend you do something for the sake of good housekeeping: **create a variable which encodes your participants**. What this will do is create a permanent record of where your data came from. Each participant will have data spread out along a particular row of the dataset, but unless you have some means of recording it, there is no way you can know from the dataset which participant this data came from originally. It is not sufficient to note the row number of the data — you will notice that on the left, each row is given a unique number. This is because some of the operations you can do in SPSS can end up shuffling the rows among themselves.

There are several reasons why this could be important: for example, if you later discover from your analysis that a particular set of data is different in some way from the rest, you may wish to retest that participant.

To create a new variable, let us call it part_no for participant number, **type "part_no" into the top cell in the Name column** (left click on this if it is not already active), and **press Enter**. That will take you to the cell directly beneath it. **Type "gender" for the second variable and "score" for the third variable, pressing the enter key after each operation.**

You now have three new variables. You may have noticed that all but one of the columns to the right which describe them have filled with default settings, some of which you will now need to change, and you will need to enter some new items as well.

(i) Go to the second row, for the gender variable, gender and left click in the "values" column. This will make a blue button appear in the right end of the cell.
Click on it. The "value labels" box will appear.
Type 0 in the value cell in this box.
Left click on the "label" box. Type "male".
Click the blue "add" button. This tells SPSS that 0 codes for the group of male participants.

(ii) Do the same but with 1 in the value box, and "female" in the label box.

(iii) Click "OK" on the value labels box.

You need to provide labels for the coding whenever you have a nominal variable, because nominal variables always represent groups or categories of some kind, and this column tells SPSS the convention you have used to represent the categories by numbers.

The reason you have to represent categories by numbers, is that SPSS can only apply statistical analysis to data that are input in the form of numbers. If you just wrote "male" and "female" into the gender column in data view, SPSS would be unable to process the information.

In some cases, two values might not be sufficient: you may need to enter in addition values for people who identify themselves as "trans", or as "trans male", "trans female" and possibly other descriptions. The main rule to observe is that these categories must be **exclusive** and **exhaustive**: that is, nobody must belong to more than one category, and every person in your sample must belong to some category.

(iv) Go to the "measure" column, second from the extreme right, and left click. A drop down menu appears with three options: scale, ordinal and nominal. **For the part_no and gender variables, click on nominal. For the final cell which refers to the score variable, click on scale.**

Note: **you could if you wished enter a description of these three variables in the "label" column.** You cannot name variables arbitrarily in the "name" column of SPSS: for example, you cannot have two words separated by spaces, nor can you use hyphens (but you can use the underscore _). If you want to use a complex description, the label column is the ideal place to do it. For the exercise, put "participant number" in the label for part_no, and "score on test 1" in the label for score. This will not appear in the data view display, but can be an invaluable aid to memory when coming back to a dataset days or even months later.

Now click on the data view label at the bottom, taking you back to the dataset, left click on the part-no column and manually enter the numbers 1 to 10. Go to the gender column and enter five 0's and five 1's, in any order. Go to the score column and enter ten numbers in it: it does not matter what you enter, this is just for the exercise. In reality of course the numbers would refer to the scores of particular participants. After typing each figure, press Enter and the active cell will go down to the next cell automatically. Enter just one number for each row where there is an entry in the gender column.

Remember the rule "one row — one participant". Each participant must have one entry for gender, and one entry for score value. Later on, you will encounter instances where some participants may not have numbers entered for each and every variable. This "missing values" phenomenon does sometimes happen, and it can create its own problems. For the moment, assume that there are no missing values.

You are now in a position to test your hypothesis, using a method called an independent groups t-test, but that will have to wait until we cover significance tests. For the moment, there are two more things which will improve the user-friendliness of your dataset. They are cosmetic rather than essential, but worth knowing about.

One is that the participant numbers and gender codes will appear by default with two decimal points. I find it distracting for nominal variables to have decimals, and you can eliminate these by clicking on the Variable View tab, and click in the decimals column for part_no. A small double arrow will appear on the right. Click the lower arrow twice so that it reads zero. Do the same for the gender variable.

If you now click the data view, you will find that the two left-hand columns no longer have decimal points.

The second thing is to click on Edit, second from left in the top row, and in the drop down menu to click on Options. There is an outlined area at the top left named Variable Lists, and just below it, two "radio buttons". If the top one is active — it is called Display labels — click the one below it, called Display names. The reason

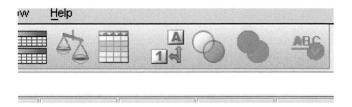

Fig. 3.2. The "value labels" icon.

for this small adjustment will become clearer when we start doing some actual analysis.

There is one final function to demonstrate at this point.

In the Data View screen, **go to the thing that resembles a motorway route marker with a red 1 and a red A and click on it.** (This is the Value Labels icon, see Fig. 3.2).

Observe that the gender variable now toggles between the encoded numbers you used and the names of the genders.

4. To save your dataset with a new name

Now you need to save your precious data. The default name will be something uninformative like "Untitled 1".

At the top left-hand corner go to File, Save As, put a suitable name in the File Name box (perhaps Exercise 1). Use the "look in" or "up one level" tools at the top of the "Save Data As" box to find a convenient file somewhere, and use the "Save" button, second one down on the right, to save your work.

When you exit the program you will be asked if you want to proceed, click yes, and if you want to save the output, where you click no. SPSS produces an output file which records everything you do with the data. When you need to report your findings, it is the Output file where graphs, tables etc. can be found to copy and paste into your report. This will happen later.

GOING DEEPER

Model construction and testing

The distinction drawn in the first paragraph of the NTK section between research which creates models, and applications which use them, is perhaps too stark. Medawar (1982, p. 34) has argued that a doctor diagnosing a patient is equally engaged in fitting a model (the disease) to the data (the symptoms), as is a mechanic trying to find the fault in a car. Essentially they are using the same method as a research team engaged in looking for a causal model for schizophrenia.

However, we would all recognise that there are differences as well as underlying similarities between these two types of activity. Perhaps it is this: the doctor or mechanic are looking for strictly local explanations, narrow models, whereas the researchers seek something of wider application: broad models. The discoveries of the doctor or the mechanic may be of immediate practical use and value to that particular patient or that specific car-owner, but not to the wider community.

The findings of the research team will therefore be *publishable*, whereas those of the doctor and the mechanic will not. In the rare cases where the doctor may discover something that is publishable, it will be because the standard framework for understanding diseases has proven inadequate in some way, and therefore her findings are of relevance to the broad model of disease.

Science and replicability

There is an important difference between the kinds of models and hypotheses studied by research scientists, and simple facts which are true at a particular place and time. A simple fact might be: "the temperature in Central London at midday on 15 June 2016 was 19°C". A causal hypothesis such as "there is a link between gender and scores on performance on the ABCD test" is a different kind of claim. If it is to be of any interest, it should be true not just at the place and time when the data were taken, but more generally. Recall that the aim of research science is to construct models, and the aim of constructing models is to be able to use the model subsequently. A model which has no validity outside the particular circumstances of its collection will not be of value, at least as a scientific model.

Not all models have this limitation. A detective investigating a crime may have a number of models (suspect 1 was responsible, suspect 2 was responsible etc.), and these models may only be relevant to a particular event: the crime itself. But in this case the models have a different aim: to account for a particular set of facts in the best possible way. Scientific models have a more ambitious aim, and so more is demanded of them: at the very least that they are applicable at a subsequent time. This requirement can be summarised in the requirement that a scientific claim, usually embodied in the form of a model, should be **replicable**. In fact it is arguable that a scientific assertion is nothing more or less than a claim that something, some event or phenomenon, is replicable.[3]

This may be the point at which to introduce, in a very broad brush way, the set of ideas known as "the new experimentalism",[4] or NE for short. The origins of this movement lie in the perceived failure of an earlier approach to the philosophy of science known as positivism. Logical positivism (and a variant called logical empiricism) attempted to formulate general statements about the world known as "covering laws" on the basis of the observation of simple facts. It was then realised that observation statements themselves depended on theories, whose validity could not be guaranteed. One way of interpreting this was that theories were essentially social constructs, and that preferring one theory to another was a matter of choice: one might say that science is basically subjective.[5]

This was a disheartening conclusion, given that objectivity is often put forward as one of the key characteristics of science.[6] The supporters of the NE approach attempted to get around the difficulty by suggesting that if science made more modest claims, they were more likely to attain these aims. In particular, the claims

---

[3] Replicability has not yet been well defined in this book. Examining the different types will be central to the later examination of the various kinds of validity that can be expected of scientific claims.

[4] A brief and accessible introduction to these ideas is a paper by Mayo to which a link is given in the Further Reading section, referred to in what follows as Mayo (1994).

[5] This is of course a very crude simplification of the sort of views attributed to Thomas Kuhn and his followers, but anyone wanting a more nuanced view should read something like Chalmers (1999).

[6] In for example, Mitchell and Jolley (2007, pp. 2–4).

might prove to have objective validity. The answer can be summarised in the phrase "experiments have a life of their own". To paraphrase, the basic unit of scientific activity is the experiment,[7] in which certain actions by the researcher lead to certain observed outcomes. The actions and outcomes are recorded and published. The claim is that if a different researcher reads the report of the experiment and undertakes the same actions, then the same outcomes will be observed.

At the risk of appearing flippant, I think of NE as the Delia Smith approach to the philosophy of science. Delia Smith publishes cookbooks that have a deserved reputation for reliability: it is said that if you follow the instructions for the recipes, you will invariably find that the results are as stated in the book. NE seems to be offering the same modest yet still vital guarantee, or rather, to be encouraging us to aim for such guarantees of replicability in our experiments, and to build science on a foundation of repeatable experimental findings. In particular, NE is immune to the one of the weaknesses that brought down logical empiricism. According to NE, the aims of conducting an experiment are independent of theory, the experimental data can be justified independently of theory, and experimental conclusions have a robustness that enables them to be retained, despite any changes in theory.

So, instead of the top down approach typical of physics, which seeks overarching laws which give a "theory of everything", the new experimentalism appears to be working from the ground up, starting with the limited aim of finding particular combinations of settings, contexts, manipulations and individual participants, which result in predictable findings. A key phrase here is "topical hypotheses" (Mayo, 1994, p. 271). In contrast to the "covering laws" of the logical empiricists, topical hypotheses refer to predictions that are local and tied to specific combinations

---

[7] I am using the word "experiment" in a broad sense here. There is a technical sense in which an "experiment" requires that independent variables should be manipulated by the experimenter. I do not wish to be that specific here: the "actions" of the researcher may simply be measurements.

of experimental circumstances. In other words, they are like the prediction that if you follow Delia Smith's recipe for hollandaise sauce,[8] you will get an excellent result, whereas the logical empiricists would have been looking for a general theory of cooking, from which the preparation of hollandaise sauce could be deduced as a logical consequence.

If this is to work, then clearly the "recipes", or descriptions of experiments, must be sufficiently clear and unambiguous to enable them to be repeated by someone who was not necessarily present at the scene. At the same time, if the results are to be of interest to the broader research community, they will need to make reference to concepts which have at least some wider relevance. A report of an experiment which records that "we played white noise at 80 decibels for 30 seconds and observed a rise in temperature of the participant's left earlobe of 0.1°C", however accurate and however repeatable, is unlikely to be of interest unless there is at least some link between this rather odd combination of manipulation and measurement, and some real world theory or concept about human behaviour. To put it in the language of cookery, the recipe needs to produce something that people will want to eat.

In fact at this point one might turn the idea on its head, and start at the other end: the conceptual end, grounded in real world concerns rather than the laboratory. It is all very well to build science on replicable experiments, but the experiments should relate at least indirectly to things of concern to the wider scientific and social community. In fact the starting point of most experiments begins with a hypothesis couched in conceptual, rather than experimental terms.

Suppose for example that a psychologist comes up with a theory of how people are able to empathise with the emotional state of other people. This theory suggests that this ability requires the simulation of the corresponding state in one's own emotional circuitry. She thinks that a good way to test this theory is to induce

---

[8] Notoriously difficult to make by traditional methods, I am told.

different internal mood states in her participants,[9] and then to see whether this interferes with their judgements of mood in others. This requires us to consider two linked issues: operational definitions and construct validity. These ideas are normally introduced independently of one another, but it seems more enlightening to bring them in as a linked pair of concepts.

Operational definitions

An **operational definition** of a variable is a **set of activities required to measure** that variable. It is two things at once. It is both a record of the actions taken by the people who conducted the original experiment, and a set of instructions that will enable other researchers to replicate those steps. It corresponds rather exactly to the part of the printed recipe in a cookbook which says "take 250 ccs of sunflower oil…". In the example in the previous paragraph, the procedure involves inducing different mood states, and then measuring the judgements of mood by the participants. The IV here is internal mood states, and the DV is the way the participants respond by judging mood. Both of these are variables, and both require measurement, and the procedures to carry out these measurements are given by operational definitions.

The use of the term "measurement" to describe a manipulation such as mood induction may appear strange, but manipulation has much in common with measurement and it seems reasonable to bend the idea of measurement a little to include it.

In the case of our notional experiment, the induction of mood states might be done by exposing the participant to 30 s of a particular extract of music. Suppose the IV has just two values, "sad" and "happy". A passage from Barber's adagio might be taken to induce a mood of sadness, and an extract from the

---

[9] This raises the question of whether she will expose each participant to just one mood induction and compare these separate groups of participants, or whether she will look at the effect of mood change on each participant. This is an important aspect of experimental methodology. The alternatives are known as between-subject and within-subject designs, and will be dealt with fully in later chapters.

second movement of Beethoven's seventh symphony to induce happiness. A clear instruction such as this is an operational definition of mood induction: it records what happened in the experiment, and will allow others to replicate this mood induction procedure. The manipulation is also a measurement, in the sense of determining a unique value of a variable. The manipulation of using the sad music corresponds to the value "sad" of the IV, and the happy music corresponds to the IV value of "happy". Establishing that a variable has a certain value is a measurement in the broad sense.

There are a number of possible ways of inducing mood changes, such as making participants read "Velten sentences".[10] Unless it is specified which alternative was actually chosen, the original experiment cannot be exactly replicated. You might ask why it needs to be replicated so precisely. If the effect of mood change on judgement is real, why should it matter how the mood changes are induced? This is a fair question: one answer might be that the effect may only work with one kind of mood induction and not others. If this is the case, the effect may still be of interest, though it may be of a more subtle nature than was originally thought.

If attempts to replicate the original experiment fail through using the "wrong" mood induction method, the cause of the failure will not be evident unless the details of the method used were included in the published account of the original experiment.[11] But if subsequent researchers *do* know the details they may find, for example, that there is an effect on judgement when mood changes

---

[10]Examples can be found online at http://idiolect.org.uk/docs/blog/negative_velten.txt and http://idiolect.org.uk/docs/blog/positive_velten.txt.

[11]The replicators can only reproduce details that were in the original report, and will fill in any gaps themselves on the basis of their own experience and resources. They may then fail to replicate the original experiment, and the reason may be that they inadvertently ignored some detail of the original setup that was crucial to the outcome. Of course the original researchers may spot the difference, and claim retrospectively that this detail explains the lack of replication. It does indeed sometimes happen that once this emerges, the replication succeeds.

are induced by music but not when they are brought about using Velten sentences.[12] This may lead to a more sophisticated understanding of the mechanisms of empathy and emotion perception.

Without the level of detail that is involved in giving a full operational definition, this level of subtlety would have been lost, all because the original research hypothesis turned out to be partially incorrect. With the full detail, however, such defects can be found and remedied. This is really all part and parcel of the NE philosophy. If we start off with modest aims, we may hope to build up to results which are reliable if unspectacular.

The measurement of the DV might be specified by showing the participant a series of ambivalent faces, which might be judged as either happy or sad, and asking them to decide whether the face was happy or sad. The actual value of the DV could then be calculated by taking the proportion of faces judged as happy. The research hypothesis suggests that this proportion will change, depending on whether the induced mood was sad or happy.[13]

Construct validity

This is the other side of the coin to the notion of operational definition. Operational definitions provide the practical counterpart of the notional concepts outlined in the research hypothesis. Construct validity is the guarantee that the practical steps given in the operational definition, really do embody the concepts given in the research hypothesis. Put another way, the operational definition of an *idea* is a *procedure*, while the construct validity of a *procedure* is the reassurance that it represents a specified *idea*.

Construct validity is a difficult thing to define clearly, perhaps because it attempts to pin down in a precise, scientific way, ideas

---

[12] To my knowledge there is no evidence for this. I merely put it forward to illustrate the point.

[13] The results of experiments suggest that the change is in the obvious direction: people in a happy mood make more "happy" judgements of faces than do people in a sad mood.

embodied in day to day informal language such as "emotion", "intelligence", or "creativity" (a particularly tricky one, this last one). Standard textbooks are not always helpful here. One popular account defines construct validity as "the extent to which the psychological constructs being proposed or investigated are valid ones". So construct validity is defined as the validity of constructs. If an otherwise masterly exposition is reduced to this level of circularity, the problem must indeed be a tricky one.

A slightly more informative standard definition is: "an operational definition has construct validity if the variable that it defines *really does* represent the concept that it claims to represent". The perceptive reader will see that this still leaves many questions unresolved, but a fuller analysis of the issue (and my own suggestion for providing a free-standing definition of construct validity) must wait until a later chapter.[14]

The procedure recommended by NE may seem unambitious, especially when compared with the hard sciences and biology. But these have the great advantage over psychology of being underlain by powerful unifying ideas. In the case of physics, Newton's laws provided an early foundation of rigour and mathematical exactness, and this character persists despite the replacement of Newton's framework by the complexities of relativity and quantum theory. Biology was in the same condition as psychology until Darwin, but his theory of evolution revolutionised that science and still underpins it, despite much subsequent modification. Geology has the theory of plate tectonics as a powerful explanatory model. These are like the backbones providing a supporting structure for the science in question. By comparison, psychology can seem formless: a jellyfish rather than a barracuda. As a science, it sometimes seems to be at the same primitive stage of development as physics as understood by Aristotle.

However, the other sciences did not reach their present stature by starting out with inflated ambitions. As Francis Bacon wrote: "If

---

[14] It will be contained in the online material.

a man will begin with certainties, he shall end in doubts; but if he will be content to begin with doubts, he shall end in certainties." It may be that psychology will one day find its Newton or Darwin. But it is certain that this will never happen unless the ground is prepared in advance by building, patiently and steadily, a foundation of reliable findings.

Chapter 4

Basic Descriptive Statistics (and How Pierre Laplace Saved the World)

SUMMARY

Descriptive statistics summarising the basic characteristics of a set of numbers: measures of central tendency (mean, median, mode) and measures of dispersion (standard deviation, interquartile range, range, mean absolute deviation). Reliability and validity of measurements. The standard error of the mean. Using SPSS to find measures of central tendency and measures of dispersion.

NEED TO KNOW

Typically, an experiment will generate a large set of data, possibly hundreds or thousands of numbers. In order to be able to handle and make sense of these sets of numbers, it is necessary to reduce them to something simpler. The most useful way of doing this is to create and compare models which can help to explain the finer structure within the data, but to begin with we need to cover something more basic: descriptive statistics. Not all statistics are descriptive: the process of model comparison uses something called inferential statistics, but for the moment we will be content to simply describe a set of data.

When it comes to writing up a set of research findings, descriptive and inferential statistics play two different roles. Descriptive statistics provide information such as the average age, IQ etc. of participants. The idea is to give data on the population or populations of participants that were sampled. Inferential statistics are used to determine whether or not the various causal hypotheses were supported by the data. However, understanding the inferential process also requires some knowledge of descriptive statistics.

The word "statistics" was already being used in the 18th century to refer to the gathering of accurate demographic data by governments. This was used to find out the size of populations, and in particular to discover details about the preoccupations of most governments: the ability of their people to pay tax, and their capacity to provide manpower to fight wars. More constructively, they were used for example to contribute to public health by categorising the causes of death among the population: the so-called bills of mortality. This explains the origins of the word as "the science of dealing with data about the condition of a state".

This approach was often concerned with producing accurate numbers: of people, of men of military age, of people dying of plague in a given year. But as the information available grew larger, it became necessary to condense these figures: in particular, to find a *single* number which represents or summarises a whole set of numbers. A ruler might, for example, wish to estimate the wealth of different provinces of his kingdom by finding out the typical size of the landholding for a single family in each province. The problem is to summarise a large list of numbers by a single number that is in some sense representative of all of them.

There are several different ways of doing this, each of which can be appropriate in different situations. These ways of summarising a dataset with a single number are known as **measures of central tendency**. The ones generally used are the **mean** (or average), the **median** and the **mode**.

A measure of central tendency gives some information about the value of the dataset: it gives an answer to the question "what single value is *most typical* of the set as a whole?" The next natural question is "given that typical value, *how* typical is it? Do the other numbers cluster closely in its neighbourhood, or are they dispersed widely around it?" If a province appears wealthy, it may be because there is a population of people who are all equally prosperous, or it may be that there are a few very large landowners, and a majority of subsistence farmers who are struggling to get by.

The possible answers to the second question are known as **measures of dispersion**. The most widely used ones are the **standard deviation**, the **interquartile range**, the **range** and the **mean absolute deviation** (or mean absolute difference). Of all these, by far the most often used are the mean, median and standard deviation.

Measures of central tendency

Average or mean

In symbols, the average of a set of k numbers n_1, n_2 and so on up to n_k, is $n_{average} = (n_1 + n_2 + \cdots + n_{k-1} + n_k)/k$, where the dots stand for the process of adding on all the other numbers between n_2 and n_{k-1}. In words, to find the mean of a set of numbers, add them together and divide the result by how many numbers you started with.

An advantage of the mean is that it is widely understood from its use as a measure of achievement in sport, it is simple to explain, and it is the easiest measure to use in doing statistical calculations mathematically. This was important prior to the widespread use of computers. A disadvantage of the mean is that it can be strongly influenced by single values in the set of numbers. If the set of numbers {1, 2, 3, 4, 5} with mean 3 is incorrectly entered as {1, 2, 3, 4, 50}, the mean will appear as 12, far from the true value even though only one figure is incorrect.

Median

The median of a set of numbers is defined as being what you get if you arrange the numbers in increasing order, and choose the number exactly half way up the list. The median of the set {2, –7, 200, 1000, –50, 3, 4, 1, 10} would be found by ordering them thus: {−50, −7, 1, 2, 3, 4, 10, 200, 1000} and finding that 3 is the median: four of the set are smaller, and four are larger. If there had been 10 rather than nine numbers, there would have been no one number exactly in the middle; in that case, find the two which are either side of middle, and take their average. For example with {−50, −7, 1, 2, 3, 4, 5, 10, 200, 1000}, the median would be the mean of 3 and 4, i.e., 3.5.

An advantage of the median is that unlike the mean, it is not strongly influenced by single values. In the example above the median of {1, 2, 3, 4, 5} is 3 and that of {1, 2, 3, 4, 50} is also 3. The fact that the median for the first set of numbers is the same as the mean in the first example, is due to the distribution of the set, which is symmetrical around the number 3: with a symmetrical distribution the mean and the median are always equal.

The median may be preferable to the mean if the numbers are distributed in a highly unsymmetrical way, or if it is suspected that there may be errors in the dataset. A disadvantage of the median is that standard mathematical results in statistics are about means rather than medians, and most statistical programs, including SPSS, use the mean rather than the median as the default measure of central tendency.

Mode

The word "mode" means among other things fashion or style. "Modish" means "popular". This may help to remember that the mode of a set of numbers is the most popular number, the one which occurs most often in the set. For example given the set {1, 2, 2, 3, 4, 4, 4, 5} the mode is 4, since that occurs three times and the others only once or twice.

If the set contains each number only once, the mode is not well defined. Sometimes there may be more than one number that is the mode: in the set {1, 2, 2, 2, 3, 4, 4, 4, 5}, both 2 and 4 occur three times, and both are modes. Such a set is known as **bimodal**, meaning it has two modes.

The mode is not commonly used in statistics for psychology.

Measures of dispersion

Standard deviation

If the mean is thought of as the *typical value of a set of numbers,* the standard deviation, often abbreviated s.d., can be thought of as the *typical value by which a number in the set deviates from the mean.*

The algebraic expression for the standard deviation may appear complicated, but it turns out that mathematically, it is the simplest possible. The expression for it is given in GD, and not included in this section since it is not essential to know it. All statistical programs, including the functions on Excel, will calculate it for you. Given that some people find it helpful to work out examples by hand, some are included in the examples section online.

The advantages and disadvantages of the s.d. as a measure of dispersion are similar to those of the mean. The s.d. is mathematically "nice" but is subject to being unduly influenced by faulty entries in the dataset. The square of the s.d. is referred to as the **variance**. It is not easy to envisage what the variance is in concrete terms, but statistical procedures often refer to the term, and you should be aware of it.

Interquartile range

If the numbers in a dataset are arranged in increasing order of size, the numbers which appear a quarter of the way along and three quarters of the way along are known as the **first** and **third quartiles,** Q_1 and Q_3, respectively. The difference between them, $Q_3 - Q_1$, is the **interquartile range**. Note incidentally that the median is at the *second* quartile, since it is just half way along the list of the numbers in order of size.

The advantages and disadvantages of the interquartile range over the s.d. exactly parallel those of the median over the mean. It is very little affected by errors in the dataset, even if they are gross errors, provided that not too many datapoints are affected. It is, however, not usually provided by the default settings of statistical programs and in mathematical statistics it is harder to work with than the s.d.

The interquartile range may be preferable to the s.d. if the numbers in a dataset are distributed in a highly unsymmetrical way, for example if there are a few very large values and a large number of smaller values, or if it is suspected that there may be errors in the dataset. It will come into its own later when we meet Tukey's box plots[1] in which it plays a key role, and box plots are vital in detecting "bad" data.

Range

This is the difference between the smallest and largest numbers in a dataset. It is seldom used in statistical calculation, but is often presented in papers and lab reports to provide a quick guide to, for example, the extreme values of the ages of participants, or their scores on some test. A small value of the range for some variable indicates that a sample of participants did not differ much in their values for that variable, and that may be an important consideration.

Mean absolute deviation

This measure of dispersion is similar to the s.d. It is not often used, but the exact definition is given in GD. A related measure is the median absolute deviation, also given in GD.

Reliability and validity for measurements

Measures of central tendency and of dispersion have an immediate application to the theory of measurements of scale variables, in particular their validity and reliability. Validity and reliability have technical meanings in this connection, which are somewhat different from their common language meanings.

Recall that any process of measurement of a quantity will involve an unknown amount of error. The error is the difference between the reading obtained by the measurement process, and the true value of the quantity. If the measurement were to be repeated

---

[1] In the online material.

on the same individual, the readings obtained would not be the same, but would differ one from another, since the amount of error is influenced by random influences which vary from one measurement to the next.

Imagine repeating the measurement process a large number of times on the same person, and by this method producing a set of numbers, each the result of one measurement. The measurement process is **valid** if the mean of this set of numbers is equal to the true value of the quantity for that individual. In practice the mean is never exactly equal to the true value, but if the difference is small we can say that the measurement has **high validity**.

The difference between the mean and the true value is the **systematic error**. It is called "systematic", because it is the error which is built into the system of measurement.[2] It can be understood as the bias in the measuring process. For example, a bathroom scales which has not been correctly zeroed may systematically be adding 2 kg to the weight of anyone using it, and the systematic error is +2 kg.

The process of repeating the measurement on a single person, described above, will produce a number of different values, scattered around the mean. The s.d. of these values measures the purely *random* component of the error. A measurement is known as **reliable** if the random error is small, i.e., if the s.d. of the set of measurements is small.

This sense of the word "reliable" differs from the usual meaning. A measurement can be highly reliable and also highly misleading, if it is of low validity. In fact a bathroom scales which reads 50 kg every time it is used is highly reliable, since the random error will be zero. But it will certainly not be useful, and this is because it has very low validity.[3]

---

[2] This discussion takes it as read that the systematic error is constant, i.e., the same for every person tested. This is not necessarily true, but it is a simplifying assumption which seems to be made by most treatments of this subject.

[3] This is a case where the systematic error will vary from person to person. Of course, one might argue that even this scales will give a valid reading for a person weighing 50 kg, but this is a point on a par with the argument that a stopped clock is right twice a day.

Note:

(1) There are several possible definitions of reliability in the statistics literature: the form described above is known as **test–retest reliability**. The precise definition enables the calculation of a number representing this, but it involves the concept of correlation, covered in the online material, along with definitions of the other common forms: inter-rater reliability, and internal consistency. Meanwhile it is sufficient to know that high reliability means small random error, and high validity means small systematic error.

(2) Test–retest reliability for a measurement can be estimated experimentally from a random sample of a given population, using the test repeatedly in the obvious way. Estimating validity on the other hand requires a separate notion of what the "correct" value of the measurement should be, and is therefore a more complex idea than reliability.

Estimating the population mean of a scale variable: the reliability of the sample mean

It is often of interest to know the average value of some quantity taken over a given population. Sometimes it is possible to discover the actual values over the entire population and simply take the mean: this may be so for a government with accurate figures for personal income, wishing to track the average income per head over time, for example. But in most cases this is not practical. For example, a psychologist may wish to estimate the average score of all first year psychology students on the Goldsmiths Musical Sophistication Index, or Gold-MSI. This is quite a complex measure of the ability to engage with music, and taking scores for the whole population is out of the question. The best that could be done in practice is to take a sample of students, and to measure their scores on the Gold-MSI.[4] The average for the sample would be an estimate for the population as a whole.

---

[4] There are in fact subscores on the Gold-MSI for such things as accuracy of singing and formal musical understanding, but the total score can be thought of as a summary of overall engagement with music.

This is in effect what pollsters do in advance of an election. They cannot ask the whole electorate about their voting intentions, but they can sample one or two thousand and find out how they say they will vote. This sample provides a more or less accurate picture of sentiment across the whole voting population. If this is going to provide a useful result, two things are necessary: that the sample should be *representative* of the population, and that it should be *large enough*.

To be representative, the sample should have been selected randomly from the population. This could be done in the case of students by drawing names randomly from a list. More on this is contained in the online material. Another assumption is that the way the dependent variable is measured does not introduce a systematic bias into what the variable is claimed to represent. If it does, the measurement will not have validity. Pollsters have made some conspicuously wrong forecasts in recent times, possibly because they focused too much on establishing reliability through large sample sizes, and too little on guaranteeing validity by ensuring that respondents answered accurately on their voting intentions, without systematic bias. For now I will ignore this complication, and concentrate on the issue of how large the sample needs to be, to ensure reliability, and — given that the measurement has high validity — to ensure accuracy.

The basic statistical result is as follows: in estimating the population average from a random sample of size N, the accuracy of the estimate improves proportionally to the square root of N, usually written $\sqrt{N}$. For example, the estimate from a sample of size 2500 will be five times as accurate as from a sample of 100, because the larger sample is 25 times as large, and the square root of 25 is 5.

This still does not tell us how accurate the estimate is from a given sample. It only tells us how much better or worse the estimate will be if the sample size is increased or decreased. It is intuitively clear that if a random sample is taken and the values of a variable such as Gold-MSI scores are measured, the variability of the values within the sample must reflect the variability within the population as a whole. Of more immediate relevance, *the variability within the sample affects the accuracy of the sample mean as an estimate of population mean.*

Suppose a small but random sample of just 20 students was taken. In the implausible event that everyone in the sample were to score within a range of, say, 49 to 51 on the measure, we could be fairly confident that the mean value of 50 was an accurate one. But if the sample revealed a spread of numbers ranging fairly evenly between zero and the top score of 100, with an average of 50, this suggests that the sample average is a less reliable indicator of the population average. A different sample might have included more, or fewer, in the extreme ranges of scores and this would have affected the mean.

So, how accurate is the sample mean? Put another way, given the sample mean, how close, or distant, is the true population mean from our estimate? The distance between the sample mean and the population mean is known as the **error of the mean**.

It turns out that we can estimate how large this is likely to be. At this point there are two estimates to keep track of and the situation is quite complicated. This is unavoidable. Recall that we have estimated the population mean from the sample mean. How accurate is this estimate, in other words what is the size of the error of the mean? Another estimate is needed. It turns out that the size of the error can be estimated from the sample itself. This estimate is known as the **standard error of the mean**, abbreviated s.e.m.

The formula for it is s.e.m. $= s.d./\sqrt{N}$, where s.d. is the standard deviation of the sample, and N is the number of individuals in the sample.

What have we achieved? Clearly we do not have an actual estimate of the error of the mean itself. Achieving that would do the impossible: it would give a better estimate of the population mean than taking the sample mean, and it is known that you cannot do better than the sample mean. For example, suppose the sample mean for the Gold-MSI score on our students was 50, and that we could estimate the error of the mean as +5. Then the sample mean is 5 points too high, and the population mean must be 45.

So if the standard error of the mean is not telling us about error of the mean, what is the use of it?

Although the s.e.m. does not tell us the *actual value* of the error — in fact it does not even tell us the sign of the error, positive or negative — it does tell us *how large* the error is likely to be. In other words, it tells us nothing about the systematic error from using the sample mean, for the simple reason that the systematic error is zero.[5] But it does tell us about the random error. And this enables us to give a range of values within which the true population mean is likely to be found. It is clearly useful to be able to say from our sample of students that the population mean for Gold-MSI is very likely to be within, say, plus or minus 3 points of 50, the sample mean.

The next question is, what do we mean by "*very likely* to be within."? How likely is "very" likely? To understand this, a digression is needed into the workhorse of statistics, the Gaussian distribution, which will have to await a future chapter.

What follows in this section is a "how to" guide on getting basic estimates for mean and other useful numbers from samples in SPSS, plus the procedure for finding the s.e.m.

Basic descriptive statistics in SPSS: the mean, median, mode, standard deviation, variance, interquartile range, range and s.e.m.

There are several ways of getting SPSS to calculate basic descriptive statistics such as the mean, variance etc. of a set of numbers. As an example of a dataset, suppose Professor A has taught a course in psychology to a dozen students, and given them an end of year exam which yielded the following results in percent: 61, 43, 52, 81, 72, 35, 49, 69, 39, 69, 58, 82.

You will need to open a new dataset and type the numbers in down the first column. Name the new variable Marks.

(1) For calculating the mean, median, s.d., variance, range and interquartile range.
   Click on Analyze, 6th from the left on the menus on the bar at the top. On the drop down menu hover the cursor over Descriptive Statistics, then left click on Explore.

---

[5] Technically, the sample mean is an **unbiased estimator** of the population mean.

Left click on the top blue arrow button that is between the two white boxes. This will move the Marks variable in the left box over to the box marked Dependent List. Click OK.

The output will contain a box marked Descriptives. Besides other numbers not yet explained, you will find values for the mean, median, variance, s.d., range and interquartile range.

(2) To find the mode, you need a different procedure.

Click on Analyze, Descriptive Statistics, Frequencies. Move the Marks variable into the Variable(s) box. Click the Statistics button on the right, and check the box for mode.

In the output, the box marked Statistics contains the value 69 for the mode. Inspection of the data reveals that this is the only mark that is repeated. You may wish to investigate what SPSS does to provide a mode when there are no repeated marks. Go back into the dataset and change one of the 69 values to 67. You will find that SPSS still attempts to provide a mode, though with an apology!

Note: I will be referring to this dataset, with the 67 substituted for one value of 69, in the GD section. I suggest you save this dataset so as to be able to follow the later example.

(3) To find the s.e.m., another menu is needed.

Click on Analyze, Descriptive Statistics, Descriptives. Move the Marks variable into the Variable(s) box. Click the Options button on the right, and check the box marked S.E. mean. Click continue and OK.

This gives an s.e.m. of 4.591. It also gives an s.d. estimate of 15.903. You can verify that the s.e.m. is what you get by dividing the s.d. by the square root of 12, 12 being the sample size.

Note: the s.e.m. in this case is not a very meaningful number. To be meaningful, there needs to be a clear statement about taking a sample from a population and attempting to estimate the population mean from the sample. Here this has not been done, but the procedure is included to show how the s.e.m. can be calculated in case you require it.

Fig. 4.1.   The recall recently used dialogues icon.

Fig. 4.2.   The go to data icon.

(4) There is one tip that will already start to appear useful. If you wish to repeat a previous operation in SPSS, there is a special icon which acts as a short cut (see Fig. 4.1).

If you hover the cursor over it, it will say "Recall recently used dialogues". Clicking on it will reveal a drop-down menu with up to twelve of the last operations you performed. Clicking on the one you want will save time going to it through the sequence of menus in the regular way.

(5) A further tip, for when you want to go quickly back to the data set from the output view, is to click on the red star, in the same row as the Recall dialogues button, three places to the right (see Fig. 4.2).

GOING DEEPER

How to find "typical" numbers

To anticipate, in chapters 5 and 6 we will meet two key elements of the modern scientific method: Bacon's idea of solving the inverse problem via the direct problem, and Fisher's notion of arriving at a positive result not directly, by eliminating its contrary. Both in a way are doing similar things: using a kind of looking-glass logic to solve a problem, by doing the opposite of the obvious. The final element in what one might call the standard experimental method is really much more straightforward than this: it is nothing more than the average. This is a notion which probably appears so obvious now that it is scarcely worth making a fuss about. Nevertheless it is a historical fact that it took many false starts before its power and importance was fully realised.

In symbols, the average of a set of numbers n_1, n_2 and so on up to n_k, is

$$n_{\text{average}} = (n_1 + n_2 + \cdots + n_{k-1} + n_k)/k.$$

An average is usually taken to be in some sense a typical value for something that may vary widely. An average number is "typical" in the sense that if you compare the set of numbers $\{n_1, n_2,$ up to $n_k\}$ with the set of numbers $\{n_{\text{average}}, n_{\text{average}}, n_{\text{average}}$ and so on repeated k times$\}$, the two sets add up to exactly the same total. Connected to this, is the fact that once you know the average of a set of numbers and how many there are, you can at once calculate what the total of the numbers must be: it is the result of multiplying these two quantities. So if a person's batting average over a season is 38, and if she has played in 40 innings over that time, she must have scored a total of 38 times 40, or 760 runs.

Moreover her average has the merit of being a reasonable measure of her general merit as a run-scorer. If she bats at number 11 and if her average of 38 is the third highest in the team, it would probably be worth putting her higher up in the batting order and ensuring that she has more opportunities for scoring runs in the following season. These conclusions suggest that the average is both convenient to calculate, and useful as a device for summarising a number of figures in a single figure. We are constantly bombarded with statistics, and anything which can reduce the need to process information is likely to be valuable. If you wish to boil down a whole set of numbers — of which there might be millions — into one single number, the average is a reasonable one to give.

However, the average is not the only possible figure of this kind; other candidates might in some circumstances turn out to be better at providing "typical" numbers. The most widely used of these is the median, defined above.

The mean and median can differ substantially. The mean and median of the set {−50, −7, 1, 2, 3, 4, 10, 200, 1000} are 129.2 and 3, respectively. Which if any is the "right" answer? This depends on the use to which you wish to put the number you come up with, and on the questions with which you begin your analysis.

To illustrate this point, suppose you wish to test whether real annual incomes in the UK increased between 2010 and 2015, and if so by how much. It would be reasonable to compare the average incomes for 2010 and for 2015, corrected for inflation, and to take the difference between these two figures as a single figure giving an idea of how much standards of living had gone up (or down) over the period. However, such a figure would have political implications, as it covers the period of a Conservative-dominated government.

If it turns out to have been positive, Conservative supporters will claim this as evidence for the success of the government's economic policies. Critics, however, will not tamely accept such a conclusion. They may claim that a single number cannot adequately represent something as complex as a national economy, and that the increase in average income disguises a growth in inequality between rich and poor, with the rise in the average being driven by a small number of people becoming much, much richer, and the majority staying the same or even declining. For them, if one must take a single number to summarise incomes, a better one to use might be the median.

The median is a measure of central tendency which is not affected by extreme values. The median of {1, 2, 3, 4, 5} is 3, and the median of {1, 2, 3, 4, one million} is also 3. The mean of the first set is 3, but the mean of the second set is two hundred thousand and two, which is really a quite meaningless result: it is roughly one fifth of the extremely large single number, and yet vastly greater than the other four numbers: it represents nothing very much.

If you want a "typical" number to represent a set of numbers which has a few extreme values, the median might be a better choice. This is because the median is unaffected by numbers at the extremes, whereas the average is sensitive to them. Numbers such as "one million" in this example are known as "outliers", and checking for their presence is an important (and often overlooked) requirement of good statistical practice which will be dealt with in a later chapter.

The third number sometimes used to characterise the "typical" number of a set of numbers is the mode, though less common in psychology than either the mean or the median. The mode is the number which is most frequent in your set of numbers. For the income distribution example, the mode is the income which is most commonly found in the population.

In our artificial examples these measures (when they are all defined) give different results, but this is not simply an artefact: it happens also in genuine datasets. This is well shown in the following figure reproduced, with kind permission of the authors, from "Life in the middle", a TUC publication available at https://www.tuc.org.uk/sites/default/files/documents/lifeinthemiddle.pdf

The figure shows the distribution of weekly incomes in Britain in 2006/7, and has several points of interest. The curve stops at the left at zero (nobody can earn a negative income!) but there is no natural upper bound, which means that going from left to right, it has a steep upwards slope to begin with and a shallower slope downwards to the right. This lack of symmetry is known technically as "skewness". The idea will become important later, but for the moment note simply that with a skewed distribution, the mean will generally be different from the median, as here. The comparatively small number of very high income earners have a greater influence on the mean than on the median, as with the example above. The mode was not marked on the original figure, but I have added an arrow at that point, corresponding to an income of just under £300 per week (see Fig. 4.3).

These three ways of measuring the "typical" value of a set of numbers all have their advantages in different circumstances.

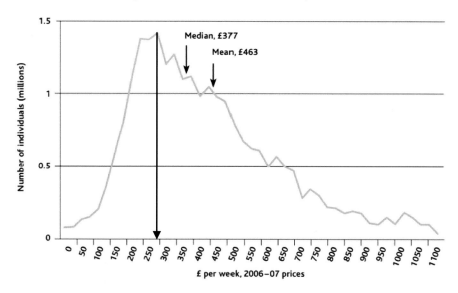

Fig. 4.3.   Distribution of weekly household incomes in the UK, 2006/7.

Source: M. Brewer *et al.*, *Poverty and Inequality in the UK*: 2008, p. 6.

Note: Income is household income, net of tax, benefits and tax credit and before housing costs are deducted.

The mean is probably the commonest, partly for historical reasons: unlike with the other two, it has a simple mathematical formula, and it was easier to use the mean when the theory of statistics was being developed, prior to the advent of powerful computers. Provided certain precautions are taken (to be described in the chapter on data checking) the sensitivity of the mean to outliers is not a problem in practice, and it will be the default choice in this book when a measure of central tendency is required.

How typical are typical numbers?

One problem with the approach of summarising a complex dataset with just one number, whether the mean, median or mode, is that it involves a gross simplification of a complex situation. In particular, it says nothing about the degree to which the other numbers tend to depart from our "typical" value. If we want to summarise a set of numbers in a way that is not too misleading, but at the same time is relatively simple, we need to give not only a typical value, but some idea of how the other values tend to spread out around it.

An analogy might be with a weather forecast for the track of a hurricane hitting the East coast of the US. Residents would want to know not only the path of the centre, but also how wide the zone of devastation was going to be. Similarly, with a set of numbers one needs to know where the centre is, and how widely the set varies around this centre. As with the measures of central tendency, there is more than one measure of "dispersion" as it is called.

The easiest measure of dispersion to understand is the "range". This is the difference between the smallest and largest numbers in the set. With {1, 2, 3, 4, one million}, the range is (1,000,000 − 1) = 999,999. If all one knew about these numbers were their mean and range, i.e., 200,002 and 999,999, one would have a better idea of the set than with the mean alone. The range would tell us that there was a wide dispersion within the set. If we are looking at the set of incomes in a country, the range will give some measure of income inequality, though probably not a very useful one: the lower end of the range will be close to the minimum needed to sustain life (or possibly even below it) and the maximum may be in the hundreds of millions. Given that there will be some very poor and some very wealthy people even in countries (such as Sweden) where income inequality is low, this does not tell us very much. The trouble is that the range is very sensitive to the presence of outliers.

What is needed is something to measure not how far the extremes depart from the middle, but how far the numbers "typically" depart from the central value. Suppose we have chosen the mean to represent this central value. The obvious choice for the dispersion might be to calculate the deviations of all the separate numbers from the mean, and take the average of these. So with the set of numbers {1, 2, 3, 4, 5, 6, 7}, the mean (and the median) would be 4, and the deviations would be {−3, −2, −1, 0, 1, 2, 3}. It is no good taking the average of these numbers as they stand, since that would give a result of zero. But if we take the deviations always to be positive, by reversing the sign of the negative numbers (a process called taking the "absolute value" of the negative numbers) we do get a sensible result. The mean of {3, 2, 1, 0, 1, 2, 3} is 12/7 = 1.7 approximately. This measure of dispersion is known as the **mean absolute deviation**, or MAD.

The MAD is a perfectly good measure of dispersion, and together with the mean, these two numbers are an efficient way of condensing a lot of useful information about a set of numbers into just two figures. MAD has the virtue of being easy to understand, but it has a technical disadvantage. The process of taking absolute values leads to difficulties when doing the maths of statistical analysis. This does not really matter when powerful computation is available, but historically the subject was developed using advanced mathematical analysis rather than computers, and it was found easier to work with a different measure of dispersion. Unfortunately, the calculation of this measure — the standard deviation — involves a couple of steps whose motivation is far from obvious.

I will try to explain how it might seem natural to go down the standard deviation route. In calculating the "average deviation" of numbers from the mean, we have seen that it is no good simply subtracting the mean from each number, and taking the mean of the new set of numbers. This is because if a number is less than the mean, this process will lead to negative numbers, and what we want is a measure of "deviation" which like distances on a map, is always positive. The simplest way of making a negative number positive is by just changing the sign from minus to plus, but this turns out to be undesirable for technical reasons.[6] An alternative way of turning a negative number into a positive one is to take its square. The square of any real number, negative or positive, is always positive. The squaring procedure has the advantage of being mathematically "nicer" than taking the absolute value. If we now add up all the squared deviations and take *their* mean, we have something that measures the "average squared deviation" from the mean. This number is known as the **variance** for the data set.

---

[6] The first derivative of the absolute value function has a singularity at zero.

We are still not home and dry, however. I can illustrate the difficulty by considering the following set of numbers: {–1000, –1000, 1000, 1000}. The mean is pretty clearly 0, and the squared deviations are one million (repeated four times) so the average squared deviation is just one million. This is a pretty odd measure of dispersion for a set whose total range is 2000. The cause of the problem is that when we squared the deviations in order to solve one difficulty (turning negative numbers into positive ones), we introduced another problem: squaring also tends to make large numbers disproportionately much larger.

However, we can get round this by undoing the effects of the squaring operation as the last stage of the process. To get our final measure of dispersion, the standard deviation, we simply unwind the squaring process by doing its opposite. The opposite of squaring a number is taking the square root of that number. So in this case, the final result is found by taking the square root of the variance. This is the **standard deviation**. It is commonly abbreviated s.d. In the case of the set {–1000, –1000, 1000, 1000}, the s.d. is the square root of one million, i.e., one thousand. Given that each number deviates by just 1000 from the mean, we would certainly expect any measure of dispersal to give 1000 as the result. This may help to make the rather complex procedure for calculating the s.d. more convincing.

Going back to the example of the exam results given in NTK, recall that Professor A's students scored exam results as follows, in percent: 61, 43, 52, 81, 72, 35, 49, 67, 39, 69, 58, 82. You are required to report on the success or otherwise of the course. The mean of the marks turns out to be exactly 59, well above the pass mark of 50%, but this number on its own does not reveal the fact that four out of 12 students failed the course, a rather poor result. Calculating the standard deviation reveals the reason:

1. find the squares of the deviations of each mark from the mean:
    $(61-59)^2$, $(43-59)^2$, $(52-59)^2$, $(81-59)^2$, $(72-59)^2$, $(35-59)^2$, $(49-59)^2$, $(67-59)^2$, $(39-59)^2$, $(69-59)^2$, $(58-59)^2$, $(82-59)^2$
2. this works out as: 4, 256, 49, 484, 169, 576, 100, 64, 400, 100, 1, 529.

3. the average of this is the sum of the numbers (2732) divided by how many there are (12), or 227.67. This is the **variance** of the original set of numbers.
4. the square root of the variance is 15.09, which is the **standard deviation**.

If the "typical" distance of the numbers from the mean is over 15, and if the mean is only 9 marks higher than the pass mark, it is no surprise that four of the students scored below the pass grade.

By contrast, Professor B, teaching a similar course to a similar class of students, tested with a similar exam, produced the following results:

$$52, 63, 55, 58, 61, 46, 56, 59, 62, 52, 58, 51, 52.$$

The mean of this set of numbers is 55.8, lower than for Professor A, yet only one student failed this exam. The reason is that the s.d. is just over 5, one third of that for Professor A. Even though the average result is lower than for Professor A's class, the marks are more tightly clustered around that average, so that more students passed the exam.

To summarise the procedure for finding these two measures of central tendency and dispersion, suppose as before that we have a set of k numbers $n_1, n_2, \ldots$ up to n_k.

The mean, often written $\bar{n}$, is equal to $(n_1 + n_2 + \cdots + n_{k-1} + n_k)/k$,

the variance is $[(n_1 - \bar{n})^2 + (n_2 - \bar{n})^2 + \cdots + (n_k - \bar{n})^2]/k$,

and the standard deviation is

$$\sqrt{\text{(variance)}} = \sqrt{\{[(n_1 - \bar{n})^2 + (n_2 - \bar{n})^2 + \cdots + (n_k - \bar{n})^2]/k\}}.$$

In practice you will seldom or never need to calculate these numbers by hand, since any statistical program you use will have the facility to do so automatically, but I think it may help demystify the ideas if you can see what the programs are working with.

Note: the mean is the same as that given above, that is, 59.0. You will notice however that the value of the s.d. is 15.76, not 15.09 as found above. Why the difference?

The answer is that the formula used for a standard deviation by SPSS is slightly different from that used above. The formula we have used above for Professor A is correct if we want to find the s.d. of a set of numbers. But if the numbers are a random sample from a larger population, then *we have to modify the formula if we want to estimate the s.d. for that population.*

It turns out that the best formula to find the s.d. for the population, from the numbers in a sample, is to modify the formula for the variance. The s.d. is still the square root of the variance, but now it is a different variance. The original variance was calculated as the mean of the squared differences, i.e., the sum of squared differences (2732) divided by how many there are (12), which comes to 227.67, which square-rooted gives 15.09 as the s.d. A better estimate is given by "Bessel's correction", found by dividing 2732 by 11, giving 248.36. Square-rooting this gives 15.76, as SPSS claims for the value of the s.d.

So the rule is, if you have a sample and want to describe variability within the sample, the correct formulae are the ones we had before, which were

$$\text{Variance} = [(n_1 - \bar{n})^2 + (n_2 - \bar{n})^2 + \cdots + (n_k - \bar{n})^2]/k,$$

$$\text{Standard deviation} = \sqrt{(\text{variance})} = \sqrt{\{[(n_1 - \bar{n})^2 + (n_2 - \bar{n})^2 + \cdots + (n_k - \bar{n})^2]/k\}}.$$

But if you have a sample and you want to make your best estimate for the variance and s.d. for the population of numbers from which the sample was drawn, the formulae are

$$\text{Variance} = [(n_1 - \bar{n})^2 + (n_2 - \bar{n})^2 + \cdots + (n_k - \bar{n})^2]/(k-1),$$

$$\text{Standard deviation} = \sqrt{(\text{variance})} = \sqrt{\{[(n_1 - \bar{n})^2 + (n_2 - \bar{n})^2 + \cdots + (n_k - \bar{n})^2]/(k-1)\}}.$$

In other words for a sample with k numbers in it, use $(k-1)$ and not k to divide the sum of squares.

The technical reason for this is that when you do not know variance and s.d. for a variable in a population, you normally do not know the mean of the variable either, and you have to estimate it from your sample. So when you estimate the variance by taking the squared differences of the numbers from the mean, you are already including a source of error in using an estimated mean. The Bessel correction is the best we can do to redress this error. This does not hold by the way if we know the population mean and are merely trying to estimate the variance by sampling. In that case, the original formula, with k rather than $(k-1)$, is the best: provided we put the known population mean in place of $\bar{n}$.

There is no complication over estimating the population mean from a sample, though. The mean of the sample is, mercifully, the best guess we can make for the population mean.

Note also that the basic descriptives menu give the maximum and minimum numbers in the sample, in this case 35 and 82, and the range can be found by subtraction to be 47.

Why the mean is so important

In the following sections I will try to show why the mean enjoys the popularity it does from a statistical point of view. If you ever go to one of the old-fashioned village fetes in the English countryside, you will sometimes find a large glass jar filled with sweets. You have to pay a small fee to enter the competition, which is to guess how many sweets the jar contains. The person guessing nearest the correct total wins a prize. Scientifically speaking, what would your best strategy be to maximise your chances of winning? Perhaps you might wish to measure the diameter of the sweets, and the dimensions of the jar, and do some complicated mathematical calculation to arrive at the result. But if you did not have an accurate measuring device, you would have to estimate all these quantities, and you would be forced into something not much better than a guess. If you have a number of friends with you, they might all have their own ideas about the number, and these estimates are likely to vary widely. Is there any way of somehow combining these estimates to produce something more accurate?

This problem in a somewhat different form faced astronomers in the eighteenth century. With the knowledge of Newton's three laws of motion, and his law of universal gravitation, astronomers had the mathematical toolkit to calculate, in theory, the position of all the planets in their orbits at any future time given their current positions and velocities. If you were wealthy and interested in science, you could buy something called an orrery (named for obscure reasons after the 4th Earl of Orrery). This was a mechanical model of the solar system, which gave a physical embodiment of the Newtonian approach. It was driven by clockwork through a system of gears, and once it was set up and put into motion, you could watch the planets slowly rotate around the sun at the centre in an orderly, predictable way.

The trouble was, the model seemed to be going wrong: it did not match the observations that astronomers were making. Reality, it appeared, was more complex than clockwork. In particular, the planet Jupiter was doing something it shouldn't be doing: the speed with which it was orbiting the sun was slowly but steadily increasing, at the expense of Saturn, which was slowing down. If Jupiter was speeding up, this meant that it had to be getting nearer to the sun: its orbit was not a closed curve like an ellipse, but a spiral. And if Jupiter were spiralling towards the sun, on its way it would cross the orbits of the four planets closer to the sun, including the Earth, and pulverise them. Naturally enough, this prospect was of concern to more than just the astronomical fraternity.

This fate was not quite certain, however. It was possible that the acceleration of Jupiter might be some kind of recurrent or cyclical phenomenon, and would be followed by a slowing down, in a regular rhythm. The only way to find out which alternative was correct, would be to calculate very precisely why the acceleration was happening, and how it would eventually develop: in the direction of stability, or of catastrophe. What was required was to calculate just eight numbers known as "orbital parameters", which would enable Jupiter's future motion to be calculated. In theory this could be done by simply measuring the positions of the planets at different times and doing the mathematics.

Unfortunately, the calculations would only be valid if the observations were precisely accurate, and astronomers had known for centuries that all measurements of position using telescopes were subject to some degree of error and approximation. This being so, the numerous available observations of the motions of Jupiter all incorporated some unknown amounts of error, different for each observation, and for each observatory. Attempting to calculate Jupiter's eight parameters would therefore give different results, depending on which observations were used in the calculations. Trying to use all the calculations at once would not work, because they would give inconsistent solutions to the equations.

This problem baffled the greatest minds of the age, until in 1787 Pierre Laplace came up with the brilliant, if simple answer.

Note: the remainder of this chapter is available in the online material for Chapter 4.

Chapter 5

Bacon's Legacy: Causal Models, and How to Test Them

SUMMARY

Three possible strategies for establishing causality: Bacon's choice. Effects as a combination of signal plus noise. Sources of noise. Criticisms of causality, and alternative forms of causality. The problem of social interactions. The qualitative option.

NEED TO KNOW

In common usage, "cause" and "effect" are defined essentially as follows.

C causes E **if**:

C's presence leads to E's presence,

and C's absence results in E's absence,

with C preceding E.

In Chapter 1, I suggested a more flexible definition in which causes and effects were identified with variables, so that saying that there is a causal link between one variable (the IV) and another (the DV) was the same thing as saying that a *change* in the IV results in a *change* in the DV.

The problem with the common usage definition is that it encourages us to think in terms of "the" cause of some phenomenon. If a factor C has been found whose presence leads to the presence of E and whose absence leads to E's absence, this seems to imply that **the** cause of E has been found. For humans, this seems to be a natural way to think. We see something, an effect E, and ask the question "why?" The reply is "because of C", and we are content if a single "C" is offered.

On the other hand, the second, variable-centred way of looking at causality invites us to consider the possibility that there may be more than one causal variable. If a change in blood alcohol level in a person leads to a slowing in their response times, this leaves open the possibility that changes in their level of tiredness may also affect their responses. Indeed, why stop there: why not look at the possibility that response times are affected by blood sugar levels, levels of anxiety and perhaps other factors as well.

But continuing this line of thought, if there may be multiple causal variables for the same dependent variable, does this not bring the whole notion of causality into question, at least for single independent variables? If we want to know whether there is an effect of blood alcohol on response times, is this not like wanting to know the effect of the violin section in Beethoven's fifth symphony? The question is not only impossible to answer, it may actually appear meaningless.

In order to give the question significance, we need to give an *operational definition* of what is meant by the effect of a single independent variable X on a dependent variable Y. The definition may to some extent be arbitrary, but it should capture as far as possible the intuitive idea of causality, while being free from ambiguity. It should also suggest a practical means by which we can *test* whether there is a causal link between X and Y.

Doing this is not entirely straightforward. The answer that is usually given is as follows. Define a dependent variable Y (for example, the response time of a participant in a computer-based performance test), and list all the possible independent variables that we think might have an effect on Y. These might be blood alcohol level, blood sugar level and anxiety level, for example. If we wish to find the effect (if any) of blood alcohol level on response times, the definition is as follows: arrange that the blood alcohol level **varies** by a certain amount, **fix** the values of blood sugar and anxiety at certain determined levels, and **measure** the change in response times. The measured change (if any) in response times will be the effect of the given change in blood alcohol level on response times. Because the other causal variables were held constant, there cannot have been any interference between them and the dependent variable: *the measured change has to be the "pure" effect of blood alcohol change on response times.*

   This procedure, simple though it may appear, conceals a number of complications, both practical and conceptual. One practical difficulty is that of how to arrange that variables such as blood sugar and anxiety remain fixed, as required by this arrangement. If the experiment is conducted on a single participant, one can imagine asking him to do the task sober, giving him a certain amount of alcohol to consume, measuring the change in his blood alcohol and then requiring him to do the task a second time. The change in the DV would then be the effect of the measured change in blood alcohol on response time. But what if his blood sugar level had fallen in the meantime? What if his anxiety level, initially high, had also fallen due to familiarity with the test and the calming effect of the alcohol? What if simply doing the test the first time gave him experience which made it easier the second time? What if he began to get bored and so did less well the second time?

   Another objection is that the definition — fix all variables but the variable of interest, and vary that one — begs the question of *at what values* the other variables should be fixed when the causal variable is varied. What if the effect of the IV depends on the levels of the other variables? What if, for example, increase in blood alcohol levels has only a small effect on response times when a person is fully rested and well nourished, but a much larger effect when the same person is fatigued, hungry and generally on the edge of collapse, when a drink may push him over into stumbling incompetence? This is no quibble, but a very important aspect of any deep investigation into causal models; to anticipate, this "interaction" of variables is key to understanding how a multifactorial[1] model operates and will be dealt with in a later chapter.

A more serious objection, at least theoretically, to this arrangement is that it involves making a list of all the independent variables which might possibly affect the DV without exception. What if some had been inadvertently left out? What if, for example, the whole process was affected by how many hours sleep the participant had enjoyed the previous night? One of the advantages of the NE approach to science, as claimed by its supporters, is that it should be independent of theory. If we have to list all the possible variables that might have an effect on the dependent variable, and furthermore if we need to assert that this list is comprehensive, surely we are making strong theoretical claims and assuming advance knowledge of causal mechanisms of a profound nature?

This argument appears at first sight to be insurmountable. But one of the great achievements of the people who developed modern scientific thinking was to discover a way of getting around both of these difficulties at one and the same time. There is a method of ensuring that we can vary one variable of interest — one single IV — and keep the other IVs constant *even if we have no idea what they are*. This is such a remarkable invention, or discovery, that it deserves a chapter all to itself and hence will be the topic of Chapter 7.

Meanwhile, there is a different angle to be explored. In what follows, I will revert temporarily to what one might call the naïve language of cause and effect, of C and E, rather than using the language of variables, referring to IVs and DVs. It makes the explanations simpler and the underlying ideas are unaffected.

---

[1] That is, with multiple independent variables. Nominal IVs are often referred to as "factors".

Bacon's big idea

If science can be defined as the systematic investigation of the link between causes and effects,[2] there are three possible ways we might begin:

(1) Start with a specific cause and look for its various possible effects.
(2) Start with a specific effect and look for its various possible causes.
(3) Start with a specific effect and a specific cause, and critically examine whether there really is a cause–effect relation between them.

It is not immediately obvious which strategy will be the most fruitful. Historically, the Greeks began with 2, which starts with an observation — the planets moved in erratic orbits — and asked the question "why?" Greek science answered this question with a series of models, which matched the observed motions of the planets fairly closely, at least by the standards of observational accuracy possible at the time.

Strategy 2 starts out with a phenomenon, chosen perhaps either because of its evident importance or because it seems so hard to explain, and seeks to understand the reasons why the phenomenon happens at all, or why it takes that exact form. Strategy 2 type questions seem to have been a characteristic feature of Greek philosophy, to the extent that it dealt with scientific topics at all, and the importance of the "why" approach is illustrated by the fact that Aristotle went so deeply into analysing the possible types of "why" questions that one might ask. (His analysis of causality into four distinct types is the subject of some comments in the GD section below and supplementary online material).

Strategy 1 might be characterised as the "what happens if…" approach. Strategy 1 is not always an intentional one. It is

---

[2] At least in the less developed sciences, of which psychology is one. Physics moved beyond this level with the work of Galileo, if not earlier.

sometimes most successful as the result of a happy accident. We do not know how cooking was invented: it might have been the result of someone placing food in or near a fire deliberately; but equally, it may have been the accidental outcome of food falling into the embers of a fire, and being later retrieved and found to be palatable. A means of making pottery might have been discovered in a similar way. On encountering new types of fruits or vegetables as a result of migration to a new land, early humans must have tried strategy 1 as a means of finding out which were good to eat. Strategy 1 is also perhaps a characteristic of children's play.[3]

Strategy 3, however, is the one which has turned out to be key for modern scientific method. Of course, it presupposes the outcome of a previous decision, which is: which causes and which effects are of interest and worth studying in the first place? In the attempt to find a cause and effect, do we begin with a cause and then choose an effect, or do we begin with an effect and then choose a cause? Either alternative leads to a closed question, different in nature from those raised by strategies 1 and 2, both of which give rise to open questions. But if we decide on strategy 3, we need to choose both the cause and the effect, and this requires some additional work to be done before we are ready to address the question at issue.

In science, we generally begin with an effect and seek the cause (or rather, taking a more sophisticated view, causes). This appears on the surface to be an application of strategy 2. However, it is not. We start with the effect, which should be something of clear interest in its own right. It might be, for example, some form of disease or mental illness: we are interested in why this happens, with a view to preventing or remediating it. On a less sombre note, it may be that we wish to find out why music has the strong impact that it does on our emotions. But before we start to apply strategy 3, we first need to select a possible cause. The process cannot begin until this has been done. So the practical phase starts not with a question such as "what is the cause of schizophrenia?" but rather, to take

---

[3]See Einstein's quote: "play is the highest form of research".

one possible example, "is childhood trauma the cause of schizophrenia?", or alternatively perhaps "is the genetic makeup of a person the cause of their schizophrenia?"

So we may indeed begin conceptually with an effect on its own, but before setting out on our scientific journey, we also need to provide a tentative cause. The outcome of this process of providing a tentative cause for a named effect is termed a **research hypothesis**, or sometimes an **experimental hypothesis**. I prefer the former version, as it can refer to studies which are not strictly speaking experimental in the sense of incorporating some form of causal variable which is manipulated by the researchers.

So although we started out with something looking like a strategy 2 approach, this was merely a first step to putting together a *combination* of cause and effect in accordance with strategy 3. Strategy 3 *does* mean that we forego the potential benefit of having an open-ended question of the form "what is the cause of schizophrenia?", for example. If we fix on the hypothesis "childhood trauma is the cause of schizophrenia" and if we find we are mistaken, the attempt will have been in vain. But that is the price of using this method, and its benefits are great enough to outweigh the costs.

Strategy 3 can be viewed as a combination of strategies 1 and 2. It was first given this explicit form by Francis Bacon, a seventeenth century writer who has been called "the father of experimental philosophy".[4] *Bacon's big idea* was that by putting together the *active* force inherent in the suggestion "let's see what happens if we do C!" with the *passive*, philosophical viewpoint of the question "I wonder what was the cause of E?", one obtains something with the virtues of both. Faced with the question about the cause of E, rather than sitting and waiting for inspiration to strike, one can actually *try out* a specific C and *see* whether it results in E.

---

[4] In for example Urbach, 1987. The phrase sounds rather dated, possibly from around Bacon's time or not long thereafter, but I have not been able to pin down its origin.

Bacon, who had been Lord Chancellor and was familiar with methods of questioning suspects which would be frowned upon today, believed in the value of what the US government terms "enhanced interrogation techniques" and actually used the interrogation of suspects as a metaphor for what scientists should do to nature. This has understandably led to a decline in his reputation, but his essential ideas are sound.[5]

This has led us rather far from the initial focus on models of nature. It was necessary to make this detour, via the concept of hypotheses, before we can return to models and to the precision that they make possible. Before that we have had to examine the idea of **testing hypotheses**, and to do that, we needed to put hypotheses in their historical context and show how they emerged from natural questions about the world.

Hypotheses do not seem to fit very easily into the way most people think about how the world works. They seem to be neither one thing nor the other, blowing both hot and cold. On the one hand, a hypothesis appears to be making a quite definite statement, for example: "childhood trauma causes schizophrenia". On the other hand, they are put forward only as a *tentative* explanation. This latter use of the word has entered common speech, as when a creationist criticises Darwin's theory of evolution through natural selection as being "just a hypothesis". If Darwin's theory were indeed only a hypothesis, this criticism would be correct: a hypothesis, in contrast to a theory, is by definition something which is not clearly established.

This dual nature of hypotheses is in fact precisely why they are so valuable. By making clear statements about the world,

---

[5] There is room for dispute about what exactly Bacon did discover about method. Medawar (1982, p. 34) claims that Bacon in fact used strategy 1. My interpretation is based on the arguments in Gower (1997, p. 45). Part of the problem is that Bacon wrote in Latin, so most of us have to read him in translation. More seriously, for all his dislike of Aristotle's teachings, his language was full of Aristotelian concepts such as species and genus that had a quite different meaning for him than for us. As a result, Bacon's works can easily become a sort of philosophical Rorschach test in which we interpret his writings in light of our own preoccupations.

hypotheses lay themselves open to challenge and testing. Bacon's contribution was to show that a definite hypothesis, put forward not as dogma but as a possibility, and presenting as it were a target for testing, could be more fruitful for the advancement of science than any number of open-ended questions of the "why?" or "what happens if?" form. This seems to have been the significance of his famous saying: "If a man will begin with certainties, he shall end in doubts; but if he will be content to begin with doubts he shall end in certainties."

Of course, having now discovered this powerful new tool for discovery, the question arises — as with any new invention — of how exactly to use it. Having formulated a research hypothesis, in the form of "C causes E", Bacon's idea is to apply cause C and observe whether or not effect E happens. If effect E does appear, the hypothesis is supported, and with sufficient support the hypothesis may be promoted to the status of a theory.[6]

The broad outline of how to test a causal hypothesis is therefore clear enough. Put in the more scientifically useful language of variables, the requirement is to ensure a change in the independent variable in the hypothesis, and to observe the dependent variable in order to find out whether or not it changes in response to the independent variable.

The next complication that arises is not so much theoretical or philosophical, as practical. Measurements in the real world involve a degree of random variation, or "noise". Noise can be defined as "the uncontrolled and generally unknown changes that a signal may suffer in the course of transmission". If you are listening to a radio tuned to an AM or FM transmitter, you will sometimes hear a slight background hiss. This may only be noticeable if you compare the sound with the same station on a digital audio band, which will be practically without noise. The hiss is a form of noise. The signal is the original transmission. Any noise present will to some extent degrade the signal. This effect is due not only to the

---

[6] Two points: this is not the language Bacon used, and this is a gross oversimplification of the process of establishing a theory out of a hypothesis.

fact that the noise interferes with the signal, but more particularly because the noise has an *unknown* effect on the signal. This means that having received the transmission, we cannot work backwards and retrieve the original signal by somehow subtracting out the noise, because we do not know what the noise is.

Measuring a variable is analogous to a transmission, where the correct value of the measurement is the "signal", and the various unknown random errors in the measuring process are the "noise", and the measurement we actually obtain at the end of it is the combination of the two.

In the situation where we are testing a hypothesis, two variables are being measured, the IV and the DV, and in the most general case either or both of these may be subject to interference by noise, though usually it is the noise component of the DV that is most relevant (there is not usually an uncertainty in measuring, for example, the age or gender of a participant). This means that a change in the DV in apparent response to a change in the IV is due to the combination of a "signal" — if there is a real causal link between IV and DV — and noise. The problem is that we do not know to start with how large the noise component is. Without some way of measuring it, we cannot answer the question about causality. If we see a change in the DV, we cannot be sure that it is not completely spurious.

Dealing with the problem of distinguishing a genuine signal from a spurious apparent signal is the topic of a future chapter. It is evident that in order to tell the two apart, we will need a means of measuring, or at least estimating, whether noise is present, and if so whether it is large enough to account on its own for the apparent effect that we are observing. The task it seems is to take our raw measurements and filter out the noise, so that the original signal — if there is one — comes through clearly.

It may seem that there is an insuperable obstacle to this aim: noise, by definition, is something uncontrolled and unknown. The demand to filter out noise before we can read the signal is therefore analogous to receiving an enemy radio transmission in an unknown code and being told to recover the original text. The task seems daunting. However, there are a couple of things working in our favour. Many random processes possess an underlying order amid the chaos. One aspect of this is contained in the so-called "law of averages", which though technical in its exact statement is important enough to have entered popular awareness in a form which is not far from the truth. If the assumption is made that the noise element follows something called the Normal or Gaussian distribution, we can take full advantage of this "law" and use the underlying mathematical theorems that have been developed to make good estimates of the size of the noise element.

The second point is that we do not actually need to know the precise form of the noise contribution to get what we need. What we need is to decide whether the measurements we obtain are enough to validate the causal link claimed in the research hypothesis. I will show later on that the key number to calculate in order to make this decision is the so-called "signal-to-noise ratio", which is the ratio of the observed effect to the noise element. This ratio of observed effect to noise is a fundamental quantity in information theory, and the concept is of much wider application than just hypothesis testing, but it does fit that application very well.

How do we calculate this ratio if we cannot measure the noise directly? It turns out that we can in fact estimate the size of the noise component quite well enough from the data themselves. This means that we can also calculate the ratio of the signal to the noise, and we can declare the causal hypothesis validated if this ratio is large enough. In most applications this ratio is either closely related to, or is actually equal to, the *F*-ratio introduced earlier. This summary of the method raises more questions than it answers, but it may be helpful at this stage to have an overview of where we are going. The use of the signal-to-noise approach will be one of the main underlying themes of this book.

Note incidentally that noise in the DV can arise from two sources. One is due to variations in the value of the DV that are due to random errors in the measurement process itself. For example, measuring the IQ of John Smith on a certain day may produce a different result depending on whether John Smith is having a hangover that day, or is incubating flu, or is depressed for some reason. Testing him on a different day will probably produce different results, but we can assume that his "real" IQ is a constant number (though it may decline slowly over time as part of the ageing process). But if we are measuring the effect of age on IQ and are comparing the IQ of a 30-year old man with that of a 60-year old, part of the difference will be due to individual differences in the people concerned, and this also represents a form of noise. There are ways to estimate this form of noise and, as importantly, to reduce it; this also will be the topic of future chapters.

GOING DEEPER

Strategy 2 is sometimes valuable

Though strategy 3 is most often the one used in experimental science, I do not mean to imply that strategy 2 is of no value. In some situations it may be the only option. Take the example of developmental amnesia (DA), a cognitive deficit in a specific form of memory, usually diagnosed in children who have markedly poorer episodic memory compared with semantic memory. In practice, they will remember facts, but are unable to recall what they were asked to do five minutes ago.

This condition, once recognised, was an effect, of which the possible cause was unknown. Strategy 2 was therefore the only option. The cause was discovered by looking in detail at the previous histories of children with DA and seeking circumstances which had happened to them, but not to children who failed to show DA. It was found that children with DA had suffered oxygen deprivation at some point. This suggested using brain imaging, and it was found that children with DA had suffered severe damage to the hippocampus on both sides of the brain, which was most likely the cause of the condition (Gadian *et al.*, 2000).

Criticisms of the causal approach

The approach to psychology outlined above, that is centred on creating causal hypotheses and testing them using quantitative methods, has come in for criticism particularly from those who favour some of the many variants of qualitative research methodology. It is important to be aware of these objections at least in outline, because they do in fact highlight some key weaknesses in the present approach.

One philosopher who has done the most to discredit logical empiricism and the methods derived from it has been Rom Harré. He has argued (e.g., in Hayes, 1997) that the analysis of causality is the wrong way to look at how human beings actually function; it makes it seem as though humans respond passively to cause–effect laws, whereas in fact they take part actively in social interactions in a conscious, intentional way. According to this view people operate socially in ways which involve rights and obligations; they use "scripts", which are established by a process of learning and socialisation; and they are acutely aware of their positioning, and that of other people around them, in any social episode. It is this positioning in a context of socialisation that accounts for how people actually behave and as importantly, communicate with one another.

Researchers who follow this line of thought tend to use qualitative methods such as discourse analysis to collect and analyse data, rather than a quantitative approach. The underlying thinking based on approaches such as positioning theory, with which Harré is especially associated, has been applied to many areas of the social sciences apart from psychology. Anyone wishing to learn more about this approach and qualitative methods generally should consult one of the many texts available. Hayes (1997) has the merit of bringing together brief descriptions of a number of different non-quantitative approaches, most of which share a mistrust, or at least scepticism, of quantitative methodology.

I am no expert on these approaches and what follows is a personal view. I think that there is much in what Harré has to say about the defects of simple causality applied to psychology. However, the answer is not necessarily to abandon the aim of modelling human behaviour, but to improve it and make it more sophisticated. Causal models of the simple kind discussed previously are no doubt crude and approximate. The hard sciences began with causality as a prominent feature and now causality has practically disappeared from a discipline such as physics, having been replaced with complex mathematical descriptions. The answer to the inadequacies of causal models in psychology is perhaps not to abandon models, but to create and test better models, possibly incorporating some of Harré's ideas about scripts and positioning.

So why not simply take over Harré's notions and build a model based on them? Unfortunately, the key feature of a model is that it should have some predictive power, and I am not clear that the notion of scripts in its present form as yet has such a capability. It is clearly possible to use the idea of scripts in analysing social interactions after the event, but I have not seen convincing evidence that this is more than a useful descriptive device. Unless it can explain, or at least predict, social behaviour in advance its value appears to be limited.

The second point of weakness in standard psychological models that is highlighted by the work of Harré and others, is that such models only claim to deal with how an individual person reacts within a certain given environment, typically a laboratory setting in which relevant factors are carefully controlled. Even if such a model is well established, it is very unclear how it would predict how a group of people would behave in a social situation, in which they will be interacting with each other, and where these interactions will affect the responses of others, and therefore the environment of each individual, in a highly involved fashion.

Just to describe this in terms of causality would be a problem. One might imagine constructing a directed graph, or diagram involving arrows from each person present to every other person, symbolising a complex web of interactions. The analysis would come up against the same sort of difficulty as weather forecasters face, where a change in conditions in one "cell" of the atmosphere has effects on neighbouring cells, which in turn feed back into effects on the first cell and so on. The difference here is that forecasters have a well-validated mathematical model of how the atmosphere behaves, which can be put into a form in which powerful computers can give relatively reliable solutions to the various equations and produce predictions which if not perfect, are at least good approximations within a reasonable forecasting period. Such abilities remain, for psychology, little more than a pious aspiration.

Meanwhile, there is a discipline called social psychology which studies the behaviour of individuals in social situations, usually within small groups. This tends to focus on looking at how participants behave in controlled laboratory conditions, typically when a participant is part of a group whose other members are "stooges" (confederates of the researcher who have been instructed to behave in programmed way), such as in Milgram's experiment on obedience or Asch's line study on conformity. While useful, the artificiality of such experiments may limit their practical applicability.

Real social interactions develop unpredictably and may rapidly go beyond the ability of simple models, based on an understanding of the behaviour of individuals, to reproduce the behaviour of the group. When psychology experiments have attempted to move to more realistic scenarios the results have not always been happy. The notorious Stanford prison experiment, in which student participants role-played as guards and prisoners, resulted in an escalation to brutality on the part of the "guards" within a surprisingly short period of time; scheduled to run for two weeks, the experiment had to be terminated on the sixth day.

One way in which experimental psychology has tried to overcome this problem is by avoiding it, and studying groups rather than individuals as the experimental "unit". Rather than explaining why a group behaves as it does, this approach treats the group as something with new characteristics which may be more than the sum of its parts. The focus is more on how the group behaves, and the effect of the group on its members, rather than on explaining the behaviour of the group in terms of its members. In order to understand the "why" of group behaviour, Harré and his colleagues may be able to offer better insights than can be obtained through strictly Baconian methods.

However, before deciding that causal explanations are flawed, it should be noted that Harré's approach via "scripts" has close similarities to one of Aristotle's four categories of causality, namely formal causes, and perhaps also with Aristotle's final causes. Baconian causality is close to Aristotle's notion of efficient cause. For a recent attempt to reconcile Aristotle's four causes with similar ideas from a classic paper by Nikolaas Tinbergen, see Hladký and Havlíček (2013).

The division of the psychology community into the majority who use quantitative methods and the minority who favour a qualitative approach mirrors a more general division across culture, well described in Gibbon (1989, pp. 129–139). In attempting to unravel the reasons behind different approaches towards archaeology, which at the time he wrote was in violent turmoil, Gibbon discusses two deep-seated ideological traditions in western thought which he characterises as the enlightenment and romantic methodological styles. The enlightenment approach focuses on general methods and the search for timeless universal laws, whereas the romantic style is more concerned with complexity, wholeness, tradition and the importance of specific context. This division is similar to that analysed by Nietzsche in The Birth of Tragedy, where he linked two contrasting approaches to art with the Greek gods Apollo and Dionysus, representing order and passion. Nietzsche believed that the highest forms of art require a combination of these two states of mind. Is it too much to expect that a mature science of psychology might aspire to a similar fusion?

Chapter 6

How Hypothesis Testing Copes with Uncertainty: The Legacy of Karl Popper and Ronald Fisher

SUMMARY

An introduction to falsificationism and the hypothetico-deductive method. Popper's views on how science progresses, and a modified view. Null hypothesis significance testing, viewed as modified falsification. The origin of Fisher's approach: the lady tasting tea. Type I and type II errors.

NEED TO KNOW

The Popperian revolution

The philosophical foundation most commonly accepted by people who work in quantitative science, including psychology, is a variant of **falsificationism**. This refers to the view sometimes attributed[1] to Claude Bernard and most successfully popularised by Karl Popper that science advances not through induction — deriving a hypothesis from data and establishing it as fact by

---

[1] By Peter Medawar (Medawar, 1982, p. 134); Medawar in fact cites several originators, but Bernard seems to have stated the idea most clearly in its modern form prior to its adoption by Popper.

further continued observation and confirmation — but by putting forward, testing and eventually refuting hypotheses, and replacing them with improved ones. Research which is self-consciously designed to use this mechanism — proposing a hypothesis, drawing conclusions from it and then testing these conclusions against reality — is known as **hypothesis-driven** research. The method as a whole is known as the **hypothetico-deductive method.**[2]

The next three paragraphs summarise Popper's views. All hypotheses are more or less in error, so the aim of showing a particular hypothesis to be true is doomed to fail, given that none of them is perfectly correct. The process of science consists not in discovering the truth but in finding a series of ever better hypotheses that approach ever closer to an accurate description of how the world works in some particular area. Hypotheses are accepted for as long as they account for the data obtained from experiments, but with the accumulation of more and more data, eventually the hypothesis will fail to be consistent with the new results.

At that point, it will be abandoned, and scientists will have to invent a new hypothesis that is, unlike the old one, consistent with all the data known up to that time including the new results. The new hypothesis will then be subject to critical testing until it in turn fails, and so the process goes on indefinitely. The classic example is Newton's law of gravitation, which was replaced by Einstein's model of gravitation — his general theory of relativity — when Newton's equations failed to account for certain astronomical facts.

When a new hypothesis has been devised in this way, initially to account for certain discrepancies unexplained by some previous hypothesis, it will be subjected to testing in its turn. At some point if it survives these challenges, it will become widely accepted as the best explanation of whatever phenomenon it claims to describe.

---

[2]At least, this is the term used by Medawar (1982). As far as I understand the distinction, it is that the *method* is hypothetico-deductive, and the philosophical *justification* for it is termed falsificationism.

At that point it is upgraded from a hypothesis to a "theory". Once confidence in a theory has been established, it will tend to be used without much question until it in turn begins to show discrepancies between what it predicts and the results of further experiments. The process of devising improved theories is sequential.

At this point the reality of how science is actually carried out tends to diverge from Popper's ideas. In practice, an obsolescent theory which has failed to predict correctly the result of some experiment is not abandoned until a better one has been found. Usually more than one alternative new hypothesis will be proposed, and there is a period when rival hypotheses will be tested and compared with one another, and against the old theory (evidently there is no profit in adopting a new hypothesis which does no better than the previously accepted one).

There is usually one winner in these contests. This becomes the dominant new theory, which is challenged in its turn when its defects become apparent with the accumulation of yet more data. In other words the process of science is not so much that of holding up single hypotheses to scrutiny one after another in a sequential manner, but more a parallel process where at any one time several hypotheses may be in contention.

"Falsification" of the null hypothesis

This brief sketch of the scientific process applies on the large scale, to hypotheses in the hard sciences which deal with powerful ideas such as gravitation, the structure of the atom or the mechanism of heredity. But the same idea of comparing hypotheses and choosing the better of two, or the best one of a whole set of hypotheses, can also be applied on a more modest scale. In the standard case where the research hypothesis is that an IV has a causal link with a DV, there are two in contention: the causal hypothesis, and the null hypothesis that there is no link.

In this instance we can state without hesitation that *either* the causal hypothesis *or* the null hypothesis **must** be true. This is a logical necessity, since the null hypothesis is the direct logical contrary of the research hypothesis. It is like stating that this apple either is red or it is not red, which I can confidently claim even without ever seeing the apple.

The idea introduced by R. A. Fisher of the **null hypothesis significance test** (abbreviated NHST) can be thought of as follows. Suppose that all apples are either red or green. If someone examines an apple and tells me that the apple is not green, then I can deduce that it must be red. If data demonstrate that the null hypothesis is false, then the causal hypothesis must be true.

This is not Fisher's approach, but it provides a step towards understanding it. A more accurate, though still incorrect approach is to say that it works not by showing that the null hypothesis is *impossible*, only that it is *unlikely*. In that case it follows that the causal hypothesis must *probably* be true, because it is the only alternative choice.

If this book used the Bayesian approach to hypothesis testing, this would be a reasonable statement of the sort of conclusions we could draw. But this would require a more complicated mathematical explanation. Orthodox statistics using the NHST is easier to apply, and programs such as SPSS are geared to apply it, but the penalty is that the fundamental idea is difficult to grasp.

The fundamental idea

Suppose we conduct an experiment to test a causal hypothesis and analyse the data. To make the example more concrete, imagine that the data can be summarised by just one single number. For example, if we were looking at the effect of gender on IQ by sampling and testing a number of students, we might take the average IQ of the female members of the sample, and the average IQ of the males, and subtract one from another. This difference is our best estimate for the effect of gender on IQ, so if there is *no* such effect we would expect the difference to at, or close to, *zero*.

We show later that assuming the null to be true, we can predict quite well where the difference in the sample averages should lie, within a range either side of zero. Suppose that if the null is true, then 999 times out of 1000 it would lie within a range of plus or minus 10 points. Suppose we find an actual value of plus 15 points (a result in favour of the women). This would be very strong evidence to suggest that women are more intelligent than men, because if the null were true it would only happen less than once in a thousand times, or 0.001 of the time. Fisher's idea is then that we declare the result **significant at the level of 0.001**. We reject the null hypothesis and claim that there is evidence for the causal hypothesis to be true.

Conventionally, this method is usually applied at a significance level not of 0.001 but of 0.05, or 5%. In other words a calculation is made on the basis of the null hypothesis, that the data obtained as the result of an experiment should fall within a certain range 95% of the time. When the data is analysed, if the data falls outside this range, the result is **significant at the 0.05 level**, and the null hypothesis is rejected. **Rejecting** the null enables us to **assert** the causal hypothesis.

Filling out the details of the argument is complicated and the mathematics involved are not easy, but at this stage it is more important to understand in a conceptual way what the NHST is attempting to achieve, and, as importantly, its limitations, which include the following:

(a) Even if the analysis shows a significant effect, the data cannot *prove* the causal hypothesis to be true. There is no such thing as totally unambiguous data. But data can provide *strong evidence* for the truth of the causal hypothesis.

(b) If the analysis fails to show a significant effect, this does not prove the null hypothesis to be true. In this case *we cannot even reliably state that the data provide strong evidence for the null hypothesis to be true*. All we can do is to *fail to reject the null hypothesis*. This is disappointingly negative, though later it will be seen that the use of confidence intervals provides a partial solution, enabling us to say something about such data.

GOING DEEPER

p-Values

It is possible to cover the topic of significance testing without mentioning *p*-values. SPSS produces exact values for these *p*-values in the output, but they can be interpreted in terms we have already met as follows: if the *p*-value is *less* than 0.05, the result is significant at the 0.05 level; if the *p*-value is *less* than 0.01, it is significant at the 0.01 level, and so on. To go further than this, it is necessary to understand what the exact *p*-value actually signifies.

I will confine attention to the situation considered above, where if the null hypothesis is true, then the average of some statistic calculated from the data will have some probability distribution centred on zero, and I will assume in addition that the distribution is symmetric. This is true in the majority of cases, and non-symmetric distributions introduce complications which are not relevant to the general principle. If you need a more concrete instance, think of the statistic as the difference between the means of the DV, compared over two groups in a randomized controlled trial.[3]

The significance test produces a positive result — allowing us to reject the null hypothesis — if the statistic is "far enough" from zero. Far enough in what sense? In the sense that there is a less than one in twenty chance that the statistic would be this far from zero — or farther — if the null hypothesis were true. For the significance test for at the 0.05 level, there will be a value, call it d, such that the result is significant at this level if the statistic is less than $-d$, *or* greater than d.[4] Otherwise, if the statistic lies within the interval between $-d$ and d, no conclusion can be drawn (recall that we cannot conclude that the null hypothesis is true given a non-significant result, we can only fail to reject it). The region of possible values of the statistic comprising the two intervals from minus infinity, to $-d$,

---

[3] With apologies for referring to randomized trials, which are not properly defined until Chapter 8.

[4] There are two alternatives, and so this is known as a two-tailed test. There are also in most cases one-tailed tests of significance available. They introduce some complications which are best dealt with on-line.

and from d to plus infinity, is known as the **rejection region** for this test: the null hypothesis is rejected at this significance level, if the statistic falls within the rejection region.

A significance test at the 0.01 level will require a new distance to be calculated, call it δ, such that there is only a one in one hundred probability that the statistic is less than $-\delta$, or more than δ, if the null hypothesis happens to be true. δ will always be larger than d, since the smaller significance level requires a smaller rejection region, and hence larger limits.

In fact, given any probability p, we can calculate a number д such that there is a probability p that the statistic will be either less than $-$д or more than д if the null hypothesis is true. This gives a mapping of p-values to values of the statistic, so that each p-value gives a number for the statistic. The mapping can be run backwards, so that each positive value of the statistic yields a p-value. When SPSS carries out a significance test it calculates the value of the statistic, call it s (I am running out of variants for d). It then works out the p-value which would have a rejection region of precisely from minus infinity to $-s$, and from s to plus infinity, and returns that as the "p-value" for the test.

All this can be summarised as follows, indeed some may find this explanation easier than the digression via rejection regions:

The p-value of a result is the probability of a result at least as extreme as that obtained, if the null hypothesis were true.

Exercise: Show from this definition that if the p-value of an outcome is less than 0.05, then the outcome must be significant at the 0.05 level, and likewise if the p-value is less than 0.01, it must be significant at the 0.01 level, and so on. This means that if one's only concern is with conventional significance testing, the p-value need only be inspected to see whether or not it is less than the conventional value, to determine whether the result is significant at that value.

More on falsificationism

One of the most influential philosophers of science, at least in his effect on working scientists, was Karl Popper. A striking example of this can be seen in the impact his ideas had on Nobel laureate Peter Medawar, and Popper's views are well set out in Medawar's books (better, some might argue, than in Popper's own works).

Scientists through the ages have regarded it as part of their task to discover the universal laws which govern the behaviour of the physical world. It was believed that careful, objective observation and analysis would enable them to do this. Newton's laws of motion, and especially the inverse square law of gravitation, were seen as successful examples of how this might work. Although this view was challenged by David Hume in the eighteenth century, when he pointed out that we had no logical warrant for assuming that regularities in behaviour seen in the past implied the existence of causal laws, or that these regularities would continue into the future, this radical scepticism had little effect on the views of working scientists.

But in the early twentieth century two developments, relativity and quantum theory, had a greater effect in undermining previous assumptions. Quite apart from showing that our whole model of space and time was flawed, general relativity demonstrated that the previously unquestioned truth of Newton's law of gravitation had been illusory. Though apparently confirmed by thousands of instances, Newton's law, it appeared, never held exactly, though it was an excellent approximation in most cases. The search for certainty about the universe, it seemed, was doomed. At best we could find "laws" which were approximately true, but the search for ultimate truth might be destined to fail. It seemed likely that a complete description of the universe in terms of universal laws was impossible, if only because the universe might be so complicated that the human brain could never form an adequate representation of it. As J. B. S. Haldane wrote: "The Universe is not only queerer than we suppose, but queerer than we can suppose".

Popper argued that this fact, if it was a fact, did not imply that science had no meaning. The search for a perfect theory is like the search for a clock that keeps perfect time. We may never find such a clock, but clocks are still useful. If we need to know the time more accurately, we improve the design of our clock accordingly.

Likewise, no laws will ever be valid in all circumstances, but the scientific process can ensure that our statements of scientific laws become ever closer to the truth, and ever more accurate and more wide-ranging. Popper's attitude might be summed up in Beckett's comment: "Ever tried. Ever failed. No matter. Try again. Fail again. Fail better."

From this basic observation, Popper could make certain deductions about how this process of "failing better" should work. It was no good proceeding as all previous scientists had done, by testing potential scientific laws and seeking confirmatory instances, whereby these laws could be established. Attempting to validate them in this way was a pointless exercise, for two reasons. Firstly, because no laws are ever perfectly correct and so one would be trying to prove something which was untrue, and secondly, because even if true, one could never prove a universal law from any number of individual confirmatory instances, no matter how many they may be. One example of this was the supposed law "all swans are white". One might observe thousands of confirmatory instances of this in Europe, but that would not make it true. One visit to Australia, where swans are black, would prove it false.

The fact that a single instance could prove a law false, deeply impressed Popper. Here at last were grounds for certainty amid a world of confusion. Descartes, despairing of finding any solid foundation for knowledge, finally found bedrock in the one thing of which he could be certain, his own existence ("I think, therefore I am"). Popper found certainty in science, he believed, by beginning with a certain class of facts: observations which proved some general statement about the universe to be false. For example, Eddington's observations of the solar eclipse of 1919 had shown that one statement of a universal law, Newton's law of gravitation, did not fit the facts. We could not be certain that Einstein was right, but we could be certain that Newton was wrong. Einstein's theory survived Eddington's observations, whereas Newton's did not.

Popper saw logic has having a privileged position in human thought, as providing certain knowledge, whereas one could never obtain certainty about laws concerning the external world. Logic might, however, enable one to make progress *towards* knowledge of the world if it was used to improve our model of the world, via this process of falsification. To clarify how this actually worked in Popper's scheme, imagine that we have a model, or theory, to describe or explain how some part of the natural world operates. We suspect that this model is imperfect, but following Popper, we regard our task as one of improving its fit with reality.

How can we improve the model? Should we look for its strongest point, or its weakest? It seems plausible that we are more likely to effect a substantial improvement by detecting the weakest point. If our roof is leaking and we need to dry out the house, it makes more sense to find the leak and to plug it, than to turn up the central heating in an attempt to make the water evaporate. How do we find the weakest point of a model? The weak points are those where it fails to describe reality; therefore, we must look for those instances in which the model breaks down: those instances are precisely those which falsify the model. Therefore we must do our best to falsify the model. Having done so, the next task is to plug the leak, i.e., to revise the model in such a way that the weakness is removed. Having done that, the new model will no doubt have weaknesses of its own. The process continues by seeking these out, through a programme of attempting to falsify the new model, and then removing the yet newer weaknesses that this reveals, and so on.

This approach, whereby falsifying theories leads to better theories, is known to philosophers as falsificationism. It may strike someone encountering Popper's ideas for the first time as paradoxical. Here we are attempting to find the truth about the external world, but we do so by attempting to show that our theories are false. This seems to be a very backhanded way of proceeding: how can we ever make progress by using such a negative method? Surely such an approach can only destroy, and never create?

It is true that Popper's approach incorporates a gap at the creative part of this process. This is deliberate on his part. Once a new observation has falsified a theory, the next step is to create an improved theory. This new theory must of course be compatible with the new observation, otherwise it would be falsified before it ever saw the light of day. But the form of the new theory is left undetermined in Popper's approach: it is the result more of psychology than logic, and is not, therefore, a proper subject for study by philosophers of science (or so he claims). It is not that the choice of new theories is completely a matter of personal taste. He suggests that a new theory, replacing one that has just been falsified, should have various desirable properties: it must for example be more than just a slightly amended version of the old one, with a "patch" to account for the new observation: Popper denounces such theories as "ad hoc" and of little value. A new theory should ideally be bold and radical, and therefore capable of making new predictions which substantially extend the range of the previous theory (Popper may once again have had Einstein's theory of general relativity in mind here). It will therefore face more challenges, and there will be more opportunities to falsify it (and so, to improve it).

So far as the new theory continues to meet these challenges without being falsified, we can continue to regard it as successful, but never as proven. "All men must die", and the same may be true of hypotheses, but with both, some credit is due for each extra day that the inevitable dissolution is postponed. And meanwhile, the surviving theories are not simply existing in limbo, uselessly as it were, passively awaiting falsification by some killer fact. If that were the case, science would indeed seem to have little point, as a futile pursuit of the forever unattainable aim of ultimate knowledge. But scientific theories spawn practical applications, and to the extent that a theory has not yet been falsified, the applications are still consistent with reality and therefore of practical value. Even highly inaccurate clocks were helpful in the fourteenth century to indicate the times of the canonical offices in churches and monasteries. As the statistician George Box wrote: "essentially, all models are wrong, but some are useful". Theories can make worthwhile contributions during their lifetimes. Popper merely pointed out that these lifetimes are finite, and that we must plan for an orderly succession, and indeed, do our best to bring it about, in the knowledge, he thought, that the succession will bring progress.

The following section, which goes in more detail to criticisms of Popper's ideas and the counter-revolution of Thomas Kuhn, is included in the online portion of this chapter.

FISHER'S STATISTICAL COUP

Accentuate the positive: eliminate the negative

Popper's argument is that the only thing we can do in the light of new observational evidence is to reject a hypothesis, never to accept it. However, there is one particular set of circumstances where we might be entitled to conclude positively that a hypothesis is true. That uses a method called "induction by elimination". The principle is not unlike the story of two men running from an enraged bear. One says to the other "it's no good — we can never outrun this bear". The other replies "I don't have to run faster than the bear — I only have to run faster than you". If we know in advance that one of two possible hypotheses is true, we only have to be able to reject one, to prove the truth of the other. Fisher, essentially, took advantage of this fact.

The method has the benefit of logical certainty, but it also has one crucial weakness. Induction by elimination makes a fundamental assumption, which may or may not be justified: it starts from the premise that we can enumerate the possible true hypotheses that might account for a phenomenon, in a list: $\{H_1, H_2, H_3, ...\}$ and so on, up to some finite number. We assume that the true hypothesis is among our list. Provided we make that assumption, the way forward is to conduct a number of experiments designed to find out which of these possibilities is the right one: a sort of Hunger Games of the hypotheses, in which we want there to be only one winner. We know from Popper that we may never be able to prove, say, that H_2 is true, but we don't have to do that; we need only reject H_1, H_3, etc., in which case H_2, as the last one left standing, must by a clear logical implication be true. By "reject", may need to use Popper Mark III[5] at this point: a hypothesis can certainly be

---

[5] Popper theories marks I, II and III are defined fully in the online material.

rejected if the observed data is *impossible* if it were true; we also reserve the right to reject it if the data is merely *extremely unlikely* if it were true.

For example, we might decide that the possible explanations for autism can be listed as: Theory of Mind, Weak Central Coherence, Enhanced Perceptual Functioning, or Extreme Male Brain. In planning an experiment to test these, the researcher must now decide on a study that will give different findings depending on which hypothesis is correct. For example, with a paradigm designed to find the characters in a "Where's Wally" book, all of the rival hypotheses might predict the same thing: that people with autism would do much better than a control group. This would be useless in evaluating the hypotheses. On the other hand, a test of the ability to recognise small changes in the contour of a melody might be good at this, because the WCC hypothesis might predict one outcome (poor performance) and the EPF theory might predict a different one (improved performance, compared with a control group). The outcome would decide which hypothesis accounted better for the data. It might of course be that several studies were needed to eliminate all but one of the hypotheses. The importance of this approach to experimental design was already appreciated by Francis Bacon. When data was available which enabled one to decide between two alternative hypotheses, he called this an "instance of the fingerpost" ("instantia crucis": he wrote in Latin), because it pointed towards one particular hypothesis out of possible alternatives.

A version of this approach is the Bayesian method, in which the possible true hypotheses are enumerated, and data is used to modify the extent to which we believe the alternatives to be true. This is often implemented in practical statistics programs by using an approximation known as the BIC (Bayesian Information Criterion). This does not involve anything so dramatic as eliminating rival hypotheses, but it may be that new data will indicate that one of the hypotheses appears a great deal more plausible than the alternatives. Though interesting, it is not an approach we have space to explore further.

Induction by elimination takes one strand of Popper's approach, that of using negative results to reject hypotheses, but appears to contradict him in another, important respect. I have suggested that we can list the possible hypotheses, and that the list will include the "true" one. Given that I have been suggesting, following Popper, that all hypotheses are false, this may appear a foolish assumption. There are two ways out of the contradiction. We may (1) decide to deal with theories that are broad enough actually to *be* true, or (2) shade our meaning of "truth".

(1) When Popper and Box suggested that all models or hypotheses are false, they had in mind models which were both general (for example, "all"-type statements such as "all swans are white") and precise (such as the formulation of Newton's law of gravitation: $F = Gm_1m_2/r^2$). But some hypotheses, which are still arguably scientific, are not necessarily of this kind.

   (a) For example, we can look at hypotheses which are precise but not general, such as "DNA-based life has at some time existed on Mars", or "some swans are black". These are liable to be confirmed by a single, well-verified observation.

   (b) Or, we can look at hypotheses which are general but not precise, such as many of those found in psychology. These include the various theories that claim to account for autism, such as those listed above, plus a fair number of others. These allow for a degree of fuzziness in their formulation, and may be true by virtue of the fact that they can each account for a wide range of behaviours. In predicting future behaviour, this type of theory specifies not a precise outcome, but rather, a wide range of possible outcomes.

(2) Or, we may decide that instead of finding the "true" hypothesis among our list $\{H_1, H_2, H_3, ...\}$, we want to find the hypothesis which is "closest" to being true. If we could define "closeness to truth", and more importantly if we could find a way to actually *measure* this quantity in practice, then we would be able to pick out that hypothesis as the preferred one. It would be the least wrong, and the most useful, by Box's criterion. This is essentially the idea behind one widely used alternative to the BIC in model comparison, namely the AIC or Akaike Information Criterion, and its variants. This attempts the difficult feat of measuring

how close a model comes to truth, without knowing what that truth actually is. This is not the place to discuss the AIC or BIC, nor the arguments put forward to support one or the other. However, they should be mentioned for completeness, and anyone sufficiently interested will find some excellent sources on both (see the further reading section at the end of this book).

Fisher's approach

The version of induction by elimination used by Fisher cleverly gets around the key potential weakness highlighted above, namely that we need to be certain that one of our listed hypotheses is actually true. It takes a list of just two hypotheses, of a rather special kind, chosen so that there is a cast iron guarantee that one of the hypotheses has to be true. It then uses Popper Mark III method (explained in the online material) in an attempt to enable us to reject one of those hypotheses, and thus to accept the other one. If you have not read about the Popper approach online, it amounts to the following argument: if something is observed which would be very unlikely on the assumption of a particular hypothesis, then that hypothesis can be rejected. The argument is given in detail below.

How can we be certain that a set $\{H_1, H_2\}$ contains one true statement? The answer may appear a cheat when you see it. We simply make the two hypotheses logical opposites of one another. Few men could claim to be as personable as a film star, though some may fantasise about it, but any man can truthfully say: "either I am better-looking than Orlando Bloom — or I am not better-looking than Orlando Bloom". For any statement you like, or any hypothesis H_1 about the world, however bizarre or plausible, I can at once give you another hypothesis H_2 such that one, and only one, of the set $\{H_1, H_2\}$ is true. "The moon is made of green cheese" might be one, and "the moon is not made of green cheese" would be the other. Fisher's idea is to apply Popper Mark III to just one of these, with the hope that it can be eliminated and give us the remaining hypothesis as something we have evidence to affirm as fact.

There is one more thing to specify before we finally arrive at what Fisher called his null hypothesis significance test, or NHST: for the method only works as intended for rather special types of hypothesis. Fortunately, this type is common in psychology. Essentially, the method can be applied when we are dealing with an experimental hypothesis of the kind "C causes E", with which we are familiar from previous chapters. For such a hypothesis, the logical contradictory can be written "there is no causal link between C and E", or equally, "C and E are independent". In this case, we have an interest in showing that "C causes E" is true, so our target for destruction by the Popper Mark III is the other one, "C and E are independent". To save space, the first or experimental hypothesis will be written H_1, and the second hypothesis will be written H_0. H_0 is also referred to as the "null hypothesis".

To sum up, Fisher's approach is as follows.

(1) Take your experimental hypothesis H_1, which we wish to be able to claim as true.
(2) From it, create a null hypothesis H_0, which is basically just "not-H_1".
(3) Construct the list $\{H_0, H_1\}$, noting that one of these must be true, and that therefore we can apply induction by elimination to it.
(4) Construct an experiment which will, if successful, enable us to apply the Popper Mark III method to H_0, rejecting it and allowing us to use induction by elimination to assert the truth of H_1.

The remaining sections will attempt to show how this can be done in practice.

Fisher's tea party

The NHST as developed systematically by Fisher originated, or so Fisher's account suggests (Fisher, 1935, p. 11) in response to the following challenge. In his own words:

"A lady declares that by tasting a cup of tea made with milk she can discriminate whether the milk or the tea infusion was first added to the cup. We will consider the problem of designing an experiment by means of which this assertion can be tested".

Clearly we will want to challenge the lady with a number of cups of tea made in different ways, and to see whether she can tell us correctly which is which. Fisher's problem is, how do we design the experiment to be reasonably certain that the lady's claim is correct? Evidently it is possible that she may pass *any* given test with flying colours, purely on the basis of a series of lucky guesses. But if the "lucky guess" hypothesis requires us to assume that something very improbable has happened, then we will reject it. Having rejected the lucky guess idea, we have no alternative but to conclude that the lady really can do what she claims.

If we were to present her with just two cups of tea, one with the milk first and the other with the milk second, and if we tell her this — i.e., if we tell her that the teas are different, but not the order in which they are presented — what can we conclude if she gets the order right? Very little: if the possible orders for the two cups are *TM* and *MT*, where *T* signifies the cup with tea in first and *M* signifies the one with milk in first, then there is a 50/50 chance that she will get the answer right just by guesswork, as in the case of tossing a fair coin. Fisher's question is, how many such trials would she have to get correct before we regard her success as reasonable evidence that her claim is valid? Answering this question amounts to a key element of the design of experiments.

There are certain aspects of the design of a good experiment which we may be able to deduce from first principles. For example, it would seem a good idea for there to be an *equal number* of presentations of *T*-type cups as of *M*-type cups. To take an extreme case in which this condition is violated, if all the cups were of the *same* type, say of type *M*, then a score of 100% might simply mean that the lady always believed the milk to have been put in first, regardless of whether this was true or not. This would be a poorly designed experiment. If we have equal numbers of cups, they should also be presented to the lady in a random order. Why? If in an extreme case we chose to present all the cups of one type first, followed by those of the other type, and if the lady had any reason to suspect that this was our very simple strategy, she would have a 50/50 chance of guessing correctly whether the order was *TT....MM....* or *MM....TT....*

The eightfold way

Fisher explains that his experiment consisted of first making eight cups of tea, half of which had the tea poured in first, and half with the milk put in first. The lady was then presented with these eight cups, in random order, and told that her task was to identify which had four had the tea put in first, and which four had the milk first. The lady knew, therefore, that there were four cups of each kind, and that the order was random (so that she would not be tempted to guess the experimenter's strategy in ordering the cups).

It turned out that the lady correctly guessed all the cups. In order to draw a conclusion from this outcome, we need to examine two possible explanations of the result.

A. the null hypothesis: the lady had no ability to tell *T* from *M*, and the result was a series of lucky guesses.
B. the experimental hypothesis: in other words, the lady's claim was correct, and the results were exactly what would be expected given her abilities.

Fisher's approach was to ask, how likely would the observed outcome be, if hypothesis A were true? Imagine the cups numbered from 1 to 8 as below, representing the order in which they are presented to the lady:

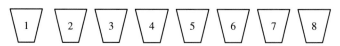

We need to allocate the four *T* cups and the four *M* cups randomly among these eight cups. We could do this, for example, by having four counters with *T* on, and four with *M* on, and drawing them consecutively out of a bag. The first cup to be presented has the symbol on the first counter, and so on for all eight cups. An example might be:

The question of how many possible presentations are possible, is simpler if approached via smaller numbers. With just two cups, there are evidently just two ways of choosing the one *T* cup out of the sequence — it can be the first or the second. Whichever cup is chosen to be the *T* one, there is no choice for the *M* cup: it must be the other. If the lady is guessing, she has a 50/50 chance of being correct in identifying the *T* cup correctly. (She knows, by the terms of the experiment, that she has to identify one cup as *T* and the other one as *M*.)

With four cups, there are six ways of choosing the two *T* cups: they can be 1 and 2, 1 and 3, 1 and 4, 2 and 3, 2 and 4, or 3 and 4. Again, having chosen the two *T* cups, the other two cups must be the *M* cups. So there are just six ways of ordering the cups. The lady, if she is guessing, now has only a one in six chance of getting the correct answer. So in an experiment with four cups, a successful outcome is beginning to suggest that there may be something in her claim. But after all, a lucky guess is still not implausible: it is the chance of throwing a six with a single die.

If now we have six cups, three each of *T* and *M*, what is the chance of the lady guessing correctly this time? Only one combination is correct, and if she is guessing, she does not know which combination we have chosen. It becomes tedious to list the number of possible sequences such as *TMTTMM* and so on, and I will rely on a fairly elementary result which says that there are 6.5.4/3.2[6] such sequences, which works out at 20. If the lady had been guessing, choosing the correct sequence out of the twenty possible ones would have a chance of just one in 20 of being correct.

Some people would already find this convincing. But Fisher went further, and prepared eight cups for the lady. If we are told

---

[6]The full stops here represent the operation of multiplication, not decimal points.

that she identified the cups correctly in this sequence of eight, we can calculate that there are 8.7.6.5/4.3.2 possible combinations, or seventy possible orders with four *T*'s and four *M*'s, such as *TTMTMMMT* or *MMTMTMTT*, etc. To have hit on the correct one by chance, would happen only once in every 70 trials on average, if the lady were guessing. The fact that she got the sequence correct, suggests that either she really does have the ability she claims, or that something very unlikely has occurred (that she is guessing, and by chance has guessed correctly). Fisher argued that the result was sufficiently unlikely on the "guessing" hypothesis, hypothesis A, to enable us to *reject* that idea. Having rejected A, we are now left with hypothesis B, that the lady really does have the powers that she claims to have.

How often will we be wrong? Fisher argued that in science, we can never be 100% sure of our conclusions, so that we have to allow some scope for error. There are two kinds of mistaken conclusions we could in theory draw about the lady.

(1) If the lady was in fact guessing, we could mistakenly decide that she has the special power of detecting if the milk was put in first.
(2) If the lady really has this special power, we could mistakenly fail to detect it.

On error[7]

Fisher chose to focus on the first kind of error, and for reasons I will deal with in a moment this is now known as a type one error, or type I error. Why neglect the second error? If we fail to detect the special power, Fisher said we could actually say — nothing! This is because the lady might have the special power to a small degree — to be better at chance at judging *T* or *M* — but that to demonstrate this we would need a large number of cups of tea, larger than we have

---

[7] Note that the term 'error' is being used here in a meaning which is quite distinct from its use in Chapter 2 as the discrepancy between a model and a set of data.

actually given her. So if we fail to detect an effect, we do not say that an effect is absent, merely that it has not been shown to be present. And of course if we say nothing, we cannot be shown to be wrong.

On the other hand, if we find that the lady has correctly guessed the eight cups, we claim that she *does* have a special power. And this, as a positive statement, can be shown to be wrong. It might just happen that she has no powers, but has guessed correctly.

To repeat: if we find enough evidence to reject the guessing hypothesis, we plump for the alternative, and announce that we have been convinced of the presence of a special power. If we do not find this evidence, we say nothing at all. We can be mistaken in the first instance, but not in the second. In that case nobody can contradict us because there is nothing to contradict. Of course there is still a problem — of the nature of a missed opportunity — but arguably this is not so serious as the first kind of error. If we say "the lady has special powers" and we are wrong, we have uttered, not a lie exactly, but an untruth, which may have consequences if people believe us. If we have said nothing, we have not said anything untrue, and on the whole this is arguably less damaging, as it does not supply false information.

There is another, later approach to hypothesis testing which takes a slightly different approach. With this, the Neyman–Pearson theory, it is not enough to think solely in terms of just one kind of error. If the lady has special powers and we fail to announce this, we have made another kind of mistake. The mistake of claiming special powers when they do not in fact exist was called by them a type I error, and the opposite mistake, of failing to say anything when in fact she does have these powers, is called a type II error. In modern approaches, this type of error is taken seriously, and we consider how to deal with it in the chapter devoted to the concept of power. But the problem of type I errors is one we need to attend to here and now, and this is the subject of the next section.

Note: the following section has been moved to the online material for this chapter.

Chapter 7
Gaussian Distributions, the Building Block of Parametric Statistics

SUMMARY

Gaussian distribution is important because it is frequent in nature, and is the basis for parametric statistics. Definition of histograms. Gaussian curves characterised by mean and s.d.. Relation between values and z-scores, and between z-scores and percentiles for a Gaussian variable. Sample mean as an estimator of population mean, and its reliability. Histograms vs. bar charts. Why Gaussian distributions are common. Non-Gaussian distributions and counter-measures. The Central Limit Theorem and probability density functions.

NEED TO KNOW

Why Gaussian distributions are important

There are two connected reasons why we need to know about **Gaussian distributions**.[1] One is that they are extremely common in nature, and therefore are worth understanding in their own

---

[1] Also known as "normal" distributions. I will use both terms interchangeably in this book. Sometimes Gaussian is better, as it is less ambiguous; but when describing something as "normally distributed" there does not seem to be an alternative: "Gaussianly distributed" sounds dreadful.

right. The second reason is that the mathematics behind most statistical methods makes the assumption that the error element of the data has a Gaussian distribution: the "assumption of normality".

Methods that make this assumption are so common that they are given a special name: they are called **parametric** statistical methods. There are other analytical methods available if it turns out that the noise distribution is not Gaussian: these are called, rather predictably, non-parametric statistics. Most of the methods described in this book are parametric.

Given that Gaussian distributions are so common, it follows that the assumption of a Gaussian noise distribution, and therefore also the use of parametric methods, is usually justified. However, we cannot just assume it to be the case, and so the assumption needs to be checked. Understanding the checking procedure requires us to understand the nature of the thing that we are checking. Hence this chapter.

As a taster for what follows, I strongly recommend you watch this short (under 3 minutes) demonstration on YouTube of something called the Galton Board, which illustrates what a Gaussian distribution is and how it can occur naturally:

https://www.youtube.com/watch?v=6YDHBFVIvIs

Histograms

Before starting to go into further detail about distributions, I need to explain a new concept: the **histogram**. A histogram is sometimes also known as a *frequency distribution.* If one is dealing with a scale variable, it is often very useful to summarise the distribution of the data in visual form, using a histogram. A histogram differs from a bar chart (see below) which relates *two* variables: it represents a *single* (scale) variable. This representation usually involves a degree of simplification, but as compensation, enables the general "shape" of the variable to be seen at a glance.

A histogram uses a division of the range of values of the scale variable into so-called "bins". An example with the distribution of ages in a sample of adults, might be to use bins comprising the ranges 20–24, 25–30, 30–34 and so on. These make up the horizontal axis. The vertical axis plots how many individuals in the sample fall into each bin's range. An image of this kind can often tell you a lot by just looking at its shape, even without calculating any numbers from it (such as its average etc). It can also tell you, at least approximately, whether the distribution of the data is Gaussian: in that case it will have the well known "bell curve" shape seen in Fig. 7.1.

An example of a real histogram is shown in Fig. 7.2.

This histogram represents the scale variable on the horizontal axis, increasing through its range from left to right. In this case it is a variable called "wordcount" from my own research. The bins are each five units wide in this case. The vertical axis represents the number of participants within each bin: this is also known as the **frequency**. The bins always include points with a score at the bottom range of the bin, and exclude points at the top of the range — those go into the next higher bin. So this histogram tells us that there are four sample points with a score of five or more, but less than ten; eight with a wordcount score of ten or more, but less than 15, and so on.

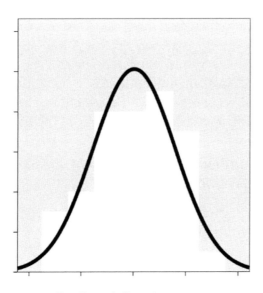

Fig. 7.1.   A Gaussian curve.

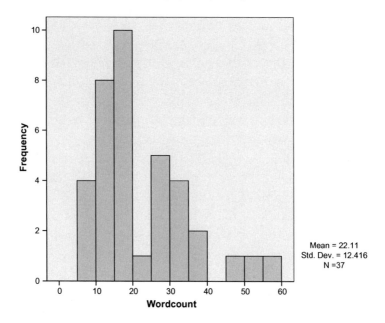

Fig. 7.2.   An example of a histogram.

There is quite a subtle process going on here regarding the decision as to bin sizes, which is taken automatically in SPSS.[2] The bin width is calculated to give a good compromise between bins which are too narrow (in which case many of the bars are either 0 or 1 unit high) and too wide (so that you do not get enough separate bins along the axis to show how the frequencies vary throughout the range of the variable: in the limit this would give a single bin, which would tell you nothing at all except for the number of points in the sample, which would be the height of the bin).

Gaussian distributions characterised by mean and standard deviation

The Gaussian or normal distribution (also sometimes known as the "bell curve") is a mathematical abstraction, but it is very close to

---

[2]The number of bins is the square root of the number of data points (rounded up), and the size of each bin is determined by the fact that the set of bins has to extend over the range of values of the variable.

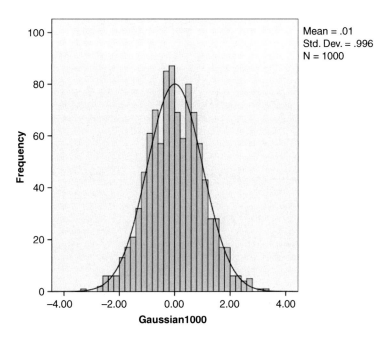

Fig. 7.3. Histogram with standard Gaussian distribution, 1000 sample points.

the actual histogram that you get when measuring a continuous variable (such as weight, height etc.) from a large population.

The curves above and below are from a computer simulation taking in the first case a sample of one thousand points, and in the second case, 5000. In each case SPSS has also superimposed a normal curve, as the best fit to the data.

As you can see from the histograms, even the larger number is only an approximation to normality, but it is much better than the smaller set (see Figs. 7.3 and 7.4).

These Gaussian distributions have a mean (on the horizontal axis) of zero and a standard deviation of one — that is, they would have in the limit if one could take infinitely many points. The 5000 point approximation is close to this, with a mean of 0.01 and an s.d. of 0.998.

You will sometimes see a normal distribution referred to by a term such as $N(4.5, 2.3)$. In this case the distribution has mean 4.5, and variance 2.3. There is only one distribution with a given mean and variance, so describing it as $N(4.5, 2.3)$ tells the reader exactly which normal distribution is being described.

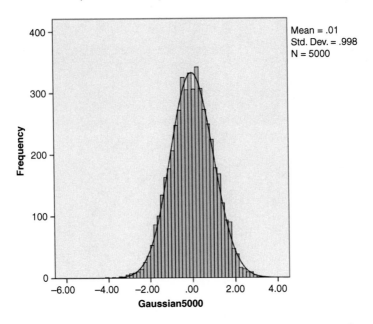

Fig. 7.4. Histogram with standard Gaussian distribution, 5000 sample points.

The normal distribution above is an approximation to $N(0, 1)$.[3]

The Gaussian-shaped distribution can describe many different distributions, such as that of IQ in the population, which is designed by the people who write these tests so that the final score will have a mean of 100 and a standard deviation of 15 for a typical population. An Excel-based simulation of this is shown below. It is obtained from the original $N(0, 1)$ distribution by simply multiplying all the numbers by 15 (the standard deviation) and then adding 100 (the mean) (see Fig. 7.5).

All normal distributions have certain things in common

They all have a similar appearance.

- In every case, the horizontal position of the "peak" is that of the mode, the mean and the median: they are all equal, in the case of the normal distribution.

---

[3] 1 is both the s.d. and the variance. The s.d. is the square root of the variance, and the square root of 1 is also 1.

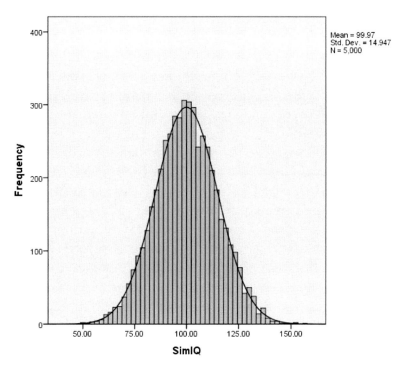

Fig. 7.5.   Histogram approximating Gaussian distribution of mean 100, s.d. 15.

- The horizontal distance from the peak to each of the "shoulders" of the distribution is equal to the standard deviation for that curve. The "shoulder" is the precise point at which the curve changes from being convex upwards, around the peak, to being concave, which it does as you go outwards towards the tails at either side.

The fact that standard deviation, and the peak to shoulder distances coincide is not an accident, by the way: it is a mathematical consequence of the formula describing the Gaussian distribution.

Recall that a standard normal distribution is written $N(0, 1)$; in the general case, a normal distribution can be referred to as $N(\mu, \sigma^2)$, where μ is the mean of the population and σ is its standard deviation. For some conventional reason the second number in the brackets is written as the variance, i.e., σ^2, not the standard deviation. So the distribution of IQ would be described as $N(100, 225)$.

All of these curves have a strong family resemblance. Some may have small variances, giving them a sharply peaked appearance; some may have large variances, making them look very spread out. Their means may vary. But mathematically, these things matter less than you might expect. For example, with a normally distributed variable, 50% of the population score less than or equal to the mean, and 50% score above the mean: this is clear when you consider that the distribution is symmetrical about the mean. It so happens that approximately 95% of the population lies between two standard deviations of the mean (you do not need to know how to prove this: simply accept it as a fact). 99.7% lies within three standard deviations of the mean. In fact if you measure numbers along the axis not in the original units for the variable, such as IQ points, but by using the normal distribution curve as a kind of landmark, you will find that certain facts like this are much easier to discover.

Using the peak of the distribution as the principal landmark, you will find yourself at the mean of the variable for the population. There are two other clear supplementary landmarks: these are the shoulders of the curve either side of the mean, which correspond to the mean plus and minus one standard deviation's worth of the variable.

For IQ, the mean is 100 and the s.d. is 15, so the left shoulder will be at $100 - 15$, the mean at 100, and the right shoulder at $100 + 15$. These landmarks at IQ points of 85, 100 and 115 are not much used in practice, but the points at two standard deviations to right and left of the mean are more popular as landmarks. Intellectual disability is sometimes defined as applying to individuals with an IQ score of two standard deviations below the mean or lower, i.e., of 70 points or below. The organisation MENSA has a membership criterion that you have to score two standard deviations or more above the mean, i.e., 130 or greater. Since 95% lie within two standard deviations of the mean (approximately), 5% of the population lies outside that limit. Since the normal distribution is symmetric about its mean, that means that equal numbers — 2.5% — lie in each of the two regions, to the left and right of the mean and 2 or more standard deviations distant from it. So around 2.5% of the population have IQ scores of 70 or less and have intellectual disability under the above definition, and a different 2.5% have scores of 130 or more, and are eligible for membership of MENSA.

These statements relating percentages to IQ scores are really statements relating percentages to **values of the variable defined in terms of the mean and standard deviation**, and since these statements are true for any normal distribution whatever, they could equally be made of the height of US adult males, weight of Lithuanian teenage females, or any other variable and population where we have reason to believe the distribution is near enough normal. So 2.5% of the population of Estonian folk-singers have a height two or more standard deviations above the average for this population, and 2.5% of them have a height two or more standard deviations below the average height for Estonian folk-singers.

This leads on to the concept of a z-score. A z-score is essentially a way of referring to the values of some variable in new units, and these units are based on the landmarks provided by some normal distribution, which has to be clearly specified. For example, with an IQ score you need to know that the score is calibrated in such a way that the mean for the general population is 100 and the standard deviation is 15.

In general, *the z-score for a value of IQ, or any other variable, is the number of standard deviations that value is above or below the mean*. For values above the mean, the z-score is counted as positive, for values below the mean, it is negative. So in the IQ example an average person would have a z-score of zero, because he is precisely *on* the mean. A z-score of +1 would correspond to someone whose score was one standard deviation more than the mean, that is to an IQ score of 115, and so on.

These z-scores are useful because of the way they are related to population frequencies. For any given z-score, there are a certain percentage of the population with scores less than or equal to that point, and another percentage with higher scores.

Table 7.1.   Relation between
IQ scores and z-scores.

IQ score	z-score
50	−3.33
60	−2.67
70	−2.00
80	−1.33
90	−0.67
100	0.00
110	0.67
120	1.33
130	2.00
140	2.67
150	3.33

These scores always add up to 100%, because for any figure you care to name, everyone — 100% of the population — scores either less than/equal to, or greater than, that amount.

For example, with IQ scores the IQ and z-scores are related as in Table 7.1.

Tables exist which tell you, for any given z-score, what percentage of the population have scores *less than or equal to* that score. This is known as the **percentile** for that z-score. Table 7.2 includes these values.

From this, which is a universal fact about normal distributions, we can construct the table of percentiles for our specific example of IQs by just putting the two tables side by side (see Table 7.3).

So someone with an IQ of 90 is at the 25.25th percentile, someone with an IQ of 110 is at the 74.75th percentile and so on. You will notice that these two percentiles add to 100%. There is a reason for this: 90 is 10 points below the mean and 110 is the same distance above the mean (see problems section).

These percentiles may seem not very useful, but they are more versatile than they appear. For example, if we wish to find the

Table 7.2. Relation between z-scores and percentiles.

z-score	percentile
−3.33	0.042912
−2.67	0.383043
−2.00	2.275006
−1.33	9.121128
−0.67	25.24925
0.00	50
0.67	74.75075
1.33	90.87887
2.00	97.72499
2.67	99.61696
3.33	99.95709

Table 7.3. IQ scores with z-scores and percentiles.

IQ score	z-score	percentile
50	−3.33	0.042912
60	−2.67	0.383043
70	−2.00	2.275006
80	−1.33	9.121128
90	−0.67	25.24925
100	0.00	50
110	0.67	74.75075
120	1.33	90.87887
130	2.00	97.72499
140	2.67	99.61696
150	3.33	99.95709

percentage of the population within any two finite limits, we can find this from the percentiles. How many people have an IQ between 110 and 120? Find the percentile for 120 (which is 90.88) and subtract that for 110 (which is 74.75), to obtain 16.13%.

The formula for calculating a z-score from something like an IQ score is quite simple, provided you know the mean μ and standard deviation σ of the score. The first step is to find out how far the IQ score is from the mean, and the second step is to express this distance in units of standard deviations.

If you start with a score X, the first step gives you $X - \mu$. for example with IQs, a score of 107.5 gets changed to $107.5 - 100 = 7.5$.

The second step asks: how big is $X - \mu$ in units of standard deviations? The answer has to be $(X - \mu)/\sigma$. Dividing by σ tells you how many sigmas fit into the distance $X - \mu$ which is the distance of your value from the mean. A score of 107.5 then goes to 7.5 under the first stage and $7.5/15 = 0.5$ under the second. So, an IQ of 107.5 has a z-score of 0.5, and so on.

To summarise, for IQ scores to z-scores:

IQ score	z-score
X	$(X-100)/15$

And in the general case:

Score	z-score
X	$(X-\mu)/\sigma$

Sampling from a population: distribution of M

Suppose now that we have a scale variable, but we **do not** make the assumption that the distribution in the population is Gaussian.[4] Suppose we still wish to estimate the value of the mean of the variable over the whole population, written μ. The obvious way to do this is to take a random sample from the population and take the mean value over that sample, conventionally written M. Our best guess for μ will then be M.

---

[4] We do, however, make the assumption that the population has a well-defined variance. For practical purposes, they all have this.

To be practically useful, we will wish to know two things about this estimate M.

1. How valid is it? In other words, is there any systematic bias in estimating μ from M?
2. How reliable is it? In other words, how close is the number M likely to be to the real value, μ? And for that matter, how is M distributed round the true value μ?

The answer to 1, and this is not a very deep result, is that the method is completely valid: there is no systematic bias in this method.[5]

The answer to 2, and this is a much deeper result, is given by the central limit theorem (CLT) discussed in more detail below. It is that *provided the sample size is sufficiently large* — and usually 30 or more is considered sufficient for this — the distribution of M is very close to a Gaussian distribution, with a s.d. of $\sigma/\sqrt{N}$, where N is the size of the sample.

It might appear that from this, we can infer that the distribution of the sample mean will be Gaussian, at least with larger sample sizes, even if the original distribution is far from Gaussian. It will appear shortly that sample means are the single most important numbers in statistics. Therefore, if these are always normally distributed, it may appear that the assumption of normality in the underlying distribution is unnecessary.

Sadly, this is not true for two reasons. Firstly, sample sizes are often less than 30. More importantly, parametric methods usually also involve the need to estimate standard deviations from the data themselves. It turns out that if the data are non-Gaussian, these estimates may be inaccurate. So the CLT is not so useful as one might have hoped. So to use parametric methods it is necessary to have distributions which approximate normality.

---

[5] In technical language, M is an **unbiased estimator** for μ. Such estimators occupy a prominent position in orthodox statistics.

GOING DEEPER

Areas under a histogram represent cases

Every "case" — that is, every individual represented — in a histogram contributes one unit to one of the bars of the histogram. From this it follows that the total area under a histogram, that is the area of the bars, is proportional to the total number of units included in the set of data. In counting the areas of the bars, each bar is like a rectangle with a base length of one. The area of that bar is therefore equal to its height, which gives the number of cases falling within the bin corresponding to that bar.

For example, in the wordcount histogram example given above, and repeated below, the numbers of cases in successive bins is {4, 8, 10, 1, 4, 5, 2, 0, 1, 1, 1} and these total to 37, confirmed by the value of N given in the output (see Fig. 7.6).

We may be interested in the proportion of cases represented, that fall between certain limits for the variable. For example, how

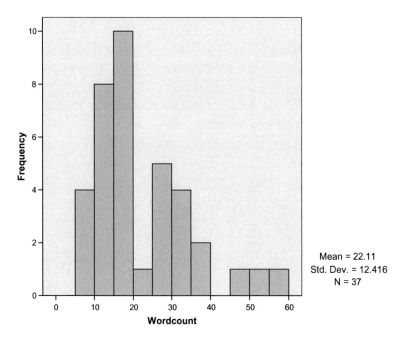

Fig. 7.6.   Histogram of Wordcount data.

many of the cases in this sample have wordcount values at the upper end of the range, between 45 and 59? Note that there are no values of 60 or more: any such would go into bins further to the right. Inspection shows there are just three cases of 45 or more. The proportion is then 3/37 or 0.081, i.e., 8.1% of cases.

We can generalise this observation: *the proportion of cases that fall between a pair of limits for the variable along the horizontal axis, is the area of the bins of the histogram corresponding to these limits, divided by the whole area of the histogram.*

If we adopt the simple trick of taking the whole area of the histogram as our unit of area, then this simplifies to: *the proportion of cases that fall between a pair of limits for the variable along the horizontal axis, is the area of the bins of the histogram lying between these limits.* All this means in practice is dividing the number of cases for the appropriate bins, by the total number of cases, and it is self-evident that this is the proportion of the total sample represented by the bins we are interested in.

This observation may seem too trivial to be worth mentioning, but the principle generalises to distributions within a larger population, where we can approximate the histogram by a continuous curve. In that case if we take the area under the curve to be the unit of area, then the area of the "slice" under the curve representing the cases that fall between a pair of limits for the variable, has an area which is just the proportion of cases in the whole population that lie between those limits.

For example, in the case of a curve representing income distribution, the proportion of people earning between £500 and £800 per week is given by the area marked out by the two vertical lines, the horizontal heavy line, and the part of the curve lying between the two vertical lines, in Fig. 7.7.

Areas under a histogram represent probabilities

There is an important fact about probabilities, which was first clearly stated by Laplace whom we have met earlier: **the probability of an event is the proportion of outcomes in which the event**

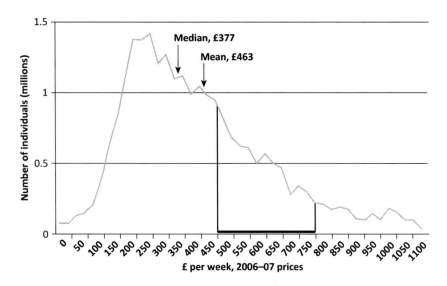

Fig. 7.7.   Proportion of households earning between £500 and £800.

Source: M. Brewer *et al.*, *Poverty and Inequality in the UK*: 2008, IFS, 2008, p. 6.
Note: Income is household income, net of tax, benefits and tax credit and before housing costs are deducted.

occurs, divided by the total number of possible outcomes, when each outcome is assumed to be equally likely.

If an individual is selected randomly from a population, then by definition of random selection, each "outcome" — i.e., each individual — is equally likely to be selected. Therefore by Laplace's definition, the probability that this individual will have certain properties (for example, being male and left-handed) is the proportion of the total population which are male and left-handed. For the more usual case where we are looking at a variable that is well defined for every member of the population, the probability that a randomly selected individual will have values that lie within certain limits, is the proportion of the population for which the variable lies between these limits. It is also the area of the histogram curve for the population that lies between these same limits, if we take the total area under the curve as one.

Histograms split between groups

Sometimes, splitting the data between different groups can reveal interesting variations between groups comprising the sample; below, the same data as above are split between a group with autism (ASD), the top histogram, and a control group, the bottom histogram, and it seems that the controls are scoring higher on the whole (see Fig. 7.8).

This does not prove anything, but it may be suggestive. As a rule, it is always advisable to visualise one's data as well as analysing it. There are a number of methods of doing this in SPSS, and the appropriate method varies with the type of data. This issue will be addressed more systematically later on, but meanwhile it is worth noting that histograms play a useful role in helping to make data more meaningful.

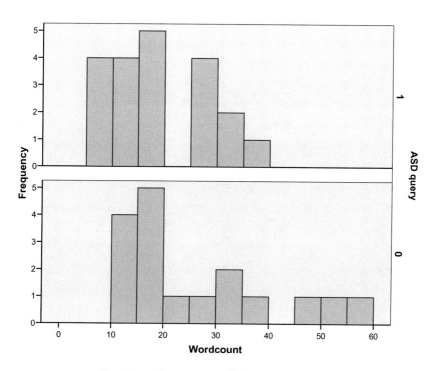

Fig. 7.8.   Histograms split between groups.

In case the concept of a histogram is still proving difficult, it may be worth looking at it from a different angle. The digital image program Photoshop will generate a histogram for you of the brightness of the pixels in an image, and this seems to me quite a good way to provide intuitively meaningful examples of histograms. In the Photoshop histograms, the horizontal axis represents the brightness of the individual pixels, ranging from totally black on the left, to maximum brightness on the right. The pixels here are the statistical population. The vertical axis gives the number of pixels of any particular brightness.

The following histogram is bimodal, i.e., there are two (bi-)peaks (or modes): it has a lot of dark pixels, and a lot of light ones, but little in between. This represents the fact that the population of pixels is very black and white, with little grey, which is clear from the image itself (see Fig. 7.9).

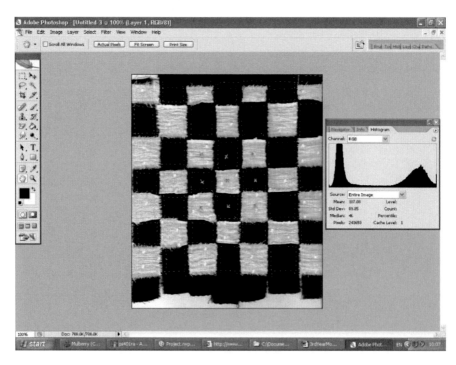

Fig. 7.9.   A digital image and its bimodal histogram.

Fig. 7.10. A more typical digital image with histogram.

You will recall that the mode is the most "popular" number in a set of data. The peak or peaks of a histogram will generally include the mode or modes.

The pixels in the following example cover a wide range from black to white, with plenty of grey scale detail. There is a rise towards the right of the histogram, representing the quite large area of bright sky at the top of the picture (Fig. 7.10).

Before going on to the next topic, I should mention that there is often confusion between histograms and bar charts, which they superficially resemble. Bar charts are commonly used to illustrate how a number of separate groups in a sample vary regarding their values of a certain dependent variable. For example, one might compare a group of men with a group of women on reaction time in a certain task (two bars, one for men and one for women, with the height of each bar representing average reaction time for that gender), which might look as in Fig. 7.11.

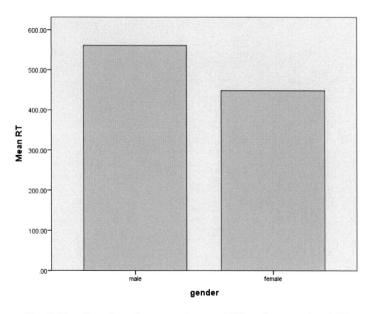

Fig. 7.11.   Bar chart for a continuous DV and two-valued IV.

The easy way to tell the difference is that the bars in a true bar chart do not touch, whereas the bars in a histogram do touch. Having said that, it may be in a histogram that there are apparent gaps due to zero datapoints in some of the bins, so you should recall in that case that the only way to be sure is to read the figure caption and work it out from that. With a bar chart the horizontal axis represents some categorical variable, and with a histogram, it will be referring to a continuous variable.

You can construct a simulation of what a normal distribution looks like for yourself by generating your own set of data using Excel, which is what I used for these simulations. This is easily done.

In an Excel worksheet, in cell A1 write the command

$$= RAND(\ )$$

In cell B1 write

$$= NORMSINV(A1)$$

Left click in A1 and drag into B1. The long rectangle formed by A1 and B1 will now have a small square nubbin at the bottom right. If you hover the cursor over this, the cursor will turn into a small black cross. If you now left click and hold, and pull the cursor vertically down, it will generate a double column for as far down as you care to go, for practical purposes. The A column generates a variable with a uniform distribution between 0 and 1. The B column generates a variable with a normal distribution that has a mean of 0 and a variance (and standard deviation) of 1, and this is the column you want.

If you go down 1000 rows you will produce something that looks close to a normal distribution in column B.

Unfortunately, Excel does not have a simple graphics for producing histograms from a column of numbers, but SPSS does it for you quite simply: once you have your data you can graph it in SPSS using the procedure described in a moment.

A Gaussian or normal distribution of the kind you produce in column B is called a **standard normal distribution**. It is often written symbolically as $N(0, 1)$.

To get your own normal histogram:

When you now go back to the top of column B, left click on the grey "B" box, then right click, "copy" and you can now paste the whole column into a newly opened blank SPSS data sheet. Then in SPSS:

1. **Go to Graphs (8th from the left on the toolbar) and left click on it.**
2. **In the drop down menu, go to the bottom, and hover the cursor over Legacy Dialogs.**
3. **On the menu that appears to the side, go to the bottom and click on Histogram.**
4. **In the left-hand box, left click on the variable you have just entered, and use the blue arrow button to move it to the Variable box on the right.**
5. **Check the Display normal curve box, and click OK.**

Why do normal distributions occur so often in nature?

There is a reason why many naturally occurring variables have a distribution which is close to being Gaussian. One illustration of the sort of thing that leads to a Gaussian is shown in the YouTube clip, cited at the start of this chapter. In this clip the demonstrator uses a device called a "Galton board", invented by Francis Galton, in which the balls all start off at the same place, at the centre of the top of the board, but are randomly jiggled to right and left by the pins as they descend the surface of the board.

This involves a fairly large number of random events, which are additive: the final position of each ball is a certain number of places to the left or right of the mid-point. You can find which point this is, as follows. Start each ball with the number zero, representing the mid-point position where it is fed into the Galton board. Imagine watching the ball falling down the board; every time that ball is diverted to the left by a pin, count that as −1 to be added to the sum; every time it passes to the right of a pin, add +1 to the running total. The final number represents the number of places the ball ends up to the left (if it is negative) or to the right (if positive). With a net score of zero the ball is exactly in the middle.

You will see that with enough pins, the plusses and minuses will tend to be roughly equal, just as when you toss a coin enough times, the number of heads will tend to be roughly the same as the number of tails: more precisely, the ratio of heads to tails will tend to one. With the Galton board, it is very unlikely that a ball will always be sent to the left of every one of twenty pins and end up at the extreme left-hand end of the board, just as it is improbable in the extreme that a coin tossed twenty times will land up heads on every occasion (unless it is two-headed!). So if you send, say, a hundred balls down the board, the distribution of the balls will tend to have a peak in the middle of the bottom row, and the number will tail off as you get further away from it on either side, which is what you see in the clip.

Why should, say, the distribution of height among adult males in the US, which also happens to be normally distributed, follow the same sort of shape as that of balls in a Galton board?

Recall that the final position of a ball at the bottom of the board was found by adding together a series of numbers representing the left and right deviations induced by the successive pins that it encounters. So a ball that experiences a series like this: {right, right, left, right, left, left, left}, represented by the numbers {+1, +1, −1, +1, −1, −1, −1}, will fall at the point at position of 1 +1 − 1 + 1 − 1 − 1 − 1 = − 1, i.e., one place to the left of centre.

It turns out that many variables are rather like the variable "final position" of a ball on the Galton board. That is, they are the result of adding together many effects, which are individually small and which each contribute some random amount to the total. For the height of adult males, this is the outcome of the combined effects of perhaps many hundreds of different genes acting together, like the pins on the Galton board, some enhancing height and some reducing it compared to the average. Of course another random effect will be added by environment, with impacts from before birth through to adulthood. Added together, it produces something very like a normal distribution: this is the content of the central limit theorem, touched on briefly below. IQ, too, is partly determined by genetic effects, with individual genes making a small contribution, and with environment and experience making another — quite large — contribution. But although environment is collectively important, its effect is the result of many small individual contributions.

For a large number of situations which are the outcome of adding many small random influences together to make the final result, the normal distribution is the inevitable outcome. A full understanding of this would require a proof of the Central Limit Theorem, but essentially it is true because the normal distribution is the "simplest" distribution with a given mean and variance.[6]

---

[6] Technically, every cumulant beyond the second is zero. The first and second cumulants are the mean, and variance respectively. The third and fourth cumulants in a general distribution are related to skewness and kurtosis, which

If you add together a whole lot of complicated distributions which are individually small, the complicated parts of the distribution (higher order cumulants: see footnote) do not increase at the same rate as the simple ones (mean and variance), which therefore end up dominating the result and yielding normality.

Non-normal distributions: their prevention and cure

This section will cover four ideas: how the distribution of a variable in a population may depart from normality, why this is a problem for statistical analysis, how non-normality might be detected from a sample of data taken from that population, and (very briefly) what can be done about it if the distribution does turn out to be non-normal.

(1) Having made a strong case for claiming that most distributions are normal, one must admit that this is not always the case. It may usually be true for naturally occurring variables such as height, IQ and so on, but something as basic as income per head may be highly non-normal, as was pointed out in Chapter 4. As a reminder, Fig. 7.12 shows this.

This graph is clearly not an actual histogram, but it is equivalent to one: the brown graph line basically just follows the tops of the columns of a histogram.

With a normal distribution, the mean, median and mode are at the same point, which is clearly not the case here. Moreover, the distribution clearly comes to an abrupt halt at the left (there is nobody with a negative income), but trails off rather gradually to the right. This reflects the fact that there are a few people with very high incomes. An unsymmetrical distribution of this kind which has the shape of a half arrow, with the arrow pointing to the right, is called **positively skewed**. If the half arrow points to the left, it is **negatively skewed**.

Positive and negative skewness represent the most important type of departure from normality, and the main one to be

---

we touch on briefly below. Skewness and kurtosis (and all higher cumulants) are zero with a normal distribution.

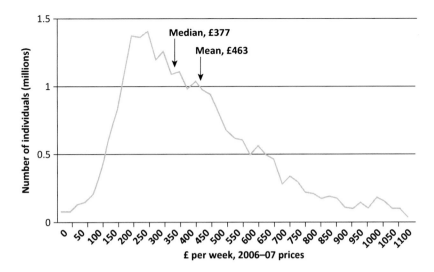

Fig. 7.12.   Graph of household incomes.

Source: M. Brewer *et al.*, *Poverty and Inequality in the UK*: 2008, IFS, 2008, p. 6.
Note: Income is household income, net of tax, benefits and tax credit and before housing costs are deducted.

safeguarded against. It is important not only because it is quite frequent, but also because it can cause the most damage to the reliability of common methods such as ANOVA. Positive skewness is quite common with variables measured in a laboratory setting such as reaction times in a test, and for a similar reason to the skewness with incomes: RTs cannot be negative, but a small number of people make take unduly long to respond so there may be some rather high values.

A less important respect in which a distribution may depart from normality, is through something called **kurtosis**. This is not so easy to describe in terms of the graph of the distribution, but it refers to the fact that the tails of the distribution may diminish either more slowly than with a normal distribution, giving "broad" tails (this is called a "platykurtic" distribution) or more quickly, leading to thin tails (giving a "leptokurtic" appearance). For most purposes, this is not worth worrying about. ANOVA tends to be more robust to the presence of kurtosis than to substantial skewness.

With a purely normal distribution, skewness and kurtosis are both zero. Both measures can be given a number, but there is no need to understand what it means, other than the fact that positive and negative values of skewness correspond to positive and negative skewness as defined above.

(2) To take a standard example, ANOVA, which analyses the conclusions to be drawn from measurements of a dependent variable across different groups of participants, makes the assumption that the DV is normally distributed within the populations corresponding to each of those groups. So a comparison of musicality between 10 and 12 year old children with Down syndrome, autism and a control group assumes that the musicality measure in use is normally distributed within the Down group, the autism group and the typically developing population. If this assumption is seriously violated for just one of the groups, the use of standard ANOVA may be unreliable.

(3) There are some standard methods of determining whether non-normality exists in this situation, and whether it is serious enough to cause trouble (ANOVA is still reliable to some departure from normality: it is "robust" in this sense). We will cover the methods in detail later, but suffice it to say here that they are attempting to derive information from each population from the samples taken from the populations: in other words, they are **inferential tests**: they attempt to infer from a sample whether the distribution of the DV in the underlying population departs from normality.

As inferential tests, they use significance testing as a key step in the process, just like other hypothesis tests. The null hypothesis here is that there is **no** departure from normality, the alternative hypothesis is that the distribution **does** depart from normality. You will notice that this is one instance where ideally **we do not want our test to be significant**: a non-significant result means that we can happily go ahead with our ANOVA or whatever other parametric test we are using, because the distributions can be assumed normal.

I should mention in fairness that this approach to testing for normality has been criticised in the literature for a number of reasons. I will not engage in the controversy here. I merely point out that testing for normality is a standard procedure at present. In practice, samples which show large departures from normality, in particular where there is substantial skewness, may be a cause for concern.

(4) If you find that the sample data within one or more of your experimental groups departs from normality, you will need to consider between a number of options. This will be covered more fully in the online material on data cleaning, but to summarise, you will need to check whether the data contains outliers and if so what to do about them (options include e.g., deleting the outliers); whether the underlying distribution is skewed and if so what to do about it (transformation of the variable is a common option); and in the last resort, whether to turn to a non-parametric method of analysis, which does not make the assumption of normality, and which can therefore be used reliably even if that assumption is wrong.

The main message to take home at this stage is that all parametric tests make certain assumptions. A good statistical analysis should include a test of these assumptions. Such tests are, in my experience, often not taught, or even mentioned, in courses on research methods, but they are important. The whole business of testing assumptions can unfortunately seem tedious and unrewarding, like health and safety at work. But like health and safety, if ignored, these beasties can come back and bite you, painfully. Be aware of them.

The Gaussian formula, for the mathematically minded

For those who feel at home with mathematics, this is the standard form of the frequency curve for a Gaussian distribution with mean μ and standard distribution σ:

$$\text{Frequency} = 1/\sqrt{(2\pi\sigma^2)} \cdot \exp\{-(x-\mu)^2/2\sigma^2\},$$

where exp stands for taking the exponent using the base of natural logarithms, *e*.

The curve depends on two quantities, μ and σ. These are fixed for a given population. Once given these two numbers, and the fact that the distribution is Gaussian, you already know everything about the distribution within the specified population.

In theory, a population can exist with any finite real number values of these two quantities.

The total set of possible Gaussian distributions corresponding to variables measured in possible populations, can therefore be seen as a doubly infinite family of distributions. Looking at a specific one from this family, with specific mean and s.d., with the horizontal axis giving the value of the variable and the vertical axis giving the frequency, then one of the numbers — the mean, μ — gives the position on the horizontal axis above which the centre of the curve is situated. The other number — the s.d., σ — gives the position above which the two "shoulders" of the curve lie: to be exact, they lie above the values $\mu + \sigma$ and $\mu - \sigma$, as shown in Fig. 7.13.

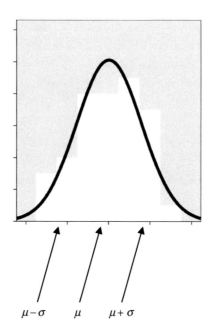

Fig. 7.13. Gaussian curve illustrating the mean, and points one standard deviation above and below it.

Recall that the shoulders are the points at which the curve changes from convex to concave. For those with knowledge of calculus, it is the point at which the second derivative of the frequency curve is zero.

The Central Limit Theorem

In a sense, the Gaussian curve is the simplest possible distribution that has the given values of mean and s.d. That is one reason why it is so common in nature. The following sketch of an explanation is impressionistic, but it might help to give a rough idea of why the central limit theorem is true, and hence, why Gaussian distributions are so basic to statistics. If the terms or reasoning do not make sense, you can skip this section without losing anything essential.

We have already met the mean and variance (or its square root, the s.d.) as important numbers which give vital information about how a scale variable is distributed over a population. But though necessary, they are not in themselves sufficient to tell us everything about the distribution. A distribution might be skewed, for example, and this fact would not be evident from inspection of its mean and s.d. alone. Which suggests the question: is there a series of numbers which is sufficient?

For almost all distributions[7] it is possible to describe them *fully* in terms of a series of numbers, starting with the mean and variance, and going on to infinity, known as the cumulants of the distribution. The useful thing about cumulants is that if you take two independent scale variables and add their values, giving a new scale variable, the cumulants of the new variable are just the sum of the cumulants of the two original variables. The mean is the sum of the original means, the variance is the sum of the variances, and so on for higher order cumulants: it couldn't get any easier than that.

---

[7]The curious may wish to look up the properties of the **Cauchy distribution** in this regard. The Cauchy distribution is sometimes described as "pathological", mainly because it is not susceptible to the methods of orthodox statistics. The Bayesian approach, however, takes it in its stride.

It turns out that if you add a series of identically distributed, independent random variables, the sum of the cumulants that is produced is dominated by the first two terms: the sum of the means and variances. The remaining sums of cumulants grow more slowly than these, and after a certain number of terms they can be ignored.[8] In other words, the distribution comes to resemble one whose third and higher order cumulants are zero: and this, a further theorem assures us, means it is just a Gaussian distribution.

To put it more loosely, though perhaps more vividly: the Gaussian distribution is the simplest kind there is, since all the cumulants after the first two are zero; and adding (or averaging) a lot of non-Gaussian variables tends in the limit to "smear out" the third and following cumulants so that they too tend to zero, at least relative to the first two, giving eventually something indistinguishable from a Gaussian distribution.

It is sometimes claimed that if 30 or more random variables are added, their sum will have a distribution that is very close to being Gaussian. This guarantees, for example, that for tests which involve 30 or more questions with a "yes" or "no" answer — each of which is clearly not continuous — the sum or total score can usually be treated as though it were continuous and Gaussian.

In practice psychologists tend to accept fewer than 30. In fact they tend to treat a variable as being Gaussian provided it is close enough. I have not defined what "close enough" means here. This will follow in the chapter data cleaning and the testing of assumptions. The important thing is not *how* the Gaussian distribution came about — whether through adding a large number of variables and being Gaussian by virtue of the central limit theorem — but simply whether it is *near enough* to being Gaussian. But the central limit theorem does provide some assurance, in advance, that most variables we encounter in practice are likely to have a Gaussian distribution.

---

[8] For those who want a full explanation of what is going on here, I recommend the proofs at: http://www.cs.toronto.edu/~yuvalf/CLT.pdf.

More on histograms and probability distribution functions (pdfs)

For anyone who has survived the excursion into the central limit theorem, this section attempts to make the connection between histograms and pdfs. It really is only for those who are keen to know more of the gruesome details.

The mathematical theory of probability on which statistics is based, generally treats variables as being continuous ones which can take any numerical values, and takes populations as being infinite. This may appear to make the problem much harder — it is hard even to imagine infinity. But paradoxically, it is often simpler mathematically to analyse situations such as this, than more realistic conditions where there is a finite population and a variable that can only take a finite number of values. The equation for the Gaussian distribution given earlier only applies, strictly, to such a case as this. The famous bell curve represents a **probability distribution function**. This is the limit to which a histogram would tend, if the population was infinite and the variable was mathematically continuous.

For most purposes, populations are large enough, and variables have sufficiently many values, that the approximation between a histogram and a continuous pdf is quite close, in the sense that the shape of a histogram is close to the shape of a pdf: and usually, they are both close to a Gaussian bell curve. However, a histogram plots frequencies on the vertical axis, that is, the number of units in the population that fall into the appropriate "bin" of the histogram at that point. Whereas a pdf is defined mathematically to relate not to frequencies but to *probabilities*.

In fact, a pdf is defined so that **the total area under the curve is exactly one**: this represents the fact that if an item from the population is selected at random, the scale variable will have *some* value. Anything that is bound to happen has probability one, and the variable is bound to have a value.

The pdf curve is very useful: it enables you to find the probability that if a random selection of a single item is made from the population, then the value of the variable for that item will be within certain limits. For example, the probability that a person selected at random will have an IQ between 105 and 106 is just the area under the pdf curve that lies *between* the vertical lines through the IQ points for 105 and 106. In practice of course this would be found not from the curve, but from tables of z-scores and p-values. This and similar examples are given in the online material to illustrate the principles involved.

The mathematical definition of the height of the pdf curve at any point involves the use of the concept of a limit, and is not easily accessible to someone who has not encountered calculus. However, it can perhaps be roughly indicated by proceeding via the notion of a histogram, which is simple enough.

Recall that when plotting a histogram, the size of the bins needs to be carefully chosen, so as to find the sweet spot between the extremes of too many and too few bins. The ideal is a histogram that approaches as nearly as possible to a continuous curve, with enough cases in each bin so that this number can be treated as a continuous variable, but with bins closely enough spaced along the horizontal axis that this too can be treated varying continuously.

With too many bins, the vertical axis which records the frequency — the number of cases in each bin — becomes too small; many bins may be empty; at any rate, the frequency will tend to vary between 0 and 1 or 2, and this is certainly not a continuous variable. With too few bins, the horizontal axis, representing the values of the scale variable, will likewise vary in a far from continuous way as the value "jumps" from one bin to another. SPSS has an algorithm which finds a reasonable compromise automatically.

In very large populations, with say one million items, one can imagine taking the values of some variable for every individual and recording it in a histogram. In any real case of course the variable will vary only between certain finite limits.[9] Suppose the

---

[9] Though mathematically the Gaussian distribution has positive values for all values of the variable. This is another instance where mathematical and physical reality part company, though for most practical purposes the difference can be ignored.

distance between these limits on the horizontal axis is divided into 1000 bins, then on average there will be around 1000 items per bin. Varying the precise number of bins will make little difference to the shape of the histogram. If the total area of the bars of the histogram is now taken as a unit of area, the histogram will correspond closely to a continuous curve, and if the underlying distribution is Gaussian, then the histogram will be close to the Gaussian pdf.

Note on the Central Limit Theorem

If you search online, you may encounter a different version of what claims to be the central limit theorem, which is that the mean value of a variable in a random sample of size N from a population tends to the true mean μ as N increases, provided that the variance exists. This is *not* the central limit theorem as properly defined: it is the so-called law of large numbers (actually the *weak* law of large numbers, in its usual formulation), which is a great deal easier to prove rigorously than the central limit theorem.

Chapter 8

Randomised Controlled Trials, the Model T Ford of Experiments

SUMMARY

Randomised controlled trials defined. Sampling and population validity. Randomised allocation as a remedy for confounding. Single blind, double blind and pretest–posttest control group variants of the RCT. Construct validity and internal validity.

NEED TO KNOW

Recall that in an earlier chapter I wrote, concerning the problems in proving a causal link between alcohol and reaction times: "One of the great achievements of the people who developed modern scientific thinking was to discover a way of getting round both of these difficulties at one and the same time. There is a method of ensuring that we can vary one variable of interest — one single IV — and keep the other IVs constant *even if we have no idea what they are*. This is such a remarkable invention, or discovery, that it deserves a chapter all to itself."

Introducing the RCT

The discovery in question is the randomised controlled trial, abbreviated from now on as RCT. This really does what it says on the tin, the two key elements being clearly stated in the name: **randomisation**, and **control**. The "control" part is easier to explain.

The logic is as follows. As before, we are looking for a causal link between two variables, an IV and a DV. The RCT is appropriate when we have the simplest possible case where this could happen: this is when the IV is a nominal variable with the minimum number of possible values, and clearly this minimum number must be two.[1] As before, and nearly always in this book, the DV is a scale variable, so there is nothing much more to be said about it.

As we are dealing with causal hypotheses, the IV should be something which can be varied by the researcher; something that can be switched on and off at will, as it were. In other words it is a variable that can be **manipulated** by the researcher.[2] Giving a dose of some medicine, or getting the participant to listen to music (or not) or to perform some task (or not) would be examples of manipulated IVs; gender or genetic profile would be IVs which could not be manipulated, and which would not be appropriate for an RCT.

The two-level IV could in theory be any manipulation, but the classic examples involve some kind of treatment or intervention. The DV might then be some measure of a health outcome, or perhaps some measure of ability. The idea typically is to see whether the treatment can improve the well-being of patients with a certain condition. I stress that the RCT is quite a general method and does not apply only to testing medical treatments, but for purposes of making the ideas more concrete I will assume a medical setting in what follows.

What are the values that the IV can and must have? Evidently one value of the IV must be something like "give the patient the treatment", otherwise the trial cannot test the efficacy of the treatment. Yet the IV must have at least two values to qualify as a variable whose causal effects are testable. If one value of the IV is

---

[1] A variable with only one value cannot change value, and causality as we have defined it involves a *change* in the IV leading to a change in the DV.

[2] And this is a necessary component of tests for causality: in a 1986 paper, Paul Holland coined the phrase "no causation without manipulation" (Holland, 1986).

"treatment is given", and there are just two values, the other value must logically be "no treatment is given".[3]

So we can see that simply proceeding from the basic conditions for the presence of a causal effect, we can see the absolute logical necessity for the existence of what is called a **control condition**: where the treatment being tested is *not* present.

Sampling and population validity

The story that a recipe for cooking hare started with "first catch your hare" is a myth, but it is true that any researcher wishing to test a causal hypothesis of this kind does need to find a suitable sample of participants before they can proceed further.

The research hypothesis which drives an RCT is a statement about a causal link between one variable (in this case treatment, vs. non-treatment) and another variable (the DV: some outcome measure) *in a specific population*. Sometimes this population consists of all patients with a certain condition; sometimes it might consist of all members of the general population over a certain age and having other characteristics (as in testing the value of statins with older people having high cholesterol levels).

The point is that if the results of an RCT are to be of the greatest possible benefit, the results should tell us something about whether the causal link between IV and DV would apply across a whole population, not just to the specific sample of individuals involved in the trial. An experimental design whose results can be generalised from a sample to a population is said to have **population validity**, and this is something we would certainly like an RCT to have. The design of the RCT itself does not guarantee population validity: in order to have this desirable quality, the *sampling process* that precedes the actual RCT should have been random.[4]

---

[3] For the sake of simplicity, I am here glossing over the possibility of giving different levels of treatment, such as different doses for a drug. That option is the topic of later chapters.

[4] Readers with good statistical instincts may at this point be asking "but what if some of the sample refuse to take part in the RCT; won't this prevent the remaining

In theory, and often in practice, it is possible to conduct an RCT with a sample that has not been randomly obtained from a population. In many instances this may be the only option. For example, a clinician who is treating patients for some rare disorder at a particular hospital may have excellent access to those patients, and rather poor, or non-existent access to patients in another hospital on the other side of the world. An RCT might in those circumstances be carried out on a sample taken from patients within that one hospital, which would then be a **convenience sample**.

From now on, I will just assume that a sample has been obtained from the population of interest. If it *has* been randomly sampled, well and good, the results will generalise. But if it has not, that does not make the RCT worthless. The word "randomised" in the description RCT does not, by the way, refer to a sample randomly selected from the population. It has a different meaning, of random allocation, to be explained below.

How the RCT concept is applied to a given sample of participants

Now, the only remaining task is to decide how to administer the two levels of the IV, treatment present and treatment absent. For short, I will call these two levels, from now on, the treatment and control levels. Logically, there are only two possibilities: administer both the treatment and control levels to the same patient successively, or give them separately to different patients. Both options are possible in experimental design terms, though they may not both be practicable in any particular case, but for present purposes I will consider only the option that *different* patients experience the treatment and control conditions, no one patient receiving both.

This decision brings with it another question: which patient, or patients, should experience the treatment condition, and which the control condition?

---

participants from being a random sample of the population?" I have an answer to this question, but it is too long for this footnote....

In practice there will always be more than one patient in each condition, so we are talking about groups of patients here. The ones undergoing treatment are said to comprise the **treatment group**, and the others make up the **control group**. So much for the semantics; the practical problem then becomes: given a set of patients, how do you choose which ones to put into the treatment group and which into the control group?

This brings in the remaining element of the RCT: *R* for randomisation: it refers to random *allocation* of participants to treatment and control groups.[5] First, I will try to explain what this achieves, and then to explain how it is done in practice. Recall the problem with which this chapter began. We are looking for the effect of an IV on a DV, and to find this, we wish to vary the IV while keeping other variables, which might affect or confound the result, constant.

The first part of the task, varying the "official" IV, has been dealt with by having a treatment group and a control group. What about ensuring that the other variables, known and unknown, play no part? How can we ensure that varying the IV does not drag some confounding variable along with it, as it were, thus confusing the issue as to which variable is really responsible for any effect that may be found?

This is where the clever bit comes in. The individual participants (I have been calling them patients, but the more general term participants is preferable since the design applies outside the field of medicine) will vary in numerous ways one from another. These represent variables which may influence the result, **confounding** variables as they are known. Some of these ways will be obvious and easily measurable: gender and age, for example. Others may be neither obvious nor easy to gauge: prior training, or genetic predisposition, which would affect their response to some treatment. But suppose for a moment that we were gifted with some

---

[5] Recall that random sampling referred to obtaining just one sample from the defined population; random allocation refers to obtaining two samples, by dividing this one sample into two groups.

kind of super power: in this case, the special knowledge of the precise makeup of each participant. How in that case would we allocate them to groups?

It should be intuitively obvious that we would prefer an allocation that balanced the two groups, treatment and control, exactly equally regarding confounding variables, so that the profiles of each group appeared similar prior to the start of treatment. That would ensure an equal playing field for the treatment which is being compared with the control. We need to compare like with like. As already noted, this is not within our gift. But look again at what we are aiming for here. That is, if we cannot balance the two groups out on confounding variables, it would at least be desirable to avoid any *systematic bias* in the way confounds varied between the treatment and control groups. *Random* differences are inevitable.

This is very similar to the previous idea of validity in measurement, which implies an absence of systematic bias in a measurement process. Here we need validity in the "measurement" — meaning allocation — of the treatment/control variable. How can we ensure that there is nothing systematic about the way the participants are distributed between the groups, in the sense that one group will have systematically older participants than the other, for example? We need a method of allocation to groups which has nothing whatever to do with any personal qualities of the participants — a method which as it were is insulated, or isolated, from any possible "contamination" by such qualities.

It is somewhat like the method of marking exam scripts in which the marker knows only candidate numbers: he or she, being ignorant of the students' identities, can only award marks on the basis of the quality of the work, not on the basis of personal likes or dislikes that are unrelated to ability. In this case we need a method of allocation to groups that has no connection with the personal identities of the participants: it doesn't "know anything" about the participants. In that case, it cannot systematically bias the allocation of participants to groups in any way at all, based on individual differences. Not only the confounds we may have thought of will be looked after, *but any confounds whatsoever*, even if we have not thought of them, and never would have considered looking for them.

So the question is, how to find a method of allocation of participants to groups which is completely independent of the identities of the participants? Suppose we start by lining up the participants in any order we please: in alphabetical order of names will do as well as any. A random number generator is a computer program which will yield a number between 0 and 1 each time it is called. Excel has such a program, for example. If this is activated a number of times, there will be no perceptible order or system to the sequence of numbers so obtained. In particular, if we allocate a random number to each participant, there will be no possible link between these numbers and the participants: and in particular, no link between these numbers and any variables that may be associated with them. *The random number assigned to each participant is in effect "blind" to any individual differences between participants.*

Take the median of the random numbers allocated to the participants. Half of the participants will score above this number, and half below it.[6] If the upper half of the participants is allocated to the treatment group and the lower 50% to the control group, then it should be evident that *there can be no systematic bias for any variable whatever*, in the allocation of participants to groups. In other words, the threat of confounding variables, due to individual differences between participants, has been eliminated.

Note that this process gives treatment and control groups that are equal in size, or differ at most by one in size. It can be shown that this arrangement is the most efficient one in terms of maximising the chances of finding an effect if one exists; to anticipate a concept from later on, it is the most **powerful** arrangement that can be found.

---

[6] I am assuming here that the sample number is even. With an odd number of participants it will obviously not be possible to have treatment and control groups of equal sizes but they can clearly be made to differ in size by only one.

To summarise what has been done so far: A research hypothesis has been proposed within a specified population, relating a two-level IV, which can be manipulated to either of the two levels, and a scale DV. A sample of participants has been selected, ideally in a random manner but possibly as a convenience sample, from that population.

The sample has been randomly allocated into two groups, equal in numbers or as nearly equal as possible: the treatment and control groups.

The next step is clearly to run the experiment. That means that the participants in the treatment group should be given the treatment, and the value of the DV for those individuals should then be measured. Those in the control group should be treated exactly the same, except that the treatment should be withheld from them, and the value of the DV should then measured also for them.

Incidentally, to avoid any misconception, the use of the word "group" for these two subdivisions of the sample does not mean that the participants are treated all together as a group. A treatment involving group therapy would not be suitable for this kind of trial.[7] It is important for the validity of the results that the outcome for one participant should not be directly affected by what happens to other participants, as might happen if they receive the treatment together and mingle socially afterwards. This might induce a group effect which would interfere with the simple IV–DV causal link that is being tested, in effect it would be a confound that would not be eliminated by random allocation.

Note that it is vital that the only variable that differs systematically between the two groups should be the treatment/control variable itself. The arrangements for the measurement of the DV should not differ systematically between the groups. In practice there are bound to be differences in the times and possibly places where the measurement of the DV for different participants occurs,

---

[7] Unless the groups themselves, rather than the participants, were treated as the experimental units. This would make for a rather complicated design but it would be possible.

if only because participants must not be allowed to influence one another. But if you have absorbed the ideas behind random allocation to groups, you will realise that this potential problem can be neutralised by using the randomisation trick yet again: all that is needed to remove any systematic influence of place and time is to randomly allocate participants to the slots available for DV measurement.

In its simplest outline, the concept of the RCT is now complete. The analysis of the results requires a further chapter, but the execution of the basic design has been described. Leaving for a moment the question of analysis, let us assume that it has been done correctly and it has been found that the treatment and control groups do indeed differ. Then an RCT will have **internal validity**: that is, we can correctly conclude that the difference is indeed due to a causal influence of the treatment IV on the DV, and not to a confound.

However, internal validity, though necessary to a good experiment, may not be sufficient. In some cases there is, for example, the possibility of a **placebo effect**. This can happen if the participant knows which group they are in. Typically, it occurs if a participant is receiving the treatment condition, and expects to experience an improvement. This produces a psychological change which may lead to physical changes. At the very least, it may lead to an improvement in mood or attitude which brings other benefits with it.[8]

In that case, there may be a genuine treatment/control group difference, caused by the treatment, but it would not be scientifically interesting, since it would have been mediated by a mechanism that is already well known. Attributing the improvement to the treatment, and not to the placebo effect, would be misleading. Such a statement would not have **construct validity**. Construct validity is quite a subtle concept which will be explored in a more

---

[8] There is, incidentally, nothing "unscientific" in claiming that changes in mental states can have effects on the body which manifest themselves physically. Medawar gives the example of blushing.

general context in the online material, but the placebo effect is a good example of something that might threaten construct validity.[9]

However, there are steps that can be taken to neutralise this threat. One is to modify the way that the control group is treated: to turn it, in fact, into a **placebo group**. This means that the participants are led to believe that they are receiving a treatment, when they are not. For example, if patients in the treatment group are receiving drugs in tablet form, those in the placebo group will also receive tablets, but which contain no active ingredients. Any placebo effect should now apply to *both* the groups equally. When the DVs are *compared* between the groups, the placebo effect will therefore not appear.

In the case of a psychological experiment, a variant of this is sometimes used. If it is claimed for example that listening to classical music can improve subsequent performance on an IQ test — the so-called Mozart effect — a control group might be exposed to listening to pop music rather have no activity before their IQ is measured. Otherwise, it might be that a difference between the group scores was due not to listening to classical music, but to listening to any music whatever. If the classical group performed better than the pop music group, then it would be reasonable to claim that it was indeed the genre of the music that was important.

The use of a placebo group is really one example of a more general principle: that participants should in general be unaware of which group they belong to, as in that case their beliefs or expectations cannot influence the result. Giving them a placebo in a medical procedure, or an apparently significant activity or stimulus in a psychological experiment, is one way of ensuring

---

[9] The experimental design literature is not totally consistent in deciding what qualifies as a threat to internal vs. construct validity. Some accounts classify the placebo effect as a confound which jeopardizes internal validity. The precise labels one uses to name these threats are not vital; the important thing is to know how to recognize them and what to do about them.

this. An experiment where participants are indeed blind to their group is known as a **single blind** trial.

It is important that participants in the two groups receive the same treatment, apart from the actual treatment IV. In particular, the person taking the DV measurements, which of course are made on all participants, should not behave differently towards those in the two groups. If the DV is taken in a standardised way this should not happen, but even a conscientious researcher can sometimes give subtle cues to an alert participant. Also a person administering a placebo pill, or a control activity, may appear less engaged than if they know that it is the genuine medication, or the real treatment activity. One way to prevent any of this from happening is to ensure that the person conducting the experiment is also blind to whether any participant is in the treatment or the control group, as well as the participant: this is known as a **double blind** design. It is sometimes said that a double blind RCT is the "gold standard" for a valid experimental design, as it is free from all of the main threats to internal validity. If it includes a properly conducted placebo group or a control activity, it is generally strong on construct validity also.

One further option should be mentioned briefly. In the case of a trial of a new drug designed to treat a serious disease, there may be ethical objections to having a placebo group which is receiving no active medication. In this case it may be more ethical, and indeed it may make more sense, to compare the new drug not with no treatment, but with the best existing treatment. After all, the key research question is not whether the new drug *works*, but whether it *works better* than any established treatment. This is still basically an RCT design, though the nature of the control group is different.

The RCT design described above is sometimes known as the **posttest-only control group design**. It is sometimes possible to have a more elaborate version of what is essentially the same concept, called the **pretest–posttest control group design**, also known as the **before–after two group design**. In this case the DV is measured twice for each participant: once before and once after treatment. It is also taken twice for the control group participants, for reasons explained below.

The advantages of this design lie in its greater power, that is, its sensitivity to detect an effect. It might seem desirable to apply this design to all RCTs, but this is not always possible, depending on the nature of the experimental situation. For example, with an RCT conducted on animals in which the DV is measured by the condition of the animal post-mortem, the DV obviously cannot be taken before as well as after treatment. But this might also be the case if the trial consisted of a comparison between a new and an existing method of teaching a new language, in which an intensive 48 hour training session was followed by a test in that language. In a pretest, all participants would score at floor and such a test would be valueless.

Such a design would however be appropriate if the measurement of the DV was of some characteristic of the individual, such that the measurement process itself did not notably affect that characteristic: such as an IQ test, or a test of reaction time responses to a computer task.

The reason for the greater power of such a design, at least in the appropriate circumstances, cannot be described in detail until I have explained the statistical ideas in a subsequent chapter, but briefly, it works because it reduces the noise component of the data, while leaving the signal component unaltered.

GOING DEEPER

The origin of the RCT

The RCT is often credited to the naval surgeon James Lind,[10] who was another of that remarkable group of intellectuals known as the Scottish Enlightenment, who contributed so much to scientific thought. Lind was working at a time when scurvy was causing more deaths in the Royal Navy than enemy action, and finding a

---

[10] The idea of a *controlled* trial had already been independently discovered by Redi as described in the online material.

cure was of the highest priority. By the eighteenth century it had been known for some time that citrus fruit could combat the disease, but this fact was not widely appreciated. Lind was the first to test the idea in a systematic way.

While not exactly an RCT, Lind's experiment did possess some of its key features. The trial was conducted in 1747 in a ship at sea, after some of the sailors had begun to show symptoms of scurvy. The choice of treatments was governed by Lind's previous reading of what had been attempted, or recommended, by previous writers on the subject. He had done in other words what we would now describe as a "literature review", which is even today one of the first essential steps in any serious scientific enterprise.

The twelve sailors selected for the trial were divided into six groups of two each. All of the men were given the same basic diet but in addition, the first pair was given a daily supplement of two pints of cider, the second pair received a measured (very small) amount of sulphuric acid, the third pair had a small allowance of vinegar, the fourth pair drank half a pint of seawater, the fifth pair each had two oranges and a lemon a day, and the sixth drank barley water. The results were clear. After just six days, one of the pair given citrus fruits had fully, and the other had almost, recovered. Of the other groups, the cider drinkers showed a lesser improvement and the other groups none at all.

Lind himself had no idea of why the citrus cure worked: or rather, he had a theory, but an incorrect one — that it countered some kind of intestinal putridity — and he himself appears to have gradually lost confidence in it (we now know that the effects were caused by the vitamin C content of the fruit, and to a much lesser extent, of the cider). However, he recognised that the validity of his underlying theory did not matter. The important thing was that the cure was effective; how it worked was not as important as the fact that it did work.

In addition to this, there were two important features of his experiment. One was that the various potential cures were tested together so that their effects could be compared with one another.

The second was that the treatments were the only thing that varied: the sailors otherwise had identical diets, and were exposed to the same environmental conditions on the same ship; moreover, the sailors were supervised to ensure that they kept to the treatments, and only the treatments, prescribed for them. Of course the sailors themselves will have differed from one another in various ways: weight, medical history and so on. However, men of similar age and occupation will tend to be similar physically, and Lind safeguarded to some extent against chance variations by treating two men per treatment. The fact that both of those in the citrus group did so much better than the others must have appeared good enough evidence for Lind, though it took the Royal Navy another forty years to accept the evidence and act on it.

The RCT today

The modern equivalent of Lind's basic experimental design will usually look somewhat different from his. The variant we are considering in this chapter has not six but just two groups, the treatment group and the control group. There will almost certainly be more than two in each group: with psychology studies a typical number is thirty per group (clinical trials may contain many more than this). The outcome will be measured in an objective way, and the measurement variable will usually be numerical. A description which Lind used such as "fully recovered" or "showed some improvement" would not be acceptable. However, the main objective, to show that a treatment does or does not have some effect, remains essentially the same.

Let us step back and ask how the need for an RCT arises. Suppose you knew nothing about vitamin C but had heard that fresh fruit could cure scurvy (through your literature review). You wish to test the experimental hypothesis that

- **there is a causal connection between administering fresh fruit, and improving or curing the symptoms of that disease.**

The corresponding null hypothesis is that

- **there is no causal connection between administering fresh fruit, and improving or curing the symptoms of that disease.**

By logic alone, one and only one of these hypotheses must be true, and our task is to discover which one that is.

These formulations of the two hypotheses make an implicit assumption: that a population exists to which they refer; in this case the population of people with scurvy. You might wish to narrow down that population to make it smaller and more specific (and if you are the British Admiralty, more useful) and call it the population of British sailors currently suffering from scurvy. Defining the population of interest is a key step in the process.

Now, you need somehow to obtain a set of experimental participants. These have to be selected from the population of interest. To be truly representative of the population they should be selected randomly from it: this involves two conditions. Firstly, prior to the actual selection every member of the population should have an equal chance of being in your sample; secondly, the selections of the different individuals in the sample should be independent of one another.[11]

The "*R*" in "RCT" does not come from the randomness in the selection process. It comes from the next step, which involves dividing our single sample into two groups, a process known as "random allocation" (vs. random sampling). *This step cannot be omitted*: it is vital. A simple method for doing this was outlined above.

Now you have the *R* of RCT, and you have arbitrarily identified two groups of individuals. One of the groups is designated as the "treatment" group, and the other as the "control" group (the *C* in

---

[11] The need for the second condition can be seen as follows. If I am investigating the population of all British adults and select my whole group from men or from women depending on the outcome of an initial coin toss, the first condition will be satisfied but the sample will all be of one gender and therefore not representative of the population as a whole.

RCT). The procedure is simply to apply the treatment to the "treatment" group, and a control condition, often simply consisting of an absence of treatment, to the control group. The final step in the process is to take a measurement of the outcome in which you are interested, which in the case of illness, is usually some measure related to its severity. In the case of scurvy, Lind recorded the change in severity in qualitative terms, but it is usually better done numerically, in some way that is objective (in the sense that the result cannot be influenced by the conscious or unconscious desire of the experimenter to make sure that the treatment "works"). The two groups now give rise to two sets of data, the outcome variable measurements for each group.

Population validity and internal validity

All we now have to do is to analyse these, but first I need to add a gloss on what has been done so far, and why. The first step described above was random sampling from the population. If the selection procedure conforms to this criterion, your sample will at least on average represent the population as a whole, and any results based on this sample will have what is referred to as **"population validity"**, meaning that deductions made on the basis of evidence from the sample can reasonably be generalised to the population as a whole. This is often miscalled "external validity", though strictly speaking, external validity is the combination of population validity with another idea, "ecological validity", which is the extent to which results from the sample will generalise to different settings, places or times.

At any event, this is the first point at which many studies, certainly in psychology, depart from this ideal: they will fail to have true population validity. Very often we are obliged to accept what is called a "convenience sample", meaning we take whoever we can get as participants provided they are from the population of interest, and this is usually a sample that is close to hand and willing, or at least able, to participate. In psychology studies, this often consists of first year psychology undergraduates who are obliged to participate in order to obtain a minimum number of course credits.[12]

In practice, this departure from randomness tends to matter less than you might think. The really vital type of validity for most purposes is not population validity but **internal validity**. This refers to the ability to claim that the inferences we can make from the sample are valid for that sample of individuals, that is, that they are not an artifact of the particular allocation into treatment and control groups. In the case of our causal hypotheses, if we claimed that our evidence supported the experimental hypothesis, then the same result would in general have been replicated had we chosen another random allocation of the sample into treatment and control groups. The effect of the treatment does not depend on the arbitrary way we divided the sample into two parts, so the effect generalises across this set of possible divisions of the sample.

The justification of this claim is via an indirect argument. Random allocation means that there cannot have been any systematic bias in how the participants were allocated. Unless we believe that the coin tossing, or selection of random numbers, or however the allocation was done, was influenced in some almost supernatural way, they cannot reasonably have been linked with any preexisting differences in the participants. And the lack of any systematic differences between the groups means that individual differences between participants should not have affected the result. It is not clear how Lind selected the sailors for his six groups, but suppose he had for example asked for volunteers and chosen the first two for the citrus group, and the next two to drink a daily ration of sea water. It is possible that the first two men were less severely ill than the next pair, and that this gave them the enthusiasm to volunteer straight away. Even had the citrus had no effect, they might have had a better outcome than the other pair, but this would have been a spurious result. Variables such as order of recruitment which might generate spurious links between the groupings and the outcomes are called **confounding variables**. Confounding variables

---

[12] A system whose ingenuity is worthy of Catbert himself.

are one of the main threats to internal validity, but the structure of the RCT, and in particular random allocation to groups, effectively insulates the causal variable of treatment from being influenced by confounds and ensures internal validity for the design as a whole.

Blinding

This is the very basic RCT design, the model T Ford version. Some incorporate a feature known as "blinding", usually in either single or double blind trials. Blinding refers to the concealing of details of treatment/control group membership from individuals. Single blind trials involve concealing this from the participants themselves. Double blinding means concealing it from both the participants and the experimenter conducting the trial. There is even triple blinding, in which the person or people analysing and evaluating the data are not told about the allocation to groups: the results may be reported simply for "group A" and "group B", and until the final evaluation and recommendation is made, the identity of the groups as treatment or control groups is not revealed.

Blinding aims to prevent confounds due to human expectations. Single blinding is particularly important in clinical trials to avoid the "placebo effect", in which merely knowing that one has received a medication can lead to beneficial health effects due to positive changes in mood. Often, those in the control group will be given sugar pills to counter this (and this group will be known as the "placebo group"). In psychology experiments, those in the control group will often be given irrelevant "treatment" interventions unrelated to the main effect being investigated, reinforced by a misleading initial briefing with an experimental "cover story" (the participants should be told the truth, however, on final debriefing after their participation is over). The aim is to avoid "hypothesis guessing", which might influence how participants behave. Double blinding helps prevent "experimenter expectation" effects. Without this, experimenters may unconsciously convey subtle cues to participants depending on which group they belong to, being for instance more attentive or positive towards treatment group participants, and perhaps a bit bored or offhand with the control group members (who are just there as a precaution, after all). Many psychology experiments are not strictly speaking double blinded. This may not matter too much if they involve the participants in quite mechanical tasks and minimal interaction with the experimenter, or if any instructions to participants are given by reading out from a script written in advance.

X–O diagram for the RCT

We can summarise all this symbolically in an X–O diagram of the kind pioneered by Campbell and Stanley:

$$R \rightarrow X_t - O_1$$
$$R \rightarrow X_c - O_2$$

Here, R together with the arrows represents the random allocation of the sample to the two groups, X represents the experimental intervention, and O the observation of the dependent variable for all the participants in that group. X is given subscripts t and c to make clear that the intervention is different in the two groups. O, by contrast, must be measured using the same operational definition in both groups. It is given subscripts 1 and 2, simply to indicate that the two sets of group observations are independent of one another.

In this diagram, X represents the independent variable (IV) and O the values found for the dependent variable (DV).[13] X varies between two values: "treatment" for the first group and "control" for the second group. In practice, X and the group variable (treat-

---

[13] X here is "independent" of the nature of the thing we are investigating: there is no systematic link between scurvy (for example) and group membership (as ensured by random allocation!). O is "dependent" on nature: it is given to us by the process we are interested in. This way round of describing things is essentially a convention. It could have been that we called X the dependent variable because it is dependent on our experimental manipulation, and O the independent variable because O is independent of us, and given by nature, but this is not how it is done.

ment group, control group) are essentially the same, and no harm will come if we identify the two concepts in what follows, though at least in a philosophical sense they are different.

Incidentally, as a general rule for understanding any paper you read (or study that you plan to carry out), it is an excellent idea to start by asking yourself these questions: what is the experimental hypothesis? What are the independent variables? What is/are the dependent variable(s)?

The experimental hypothesis in an RCT is that the group IV has a causal connection with the DV. In most cases, and in all cases treated in this book, the DV will be what SPSS calls a "scale" variable, i.e., an interval or ratio variable: in essence, you can think of this as a continuous number running along a scale. For such a variable, we will usually assume (until proven otherwise) that such variables are normally distributed within each population of interest. "Causal connection" here will be causal in Aristotle's sense of a "change or movement" in the DV in response to a change in the IV. With the assumption of normal distributions, the correct way to measure this change between the two groups is to take the means of the DV in the two groups and compare these means with one another. With non-normal distributions, the mean is not always the best measure: taking medians might prove better, for example. But with our "parametric" assumption, this is unnecessary.

Controlled variables

The word "controlled" in the term RCT comes from the presence of a control group. Another sense in which RCTs are often "controlled" is that certain variables may be controlled, that is, held constant, in the experimental environment. For example, participants performing a perception task on a computer screen may have to place their chin on a rest, at a fixed distance from the screen, to ensure that all participants do the test with their eyes at the same distance from the screen. An audio-based experiment may conducted in a sound-proofed room, to prevent interference from external sounds, with stimuli delivered at a precise average decibel level.

In planning an experiment, it is necessary to specify not only the experimental hypothesis and dependent and independent variables, but also the control variables which may affect the result and are to be held constant. Failure to control these variables may result in spurious effects due to variation in control variables across groups of participants, which would be a threat to internal validity; at the very least, uncontrolled variables may add to the variability in the data and hence increase the noise component in the signal-to-noise ratio, making the signal, if any, harder to detect.

On the other hand, one could argue that over-control of extraneous variables may restrict ecological validity. To the extent that the researcher wants to generalise her results across different settings, it might be argued that it is more realistic to allow some variation, provided this is not confounded with the treatment variable. This may require a larger sample to achieve significance, but the benefits in terms of external validity may be worthwhile. I suggest that a strategy of controlling extraneous variables is generally the wise choice, but be aware that in some situations (such as natural experiments) it may not be possible; this does not necessarily render the results invalid.

Chapter 9

The Independent Samples *t*-Test, the Analytical Engine of the RCT

SUMMARY

RCTs can be analysed by two equivalent methods, using the t and F statistics. Raw effect sizes. The t-statistic as a signal-to-noise ratio. Implementation of the t-test in SPSS. Fitting the t-test into the model comparison framework. Why $F = t^2$. Models and hypotheses revisited. More on the justification for Occam's principle.

NEED TO KNOW

The aim of an experiment is to provide an answer to a particular research question. Finding the answer involves two steps, gathering and analysing the data. In the simplest case of the RCT, the gathering part was dealt with in Chapter 8. This chapter deals with the analysis. The standard method of analysing RCT data is the independent samples t-test, which provides a way of deciding whether we are justified in claiming a causal link between the IV and the DV, or whether, alternatively, there is insufficiently strong evidence to do so, in which case the Occam's razor principle tells us to prefer the simpler of the two hypotheses. This is the null hypothesis, which states that there is no causal link.

The t-test works on the basis of comparing the means of the treatment and control groups. If the two means are sufficiently different, the test gives a significant result, and we decide to prefer the causal hypothesis to the null hypothesis. A causal hypothesis is compatible with a multitude of models, and one of these needs to be chosen as the model which best fits the data. This is termed the alternative model, m_1. If the data is insufficiently clear to favour the causal hypothesis, orthodox statistics tells us that we can make no definite claims, though in the Neyman–Pearson variant, we can be more definite and come down in favour of the null hypothesis. In that case, there is a model of best fit to the null hypothesis as well, provided by the overall sample mean, a model we can refer to as m_0.

The process of analysing the data can also be seen as one of comparing the two models m_0 and m_1. m_1 will always fit the data better than m_0, but the Occam's razor principle in effect "handicaps" m_1, so that it has to do not just better, but significantly better than m_0, if we are to prefer the causal hypothesis to the null hypothesis. This comparison process is shown to be equivalent to the usual test of significance provided by the t-test.

At this point, I find myself in a dilemma. The most logical way to proceed would be to apply the model comparison approach outlined in Chapter 2, to the data from an RCT. This would lead, via the F-ratio, to Fisher's great invention: the analysis of variance, or ANOVA, in its simplest form, with one two-valued IV and one DV. However, historically this is not what happened. This simple case was first analysed by someone named William Gosset, who in the early 20th century worked for the Guinness brewing company. He published under the pseudonym "Student", and the method of analysis is now known as "Student's t-test".

The standard explanation of how the t-test works found in most statistics books does not involve model comparison. It appears to work on an entirely different principle: the calculation of a t-statistic, together with a test of significance. This test gives a positive result if the statistic is larger than a certain critical value. In that case, we can reject the null hypothesis, which means that there is indeed a causal link between the IV and the DV.

There is, it turns out, a simple connection between the t-test statistic and the F-ratio for a set of data from a two group design.

The *F*-ratio is just the square of the *t*-value. It is also possible to view the *t*-test as a kind of signal-to-noise ratio in a natural way. This is shown below. And underlying the whole process there is in fact a model comparison going on. Provided the standard *t*-test gives a significant result, the conclusion is generally to assert the validity of a causal model. It is just that most treatments do not make this fact very clear.

There is another idea to be introduced here. I am asking you to imagine that the raw material for the analysis we are going to carry out, has arisen as the result of carrying out an RCT. So there have been two groups, composed of participants randomly allocated to one of two conditions, the groups being of equal sizes. The values of the DV have been measured for each participant, after undergoing the treatment or control condition. To anticipate, if the DV appears to be systematically different between the two groups, we will conclude that the IV has a causal link to the DV. But this apparently simple statement can be further analysed into two claims: the first is that the DV *differs* between the two groups, and the second is that this difference comes about due to a *causal impact* by the IV acting on the DV. The justification for these two claims involves quite different arguments, and I will try to tease these apart.

In the case being considered here, of an RCT, the conclusion as to causality is justified because of the way the experiment has been carried out, namely using random allocation to groups. On the other hand, the conclusion as to a link between IV and DV (not necessarily a causal one) is justified by the way the data is analysed, provided the analysis gives a significant result. So claims about *causality* are based on experimental *design*, and claims about *significance* are based on statistical *analysis*.

To say that these two claims are separate raises the question of whether they are independent: can there be statistical significance without causality? Can there be causality without statistical significance? The answer to the first question is a positive "yes". The answer to the second one is also "yes", though a full understanding of this will require a treatment of the idea of power, in the online material.

Can there be group differences without causality? Yes, at least if the groups are of a certain kind and if "causality" is understood in a certain way. An RCT always involves causality, but two-group designs can also arise where the groups are not randomly allocated, for example if they consist of naturally occurring groups: male and female would be an obvious one. Clearly individuals cannot be randomly allocated to male and female genders, so any group differences may be due to factors which are not directly due to gender.

However, one thing we can still say if the groups differ on some DV: that *information* as to which gender a person is, provides *information* as to their score on the DV. This statement remains true even if the link is not causal. An artificial example might illustrate this better. Suppose we were to investigate the link between two groups of workers in a factory (a nominal variable, the IV) and their monthly pay (the DV). The two groups consist of those who wear suits and ties, and those who don't. It is a fair bet that the suits group would have a higher average salary than the non-suit group. But it would be unsafe to conclude that wearing a suit causes a rise in salary. The most likely explanation would be that managers tend to be more highly paid than non-managerial staff, and that by convention, managers also tend to wear suits.

The IV is a two level variable, and it is linked to the DV, but evidently this link is not causal from IV to DV. But there is still a link, in the following sense. If one observed people at random in the factory and the only information one had was whether or not they were wearing a suit, this information would have value in terms of predicting their monthly salary. Without this information, being told only that the person was an employee of the factory, the best estimate one could make of their income would be to predict it to be the average of all salaries of all the workers. This would amount to using the null model. But if one had the further detail as to what the person was wearing, this information would enable one to use a better model. A suited person could be predicted to have an income which was the average of the suited group, and a non-suited person, the (lower) average income of the non-suited group. This model would be a better fit to the data than the null model.[1]

Therefore, knowledge of the IV would still lead one to make a better prediction of the value of the DV than one would without such knowledge, even though there is no causal link, certainly no direct causal link, between the two. The way the *t*-test works, conclusions are still valid even if the link between IV and DV is not causal, suggesting that analysis involves concepts from information theory. Information theory has intriguing overlaps with statistics, of which this is one example, but taking this idea further would go beyond the scope of this book.[2]

In what follows, you can assume that the data comes from an RCT involving two groups, and that we are testing a causal hypothesis that the IV (treatment vs control) has a causal impact on the DV. But bear in mind that the statistical analysis will still be valid even if we are not dealing with an RCT, but merely with a two valued IV and a DV. A significant result in that case will still tell us something, but the "something" is different from, and usually more complex than, a simple cause–effect relationship. From here on, the NTK section will tell you how to analyse the data using a *t*-test. The GD section will put this into the context of model comparison.

Analysing the data

Having conducted an RCT, we now have the data from the treatment and control groups, that is, we have taken and recorded the measurements of the DV taken at the end of the period from both groups. But data on its own is mute. The work is not completed until we can use the data to answer the research question with which we began.

---

[1] Since we assumed that we know the income data for the whole factory, Occam's principle does not apply: we are not sampling from a population, but we have all the data. In that case, more complex models are always better.

[2] And beyond the scope of this author.

This question was whether the causal hypothesis was true or not. Put in a way more compatible with the model comparison approach, the question is whether we should prefer to accept the causal hypothesis, or in accordance with Occam's razor, stick with the null hypothesis.

Recall that the causal hypothesis is that a change in IV leads to a change in the DV. That is, the DV should be different, for the two different levels of the IV. In other words, the DV for the treatment group should differ from that for the control group. But what is meant by "the DV for the treatment group" and "the DV for the control group"? The expression "the DV..." implies just a *single* number (otherwise it would have been "the DVs....". But the treatment group may comprise many different values of the DV, as many as there are participants in that group, and likewise for the control group. There seems to be a contradiction.

If there had been just one participant in each group, the contradiction does not appear. If John Smith is in the treatment group and Jack Jones is in the control group, we would simply measure the DV for Smith, and that for Jones, and subtract the one from the other. This difference score is a measure of the *change* in DV corresponding to the *change* in the IV. But of course in any reasonable experiment comparing treatment and control groups, there will be many more than one participant in each. So we are back to the question, how do we calculate "the DV" when we have not a single individual, but a group of people? How to obtain a single number out of a whole set of them?

This is not in fact a new problem. We were earlier faced with the challenge to summarise a complex set of numbers by a single number, and such a number is precisely what was referred to earlier as a *measure of central tendency* of the set of numbers. Other than the mode, which is seldom used, there are just two practical choices of how to calculate such a measure: to adopt the mean, or the median. Both options are widely used. The commonest choice, and certainly the one used by the t-test, is to take the *mean* of a group. This means that "the DV for the treatment group" can be translated into "the mean of the DV for the treatment group", and likewise for the control group.

We now have two single numbers, the means of the DV values for the treatment and control groups, and it is a simple matter to calculate the "change in the DV" corresponding to the "change in the IV": it is the *difference between these two numbers*. This is also known as the **raw effect size**. It is an effect size because it measures the effect of the change of IV on the DV. It is raw, because it is measured in the same units as the DV; later we will encounter the alternative, the standardised effect size, which is often more informative. But for the moment, the raw effect size is all we need.

Sample means are often referred to using the letter M, so with an obvious notation, the raw effect size can be written as:

$$\text{Raw effect size} = M_t - M_c.$$

We can look on the raw effect size as the "signal" being transmitted by nature to us, the researchers, via the experiment. The signal goes in at one end — via the change in IV — and comes out the other — via the change in DV. The question is, does the signal really exist (research hypothesis) or is it just random noise (null hypothesis)? The signal — if it truly is a signal — is measured using the previous definition for a measure of central tendency, namely the mean, and taking the difference in means for the two groups. What about the noise? The second characteristic of a set of numbers was a measure of dispersion for those numbers, and intuitively a measure of dispersion seems to be a good way of determining the amount of noise in the data.

There are several possible choices for a measure of dispersion, but just as the mean is the most popular measure for a measure of central tendency, so the standard deviation is the usual way of measuring the noise component. But there is a subtlety. The noise component refers to the variation in the signal due to random processes. The signal is $M_t - M_c$: how does this vary randomly? The answer is complicated by the fact that we have not one but two elements, M_t and M_c, and the uncertainties in both contribute to the uncertainty in the raw effect size $M_t - M_c$. I will omit the calculation here: more details are given in additional online material.

Even without going into the details of the calculation, however, there is one complication that does need to be faced. It arises from the question, whether the standard deviations in the treatment and control group are the same or different. The noise calculation is slightly different in each case. Again, details are in the online material but you do not need to know these: you just need to know that there is a choice to be made. And the correct choice is indicated by the output in SPSS, in a way to be demonstrated shortly.

I have given the "signal" — the difference $M_t - M_c$: what is the "noise"? I will give the formulae which calculate noise, below. Before doing so, let me say that there is a much easier way of getting to this result, via the model comparison approach, which will derive what turns out to be essentially the same result in the GD section. This is to my mind yet another huge benefit for taking the model comparison approach. Proving the formulae for the t-statistic directly is tedious, though not conceptually that complex. But it is nice to see them fall out of a more general principle.

Anyhow, here they are, for the record. Assuming the simpler case where the variances in the two groups are not significantly different, the first step is to derive an estimate for the common value of this variance, which is found by calculating the so-called "pooled variance" estimate from the data, s_p^2:

$s_p^2 = \{(N_t - 1)s_t^2 + (N_c - 1)s_c^2\}/(N_t + N_c - 2)$, where s_t^2 is the variance as estimated from the treatment group, s_c^2 is the estimate from the control group, and N_t and N_c are the sample sizes for the treatment and control groups respectively.

The noise component is now given as follows:

$$\text{Noise} = s_p\sqrt{(1/N_t + 1/N_c)}.$$

Given that the signal term is $M_t - M_c$, the signal-to-noise ratio, finally, is

$$t = (M_t - M_c)/\{s_p\sqrt{(1/N_t + 1/N_c)}\},$$

that is, the signal-to-noise ratio is equal to Student's t for this case of equal variances.

The next step is to demonstrate how to do the test in SPSS.

Independent samples t-test in SPSS

The scenario is as follows. A researcher came up with the research hypothesis that training students on a visual-spatial memory task would affect their ability to rapidly assimilate and then recall new information. A sample of students were divided randomly into two groups. The treatment group was given three sessions of 60 minutes' consecutive training on a commercially available computer program advertised as boosting memory levels. The control group was given three papers on the mechanism of short and long term memory to study over three sessions of the same length.

One week later, all students were presented with a list of one hundred facts about the economy of Azerbaijan, and after being permitted to study this for 20 minutes, they were given a multiple choice question paper designed to test their recall of these facts.

Just to check that you have assimilated the ideas so far, ask yourself the following: in this design which is the IV, which is the DV? Would it be practical with this design to implement it as a double-blind RCT?

The scores on these papers were as follows:

Treatment group: 27, 24, 25, 26, 23, 29, 28, 22

Control group: 18, 10, 22, 19, 21, 12, 25, 17

You are given the task of determining whether the experimental hypothesis was confirmed by the study.

This was clearly an RCT, where the IV is the treatment/control group variable, and the DV is the score on a test on which the students could be expected to know nothing in advance, so it really is a test of assimilation of new information. Note that the exam scores are in a sense a surrogate measure for the construct of "ability to rapidly assimilate and then recall new information": the design might be challenged by someone who thought this measurement did not represent the construct adequately, i.e., they might criticise the experiment for not having **construct validity**. The fact that the control group is given a task to do, means that it would be practical to conduct this as a double blind RCT: the control group would have no easy way of "hypothesis guessing" and discovering that they were in fact the controls, and the marking of the papers could be done by someone with no knowledge of who was in which group.

In order to test whether the data give support to the hypothesis, we need to enter them into SPSS. Opening a new blank dataset, you need to put in two variables, one representing the IV, and one, the DV. The IV is a nominal variable with two levels. You can code these any way you like, but it seems logical to give control participants the coding zero, and the treatment participants, the coding 1. After naming the variable something appropriate, you need to tell SPSS the names of the groups. Actually this is not essential to get the results, but it helps later on if you publish your results because then SPSS will create nicely labelled tables for you. So go into the "variable view" tab and encode your group variable, using the "values" column.

Now create a new variable, which in this case is a second column in the dataset, by entering a new variable name in the variable view window: I called mine rather unimaginatively "score", and label it as a scale variable. The variable view window now looks as shown in Fig. 9.1, and the data view window looks as shown in Fig. 9.2.

Now you just have to conduct the test. This is found by going to Analyze ≫ Compare means ≫ Independent samples *t*-test (see Fig. 9.3), clicking on the *t*-test command gives you the box as shown in Fig. 9.4.

In SPSS it is a general rule that the IV goes in one of the lower windows and the DV goes in the top window. So here, you need to left click on "score" and use the upper blue arrow to move it into the upper box. This is labelled "test variable(s)", but don't be misled: SPSS uses a completely arbitrary set of names to describe IVs and DVs. In this case "test variable" just means DV.

Then, using the lower arrow, place the IV — here, the group variable — into the lower box. SPSS calls the IV a "grouping variable" here. In other commands it can be called a "fixed factor"; sometimes the IVs box is just labelled "independents". SPSS has this playful way of messing with your brain.

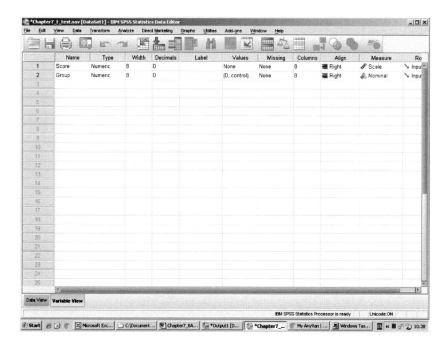

Fig. 9.1.   The variable view window.

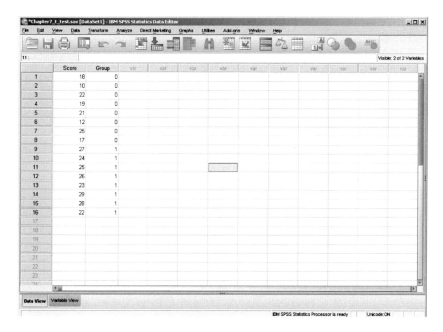

Fig. 9.2.   The data view window.

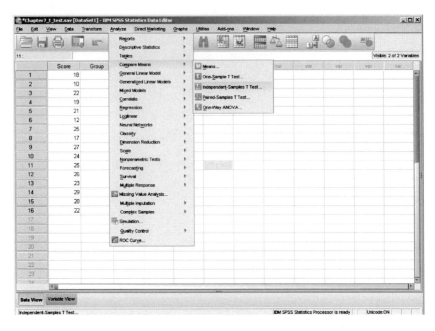

Fig. 9.3. The independent samples *t*-test command.

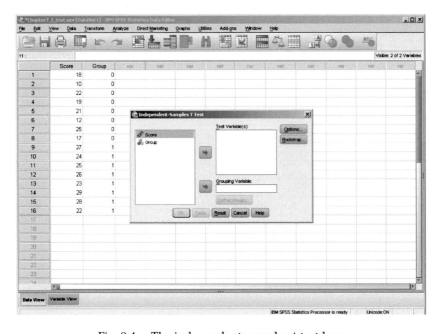

Fig. 9.4. The independent samples *t*-test box.

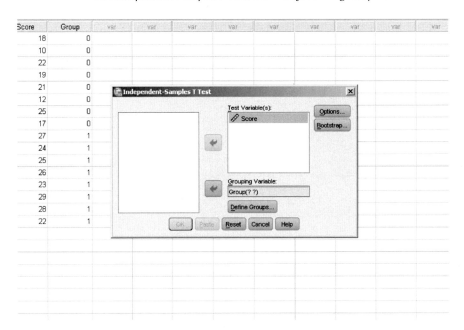

Fig. 9.5. Completing the grouping variable entry.

You are still not quite done, because SPSS has another request for you. At this point the window will look as shown in Fig. 9.5.

The two ?'s in the grouping variable box need to be dealt with. They refer to the coding numbers of the two groups that you want to compare, in this case 0 (for the controls) and 1 (for the treatment group). Just under the grouping variable window is a button marked "define groups".

Make sure the grouping variable window is coloured yellow as above (if it isn't, left click on it) and then left click on the define groups button: yet another box, also called "define groups" will pop out, with little windows in it marked group 1 and group 2.

Put 0 and 1, the values of the groups in these two windows (in either order), by left clicking in each window and typing the number for that group, as shown in Fig. 9.6.

Then press the "continue" button in the define groups box and then the OK button in the independent samples *t*-test box. At last, you will obtain an answer to your question in the output sheet.

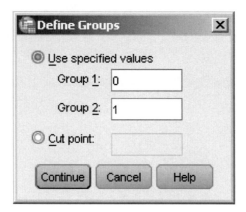

Fig. 9.6.   Specifying the group values.

Table 9.1.   The group statistics output.

	Group	N	Mean	Std. deviation	Std. error mean
				Group Statistics	
Score	Control	8	18.00	5.014	1.773
	Treatment	8	25.50	2.449	0.866

There are two output tables (Tables 9.1 and 9.2), both of which are important.

It gives you the name of the groups (this is because you entered them as group labels in the values column for the group variable; you can now see why that was useful). It also tells you how many cases were present in each group, and the means of the DV for the two groups, and the standard deviations for the groups, calculated separately for each. The standard error of the mean (or SEM) is simply the standard deviation divided by the square root of N, as you can check for yourself.

The SEM tells you basically how close the mean for any particular group is to the true population mean, though you will not normally have cause to use this. You could interpret this as telling you, roughly, that the treatment group mean of 25.50 in our sample is probably within around two SEMs of the actual population mean. Population mean here signifies the mean score we would

Table 9.2. The independent samples *t*-test output (incomplete).

		Levene's test for equality of variances							95% confidence interval of the difference	
									of the difference	
				t-test for equality of means						
		F	Sig.	*t*	df	Sig. (2-tailed)	Mean difference	Std. error difference	Lower	Upper
Score	Equal variances assumed	2.333	0.149	–3.801	14	0.002	–7.500	1.908	–11.717	–3.533
	Equal variances not assumed			–3.801	10.161	0.003	–7.500	1.908	–11.967	–3.283

Independent samples test

find if we had tested all students in the population, instead of just our small sample. Actually things are a bit more subtle than this, and in any case we are not so much interested in finding the population mean, as discovering whether there is an effect of treatment. So, it is the difference between the means that is of interest, not their actual values.

However, there is one absolutely crucial thing which this box tells you: the **direction** of the difference. In this case, the treatment mean is greater than the control mean. As yet, we do not know if this difference is statistically significant, however. It might be due to some random variation in the two sample means. The answer to this is given in Table 9.2.

The column to the right, mean difference, gives the result of subtracting the second from the first of the means in the group statistics box, which is 18.00–25.50. It is negative because the treatment group scored higher than the first group, and because I put the group numbers in the "define groups" box in order 0, 1. If I had put them there in the opposite order, the groups would have been reversed, and the mean difference, positive.

The next step is not straightforward, because we need to know whether the effect is significant (i.e., whether the means really are different) and there are two possible values given in the column recording significance, labelled here "Sig. (2-tailed)". As it happens, both p-values are less than 0.05, so both results are significant at the conventional level of 0.05, but what are the two values doing here?

The key is given in the second column, which contains two row headings: "equal variances assumed" and "equal variances not assumed". There is in fact a subsidiary test of significance going on here. Rather than discuss this right now, I will postpone this for a moment and just give you the rule for deciding which row to read in order to obtain your result.

1. If the number in the column labelled "Sig.", in the window under the heading "Levene's test for equality of variances", is **not significant**, i.e., if it is greater than or equal to 0.05, read

along the **first** row until you get to the "Sig. (2-tailed)" column, and look at the number. **If this is less than 0.05, your result is significant.**

2. If the number in the column labelled "Sig.", in the window under the heading "Levene's test for equality of variances", **is significant,** i.e., if it is less than 0.05, read along the **second** row until you get to the "Sig. (2-tailed)" column, and look at the number. **If this is less than 0.05, your result is significant.**

Applying this rule here, we see that the first significance test gives 0.149, larger than 0.05, so it is not significant, and we can read across to find $p = 0.002$, less than 0.05, so the difference between the group means is significant.

Finally, the result could be written up in a lab report or a paper for publication in some form such as this:

"On average, participants in the experimental treatment group scored higher in the memory test ($M = 25.5$) than the control group ($M = 18.0$), and the difference was significant: $t(14) = 3.801$, $p = 0.002$". (For an explanation of the number 14, see below).

Some unexplained aspects remain to be tidied up.

1. The main assumption of any parametric method in statistics is that relevant sets of numbers are normally distributed. This assumption needs to be checked, and I have not done this here. The method for checking this will be postponed to a later chapter, which deals with this and other problems with data that you may encounter. I thought it better to bring these together in one place. However, I would like to make the point now that checking for normality is best practice, although not many published papers mention it and it remains, I suspect, something neglected by a substantial number of experimental psychologists.

2. The second point is to explain what Levene's test is doing here. SPSS does not prompt you to check for normality but it *does* compel you to check for another assumption of the standard t-test: namely that the variances in the two groups do not differ by too

large an amount. If the two variances are widely discrepant, then the *t*-test may give you a misleading result. As it happens, there is an alternative statistical test which SPSS brings out of the hat to deal with this, sometimes called the Behrens–Fisher *t*-test, which can cope with the situation where the variances differ. In fact, it is more correct to call this the Welch test. Behrens and Fisher examined the problem that arises when the variances in the two groups differ, and Welch found an approximate solution, which is the method that SPSS uses. If the variances do not differ "too much", then the standard method is appropriate, but if they do differ substantially, the Welch approximation should be used. The test for whether the variances differ "too much" is Levene's test. The null hypothesis with this test is that the variances are equal. (That indeed is why it is called "Levene's test for equality of variances".)

If the result in the first "Sig." column is not significant, then the null hypothesis cannot be rejected, and therefore we can assume that the variances are equal. In that case, we can just read off the results in the first row, helpfully signposted "equal variances assumed". If the result in the "Sig." column is significant, this means that the hypothesis of equal variances can be rejected, so the second row, "equal variances not assumed", is the correct one to read. The whole thing is confusing at first meeting but is, in fact, perfectly logical once you know what is going on.

3. The result was reported as "the difference was significant: $t(14) = 3.801, p = 0.002$". This is a standard format, though some people maintain that it is better to just report whether the *p*-value is less than your predetermined cut-off value. If this is 0.05, this school of thought says one should report "the difference was significant: $t(14) = 3.801, p < 0.05$". You can get away with either convention. Giving a *p*-value is more informative, though if you also give a standardised effect size (to be discussed later) that is more informative still. The second point is to indicate where the numbers come from. The number within brackets in $t(14)$ tells your readers the "degrees of freedom" involved in the test. This happens in this case to be the number

of participants minus two. The distribution of the t-function depends on it. Unless you are interested in the details of the statistics, that is all you need to know. You find the value for the degrees of freedom in the "df" column of the output. In this case we are reading the first row, so 14 is the df for this test. The value of t appears in the column to the left of the df column, and that is the value you give for t.

4. In the event that Levene's test had been significant, you would have read the second row. You will notice that it has a different number in the df column. That is because what SPSS is doing here is in fact calculating a Welch's approximation to the Behrens–Fisher t-distribution. The approximation is that the distribution is that of the usual t-distribution *but with a different df*. It turns out that this is an excellent estimate of p-values for most purposes. If you do need to use the second row, you just report the result of the t-test as before, but with the new, fractional df, and you could mention that Levene's test was significant and that therefore Welch's approximation was used. Incidentally, Welch's test still assumes that the distributions are both Gaussian. It copes with non-equal variances, but not with non-Gaussian distributions. That problem has to be resolved differently, with either a transformed DV or a non-parametric approach, both dealt with in the online chapter on data cleaning.

GOING DEEPER

How does the t-test approach fit into the model comparison framework? The signal-to-noise calculation above takes the "signal", which is also the raw effect size, to be the difference in group means. This is an intuitively persuasive choice: the larger the difference, the more insistently the data seems to be telling us that the population means from which the groups are sampled, do indeed have different means. With this definition of the signal, the noise component becomes as stated above:

$$\text{Noise} = s_p \sqrt{(1/N_t + 1/N_c)},$$

where $s_p^2 = \{(N_t - 1)s_t^2 + (N_c - 1)s_c^2\}/(N_t + N_c - 2)$, with s_t^2 the variance as estimated from the treatment group, s_c^2 the estimate from the control group, and N_t and N_c are the sample sizes for the treatment and control groups respectively.

How does this signal-to-noise ratio compare with that calculated from the model comparison viewpoint in Chapter 2?

To find this, we need to find the lofsos of the null model, and of the causal model. The null model is the one which attempts to fit the data by a single value: the overall mean of all the data. The causal model is the one which fits the data by giving a participant the treatment group mean if they are in the treatment group, and the control group mean if they are in the control group. With the previous example, the overall mean is 21.75, and the two group means are 25.5 for the treatment group, and 18 for the control group. The lofsos for the null model turns out to be 443, and for the causal model, it is 218. Note that if you are following this calculation on Excel, there is a function, DEVSQ (sum of squares of deviations from the mean), in Excel which calculates the lofsos of any set of data. For the null model, apply DEVSQ to the whole dataset, and for the causal model, calculate the DEVSQs separately for the treatment and control groups, and add them.

Now all we need to calculate the signal-to-noise ratio, or the *F*-ratio, for the causal model is to find the difference between the parameter numbers for the null and causal models, and the causal and saturated models. The null model has one parameter compared with the causal model's two, so that difference is one. The saturated model has N parameters, where there are a total of N datapoints, so the difference with the causal model is $N - 2$. Here, $N = 16$.

So the slope of the line joining the null and causal models is the vertical drop divided by the horizontal distance, or $(443-218)/1$, i.e., 225. The slope of the line joining the causal and saturated models is $218/14$ or 15.57. The ratio of the two is then

$$F(1, 14) = 14.45.$$

The diagram for this situation is given in Fig. 9.7.

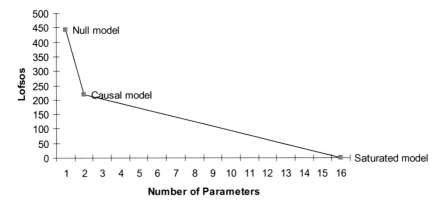

Fig. 9.7. Model comparison chart for the *t*-test example.

The value for the *F*-ratio is the square of 3.801, the value found above for the value of Student's *t*. This coincidence of course proves nothing, but it is at least an indication that we are on the right track. And the fact that it falls straight out of the model comparison approach suggests that a proof of the validity of the formula for Student's *t* should be available via the model comparison approach. So let us try doing that.

The algebra involved is a little involved — full details in the on-line material — but the point is that it is conceptually very simple. It just requires using the ideas we have already found, of model comparison and slope ratios, and doing some tedious manipulation. The only hard bit is calculating the vertical drop when going from the null model to the causal model. This simplifies after some calculation to the following:

Lofsos(null model) − lofsos(causal model) = $(M_t - M_c)^2 \cdot N_t N_c / N$, where *N* is the total number of participants.

Since the difference in parameter numbers is one, and dividing by one leaves the quantity unaltered, the slope of the first line (connecting the null model to the causal model) is also $(M_t - M_c)^2 \cdot N_t N_c / N$.

The slope of the second line (connecting the causal to the saturated model) is the sum of the within-groups squares of the deviations from their respective means. At this point we can use the fact that there is a link between these sums of squares and the formulas for the within-groups variance estimates, s_t^2 and s_c^2. In fact, given Bessel's formula for how these variance estimates are calculated, it is immediate that the total squared within-groups deviations is just

$$\text{Lofsos(causal)} = (N_t - 1)s_t^2 + (N_c - 1)s_c^2.$$

The slope of the second line is equal to lofsos(causal) divided by the horizontal distance between this model and the saturated model, which is the difference in the number of parameters for the two models, $N - 2$, so the slope is $\{(N_t - 1)s_t^2 + (N_c - 1)s_c^2\}/(N - 2)$. Since $N = N_t + N_c$, we can see that the slope of line 2 is simply the pooled estimate of population variance, s_p^2, from the earlier formula.

The previous approach suggested that the thing of interest was estimating the population variance by looking at the sum of squares within the groups. The present approach reverses this: the thing of interest is looking at the sums of squares within the groups, and it happens that this can be found by looking at the estimates of population variance.

The ratio of the two line slopes, or what we know as the *F*-ratio, is now

$$(M_t - M_c)^2 \cdot N_t N_c / N \text{ divided by } s_p^2.$$

A simple manipulation, using the fact that $N = N_t + N_c$ reveals this to equal

$$F = (M_t - M_c)^2 / \{s_p^2(1/N_t + 1/N_c)\}.$$

Compare this with the formula for *t*: you will see that it is the square of this:

$$F = t^2.$$

So why bother with model comparison?

At this point it may not appear that there is much advantage in the model comparison approach, and using the *F*-statistic rather than the *t*-test. If we were only ever interested in the analysis of two group designs this would arguably be the case. But the benefit of model comparison, and the associated F-statistic, is that it can be applied across the board to the analysis of designs with nominal IVs, including when there are multiple IVs.

It also applies when the IVs are repeated measures: for example, when instead of having separate treatment and control groups, the same set of participants is exposed to both conditions and the DV measured on both occasions. The standard analysis in these cases involves what may seem to be a series of *ad hoc* statistical tests, with no underlying rationale. Model comparison, however, provides a leitmotiv which helps in understanding the common processes that are going on.

Models and hypotheses: from hypotheses to models

In the example above, the value of the t-statistic (and F-ratio) was large enough to enable us to reject the null model in favour of the causal model. However, if you are familiar with the way results are actually reported in research papers this is not at all how they appear. Instead, it is stated that the null *hypothesis* can be rejected, and that there is support for the research *hypothesis*. I need to revisit the connection between models and hypotheses at this point, to provide a link between the treatment so far, and the approach in most books which looks at hypotheses, not models. So this section will look at the previous data from the hypothesis viewpoint. Before doing this I have to make clear a new definition.

In the RCT example above, there was an original sample of students, which was then randomly allocated to two groups. The null and causal models each represent an attempt to fit the limited data obtained. But to even state the relevant hypotheses, I need to move outward from the idea of a sample, to that of a population: or rather, two populations. What follows is clearly impossible, but look on it perhaps simply as a thought experiment.

Imagine that we were to perform the treatment condition from the experiment on the whole population from which the sample was drawn: say, the whole population of students. A large set of data would be obtained on the DV measurements, and this data would have a mean: the population mean for the treatment condition. Now imagine that instead, the entire population was to be submitted to the control condition. Another data set would be obtained, and from this, a different population mean could be calculated. Of course this is not practical, both because whole populations are too big to be tested, and because the idea is that the same people cannot be tested twice: on being tested, they should not have been previously exposed to the testing situation. The sole aim of this thought experiment is to introduce the idea that what an RCT is "really" doing is to estimate two numbers — the means of the DV in two populations — and that the underlying question is, are these two numbers the same or different?

Putting this question into the form of two hypotheses, they are:

(1) the null hypothesis: the means of the two populations are identical,
(2) the causal hypothesis: the means of the two populations are different.

Note however that each of these hypotheses is somewhat vague. For the null hypothesis we might ask: yes, but *what is* the common value of the two means? And for the causal hypothesis, if we accept that the population means are different, we might ask — how different? Or more generally, what *are* the two population means?

If the null hypothesis is true, it is consistent with a potentially infinite number of null models, one for each value of the population mean. The causal hypothesis is also consistent with an infinite number of models, which have in common only the fact that the population means differ from one another.

For people who like concrete illustrations of abstract ideas, the following may be helpful. One can view the experimental hypothesis and the null hypothesis as opposing armies, in which the individual soldiers are individual models. They are rather large armies — in fact infinitely large — but don't worry about that. The individual models all provide different ways of matching the data, but all the models in the null army are compatible with the null hypothesis — that is they predict zero difference between the population means. But the different individual models predict *different values* for that common population mean. So two models in the null army may predict a common value of 20 in one case, and 21 in another case, for both treatment and control groups.

The models in the research hypothesis army all predict population means which are different, but the values of those population means will differ from one model to another. So one model may predict a score of 25 for the treatment group and 23 for the control group, whereas the other predicts 21 in the treatment group and 17 in the control group. Not all will predict a result in the same direction: yet another model will predict 15 in the treatment group and 24 in the control group. But in each case, the two means will be different.

The idea will be that when the armies meet, they decide to do something apparently quite common in antiquity: they each nominate a champion, and agree to let the champions fight it out together; whoever wins, this decides the outcome of the battle (as in the famous encounter between David and Goliath). So the causal hypothesis army will nominate the model from its ranks which fits the data best, call it m_1, and the null hypothesis army will also select the model, call it m_0, which best matches the data from among the whole set of null models. The two will then go head to head.

This raises two questions. How does each army select its champion, and how do we decide which of the two champions has won the contest. In effect I have already answered both questions. For the question of choice, the null model that has been chosen from the beginning is the one that takes the *overall* sample mean to be the number that it predicts for the DV means of the two populations, the "treatment" and "control" populations. The causal model takes the means of the two *sample* groups separately to be the means of the corresponding *population* means.

So the answer to the first question is: m_0 is the model we get by taking the grand average of the whole sample. The null hypothesis states that there is only one population mean, and if this is written μ_0, then the model m_0 is just the following:

m_0: take μ_0 equal to the mean of the entire sample, which in this case is 21.75.

It is important to realise what a model is doing in this situation. Each of the null models will have a single number attached to it — the number which it claims to be the common mean of the two (theoretical) populations. So a model is not just an attempt to fit a certain limited set of data, it represents a claim about the wider world.

For the causal model, the means of the control and treatment groups are 18.0 and 25.5. So the champion for the causal hypothesis army is model m_1: take μ_c equal to 18.0, and μ_t equal to 25.5.

It may help to visualise this situation not only in terms of the lofsos/parameter plot, but also directly as a scatterplot. In Fig. 9.8 below I give a picture of the null model. The model is actually the dotted horizontal line, drawn at a score value of 21.75, which is the

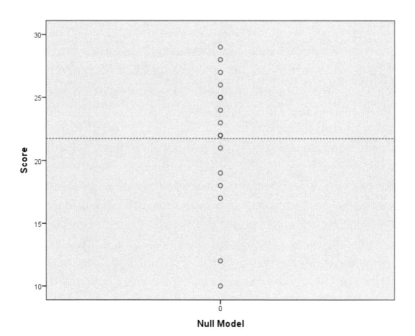

Fig. 9.8.   Illustrating the null model of best fit to the data.

sample mean. The lofsos is a measure of how far in total the individual points are distant from the dotted line.

It may appear from this chart that the dotted line is too high up and a better fit could be found by moving it lower down, but this is an illusion. The mean is the model of best fit using the lofsos measure, a mathematical fact which can be verified in any advanced text on statistics.

Compare this now with the corresponding diagram for the best fitting causal model, in Fig. 9.9 below. This more complex model can be visualised as follows, where the dotted line gives the overall mean and the heavy lines represent the means of the two groups. This time I have separated the data points into the two sets from the treatment and control groups, control group on the left and treatment group on the right (see Fig. 9.9).

The model now matches the data better, because it is allowed the freedom to match the two groups separately. The lofsos with

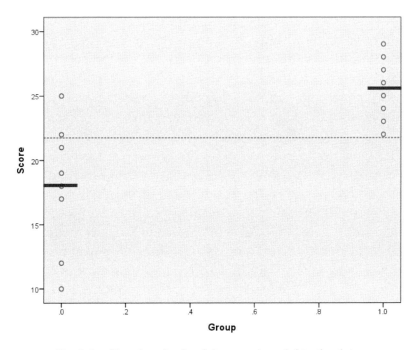

Fig. 9.9. Showing the fit of the causal model to the data.

this model turns out to be lower than with the null model. This is because for each number in the control group, it is being compared not with 21.75 but with 18.0, which is in most cases closer to it. For example, the low score of 10 in row 2 of the dataset is distant only 8 from this mean, compared with 11.75 for the overall mean. That implies that this point adds only 64 to the lofsos for the alternative model, compared with 138 to the lofsos for the null model.

Similarly, every number in the treatment group, e.g., the value of 28 in row 15, is being modelled by 25.5, not by 21.75. The mean of the treatment group is always going to be the best approximation to the data in the treatment group, and likewise with the control group. So if we are allowed to use separate approximations for the two groups, they are always going to be better than any single number applied to both groups.

Models and hypotheses: from models to hypotheses

To sum up what we have achieved so far. We have stated two hypotheses, one and only one of which must be true. Either the population means differ or they do not. To decide between them, we have found two models, each of which provides the best fit to the data consistent with the hypothesis that they represent. We have then found a way of determining which of the models wins in a head-to-head battle over how well they fit the data.

But that is only part of the way to where we would like to be: it is certainly not how analyses are reported in most published papers. There, most results appear in the form of rejecting the null hypothesis and affirming the causal hypothesis. Suppose we have found that the causal model is preferable to the null model: then it is but a short and logical step to affirming the causal hypothesis. However, you may object that to reduce the outcome to merely claiming a causal link between IV and DV amounts to degrading the quality of the result that we actually obtained. The actual result gave a clear description of the causal model, with values for the sample means, which must represent more or less closely the actual values for the population means. And surely it is highly desirable to know these values. At the very least, it is desirable to know the value of $\mu_t - \mu_c$, the raw effect size of the treatment (versus control condition) in the whole population.

In the present case this might not appear vital, but if the RCT involves a trial of a cancer drug, and if the population means represent survival times, it is clearly essential to find out whether the raw effect size — the extent to which the drug can prolong life compared with a control treatment — is measured in days, weeks or years. A simple statement that "drug A is effective" is not sufficient. What if, after reporting this fact, we found that another drug, drug B, was also "effective" in this sense? In choosing whether to invest in production of A versus B, we will need to know which is *more* effective. One way would be to run another series of trials comparing drug A directly with drug B, but this would take time and money: how much better if the original trial of drug A had reported the effect size found, which could then be compared with the results from drug B directly.

Arguments like this have led to a change in recommended best practice in reporting statistical results. Rather than simply stating that the null hypothesis was rejected, it is now suggested that papers should give the actual effect sizes found. For instance, in the memory experiment example, we would not simply report that the null hypothesis was rejected and that an effect was present, but also the size of the effect. Given that the sample means were 18 and 25.5, the raw effect size is the difference between the two, namely 7.5 units. Note by the way that it is the difference in the means that is important: the comparison between the treatment and control means that tells us how effective the treatment is. Do not be confused by the fact that there are two levels of comparison going on here. The null model has been compared with the causal model: and found wanting. Having adopted the causal model, we are then making a statement about how the treatment condition compares with the control condition: and the conclusion is that it is superior, to the tune of 7.5 units, in the particular memory scale that was adopted for the experiment.

But hang on. Haven't we gone too far in our claims at this point. We have stated that the effect size of the treatment is 7.5 units in the whole population. And the evidence only states that it is 7.5 units *in the particular sample that was chosen*. What right have we to extrapolate to the population as a whole? The answer is that we have no such right.

This may seem a worrying conclusion. So far, I have suggested two ways forward, both of which are flawed. One is simply to state that the null hypothesis can be rejected, and therefore that the effect size of the treatment in the population is not zero. This is too vague. The second was to state that the effect size in the population is 7.5 units. This is too specific. Is there a third, middle way, which includes the advantage of being more specific than the first alternative, while avoiding the trap of being too precise, which we fall into if we choose the second option?

The compromise, which seems to enjoy the best of both worlds, is to use something called a confidence interval, usually abbreviated to CI. This is to state that the actual size of the raw effect, in the population, lies between certain limits.

The CI, in the case of the *t*-test example given above, is provided automatically by SPSS. It appears at the right hand end of Table 9.2, page 217.

The "mean difference" is 7.5 units, which is simply the difference between the sample means. But in extending this to a claim on the difference between the population means, we need to be more cautious. Here, the relevant numbers are those in the two right hand columns, headed "95% confidence interval of the difference". Since Levene's test is not significant, we can read the top of the two rows of output. The result is that the CI for the difference between the population means lies between 3.27 and 11.73 (I have taken just two places of decimals as being sufficiently accurate for this purpose).

So finally, we can produce a statement which has some precision, but not too much: we can be 95% confident that the raw effect size in the population lies between 3.27 and 11.73 units.

This statement raises the question of what exactly a confidence interval is, and how it is calculated. To answer this question properly requires a digression, which I have moved to the online material. However, in brief it does *not* state that there is a 95% probability of the true population effect size lying between the limits of 3.27 and 11.73. Rather, it states that if one uses the 95% CI criterion in making statements about the limits of population effect sizes, one will be correct 95% of the time on average. If the subtlety of this distinction escapes you, I suggest you do not worry too much about it.

Perhaps the best way to look at CIs is as a way of reporting results in statistics that ensures that one will not be wrong more than 5% of the time. To that extent, it has something in common with the use of significance testing, where the type I error rate is limited to 5%. In fact, there is a close link between CIs and null hypothesis tests. You will notice that the range from 3.27 to 11.73 does not contain zero: all the possible raw effect sizes numbers within this range are positive. This is not compatible with the null model (for which the effect size would be zero). So in this case, we know both that the outcome is statistically significant, and that the CI is incompatible with the null model. It turns out that this is always the case: whenever a statistical result is significant at the 5% level, the corresponding CI does not contain the point corresponding to the null hypothesis, and vice versa. This is of course what one would expect, but it illustrates the fact that confidence intervals give one all the information that one would obtain from a simple significance result, together with a lot more besides: an actual range of probable values.

Occam's principle revisited

This chapter has covered a lot of ground, in terms of applying general principles to a specific case, and readers may be confused at this point. Before attempting to summarise the argument and hopefully make it clearer, I want to look more closely at the Occam principle, which is fundamental to everything and therefore worth all the useful attention I can give it.

First I want to repeat the message of Occam's principle, and then to give two quite different reasons why it should be followed. Until now we have not really had the concrete examples to do more than argue in general terms why it should be a good thing. Hopefully in the light of the analysis in this chapter, the rationale for it should start to be more convincing.

Restating Occam's principle

A model can be viewed as an attempt to reproduce a given set of data. In practice, all models include numbers, called parameters, that can be adjusted to give the best possible fit to the data. In general, the more parameters a model has, the better fit can be obtained to the data. It may help to revisit the photographic analogy mentioned earlier. A digital photograph in black and white consists of a number of pixels, each of which is given a certain intensity. A digital photograph with just one pixel would be a very poor reproduction, but if it had the same intensity as the average intensity of the original scene, it would at least provide some information about that scene.

The null model for a dataset, in which every data point is approximated by the average value for the set as a whole, corresponds in this analogy to a photograph with one pixel. If the dataset represents the outcome of a two group experiment, then the causal model corresponds to a digital photo with two pixels. The first pixel represents the values for the DV in the treatment group, and its intensity is the average value of the DV for that group. The second pixel represents the control group values, and its intensity is the average for the control group. This model is the best "photograph" that can be provided for the data, given that one "pixel" must represent the treatment group and one "pixel" represents the control group.[3] Occam's principle states that given the choice

---

[3] It is possible that a "better" two-pixel image of the data could be obtained if the pixels were permitted to represent arbitrary members of the dataset, but in this analogy the pixels can only be allocated according to specified values of the independent variable; just as with a real camera, the pixels correspond to specified positions of the image in the field of view.

between a number of models with differing numbers of "pixels", or parameters, one should prefer a simpler model over a more complex model, unless the complex model reproduces the data so much better than the simple one that the better fit to data justifies its greater complexity. This pixel analogy may seem strange, with a maximum example of two pixels. We will see later with multi-factorial ANOVA, how it may appear a little more plausible, however.

Reasons for accepting Occam's principle

As applied to the situation in this chapter, where a two-level IV is being tested for its effect on a DV, the principle takes the form: choose the null model to represent the data unless there are compelling reasons to choose the causal model. What reasons are there for believing this to be a good policy?

First reason

To illustrate one reason, let us compare two policies at the opposite ends of the spectrum. Suppose we have two professional data analysts, A and B. A, the ultra-Occamist, always prefers the null model, no matter what the results of the experiments, whereas B, the risk-taker, always rejects the null model and recommends the model that fits the data better, which in practice will always be the more complex model.

There are two kinds of errors one can make when faced with a set of data. One is to adopt the more complex model, when in fact there is no effect because the null hypothesis is true. The second is to prefer the null model when there *is* a real effect. These kinds of errors are known as type I and type II errors, respectively. Faced with the same set of data to analyse, A and B will always come to opposite conclusions. Sometimes one will be correct, and sometimes the other, though never both at once. The only errors that A will ever make are type II errors, and the only errors B will ever make are type I errors.

Evidently neither A nor B is making much of a contribution to science, but faced with choosing one or the other, which would we prefer? Probably, if one had to make such a choice, one should choose the ultra-Occamist, A. One reason is that it is on the whole more damaging to make a type I error, and to claim that a causal effect exists when it does not, than to make a type II error, by failing to identify an effect that does exist. Claiming the presence of a non-existent effect is particularly damaging in the field of medicine: it is exactly what purveyors of ineffective alternative treatments have done through the ages.[4] Proliferating claims from practitioners of ineffective treatments are damaging, both because they involve expense and sometimes damaging side-effects for the patient, and because they make it harder to detect genuinely effective treatments among a mass of competing claims. This disadvantage also applies to "pure" research. A false claim of the presence of an effect can involve years of acrimony while the effect is laboriously proved not to exist. The history of cold fusion illustrates this point.

A false claim causes confusion and much effort in its refutation, whereas a type II error is at most provisional. It does not state that no effect exists: it merely states that the evidence does not (yet) support the conclusion that an effect is present.

To sum up: one justification for Occam's principle is that the type of error we are liable to make by following it (type II error) is less damaging than the type of error we are liable to make by ignoring it (type I error). Without going to the extremes of either A or B above, it seems a reasonable compromise to adopt Fisher's policy on null hypothesis significance testing. This ensures that the type I error rate will be confined to 5%, in the sense that on average, when faced with a case where the null hypothesis is actually true, we will mistakenly reject it in favour of the more complex hypothesis just one time in twenty. This provides no direct control over the type II

---

[4] These treatments may sometimes lead to improvements, but it is likely that these are the result of the placebo effect. There is as yet little reliable empirical evidence for the effectiveness of most alternative therapies. Effective alternative medicine is incorporated into conventional practice, though sometimes with a significant delay, as the history of antisepsis shows.

error rate, but if we regard type I errors as so much more serious, it makes some sense to focus on limiting their incidence.[5]

Second reason

The second way of approaching Occam's principle is to ask a rather different question from the fundamental one: "is the null hypothesis true?" This is to ask instead: "which of the two models constructed from the set of data, the null and causal models, has better predictive accuracy?"

Suppose for simplicity that the data is taken from a two group design, so that the experiment is designed to detect whether the populations from which the two groups are sampled have different means, and if so, by how much they differ (i.e., what is the raw effect size). Suppose for simplicity that the two groups are of equal numbers of participants, and that the overall data mean of the values of the DV is M, and that the two group means for the DV are M_t, and M_c for the treatment and control means respectively. Then the null model predicts: "every member of the population has the value M for the DV", and the causal model predicts: "for every member of the treatment population, the DV has the value M_t, and for every member of the control population, M_c". How good will these models be, in the real world, at predicting the actual values of the DV?

It may seem that this question is unanswerable, unless we happen to know in advance what the real world population means happen to be. Otherwise, we are in danger of arguing in circles: we use the limited data we have to formulate models, and then we judge those same models by the limited data that we have. It looks like an attempt to hoist ourselves up by our own bootstraps. But there is nothing to stop us considering how well the models would do under certain hypothetical real world conditions. If it turns out that the null model is always better, or if it is better under nearly all

---

[5] The job of controlling type II errors is indeed important, but the subject of a separate treatment: see the chapter on power in the online material.

circumstances, we would be able to deduce Occam's principle in a very strong form. If, on the other hand, the causal model is better in all but a very limited range of cases, severe doubt would be cast on the principle.

It can be shown, and I have included this in the online material, that if the null hypothesis holds, then the null model will *always* be a better predictor than the causal model. This is still true even if the null model does not hold, but if the population raw effect size is relatively small. There will come a point, if the effect size is increased, where the causal model will, on average, be a better predictor than the null model. But for small effect sizes, this is not the case. Occam's principle is a way of expressing this fact.

I do not claim that this approach, of assessing the two competing models on the basis of their predictive value, is how the orthodox method actually works. Statistical significance testing does involve something which amounts in practice to Occam's principle, because it tells us only to choose the causal model if there is good reason to reject the null model: that "good reason" being the positive outcome of a significance test.

One could argue that any valid approach to experimental science has to adopt something equivalent to Occam's principle, if only to avoid the situation where we accept every possible claim for a causal connection, thereby hopelessly confusing correct theories with bogus claims. All I am saying is that another criterion, which appears to be quite reasonable, even though different from orthodox statistics, gives qualitatively similar results in terms of justifying Occam's principle.

The approach I have tentatively outlined in fact leads in two directions, with two different criteria embodying Occam explicitly. These are known as the AIC and BIC, or Akaike Information Criterion and Bayesian Information Criterion. There is controversy as to which is "better". There is no clear agreement on this, nor indeed whether either approach is superior to orthodox significance testing. An internet search will produce ample background on the AIC and BIC for anyone who wishes to explore the matter further. See also the Further Reading Section.

One further point on effect sizes. I have mentioned the raw effect size in the sample, which is the difference between the two group means. There are other ways of measuring effect sizes in statistics, and one of the most common in the two-group case is known as Cohen's d. This is closely related to the raw effect size, but requires some explanation, which will be provided online. One complication with Cohen's d, is that an accurate calculation of a 95% CI for this measure is complicated, whereas the 95% CI for the raw effect size is given automatically in SPSS. However, it is important practically and conceptually in power calculations, and a treatment of this is included in the relevant online chapter.

Causality, counterfactuals and why comparing means is meaningful

A thorough treatment of causality seems to require the notion of counterfactuals, that is, consideration of what might have happened if things had been different. With RCTs, this includes the idea that in generalising the effect of a treatment vs control on a sample, we need to work with the concept of a having two populations, identical to one another, but one of which undergoes the treatment condition, and one, the control condition.

Analysing the outcome of the RCT involves comparing the means of the dependent variable in the two sample groups, with the aim of drawing inferences as to whether the means of the dependent variable across the two "populations" differ, and by how much. It may not be obvious that the correct way to estimate the effect of the treatment compared to the control condition is to notionally compare the means of the DV between these two populations. What follows is not a formal proof that this is so, but an argument that may suggest why it is at least plausible.

In constructing the hypothetical "treatment population", we may imagine cloning the actual population so that one of the clones undergoes the treatment condition, and the other one experiences the control condition. Since each member of the population exists in two states, as it were, or two clones, one in each population, it makes sense for a particular pair of identical individuals to compare the actual value of the DV measured for the "treatment clone", and to subtract from it the value of the DV measured for the corresponding "control clone". This is clearly a reasonable measure of the effect of the treatment for this particular pair of clones, since it excludes all the other personal variables (both individuals are the same "person"), leaving only the difference between treatment and control to be measured as the effect. Call this the individual raw effect size.

Now consider all these individual raw effect sizes, taken over the whole set of pairs of clones in the populations. It makes sense to take, as a measure of the overall effect of the treatment, the *average* of all these individual effect sizes taken over every pair of identical clones. But a moment's consideration will show that this average individual effect size is precisely equal to the difference between the means of the "treatment population", taken as a whole, and the "control population", taken as a whole. In other words, the mean of the differences is equal to the difference of the means. This is simply an algebraic necessity. So, in estimating the difference between these population means, we are calculating something with real significance in terms of treatment effects on individuals. Population means really do signify something important, and so sample means are also important, as an estimate of population means.

So far I have introduced several quite complicated ideas in the course of the past three chapters, as well as applying them in the present chapter to a particular type of experimental data. The next chapter will begin by reviewing the story so far, and then will embark on the basic form of what might be called Fisher's masterpiece, the method known as the Analysis of Variance.

Chapter 10

Generalising the *t*-Test: One-Way ANOVA

SUMMARY

Extending the two group design to multiple groups. Group difference designs. Generalising the *t*-test: the omnibus *F*-test of one-way ANOVA in SPSS. Plotting group means. Meaningful comparisons via contrasts. Homogeneity of variance assumption and testing for it. Contrasts comparing groups of means. Inflation of type I error rates with multiple comparisons, and the Bonferroni correction. Post hoc pairwise comparisons of means in SPSS. Contrasts and trend analysis. Effect parameters.

NEED TO KNOW

Summary of progress to date

I will set out the ideas that we have encountered so far, to try to make it clearer what has been achieved.

(1) A typical problem is to determine whether a treatment does, or does not have an effect on some condition. The claim that an effect is present, is known as the causal hypothesis, and that there is no effect, as the null hypothesis. The effectiveness of the treatment must be defined in operational terms, as the

effect on a specific outcome variable (or variables) which represents the level of the condition in question.

(2) The randomised controlled trial is a good way to check whether the causal hypothesis is true. It involves sampling participants from the population of interest, and randomly allocating half of them to a treatment group and half to a control group, following which a measure is taken on all participants of a suitable outcome variable which represents the condition in question. The group variable is known as the IV, and the outcome variable, as the DV.

(3) Having obtained the data, the hypothesis is tested by attempting to fit the data using two models, one of which approximates the value of the DV for every point by the overall mean (the null model), and the other of which approximates the DV for every point of the treatment group by the treatment group mean and the DV for every control point by the control group mean (the causal model). The raw effect size for the sample is the difference between the treatment and control group means.

(4) The null model is the best fitting model consistent with the null hypothesis, and the causal model is the best fitting model consistent with the causal hypothesis.

(5) The question now becomes, is the evidence strong enough to enable us to reject the null model, thereby justifying us in adopting the causal model and asserting that the causal hypothesis is true.

(6) Occam's principle tells us not to accept the causal model unless there is strong evidence to reject the null model. The causal model will always fit the data at least as well as the null model, and in fact will generally fit it better than the null model, even if the null hypothesis is true.

(7) Applying Occam's principle involves calculating Fisher's *F*-ratio. If the *F*-ratio can be shown to be greater than 1, then a plot of the causal model on a diagram representing goodness-of-fit and parameter complexity, must lie below the Occam line.

(8) However, due to the fact that the data is sampled from a population and therefore involves an element of randomness, it is not sufficient to establish that the *F*-ratio is greater than 1. Significance testing involves showing that the result is significant at a certain level of probability, conventionally at the 1 in 20 or 5% probability level. The *F*-ratio should be large enough, that if the null hypothesis were true, such a level would not be exceeded by chance more than 5% of times on average.

(9) If the *F*-ratio exceeds a certain figure — the precise value of which depends on the number of parameters in the model and the sample size — then the result is declared to be significant and the *F*-ratio can be confidently stated to be greater than 1. A significant *F*-ratio justifies the statement that the null hypothesis can be rejected and therefore, that the causal hypothesis can be asserted.

(10) In the case of a two-group RCT, a statistically equivalent way of testing the causal hypothesis is to calculate the value of the *t*-statistic, which is related to the *F*-ratio in the two-group case by the equation $F = t^2$. If the value of the *t*-statistic is significant, the null hypothesis can be rejected and the causal hypothesis asserted.

(11) If the result is significant at the 5% level, there is an alternative to simply asserting the causal hypothesis. This is to give the lower and upper limits of the 95% confidence interval for the raw effect size in the population. The raw effect size in the population is the theoretical difference between the average for the DV for the whole population in the control condition, and the average for the DV for the whole population in the treatment condition.

(12) The 95% CI for the raw effect size in the population will contain the actual raw effect size found in the sample, and if the result is significant, it will not contain the value zero which corresponds to the null hypothesis.

This is the basic tool kit, one might call it, for the simplest experimental design and analysis, and for its justification and interpretation. There are some more comments which help to put it in context, and which are more applicable to the current chapter where multi-group designs are considered.

(13) Although the most commonly used experimental design is the two group RCT, it is possible to apply the *t*-test method of analysis to two groups even if they are not randomly allocated, for example, if the groups represent samples from naturally occurring groups within the overall population, such as male and female. It can also be applied where one of the population groups is a clinical group, such as the set of all people with autism in that population, and the other group consists of unaffected individuals. In this case, the alternative to the null hypothesis is not a causal hypothesis, but the hypothesis that the averages for the DV in question are different within the two populations, corresponding to these two groups.

(14) If the two groups are given naturally rather than as part of a treatment/control concept, then if the data justify the assertion of a significant link between IV and DV, the relation between IV and DV cannot be considered as a directly causal relationship, because the IV has not been experimentally manipulated in this case. It is the experimental design that allows us to proceed from a significant result in an RCT, to the assertion that a causal link has been established. In an non-experimental two group design, the presence of a significant link between the IV and the DV allows us only to claim that the population means differ.

Generalising the two group design to more than two groups

The previous chapter considered the case where there were two groups, to be compared on the value of some DV. This chapter generalises this to any number of groups. The group variable is, as before, the nominal IV, with the different groups comprising the different levels of the IV.

The nature of the groups is not important for the purposes of the most basic analysis, which extends that of the previous chapter.

However, the fact that there are more than two groups does open up other possibilities that were not there with just two groups. For example, with three groups, one might want to compare groups 1 and 2 with one another and ignore group 3, or to compare groups 1 and 3, or groups 2 and 3.

Experimental designs

Something should be said about how the groups are selected. As with the *t*-test, the analysis of three or more groups can be applied to a purely experimental design, where individuals are taken from a single population and randomly allocated to one of the several groups. An example would be if a drug trial took patients and allotted them to treatment with a new drug (group 1), treatment with the best currently available existing drug (group 2), or treatment with a placebo (group 3). The IV is then a nominal variable with these three levels. The question the experiment is designed to address is a complex one. The design ensures that it may be possible to draw conclusions as to the causal link between treatment and outcome, but the addition of an extra group means that more complex links can be explored.

This trial can be seen as an extension of the RCT with not one but two "control" groups. It is standard in clinical tests to include a placebo group in which patients are given an inactive medication. This is because any new drug is likely to have its own placebo effect on patients; comparing group 1 with group 3 can then answer the question of whether the new drug has any "real" effect above and beyond that of the placebo. But the inclusion of a second drug group answers a different and possibly more important question. Suppose the new drug is more effective than a placebo. There is still little point in using it, if it is no better than alternative drug treatments (though it may of course be cheaper and thus worthwhile even then). The inclusion of group 2 should answer this question. It might be argued that with group 2, group 3 is then redundant. But it is of course possible that existing drug treatments actually make patients *worse* (this has happened). With three groups, we have all bases covered.

Group difference designs

As with the two group design, it is possible to have multiple groups selected from different populations. With clinical or other fully experimental trials, it is important that the individuals are as similar as possible, so that what is being measured is the effect of the treatments, rather than that of individual differences between patients. This is ensured by taking a sample from a single population and allocating randomly to groups. The results are then interpreted in terms of treatment effectiveness. But it is also possible to ask in what ways separate populations differ in certain respects, and for this it may be necessary to have more than one comparison group.

For example, children with Williams Syndrome are often characterised as having low general IQ but normal or superior language ability. To test this, we may wish to take a sample of WS children (group 2) and to compare them both with a group of typical children matched by age with the WS group (group 1), and with a group of typical children matched on IQ with the WS group (group 3). The IV will then consist of these three groups. The DV would be a measure of language ability.

Such a design might enable us to answer two different questions: is the language ability of WS children impaired *for their age* (compare groups 1 and 2), and is the WS language ability greater than would be expected for children *in their IQ range* (compare groups 2 and 3). These are related but distinct questions: it is possible that WS children have impressive language levels given their IQ, but are still impaired when compared with their age-matched peers.

Statistical analysis: generalising the t-test

Although the randomised and group difference designs are in some ways radically different, the possible options for analysing the data are the same in these two cases. Which options are chosen depends on the details of the research questions that are being asked.

Before proceeding to discuss the question of fitting models to the data, I should introduce a different terminology for the model provided by the group means. I have previously compared the null model, in which the data entries are approximated by the overall data mean, with what I called the causal model, in which the data was approximated by the individual group means. When dealing with RCTs, this terminology is appropriate, but the word "causal" is really only applicable when a randomised design is in use. For group difference studies it can be misleading. So I suggest using the term "IV model" to describe the obvious generalization of the causal model to the multiple group case.

The most basic question that might be asked is, whether we can reject the null hypothesis in favour of some more complex hypothesis. As in the case of the *t*-test analysis, this can be tested by comparing the null model (the best fitting model that we can find from the data, consistent with the null hypothesis) with the best fitting model that we can find from the data, based on the information we have on the value of the IV for each case (in other words, what I have called the IV model). An *F*-ratio can be calculated as the ratio of the slopes of two lines, bearing in mind that the number of parameters of the IV model is the same as the number of groups, as there is one parameter per group mean. If the *F*-ratio is significantly greater than one, the null model can be rejected in favour of the IV model. In terms of the original question, this means that the null hypothesis can be rejected.

As an example of how this works, the dataset (available online as Dataset 1) contains some notional data comparing a WS sample with age and IQ matched controls on a measure of language ability.

The simplest way to get SPSS to carry out the basic *F*-ratio calculation on a one-way ANOVA is to use the sequence Analyze >> Compare Means >> one-way ANOVA. Move the Score variable into the Dependent list window, and the Group variable into the Factor window. Note that in this menu, SPSS refers to nominal IVs as factors. Press OK and you obtain a single output box (see Table 10.1).

Table 10.1.   Output of one-way ANOVA test.

Score	Sum of squares	df	Mean square	F	Sig.
		ANOVA			
Between Groups	5474.067	2	2737.033	6.777	0.004
Within Groups	10904.100	27	403.856		
Total	16378.167	29			

The interpretation of this is as follows. The row headed "Total" refers to the null model, the "sum of squares" column showing the lofsos amounts, so 16378 is the sum of squared differences between the overall mean for the whole set of data, which is 58.8, and the individual data entries. The df figure of 29 is the difference between the parameters for the saturated model (30, as there are 30 data points) and the null model (just one, the full data mean).

The "Within Groups" row refers to the lofsos total for the IV model, the one modelling the datapoints by the group means. These group means are 77.2, 45.1 and 54.2. The df figure refers to the parameter difference between the saturated model and the IV model, which has three parameters corresponding to the group means: 27 = 30 − 3. The "Between Groups" sum of squares is the reduction in lofsos when going from the null to the IV model. The IV model improves on the null model by 5474, in other words. The df figure is the distance, in parameter terms, between the null and IV models.

The whole situation can be summed up in the lofsos-parameter plot (see Fig. 10.1), with the IV model appearing to lie comfortably below the line (not included here) joining the null model plot to the saturated model.

The slope of the left-hand line is the between group sum of squares divided by the between groups df, and this is shown in the output as the "Mean Square" for the between groups row, at 2737. The slope of the right-hand line is the within groups sum of squares

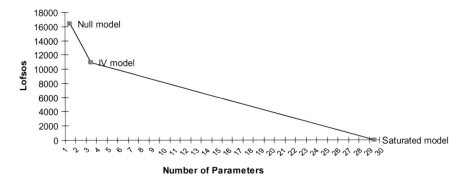

Fig. 10.1. Graph of null, IV and saturated models.

divided by the df, which the output calls the "Mean Square" for the within groups row, which is 403.9. The ratio of the two slopes is 2737/403.9 or 6.78, which is entered in the "F" column.

The only remaining number is under "Sig.", for significance. This is the *p*-value of the result, which is the probability that an F-ratio could be as high, or higher than 6.78 if the null hypothesis were true. It is 0.004, which is less than 0.05, and therefore we can safely conclude that the IV model is indeed a better fit to the data, and *the null hypothesis can be rejected.*

The test is often referred to as an "omnibus" test, from the Latin word meaning "of all": so it is a test of whether the model involving all the group means is preferable to the null model.

This test can be seen in two ways. The traditional way is to regard it as a test of the null hypothesis. The model comparison approach looks on it as a test of whether the model provided by all three group means, is better than the null model. The null hypothesis significance test or NHST is, however, less suggestive. Having rejected the null, what do you do next? The test offers no clues. But with the model comparison, the obvious answer as to what to do next, is: propose the IV model as the correct model for the data.

The problem is, that it is not clear how the model answers our original questions. To remind you of what they were: is the language ability of WS children impaired for their age (compare groups 1 and 2), and is the WS language ability greater than would be expected for children in their IQ range (compare groups 2 and 3).

The outcome of the omnibus test is not very helpful in answering these. The IV model, it seems, is superior to the null model, but where does its virtue lie, and how is it relevant to the original questions? With a two-group design, analysed with an independent samples *t*-test with a significant outcome, the answer is clear. The IV model in this case is just the two group means. If the group mean for the treatment group (in an RCT design) is higher than that for the control group, then we say that the hypothesis "the treatment has an effect" is confirmed, and we also know the *direction* of the effect: positive for the treatment concerned. The answer is direct because there is a simple correspondence between hypotheses and models: if the model shows a positive effect, the hypothesis is confirmed in one direction, and if negative, it is confirmed in the other direction. But here, the fact that the IV model wins over the null model means that in the language of hypotheses, we can only say: "*something* is happening". And unfortunately, that does not help.

The reason why the two group case was simpler, is that there is only *one* extra parameter in the IV model compared with the null model (two group means compared with one overall data mean), so in the conventional language of statistics, there is *one* degree of freedom for the independent variable. One degree of freedom can be viewed as a single quantity varying along one axis of numbers: a one-dimensional entity. In effect, the one degree of freedom can be identified with the difference between the group means, or what we earlier called the raw effect size.

When something varies along a single line, if you know its value you can say at once whether it is greater or less than zero. The only sensible research questions you can ask with just two groups is: are the group means different, and if so in which direction? And the result of the *t*-test tells you this at once. The problem with the present situation is that the IV model has not two, but three parameters, two more than the null model. And this means that the fact that the IV model is better, tells you nothing directly about the sort of research questions posed above.

To answer these, we need to somehow reduce the model comparison to something involving just one degree of freedom. The answer may seem obvious: just do a couple of *t*-tests back to back, comparing groups 1 and 2, and then comparing groups 2 and 3. And indeed this is quite possible. In the present case, in fact, it turns out that this gives results which are identical with the more elaborate alternatives. However, there are situations where this is not the most powerful way to analyse the data.

In fact two alternatives exist, appropriate for different situations. The first, involving "contrasts", can be explained quite naturally using the model comparison framework, and it is generally the most powerful technique for analysing data in cases where you have specific research questions regarding group comparisons as in the present case. The second, which uses so-called "post hoc" tests, is used in a different situation, and I will cover this method in the GD section.

As a preliminary to looking at contrasts, I find it always helps to do one simple thing first of all: to represent the data in visual form. The means are the important thing, and they can be seen in the form of a "means plot". This is accessed via the Options button in the one-way ANOVA menu, and checking the Means plot box (see Fig. 10.2).

On pressing Continue and OK, the output in Fig. 10.3 is produced.

So it looks as though the age matched controls did a lot better than the WS group, and the IQ matched controls just a little better. But the significance of the omnibus test does not allow us to conclude this immediately.

Rather than trying to derive a relationship between groups 1 and 2, say, from the IV model compared with the null, might it not be better to construct a pair of models directly which represents the comparison between groups 1 and 2?

If we were in the two group situation, we could imitate the model comparison for the *t*-test and compare the null model with

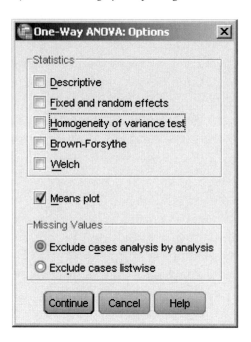

Fig. 10.2.   One-way ANOVA options menus.

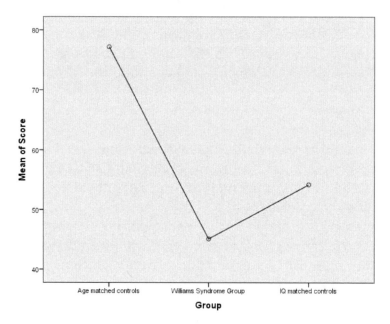

Fig. 10.3.   One-way ANOVA means plot.

what I called the "causal model" above. The null would attempt to reproduce the data for groups 1 and 2 by assigning every participant in those groups the overall (group 1 plus group 2) mean, and the causal model would map everyone in group 1 to the group 1 mean, and everyone in group 2 to the group 2 mean. But here the dataset also includes values of the DV for group 3, and any models to be included in our comparison must also attempt to reproduce the data in group 3. Group 3 is not doing anything much in the comparison, since what is being compared are the first two groups, but it cannot be forgotten. I will try to explain in more detail later the reasons for this choice but a natural decision would be to model every data point in group 3 by the group 3 overall mean.

So in seeing whether groups 1 and 2 differ in their population means, we compare the more complex model A, say, with the simpler model B, where A and B are defined as follows:

A: model every point in the dataset by the *mean of the group to which it belongs.*
B: model every point in groups 1 and 2 by the *mean of the two groups combined,* and model every point in group 3 by the *mean of group 3.*

To see what is going on here, I have attempted to represent models A and B in the scatterplots below, in which the values of the group variable are given along the horizontal axis, the DV along the vertical axis, and the dotted lines represent the group means. So for model A, every point in group 1 goes to the value given by the first dotted line, and so on (see Figs. 10.4 and 10.5).

It does not really matter what the actual means are. What matters is the concept.

Model B is a null model as far as groups 1 and 2 are concerned, as it does not distinguish between them. But it is more complex than the *real* null model, because it distinguishes between points which are in group 3 and points which are not, whereas the true null model just gives every point the same value, the overall mean.

Model A in fact turns out on a moment's reflection to be none other than the IV model that was used above in the omnibus test as

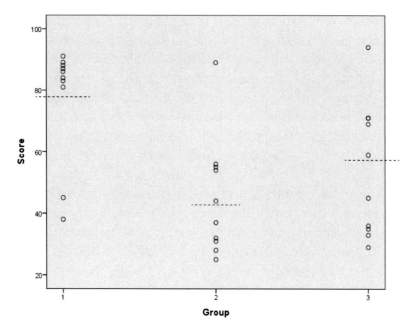

Fig. 10.4.   Illustrating model A.

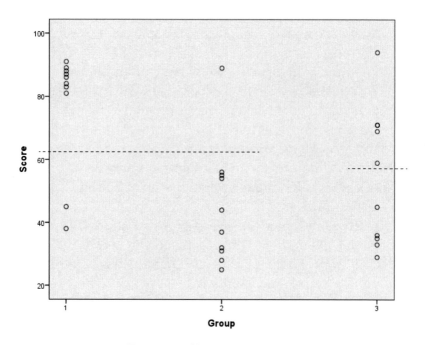

Fig. 10.5.   Illustrating model B.

the comparison with the true null model. So, what we are doing here is comparing the IV model with a sort of pseudo-null model; it is sometimes called the **reduced** model. And the point is that model A has three parameters and model B has two, so the difference is one, and this means that the comparison is similar to the basic *t*-test: the comparison will give us a direction of difference which can be interpreted directly in terms of hypotheses, just as with the *t*-test.

This illustrates an important point. All the comments previously about the Occam principle applied to the null model and more complex models, apply equally to the comparison between model B, and model A. That is, when plotted on a lofsos-parameter diagram, in order for model A to be preferred to model B, model A must plot below the line joining model B to the saturated model. This line is in fact the Occam line for the purposes of this comparison. And just as for previous comparisons, we can calculate an *F*-ratio as the ratio of the slopes of two lines, and demand that it be clearly greater than one, if we are to prefer model A. It is just that this time, the first line joins model A to model B, not to the null model. The second one joins model A to the saturated model, as before.

To create the diagram, we need to know the lofsos values for model A and model B. As model A is the IV model we already have this number from the omnibus *F*-test above: it is the "within groups" sum of squares, 10904. The sum of squares of model B can be calculated in Excel quite simply as 16056 (don't forget to add the sum of squares contributed by group 3 from its mean). The difference in parameter numbers is one, so the slope of the left-hand line is (16056 − 10904) = 5152. The slope of the right-hand line is the same as before, 403.9. This gives an *F*-ratio of 5152/403.9, or 12.76.

More accurately, we can write $F(1, 27) = 12.76$.

The plot of these two models on the lofsos-parameter diagram is shown in Fig. 10.6.

We know that the significance test for the *F*-ratio in this case is the same as for the *t*-test, with the same number of error degrees of freedom, where the value of *t* is found by taking the square root of the *F*-ratio, so in this case we can write $t(27) = 3.572$. And

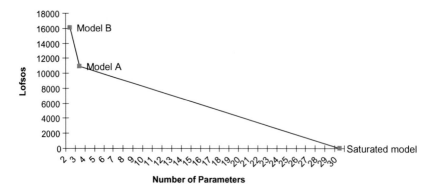

Fig. 10.6.   Graph of model A, model B and saturated model.

consulting the relevant tables shows that this is significant at the 0.05 level, with a *p*-value in fact of 0.001.

Now, we can safely interpret the result as follows: the age matched controls did indeed outperform the WS group in the test, and the difference is significant: so that it is unlikely to be due to chance alone. Provided the samples are representative of their respective populations, the result can be generalised to those populations: children with WS (within the age group chosen for the study) do indeed perform less well than their typical age matched peers.

Two tasks remain in this section, firstly to explain the benefits of this procedure, and secondly to demonstrate how to carry it out using SPSS, rather than by hand as above.

(1)   We could have simply done a *t*-test on the two groups in SPSS. After entering the IV, SPSS requires you to state the two levels of the IV that the test will be done on. If you put in 1 and 2 in these windows, the test will proceed to compare the age matched controls with the WS group. If you do this for yourself, you will find a rather similar result for the *t*-value, at 3.74. You will notice in that case that the degrees of freedom for this test are 18, compared with 27 for the calculation above. And herein lies the reason for the long-winded procedure. Statistics makes assumptions, and one of the assumptions commonly made in group comparisons is homogeneity of variance (or

HOV), mentioned in the *t*-test chapter, that is, that variances don't alter much from group to group.

This is usually a good bet on theoretical grounds with randomised designs, as the same population of participants is being used in the different groups, and can be expected to have much the same spread of individual differences in whatever condition. With group difference designs such as this one, the assumption is much more questionable, though it does no harm as long as the assumption is tested at some point. But bearing this in mind, just for the sake of the argument suppose the assumption is reasonable. How does the sum of squares calculation above differ from the two group *t*-test? By including the data from group 3. Why does this help? Because if we assume the HOV variance condition, then including the apparently redundant data from the third group performs one useful role: it helps to firm up the calculation of what the value of this unknown variance is. The variance can be estimated separately in each group, and the more groups, the more estimates there are. And the more estimates there are, the closer the mean of these estimates will approach the true value in the populations.

Variance is a source of noise in our data. But if the variance is known precisely, the amount of noise is known to lie within certain limits. Vague values for variance lead to uncertainty about the true value of the noise element. Using the language of Donald Rumsfeld, a known unknown is less unknown than an unknown unknown. The more groups you can include in the model, the more known the unknown variance is. In the model A/model B calculation, the unknown variance can be more precisely known than the unknown variance in the two group *t*-test, a fact which is encoded in the larger df value for the model A/model B calculation. A proper explanation would involve the sort of mathematics which you can find in advanced statistical texts, but I hope this may at least give a flavour of the concepts at work behind the maths. Of course, to estimate this "thing", there has to be just one "thing" to estimate, or you are combining apples and bananas. Hence the need for the HOV assumption.

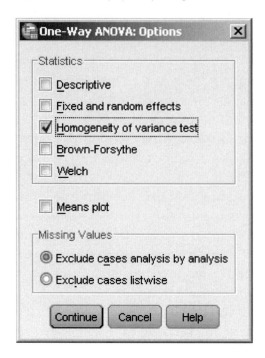

Fig. 10.7. Calling for the homogeneity of variance test.

In order to test this assumption with our data, go to Analyze ≫ Compare means ≫ One-way ANOVA, click the options button, and check the homogeneity of variance test (see Fig. 10.7).

Click Continue and OK, and the output will show the result of the test. It is non-significant, so the assumption of HOV has not been violated; we are safe to go ahead (see Table. 10.2).

(2) The comparison between models A and B is, as stated above, known as a **contrast**. Contrasts can be described in two ways. One uses the conceptual route, using model comparisons. But every contrast can also be translated into a series of whole numbers,[1] and in fact to persuade SPSS to calculate them for you, this is what you will need to do. These numbers are a

---

[1] This is not strictly true, as the experts will immediately realise. However, it *is* true of the type of contrasts that I will be using in this book.

Table 10.2. Output for Levene's test for homogeneity of variance.

	Test of homogeneity of variances			
	Levene statistic	df1	df2	Sig.
Score	0.471	2	27	0.629

way of encoding the model comparison task in a way that SPSS will be able to understand.

Contrasts are essentially just *t*-tests, but rather special ones. In the present case, we want to compare group 1 with group 2, but taking account of group 3. In an ordinary *t*-test, a key number is the raw effect size: the difference in the sample means of the two groups. A *t*-test is a test of significance to see whether this difference — the "signal" — is large enough compared with the "noise" that we can take it as a reliable indication that the group means really do differ in the populations from which they come.

This suggests that a first step in doing our comparison of group 1 with group 2 is to take the group mean for group 1, and subtract from it the mean for group 2. So we need to tell SPSS: "calculate $M_1 - M_2$", in the usual notation. But SPSS can't understand this. Instead, you need to simplify this to what are termed the **coefficients** in this expression. M_1 appears on its own, so its coefficient is just 1. M_2 appears with a negative sign in front, so its coefficient is −1. The coefficients are written in the numerical order in which the groups are encoded in the dataset, so the coefficients will appear in the order 1, −1.

But we are not quite done. SPSS will demand one coefficient for each group encoded in the IV, and that means group 3 needs to be included. That is easy, however: it is not to be part of the calculation of the "signal", so it just gets a zero. The full sequence for groups 1, 2, 3 in that order is therefore 1, −1, 0. This is usually written in brackets thus: Contrast = (1, −1, 0). This is something that SPSS can eat. To feed it, go to Analyze ≫ Compare means ≫ One-way ANOVA as before, and now after moving Score to the

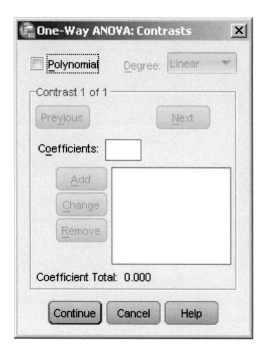

Fig. 10.8.   One-way ANOVA contrasts box.

dependent list and Group to the factor list windows, click on the Contrasts button to bring up the box as shown in Fig. 10.8.

Click in the Coefficients window to activate it and input the coefficients in order. Start with 1, and click the blue Add button which now becomes active, then −1, then 0, and you will see this as the end result (see Fig. 10.9).

Ignore the Next button for the moment, and the polynomial check box. Click Continue, OK in the one-way ANOVA box, and three boxes will appear in the output. The first one is the result of the standard omnibus *F*-test, which we have already done. The second one just confirms for the record the coefficients for the contrast that you asked SPSS to do (see Table 10.3).

It is contrast 1 in the left-hand column, because this program allows you do to many contrasts at the same time. The final box is the key one (see Table 10.4).

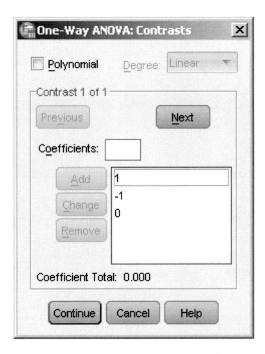

Fig. 10.9. One-way ANOVA with contrast coefficients included.

Table 10.3. Output of contrast coefficients in one-way ANOVA.

	Contrast coefficients		
	Group		
Contrast	Age matched controls	Williams Syndrome Group	IQ matched controls
1	1	−1	0

Since we have tested negatively for violation of HOV, we can assume equal variances, and read the first row. One thing to note is that the value of t is identical to that calculated above by hand using the F-ratio, which is reassuring. The "Value of Contrast" column gives a total which in this case is the expression represented by the contrast, namely $M_1 - M_2$. It is the raw effect size of comparing these two groups, and the important thing to note is the sign: it is positive, so the mean of the first group is larger than that of the second group (by

Table 10.4.   Result of tests of contrast in one-way ANOVA.

			Contrast tests				
		Contrast	Value of Contrast	Std. error	t	df	Sig. (2-tailed)
Score	Assume equal variances	1	32.10	8.987	3.572	27	0.001
	Does not assume equal variances	1	32.10	8.592	3.736	17.998	0.002

32.1 units). This means that as with all contrasts, having one degree of freedom, the model comparison significance test can directly be translated into a meaningful statement about the real world. You need not be too concerned about the standard error column.[2]

This trick of using coefficients to represent contrasts, and using contrasts to explore a variety of different and interesting questions about data in one-way ANOVA, will be taken up in the GD section.

Incidentally, you may care to ponder the following question: if the comparison of model A with model B addresses the question: "do groups 1 and 2 differ significantly from each other?", what question would be addressed if we compared model B with the null model?

GOING DEEPER

Contrasts have much wider applications than just as a more efficient way of comparing two groups. There is a whole class of problems that can be solved with them, involving the comparison of sets of population means. In a typical practical context, this involves *comparing the effectiveness of one set of treatments with that of another set of treatments.*

As a notional example, suppose an experiment was conducted among a sample of patients with depression, to compare the results

---

[2] It is the noise component, the contrast being the signal component. The value of t is the signal to noise ratio.

of four types of therapy: Freudian, Jungian, CBT (cognitive behavioural therapy) and REBT (rational emotional behavioural therapy). The outcome variable is a measure of the amount of improvement in condition in 40 patients, of whom ten were randomly allocated to each of the four therapies. (Note: the DV here is a derived variable, the **gain score**, or the difference between the posttest and pretest measurements of depression. Using a pretest–posttest design of this kind is fairly common in clinical trials, and comparing gain scores between groups provides a simple way of analysing the result. An alternative more complicated method, using the analysis of covariance or ANCOVA, will be covered in the online material).

Your research question is: do the psychodynamic theories (the first two in this list) differ, collectively, in effectiveness from the behavioural therapies (the final third and fourth in this list), and if so, in which direction?

The dataset for this example is included online as Dataset2.

As before, the question could be answered by merging the data for the two psychodynamic theories into one group, and merging the CBT/REBT into another group, and just doing a standard *t*-test. If this is done, then as you can test by using the MergedGroups variable in the dataset as the IV, the result falls short of significance. However, contrasts can come to our aid. Merging groups in the analysis does one avoidable harm to the data: it loses information. Contrasts don't lose information.

Firstly, what models are we comparing here? We are bundling up the first two therapies into a set, and the second two into another set, and asking if they differ or not. If they do not differ, then we have in effect the null hypothesis: there is no effect of group. If they differ, then the model found by taking the mean of groups 1 and 2 to approximate the data in those two sets, and the mean of groups 3 and 4 to approximate to those items of data, will be significantly better than the null model which just uses the overall mean to estimate everything.

But hang on: comparing these two models is surely just what we did previously in justifying the two groups *t*-test, and we have seen that this produces a non-significant result. So what can a contrast do that a *t*-test cannot?

Model comparison provides the answer. But we need to choose different models to answer this question in the most efficient way possible. I will give two models, which differ in just one respect: in one model the overall mean of groups 1 and 2 is held to be the *same* as groups 3 and 4, and in the other it is allowed to be *different*, but where the models contain as much information as possible subject to this requirement. If the second model improves significantly on the first one, then we can deduce that the overall means of 1 and 2 versus 3 and 4 do indeed differ.

A word of warning. What follows is somewhat elaborate. *You do not need to know the details in order to do perfectly adequate contrast calculations in SPSS.* The aim of what follows is to show that underlying the clever stuff in the program, there is something that can be understood conceptually as a model comparison. If you prefer to skip this section and go directly to the next, where the contrast is demonstrated using SPSS's slick program, you will not lose too much by doing so.

Model A is going to be the IV model, which as usual attempts to reproduce the data by allotting every point to the mean of its individual group, 1 through 4. Model B is identical to model A, except that I am going to nudge the group means for 1 and 2 up a bit, and the means for 3 and 4 down a bit, so that the overall mean of combined groups 1 and 2 is now the *same* as groups 3 and 4. So comparing model A with model B will tell us whether the observed difference between the means of 1 and 2 versus 3 and 4 is significant, because in comparing these two models, that difference has been isolated out. If there is a difference between the models, it can only be due to the {1, 2} versus {3, 4} mean difference.

Let us give the actual figures. The means of the four groups, which you can find by using the Analyze >> Descriptive Statistics >> Explore command and putting Gain Score into the Dependent window and Therapy Type into the factor list, are:

(71.6, 102.3, 115.2, 95.5) for the four groups in order of group. The mean of the first two means is 86.95, and of the second two is

105.35. The difference between these is 18.4. If we now nudge the first two means up by half this, 9.2, and nudge the last two means down by the same amount, then everything else will be unchanged, except for the fact that groups 1 and 2 will now have the same combined mean as groups 3 and 4. But the overall mean will remain the same. And the difference between the means of groups 1 and 2 will also be unchanged (both means have been nudged by the same amount, so this will cancel out when you subtract one from another). Likewise for the difference between group means 3 and 4.

So model A represents the groups by their actual means, which are

(71.6, 102.3, 115.2, 95.5),

whereas model B represents the groups by their nudged means of

(71.6 + 9.2, 102.3 + 9.2, 115.2 − 9.2, 95.5 − 9.2),

which works out at

(80.8, 111.5, 106, 86.3).

Since model A is just the IV model, its lofsos of model A can be found conveniently by running a one-way ANOVA in SPSS, where it will appear as the within groups sum of squares total in the output (see Table 10.5).

So the lofsos of model A is 28596.6. The lofsos of model B is a bit more difficult to calculate by hand, but it can be done in Excel with a little labour. The individual sums of squares in the four

Table 10.5. Sums of squares and *F*-test in one-way ANOVA.

Gain Score	ANOVA				
	Sum of Squares	df	Mean Square	*F*	Sig.
Between Groups	10038.500	3	3346.167	4.212	0.012
Within Groups	28596.600	36	794.350		
Total	38635.100	39			

groups are found by taking the DV values, subtracting from them the appropriate number from (80.8, 111.5, 106, 86.3) depending on group, squaring and adding over the group, then adding the results for the four groups. I calculate the result of all this to be 31982.2.

The difference in lofsos between the two models is therefore 31982.2 − 28596.6 = 3385.6, in model A's favour: model A is closer to the actual data.

Now we just need to work out parameter numbers. Model A clearly has four parameters, the group means.

Model B, on the other hand, has just three. To see this, observe that to construct the four numbers in model B we just need to know the overall data mean, and the differences in the group 1 and 2 means (which is 80.8 − 111.5 or −30.7) and the differences between group 3 and 4 means (which is 106 − 86.3 or 19.7). I will put more on how this actually works online, and show how the numbers for model B can be reconstructed from just three parameters. Conceptually, in losing the difference between the amalgamated means of groups {1, 2} and {3, 4}, you have lost a degree of freedom.

So we can now draw the usual lofsos diagram. The parameters for the saturated model are the number of data points, in this case 40 (see Fig. 10.10).

The slope of the line joining A and B is 3385.6/1 = 3385.6, since the parameters differ by one. The slope of the line joining A to the saturated model is 28956.6/36 = 794.35. The denominator is 36,

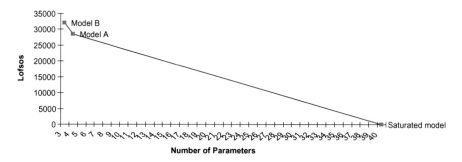

Fig. 10.10. Model comparison graph in one-way ANOVA.

because model A has four parameters, and the horizontal distance between it and the saturated model is $40 - 4 = 36$.

The F-ratio between these two slopes is 4.212: $F(1, 36) = 4.212$.

You could just look this up in a table of F-values and find that it is significant. An alternative, since models A and B differ by just one parameter, is to derive an equivalent t-value, and this is useful to compare with the result given by SPSS in the next section.

Taking the square root gives a t-value of 2.064, with 36 parameters. This too is significant at the 0.05 level. So finally we can say that yes, taken overall, the two groups representing behavioural therapies do differ in effectiveness from those representing psychodynamic therapies. To find the direction of the difference, compare the combined group means: that of the first two is 86.95, and of the second two is 105.35, so given that a higher number represents a better outcome, the cognitive therapies did better.

I am now going to show how this particular example works in SPSS. Then I will generalise the notion of comparing one group of means with another group of means, using contrasts. By the way, in case you have come across the notion of complete sets of orthogonal contrasts, this too can be represented using models. In the online material, I will show how a set of orthogonal contrasts corresponds with a nested set of models, with each consecutive pair of models furnishing one contrast, so that you can proceed from the null model all the way to the IV model in one parameter steps. In Appendix B, I will also introduce another fruitful way of viewing models in terms of transformations of the data. It will turn out that orthogonal contrasts correspond to transformations which commute with one another. Note that this result obtains in general only if the group sizes are all equal. Unequal group sizes introduce complications which I hope to cover in the online material.

Contrasts comparing one group of means with another group of means in SPSS

In comparing groups 1 and 2 with groups 3 and 4, we are in effect creating a t-test between two supergroups, {1, 2} and {3, 4}, while keeping the detail of the internal structure of the supergroups intact. Groups 1 and 2 are being treated together, and set against groups 3 and 4.

With an ordinary *t*-test, the "signal" part of the calculation requires us to find the value of $M_1 - M_2$. The "noise" calculation is based on the variance of the population, calculated by pooling the variances within each group. With a group of means comparison, such as the case here, the signal component can be found by substituting the sum of the first two group means for M_1, and the sum of the second two group means for M_2, giving the number $(M_1 + M_2 - M_3 - M_4)$. If we omit the cumbersome M suffix notation, this can be represented more simply as (1, 1, −1, −1), sometimes known as a row vector, with the numbers being the coefficients of the group means.

The "noise" part of the calculation involves looking at the within groups variance, but SPSS takes care of that automatically for us once we have input the row vector.

This is done as follows. Analyze >> Compare Means >> One-way ANOVA. Click on the Contrasts button and input the numbers in the row vector in sequence, remembering to click the Add button each time. Press Continue. Press the Options button and check homogeneity of variance test.

The output will show that HOV is not violated (the Levene statistic is not significant), and so you can use the upper row of the contrast result (see Table 10.6).

You can verify that the number in the "Value of Contrast" column is equal to $(M_1 + M_2 - M_3 - M_4)$, as a check against error. The *t* score is negative, since the value of the contrast is negative, but the value and df number are the same as that found above by the model comparison route. As before, the result is significant, showing that this method is more powerful than a brute force *t*-test comparing the amalgamated groups 1 and 2 with the combined groups 3 and 4.

There are other contrasts which might be appropriate here. For example, having established that behavioural therapies are better as a group than psychodynamic ones, that is the *between* group

Table 10.6. Single contrast test in one-way ANOVA.

Gain Score	Contrast	Value of Contrast	Std. error	t	df	Sig. (2-tailed)
			Contrast tests			
Assume equal variances	1	–36.80	17.825	–2.064	36	0.046
Does not assume equal variances	1	–36.80	17.825	–2.064	32.169	0.047

effect, we might reasonable enquire what the difference is *within* groups: is Jungian therapy really superior to Freudian, as the group means suggest, or might the difference be due to chance? And likewise with CBT and REBT.

The nice thing is that we can ask all these questions at the same time. If when entering the coefficients for the first contrast (1, 1, –1, –1), you press the Next button, the coefficients window clears, and you can enter coefficients to compare groups 1 and 2, ignoring 3 and 4, and then having pressed Next again, to compare groups 3 and 4, ignoring 1 and 2. The coefficients for the first contrast are (1, –1, 0, 0) and for the second, (0, 0, 1, –1).

The results you should get are given in Table 10.7.

This shows that there seems to be one other significant result: the comparison in contrast 2, which has a negative value of –30.7. Contrast 2 was (1, –1, 0, 0) so that the negative value is the one you obtain by taking the mean for group 1 (the coefficient is 1, so it is unchanged) and adding the negative of the mean for group 2 (the coefficient is –1, so it is negative). The only way this can produce a negative outcome is if the mean for group 2 is greater than for group 1. You can of course simply examine the group means in this case to confirm this result, but in more complex cases it can be useful to have the value of the contrast worked out for you.

So what this seems to say is that not only are behavioural therapies better than psychodynamic ones, but also that Jungian therapies are more effective than Freudian.

Table 10.7. Multiple tests of contrasts in one-way ANOVA.

		Contrast tests				
Gain Score	Contrast	Value of Contrast	Std. Error	t	df	Sig. (2-tailed)
Assume equal variances	1	−36.80	17.825	−2.064	36	0.046
	2	−30.70	12.604	−2.436	36	0.020
	3	19.70	12.604	1.563	36	0.127
Does not assume equal variances	1	−36.80	17.825	−2.064	32.169	0.047
	2	−30.70	13.638	−2.251	17.798	0.037
	3	19.70	11.479	1.716	14.528	0.107

If you can sense a "but" coming, you are correct. In fact with this multiple simultaneous use of significance tests, we have the first instance so far of an unpleasant obstacle to the NHST routine of something called "inflation of type I error rates". This sounds, and is, potentially painful and damaging, and requires a brief digression to explain the problem, and one possible solution to it.

Inflation of type I error rates through multiple testing

The basic principle is humorously illustrated in a website devoted to demonstrating the dangers of indiscriminate use of statistical tests:

http://tylervigen.com/spurious-correlations

Here you can find how per capita cheese consumption correlates significantly with the number of people who died by becoming entangled in their bedsheets; how the divorce rate in Maine correlates with per capita consumption of margarine; and how the number of world-wide non-commercial space launches correlates with the number of US sociology doctorates awarded between 1997 and 2009. The message of course is that if you run enough pairs of correlations between variables, you will eventually find significant ones, but that these are almost certainly artifacts of repeated testing: type I errors in other words.

The objective of using a *p*-value of 0.05 in a significance test is to reduce the type I error rate to 1 in 20. That is the so-called PC, or **per-comparison error rate**. This does not of course mean that 1 in 20 of all statistical tests will produce false positives. It means that on average, out of all the statistical comparisons made *for those instances in which the null hypothesis happens to be true*, one in twenty such comparisons will produce a significant result; and a significant result when the null hypothesis is true, constitutes a type I error. In practice, in a given research project it is conceivable that no type I errors are ever made, because the null hypothesis is always false. In the opposite extreme where the null hypothesis always turns out to be true, one in twenty tests will still yield significant results and they will *all* be false positives.

In advance, researchers setting out on a series of experiments evidently cannot say with confidence where the true situation lies in their particular case. It may seem that there is not much that can be done to guarantee the quality of the results. However, there is one precaution that can be taken. When faced with a particular set of data to analyse, there are often a number of different statistical tests that could be applied to the data, often involving a repeat of the same method over different sections of the data. Given values of some dependent variable over, say, five different experimental groups, one might do *t*-tests comparing each possible pairing of the groups — there happen to be ten such pairs — and looking for significant results. Or given a set of, say, five variables measured over some sample, one could do correlations[3] over every pair of variables, of which there are again ten possibilities.

If you had seven groups, or variables, to start with then there are 21 possible pairings. If you were analysing such data and were tempted to carry out pairwise *t*-tests over all seven groups, using 21 separate tests, it would be quite likely to yield at least one

---

[3] Or at least, you could if you know how to do this on SPSS. I have included a section on correlation in the online material. It does not lend itself so easily to the model comparison approach, except via a rather long detour taking in linear regression, so including it in the book was not an option.

positive result even if the null hypothesis was true, and all seven population means were equal. The practice of examining your data from all possible angles and squeezing the last drop of significance out of it is known as "data dredging". One might suppose that making the best use of the data was a virtue, not a vice, but it brings with it the danger of spurious results.

There is, however, a way — or rather, several ways — of neutralising this danger. The simplest to explain involves the Bonferroni correction.[4] With this, when you are carrying out multiple tests on the same set of data, you use a threshold p-value not of 0.05, but of $0.05/n$, where n is the number of tests. For example, if you were to want to do pairwise t-tests on all 21 pairings of seven groups, the only tests that would qualify as "significant" using this correction would be those with a p-value of less than $0.05/21 = 0.0024$.

Two questions suggest themselves: what does this achieve, and how does it work? As to the first question, this method reduces the so-called **familywise error rate** to 0.05 (sometimes known as the FW error rate, as opposed to the PC or per-comparison error rate). The FW error rate is the proportion of type I errors that will appear in a whole set of tests applied to data, as opposed to a single test. So out of all the cases where the null hypothesis is true, if the FW error rate is restricted to 1 in 20, the proportion of false positive tests will be limited to one twentieth of the *total number of families of tests*, rather than the total number of tests. To see the effect, suppose each family includes 21 tests, as with the seven group situation. Using the PC criterion of 0.05, on average it is possible (in the worst case where the null hypothesis prevails) for each family to include a false positive. Using a FW error correction, this is limited to just one family in twenty.

The definition of what constitutes a "family" seems to vary in the literature. One that seems to work quite well is that all the tests involving a particular independent variable should be considered as one family. In the case of one-way ANOVA that means all tests

---

[4] The best alternative known to me uses the concept of the False Discovery Rate, see the online material.

possible with the data, though when we encounter multi-factorial ANOVA, this means that there may be several families for one set of data. In fact, I think this approach may be overly generous in that case, but that is a matter for the next chapter.

The way it works can be seen conceptually as follows. Imagine a game of Russian roulette, where there are twenty chambers in the revolver and just one bullet. The chamber is spun and the trigger is then pulled. A single session, which involves playing the game once, means a 1 on 20 risk of death to the player. This is like the PC type I error rate. It might be that for a large enough reward (or as the alternative to something even worse, like being thrown into a cage of crocodiles) you might be prepared to take such a risk. But if a "session" involved playing the game five times, or ten times consecutively, you would be much less happy about playing: the risk of death (the FW error rate) would go up roughly in proportion to the number of plays. However, if you were given a revolver with *one hundred chambers* and just one bullet, then a session of five plays would not seem too dissimilar to a session of one play with a revolver with 20 chambers. And this is the principle of the Bonferroni correction. With five sessions, divide the 1 in 20 error rate by 5 to reach 1 in 100. Then each play (each test) has a death rate (PC error rate) of 1 in 100, and the probability of death in a session (FW error rate) is back at 1 in 20.[5]

Application to multiple contrast testing

This suggests that if we wish to use more than one contrast test with an IV, we should regard these tests as belonging to a single family, and that we need to apply a correction to avoiding inflating the FW error rate. With four groups to analyse, the first two groups can be compared with the second two, as above comparing the psychodynamic with the behavioural therapies. Then the two psychodynamic therapies can be compared with one another, and

---

[5] In fact, it is very slightly less than 1 in 20, but this is an error in the right direction, and in practice it makes little difference anyway.

finally the two behavioural therapies with each other. That makes three contrasts, and if we do all three, then we need to apply a Bonferroni correction using a cut-off p-value of not 0.05, but $0.05/3 = 0.017$. Unfortunately, if we do this then none of the three results above is significant by this new criterion.

That does not matter if — and it is an important "if" — the research question was clearly stated at the outset, as being to compare the two types of therapies and nothing else. Setting out to test a single contrast does not risk inflating FW error rates, because the "family" of tests has just one member, so FW and PC error rates are the same. It would be similar if all you were planning to do was to compare the two psychodynamic therapies with each other, and the two behavioural therapies. In that case there would be two planned contrasts and the p-value criterion would be 0.05/2 or 0.025. In such cases we talk about *a priori* contrasts: *a priori* meaning literally "from the earlier", which refers to tests that we propose to do *before* the data is analysed. If you have just one *a priori* contrast, it can be tested without using a Bonferroni correction; but what you cannot do is eyeball the data, notice some clear trend and then decide to do a contrast on that on its own without any further correction. The test has to be determined in advance.

By the way, it may occur to you that it is OK to look at the data, and then decide to do a certain set of contrasts and apply a Bonferroni correction appropriate just to this specific set of contrasts. This is however not the case. In eyeballing the data, you have in effect done a full set of tests, and it makes no difference if you are only admitting to the interesting ones. The laws of statistics are firm on this point.

Post hoc pairwise comparison of means

A priori contrasts are often a very nice way to analyse multi-group designs. Their appeal is that since any contrast has just one degree of freedom, a significant result can be interpreted unambiguously in terms of a simple hypothesis, essentially telling you that some number of interest is larger, or smaller, than another number of interest.

The one degree of freedom means that things are varying along a line, and so the alternative to the null hypothesis is a single number, and it is often mainly the sign of this number (plus or minus) that is of interest: does something have an effect, and if so is it positive or negative? So the result of a contrast is easy to interpret.

However, sometimes it is too restrictive to insist that tests are formulated in advance in this very specific way. Sometimes the aim of an experiment might simply be to detect *any* differences between the group means. There is no attempt to single out any one pair of groups that might be of interest: potentially, they all are. Because there is no attempt to spell out hypotheses in advance — other than to express a general interest in pairwise differences — this situation is described as *post hoc* testing, *post hoc* meaning "after this", so that any conclusions are drawn after all the data is available for testing.

Pairwise comparisons could be done using ordinary *t*-tests, or possibly the more powerful contrast equivalent, together with the application of a Bonferroni correction to prevent inflation of FW error rates. However, it turns out that there is a better way, using a method that is purpose built to deal with this particular problem. One of the many contributions of John Tukey to statistics was the development of a more powerful test of multiple pairwise comparisons of means, known as Tukey's HSD or honestly significant difference test.

The idea behind the test is that given a set of sample means where the null hypothesis holds — i.e., each of the population means is equal — the *range* of the means (the difference between the largest and smallest) should be less than a certain value, 95% of the time. The actual calculation of this range limit is somewhat complicated: doing it by hand involves calculating the sample standard deviation, and looking up tables of critical values of the "studentised range statistic" q, for the number of groups involved. Fortunately, SPSS does the calculation for you.

The value of this test is that if a given pair of means — say M_2 and M_4 — differs by more than this amount, then we can deduce that the null hypothesis can be rejected. That is because if these two means already differ by more than the critical range limit, then certainly the range of *all* the means must be at least that large. Adding numbers to a set of numbers can only increase the range, never decrease it. So we can conclude that at least *one* pair of means must differ.

We appear to be concluding rather more than this: that M_2 and M_4 must differ. But if the range test is significant, the probability that the null hypothesis is violated in some *other* way but *not* by M_2 and M_4 can be shown to be small. Using the criterion to test all pairs of means, and declaring a significant effect for *any* pair if they differ by more than the critical amount, can be shown to keep the FW error rate down to 0.05, at least in most cases. And this allows us to test multiple pairs of means, indeed all of them, without getting into trouble.

The test is both a powerful and reliable one, though it does make an assumption of HOV. Fortunately, if HOV is violated there is an alternative which is immune to this problem, called the Games–Howell test.

A useful procedure then, if you have a one-way ANOVA and wish to do a *post hoc* comparison of means, is to go into the one-way ANOVA program in Compare Means, and tell SPSS to do three things simultaneously: check for HOV, do the Tukey test, and do the Games–Howell test. In the output, look and see if the HOV assumption is violated (Levene's test significant) or not. If not, examine the output for the Tukey test. If it is violated, examine the output for the Games–Howell test. One or the other will tell you what you need, and doing this all at one pass saves time. I will demonstrate this for Dataset2 at the end of this section.

You may be wondering, if Games–Howell is valid whether the HOV assumption is justified or not, why not save even more time and just do Games–Howell, ignoring Tukey? The reason is that the Tukey test is generally *more powerful* than Games–Howell, so that it can pick up significant differences that Games–Howell might miss — *provided it can be validly used*. So if the HOV assumption can be made, it is worth using Tukey because it is better (more powerful). If HOV is violated, it is better to use Games–Howell because it is better (more valid). There is a delicate balance between power (reducing type II errors) and safety (keeping type I errors within bounds). That is why the choice of test is conditional on the validity of the assumptions.

This trade-off happens on other occasions too. For example, if the basic normality assumption of parametric statistical tests is violated there are non-parametric alternatives, but these are usually less powerful, and so should be used only when necessary.

It may seem odd that I have not mentioned model comparisons in connection with post hoc tests, having highlighted them so consistently up to now. The reason is that pairwise means testing seems to be one area where this approach is not helpful. It might be possible to think up a set of models, representing every possible situation where some means differ and others don't, but the set would be very complex to describe. Imposing it on Tukey's test would be like putting a saddle on a cow. Even the redoubtable Maxwell and Delaney (see Further Reading) in their chapter on multiple comparisons do not attempt this.

For those who like this kind of thing, I suspect that the reason is that the various pairwise comparisons are not independent of one another (more precisely, the set of comparisons is not orthogonal). Knowing that mean 1 is significantly less than mean 2, and that mean 2 is significantly less than mean 3, we can deduce immediately that mean 1 is significantly less than mean 3. More problematically, means 1 and 3 may differ significantly, but mean 2, in the middle, may not differ significantly from either 1 or 3. It seems rather difficult to represent this as a model.

Models seem to work well where the variability in a dataset can be carved up into non-overlapping chunks, with each extra chunk representing the step from one model to the next most complicated one. I will demonstrate this at the end of this chapter with a set of contrasts, moving in single steps from the null to the full IV model. But this requires an orthogonal set of comparisons, which guarantees that the chunks of variability are non-overlapping, and so each chunk corresponds to one pair of models. Where the variability overlaps, this option is not available.

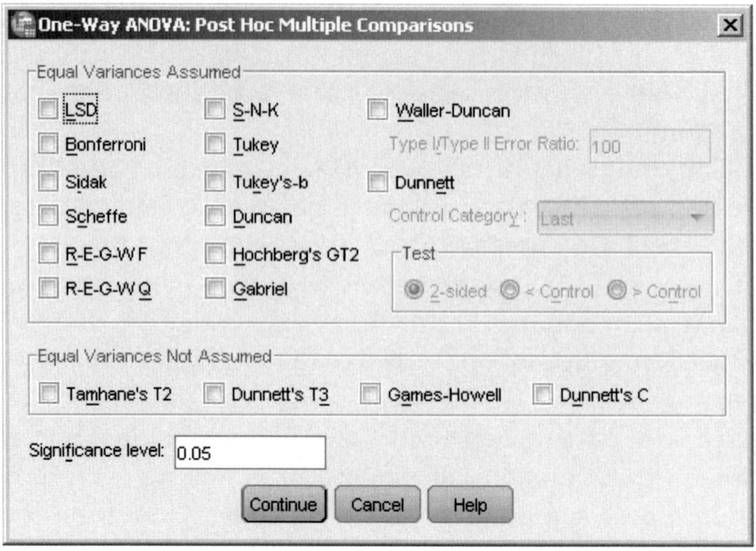

Fig. 10.11.   Post hoc multiple comparisons options in one-way ANOVA.

I will now demonstrate the procedure for Dataset2, comparing all possible pairs of means. Of course, analysing the data in this way is something that you should have decided in advance, rather than as a consequence of the failure of the contrasts method.

In the one-way ANOVA box click the Post Hoc button (see Fig. 10.11).

In this rather busy box, check the Tukey and Games–Howell tests. Note, it is the Tukey and not the Tukey's-b that you need. Note also that the box reminds you that the Tukey test requires the HOV assumption to be satisfied, and Games–Howell does not. Click Continue, and now go to the Options button and click on the HOV test (in fact we have already done this, but this is the general procedure if you are moving straight to *post hoc* tests). Click Continue and OK, and under the Levene's test (confirming that HOV may be assumed) and the omnibus ANOVA test, you will find a rather complicated set of results including both the Tukey and Games–Howell results. Given the HOV result, we know that we can read the first, Tukey set of results, but you might care to glance at Games–Howell too. You will find that in most cases the standard error for a particular comparison in Games–Howell is larger than the same comparison for Tukey, though not in all cases. This indicates that the Tukey test is more powerful.

The output in these tables has a lot of redundancy. Each pairwise comparison is given twice, for example Freudian therapy is compared with Jungian, and Jungian with Freudian. The results in both cases are identical, except of course that the difference between the means has the opposite sign in the Freud–Jung comparison relative to the Jung–Freud comparison. The difference is only meaningful, however, if the *p*-value at the right in the Sig. column is less than 0.05. So the fact that the Freudian mean minus the Jungian mean is −30.7, so that the Freud sample mean is 30.7 less than the Jung mean, cannot be interpreted as showing the superiority of Jungian therapy. In fact the only comparison that is significant is that between Freudian therapy and CBT, where the difference between the means is 43.6 in favour of CBT, because in this case the *p*-value is 0.007. All this can be seen in the Table 10.8.

The 95% confidence interval section at the far right of the table gives limits within which the mean difference can be taken as lying. People sometimes find this a difficult idea. With the Freudian–CBT comparison, the means differ in this sample by 43.6 in CBT's favour, but the means in the actual population of patients might not differ by this at all: in fact given unavoidable sampling error, they probably will not. The 95% CI attempts to quantify this uncertainty. The mean difference measures the true level of superiority of CBT over Freudian therapy and we can be fairly certain that this quantity lies somewhere between the limits of 9.65 and 77.55 in CBT's favour. This may seem a wide range, and it is, but the key point is that all points in this range are positive. None of them is zero. This is exactly what we would expect, given that we know the mean difference is significant. If you examine the non-significant pairwise comparisons, you will see that in every case the limits have opposite signs: this means that they sit either side of zero, and therefore *include* zero within the limits of what is plausible. This is precisely the same as saying that the result is not significant.

Table 10.8.   Output of multiple comparison tests using Tukey's HSD.

Multiple Comparisons

Dependent Variable: Gain Score

Tukey HSD

(I) Therapy type	(J) Therapy type	Mean Difference (I–J)	Std. error	Sig.	95% confidence interval	
					Lower bound	Upper bound
Freudian	Jungian	−30.700	12.604	0.088	−64.65	3.25
	CBT	−43.600*	12.604	0.007	−77.55	−9.65
	REBT	−23.900	12.604	0.248	−57.85	10.05
Jungian	Freudian	30.700	12.604	0.088	−3.25	64.65
	CBT	−12.900	12.604	0.737	−46.85	21.05
	REBT	6.800	12.604	0.949	−27.15	40.75
CBT	Freudian	43.600*	12.604	0.007	9.65	77.55
	Jungian	12.900	12.604	0.737	−21.05	46.85
	REBT	19.700	12.604	0.412	−14.25	53.65
REBT	Freudian	23.900	12.604	0.248	−10.05	57.85
	Jungian	−6.800	12.604	0.949	−40.75	27.15
	CBT	−19.700	12.604	0.412	−53.65	14.25

*The mean difference is significant at the 0.05 level.

So in one sense the CI limits are telling us what we already know, but the additional information as to the likely size of the difference may be very useful. The difference is what I earlier referred to as a raw effect size. Knowing effect sizes is often helpful in decision making. If for example CBT turned out to be a lot more costly than Freudian therapy, the fact that the raw effect size might be as small as 9.65 could have a bearing on whether to fund a policy based on replacing Freudian with CBT treatment.

The output named "Homogeneous Subsets" is not in my view very useful, but I will try to explain its meaning in the online material.

Before leaving the topic of one-way ANOVA, there are three more topics to cover briefly: the use of contrasts in general comparisons of means, contrasts in trend analysis and the difference between fixed and random factors.

General comparisons of sets of means

The therapies analysis gave one example of a more general problem, where the hypothesis is typically that one set of treatments differs in effectiveness from another set of treatments. This can be solved using a contrast. In the therapies case, the contrast was (1, 1, −1, −1). Suppose now we have seven groups and we want to test the first 3 means in a group, against the next 2 means, leaving out of account the final two groups. The test involves taking the average of the first 3 group means and subtracting from this, the average of the next two group means. We will wish to test whether the result is significantly different from zero.

It turns out that the appropriate contrast to use will be (2, 2, 2, −3, −3, 0, 0). Detailed justification will be given in the online material. And from this you should be able to see the general form of such a contrast. If there is one group of m means, and a second group of n means, the contrast will consist of putting an n at each point corresponding to the first group, a minus m for each mean in the second group, and zeroes elsewhere. The contrast can be input via the one-way ANOVA contrasts button as before. If the contrast value is positive and significant, then the first group of means has a higher overall mean than the second group, and vice versa if it is negative and significant.

Note by the way that the coefficients in any such contrast should always add to zero. If it does not, you have made a mistake somewhere. The contrasts window makes a running total of the coefficients near the bottom at Coefficient Total, and this provides a check against gross error at the end. If the running total is nonzero there has been a mistake.

The use of contrasts to compare groups of means in this way is fairly common in textbooks, though I am not sure how useful it generally is in practical applications. Where you have a situation where each set of treatments has some different thing in common (such as being psychodynamic vs. behavioural) some would argue that it is more interesting to analyse the data using a random effects model rather than a fixed effects model. The whole issue is interesting and important but rather beyond the scope of this book, but you should be aware that it exists. Random effects models assume that the treatment levels are randomly sampled from a population of treatments, and in comparing two treatments, would include this source of variability as well as simply the variation between individual participants. Fixed effect models assume that the treatment levels are fixed, and the only source of variation is from the participants.

Contrasts in trend analysis

There is a use for contrasts in something called trend analysis, which may be of value in cases where the levels of the IV correspond not to dissimilar groups, but where they can be described using numbers varying along a scale. Typically, the scale might represent the effects of administering a drug, usually by increasing the dose in equal increments. In such a case a research question might be: what effect is produced by the drug when the dose is changed? Usually, increasing the dose starting at a low base level will increase the (hopefully beneficial) effect of the drug, but there will come a point at which this trend levels off, and it may even decline: high enough doses may start to become toxic. Other interventions which can be graded on a scale also often show such an effect — good to start with, then detrimental.

   These possibilities need to be interpreted in a more mathematical way before we can make sense of the trend analysis program in SPSS, but before doing this I will take a specific example, though the actual data are (as in most cases in this book) purely fictional. The results are supposed to represent the result of tests on four separate groups of patients given increasing doses of some drug, at 200 mg, 300 mg, 400 mg and 500 mg respectively for the four groups. The outcome variable in this case represents the level of

Fig. 10.12.   Contrasts in univariate ANOVA.

Fig. 10.13.   Polynomial contrasts in univariate ANOVA.

some symptom, let us say, with a reduction in the variable as the dose is increased showing an improvement. The dataset itself is available online as Dataset3.

I will work through the actual analysis and then describe how the results answer the research question. Finally I will at suggest how the analysis uses contrasts to arrive at the answers, and give a demonstration of how this can be seen in terms of model comparisons.

To do the trend analysis, we need to activate the one-way ANOVA procedure, but in this case the program we have used so far is not the best available in SPSS. SPSS contains a great deal of redundancy: there are usually several ways of getting a result, and one-way ANOVA is no exception. In this case it is better not to go via Analyze >> Compare Means, but to use Analyze >> General Linear Model >> Univariate. The General Linear Model is immediately below Compare Means in the dropdown menu.

In the box that appears, move the Outcome variable to the Dependent Variable slot, and the Dosage variable to the Fixed Factor(s) slot. Note that this program gives you a Random Factor alternative, but I will not be using this in the book. The Dosage variable has been entered as an ordinal variable, since it makes sense to think of it as varying along a scale: it might even have been described as a scale variable.

Now click on the Contrasts button, we get the box as shown in Fig. 10.12.

Click on the blue button marked "None" next to "Contrast:" in the Change Contrast area. At the bottom of the dropdown menu that appears click Polynomial, and then click the Change button on the right (if you omit this step, nothing will happen). You now get the box as shown in Fig. 10.13.

Click on Continue and OK. Included in the output is an *F*-ratio test, which is simply the *F*-ratio of the IV model compared with the null model, but more relevantly for our purposes there is also a table giving the contrast results. The key things to note from this are the following:

(1) The program includes tests for three contrasts, labelled linear, quadratic and cubic.
(2) The linear contrast has a negative value (the "contrast estimate" is −192) and the test is significant: the *p*-value is given as 0.000, which really means simply that it is less than 0.001, therefore certainly significant at the 0.05 level.

Table 10.9.   Output of tests of polynomial contrasts.

Contrast results (K matrix)			
			Dependent variable
Dosage polynomial contrast[a]			Outcome
Linear	Contrast estimate		−191.631
	Hypothesised value		0
	Difference (Estimate − Hypothesised)		−191.631
	Std. error		6.488
	Sig.		0.000
	95% confidence interval for difference	Lower bound	−204.790
		Upper bound	−178.472
Quadratic	Contrast estimate		51.300
	Hypothesised value		0
	Difference (Estimate − Hypothesised)		51.300
	Std. error		6.488
	Sig.		0.000
	95% confidence interval for difference	Lower bound	38.141
		Upper bound	64.459
Cubic	Contrast estimate		−8.721
	Hypothesised value		0
	Difference (Estimate − Hypothesised)		−8.721
	Std. error		6.488
	Sig.		0.187
	95% confidence interval for difference	Lower bound	−21.880
		Upper bound	4.438

[a]Metric = 1.000, 2.000, 3.000, 4.000.

(3) The quadratic contrast is positive, and it is also significant.
(4) The cubic contrast is not significant, so its value can be ignored.

The Hypothesised Value is zero in all cases: this represents the null hypothesis, that there is no effect of this contrast (see Table 10.9).

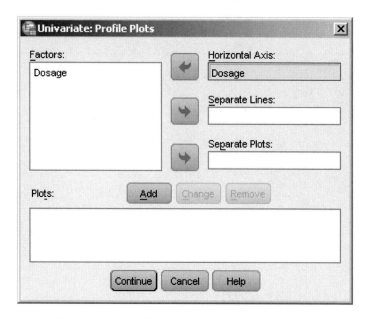

Fig. 10.14.   Profile plots in univariate ANOVA.

In order to understand what all this means, it will be helpful to give a visual plot of the means for the different doses. For this, go back into the program, click the Plots button, and in the box that appears move the Dosage variable into the Horizontal Axis slot using the blue arrow button (see Fig. 10.14).

Now click the blue Add button — or you will get an error message — click Continue, OK. The plot as shown in Fig. 10.15 will appear.

Even without the contrast results, it seems fairly clear what is happening: the outcome variable seems to be dropping (showing an improvement in condition) as the dosage increases, though there is a suggestion that the improvement is levelling off for the higher values of dosage. Incidentally, one should use a Bonferroni correction with these multiple contrasts, but even then the two significant results are still significant.

How does this correspond to the contrast results? The negative linear contrast abstracts out of the data the fact that overall, the trend in the DV is *downwards* as dosage increases: this is the

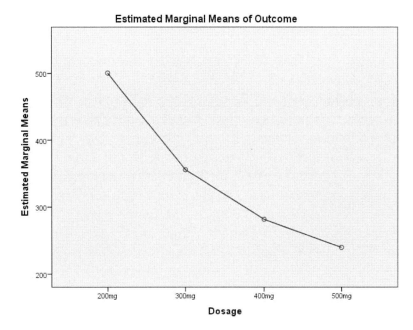

Fig. 10.15.   Means plot in univariate ANOVA.

meaning of the negative contrast, which tells us that if we attempted to fit the data means with a straight line (note it is "linear" contrast), the slope of the line would be negative.

The quadratic contrast represents the fact that the plot of the means is concave or U-shaped. "Quadratic" is from the fact that the basic U-shaped curve can be written in the form $y = x^2$, a quadratic expression. The positive value of the contrast means that the U is upright; a negative quadratic contrast would have indicated an inverted-U component. The overall means plot is well approximated by these two trends added together.

If the cubic contrast had been significant, it would have suggested that a trend was present that could be described as an S-curve, or more technically this would be called a **sigmoid** trend. But the non-significance of the cubic contrast shows that we can ignore this.

Note by the way that for this to work, the successive levels in the IV should represent equal intervals in dosage, or whatever the variable represents. This particular program in SPSS makes that assumption. There is a mathematical work-round if the levels are not in equal steps, but this requires a bit more work. I will not attempt to cover it here (oddly enough, the polynomial contrast program in the simpler, Compare Means version of one-way ANOVA *can* automatically compensate for unequal steps: another example of the unpredictability of SPSS).

You may be sceptical about the point of doing a trend analysis. Why bother to get these rather mathematical statements about how dose affects response? Well, at least the implications of a linear trend are probably clear, and the need convincing: to be able to conclude "more means better", or "more means worse", is surely worth doing, and the value of the contrast makes it possible to quantify how much better, or worse, the outcome is for each unit change in the dosage. The use of a significance test means that any claim of "more means better" can be backed up with real evidence, and quantifying it means value for money estimates can be made with at least a basis of fact. A quadratic trend may also be useful in predicting the effect of different doses. The mathematical nature of the contrasts means that the effects can be extrapolated to dosage values not included in the original experiment. And claims about the effects are testable, and do not depend on the intuition involved in "eyeballing" the data, useful though that may be.

Building the IV model from the null model using contrasts

The way trend contrasts work is rather technical, but it is worth knowing that they are independent of one another — they are orthogonal — and that together, the contrasts account for all of the variability in the group means.

Put another way, the IV model can be constructed from the null model by adding together the effects of the different polynomial terms, step by step. In this case, there are three polynomial contrasts, each adding one degree of freedom. Together they account for the three degrees of freedom that separate the one parameter null model from the four parameter IV model. I will show this

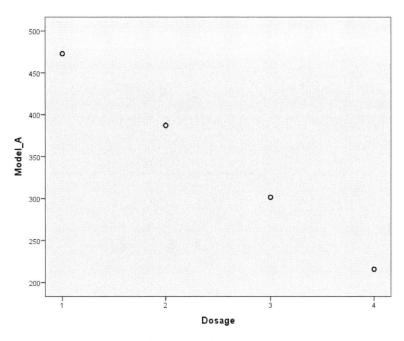

Fig. 10.16.   Illustrating the straight line model of the data (model A).

below. Note that this construction of the full IV model from the null model by successively adding contrasts, can be done with any complete orthogonal set of contrasts.

In this particular case the linear model consists of mapping each element of each group onto a number, one per group, such that these points lie on a straight line when plotted with Dosage on the horizontal axis. In the figure, the levels 1–4 of Dosage represent the amounts of 200–500 mg. I have named this, model A. The numbers corresponding to the groups are 473, 387, 301 and 215, decreasing by 86 units at each step (see Fig. 10.16).

So all the points in the group that got the 200 mg dose are approximated by the figure of 473, those in the second group by 387, in the third group by 301, and in the fourth group by 215 (I will omit the actual calculation of these numbers here).

The linear plus quadratic model, model B, can be represented by adding 25.65 to the linear model numbers for groups 1 and 4,

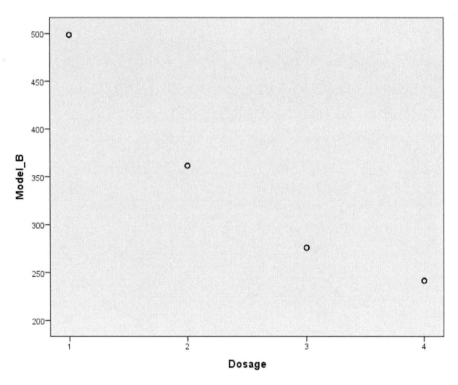

Fig. 10.17.   Illustrating the linear plus quadratic model of the data (model B).

and subtracting it from the numbers for groups 2 and 3 (I will explain how this is found in the online material) (see Fig. 10.17).

The final model, incorporating all three polynomials, brings us up to the IV model, where the predicted value within a group is the group mean.

This series of models leading from the null to the IV model can be represented graphically as shown in Fig. 10.18 (the calculation of the lofsos figures is explained online).

In this figure I have compressed the horizontal distance between 4 and 40 parameters to show the more important details. Model A is evidently considerably better than the null model: it accounts for most of the discrepancy between the null and the actual data. The improvement is due to the application of the linear contrast.

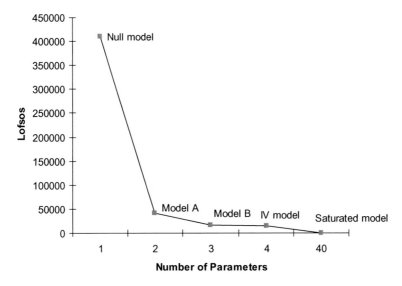

Fig. 10.18. Graph of all models of the data.

Model B is also doing useful work: it accounts for over half of the remaining sum of squares discrepancy, and this improvement is due to the quadratic contrast: Model B is just model A *plus* the effect of this contrast. Adding the cubic contrast gets us to the IV model. (The fact that a linear plus quadratic plus cubic polynomial can perfectly reproduce four group means is the mathematical truth that makes this whole thing work).

The improvement of the IV model over model B looks, and is, small and non-significant.

F-ratios are calculated by the ratio of two slopes. The first of these slopes, the number that goes on the top line of the ratio, is the slope of the line connecting the model to the previous model in this sequence. This slope represents the improvement provided by the new model. So the first slope for model A is the line connecting it to the null model, that for model B is given by the line connecting model B to model A, and that for the IV model is that connecting it to model B.

Now the big question is: *what is the second slope?*

The first answer that may occur to you is that when judging the value of model A for example, we should use the line joining model A to model B as the second slope, so that the F-ratio is F = (slope of line joining null model to model A)/(slope of line joining model A to model B). However, that is not correct. If we look on the F-ratio as a signal-to-noise ratio, the first slope being the signal and the second slope being the noise, then this cannot be correct. The difference between model A and model B is not error: it is just an extra chunk of the variability that is accounted for by the quadratic term. Only if model B were the saturated model, could we justify treating the slope as noise.

The next answer that might suggest itself is that the second slope should refer to the straight line joining model A directly to the saturated model. That would be correct if the only information we had was from model A, but there is additional useful data on the exact values of the group means, and we do not wish to throw this away.

The final answer is that the line whose slope gives the bottom line of the F-ratio is the noise component that we identified right at the beginning: **the line joining the IV model to the saturated model**. In the figure above, this slope looks steeper than it really is: that is an artefact of the way the horizontal axis has been compressed between the 4 and 40 parameter points. In fact if the axis could be represented in its actual length, this line would look nearly horizontal. The flatness of this line means that the noise component in the F-ratio is as small as we can make it. The sums of squares unaccounted for by the IV model is quite small, and the slope in question is this small sum of squares divided by 36, the horizontal distance.

The take home message from this is that when you put together a series of orthogonal contrasts in this way, the contrasts work together, as it were, in reducing the size of the error term, so that each contrast benefits from the combined efforts of all the others, and each significance test is more powerful in combination than it would be on its own. In combination, the contrasts get you all the way from the null model right down to the IV model, so the error term for each contrast is the error term for the IV model, which generally gives rise to the smallest amount of "noise" that it is possible to get from the data.

Another way of seeing this is to represent the way contrasts work in a diagram, sometimes called a "Venn diagram". The area of the circle in figure 10.19 below represents the lofsos of the null model, or the "total sum of squares". The quadrants individually also represent sums of squares, in a way shortly to be explained, though of course the diagram is purely schematic: the areas are not intended to be exactly proportional to the sums of squares.

Applying the first, linear contrast, which gives brings us to model A, the amount of lofsos represented by quadrant 1 is subtracted from the original amount. The area of quadrant 1 is the drop in lofsos going from the null model to model A, in Figure 10.18. The lofsos of model A is now what remains when quadrant 1 is removed, which is of course just the sum of the areas of quadrants 2, 3 and 4. Applying an additional second contrast, producing model B, the lofsos is now reduced by the area of quadrant 2, representing the drop in lofsos between model A and model B in Figure 10.18. The lofsos of model B must then be what remains, i.e., the areas of quadrants 3 and 4 combined. The third contrast takes us from model B to the IV model, a further reduction in sums of squares represented by quadrant 3. The remaining sums of squares is represented by quadrant 4.

What this means is that the error component — the lofsos in other words — has been reduced from the whole circle with the null model, to just quadrant 4 with the IV model. But this has another implication. It might seem that the value of the first contrast — which takes us from the null model to model A — should be judged on the basis of the "error" term for that model alone: in other words, the whole of quadrants 2, 3 and 4. That is how the *F*-ratio is calculated when the null model is compared with a more complex model on its own. So the value of the contrast (the reduction in error, that is, quadrant 1) should be compared with the whole of the remaining area as the error term.

But the clever thing about using the contrasts together, is that the correct error term for this one contrast is *just quadrant 4 on its own*. It benefits from the fact that quadrants 2 and 3 are not really error components, since they are swept up by contrasts 2 and 3. The contribution of the first contrast is still the area of quadrant 1, but now the error term is quadrant 4, not the sum of quadrants 2, 3 and 4. Likewise, the contribution of the second contrast — which accounts for the improvement from model A to model B — is still given by the area of the second quadrant, but the error term is just quadrant 4, not quadrants 3 and 4 combined. This has a direct effect on the F-ratios for the three contrasts, since the bottom line for the F-ratio (the "noise" component) is just the error term divided by the remaining parameters — in this case 36 — separating the IV model from the saturated model. A smaller error term means a smaller noise component, and a larger signal-to-noise ratio (see Fig. 10.19).

All this may seem a somewhat elaborate way of expressing a basic truth about contrasts. However, the principle is of more general application. The fundamental idea is this. With any set of data, there are usually various different "ways" in which you can try to explain the variability in the DV. For any particular "way", it will explain a chunk of variation, and will fail to explain the remainder: that remainder is "error". However, if you have several ways of

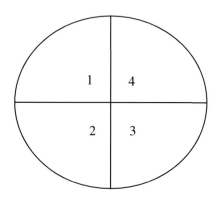

Fig. 10.19.   Dividing the null model lofsos into three contrast contributions and one error term.

explaining variation which are non-overlapping, then they can be made to work together, so that the error term is the *intersection* of the individual error terms, usually a much smaller area. Each "way" can now be tested against an error term which is not the variation that is not explained by that "way", but the error term consisting of variation which is not explained by *any* of the "ways". The error term is like a herd of rabbits which is crowded into a smaller and smaller part of a hay field as the hay is harvested. Each "way" harvests its own bit of hay, and they all benefit from the small area left at the end.

The reason for the importance of the principle will be evident in the next chapter, where multiple IVs are considered. The power of Fisher's analysis of variance method is that it uses as many "ways" as possible to account for variance, leaving the smallest possible error term, from which all the "ways" benefit. And the "ways" themselves are not arbitrary ideas: they can be understood in specific, meaningful contexts.

I have ignored one contentious issue in this chapter: that of whether one needs to find a significant result in the omnibus *F*-test in one-way ANOVA **before** proceeding either to *a priori* or to *post hoc* testing. The smart money favours the answer "no" to this question (See Wilkinson *et al.*, 1999 in the further reading section). The reason why it is traditional to do an omnibus test first is due to a misunderstanding concerning Fisher's so-called LSD, or least significant difference test. The topic is covered in the online material.

Effect parameters

Most books on statistics define models in terms of an algebraic equation giving the values of the data in terms of what are known as effect parameters. These equations probably do not have much impact on the non-mathematically minded, but I need to touch on them here simply in order to define effect parameters, which are required in Chapter 12 and which may also help to understand what is going on in one-way ANOVA from a somewhat different point of view. And those readers who like algebra will probably find this approach useful.

In Chapter 2, I stated the basic conceptual equation relating a model to its underlying dataset in the form:

$$\text{Data} = \text{model} + \text{error.}$$

In the case of one-way ANOVA, the null model approximates everything by μ, the grand overall mean of the whole dataset.

If the dataset is divided into n groups, the null model can be written:

$$Y_{ij} = \mu + \varepsilon_{ij},$$

where Y_{ij} is the ith observation in group j, and ε_{ij} is the error term (that is, the difference between Y_{ij} and μ).

How does the IV model appear in this format? Suppose the group numbered j has a group mean of m_j. Then the IV model can be written:

$$Y_{ij} = m_j + e_{ij},$$

where now e_{ij} is the error term for the IV model, which will always be no larger than the previous error term ε_{ij}, and in general will be smaller.

This can be written in another way, which shows the linkage between the two models in a clearer manner. To discover this, first write m_j in terms of the grand mean μ as follows:

$$m_j = \mu + (m_j - \mu).$$

This is of course a simple algebraic identity and tells us nothing. But now consider the quantities $(m_j - \mu)$, as j varies from 1 to n. These numbers are known as the **effect parameters**. If, using some different symbolism they are written α_j, then the previous equation can be written more meaningfully as

$$m_j = \mu + \alpha_j.$$

The IV model can now be restated as follows by substitution in the previous equation:

$Y_{ij} = \mu + \alpha_j + e_{ij}$, where the connection with the previous null model is now more apparent. The IV model differs primarily according to the effect parameters, plus a different set of error terms. The error terms represent random noise, and the effect parameters represent the differences between the group means.

The effect parameters, in other words, show how the individual group means vary away from the overall grand mean μ, and they arguably have a more meaningful interpretation than the individual group means. They show for each group how far that group mean is from the overall mean, and indicate, if you will, how *untypical* that group is, in the sense that an effect parameter of zero signifies that group differs not at all from the overall mean, whereas a large effect parameter (whether large and positive, or large and negative) suggests that the group is not adequately represented by the group mean.

Of course, in any given sample the effect parameters are themselves subject to random noise. Effect parameters are *estimates* as to how far, if at all, the groups are genuinely drawn from different populations. The null hypothesis states that the true values of the effect parameters are all zero. If the IV model is significantly better than the null model by the *F*-ratio test of significance, this is telling us that the effect parameters are *not* all zero.

For the mathematically inclined, I should mention one fact about model comparisons which can sometimes be quite useful in calculations, and which is of theoretical interest as well. I will not discuss this in detail here, but will only mention that the *difference* in the lofsos distances from the data for a pair of models can sometimes be calculated without knowing the actual data, provided only that the models are known and one is nested inside the other in a particular way. For example, the between groups sum of squares in one-way ANOVA, which is the difference in the lofsos values for the null and IV models, can be calculated by as the sum of the squared differences between the grand mean and the group means, weighted by group sizes. One does not have to know the actual data values to find this. This corresponds to the fact that in a certain vector space, two vectors are orthogonal, and that the vectors obey a generalisation of Pythagoras' theorem. This will be explained in the online material.

Chapter 11

Multifactorial Designs and Their ANOVA Counterparts

SUMMARY

Additive effects for multiple IVs, and interactions. Balanced designs. Inputting multifactorial data in SPSS. The full model, and its characteristics in the SPSS output. Main effects illustrated in 2×2 ANOVA. Omnibus model testing as safeguard against type I error rate inflation. Simple main effects. Three way and higher order ANOVA. Three way interactions from means plots. Building up the full model from main effects and interactions. Qualitative and quantitative interactions.

NEED TO KNOW

In this chapter, we will extend the simple one-way ANOVA, which deals with just a single IV, to the case of two or more IVs. Why do we need to do this? Because some experimental hypotheses are too complicated to be tested with just a single IV. For example, some diseases, such as TB, are becoming resistant to treatment with any one antibiotic on its own. We may need to find out about so-called multidrug therapies, in which various combinations of medications are administered. Or it may be that in examining the emotional effects of music, we wish to look at the combined effects of two variables on mood: major/minor key and fast vs. slow speed.

Such effects are called **multifactorial**, that is, they are affected by multiple IVs, or factors.

Incidentally, do not be confused between the words **multifactorial** and **multivariate**. In statistics, multivariate refers to an analysis in which there is more than one *dependent* variable, and multifactorial to more than one *independent* variable. In regression, where there is more than one independent variable it is called multiple regression. In this book we will not be treating multivariate statistics.

Traditionally, science has focused on manipulating just one independent variable at a time while keeping all the others fixed, but this is not always the most useful way of exploring causal relationships.

It may be that the introduction of additional IVs is inevitable, as it is dictated by a requirement to describe a complex reality, but this does not make it any easier to understand the concept of causality. The notion of a causal link between an IV and a DV is quite intuitive, but it does not extend in a simple way when more IVs are introduced. You might think that the only question that arises is whether the new IVs each have a separate causal link with the DV, and that the task is completed when one specifies for each IV whether such a link exists. For example, if the DV is happiness and the IVs are state of health and income, it makes sense that going from being ill to being well will make you happier, and going from being poor to being rich will also make you happier, and that this is all we need to know.

Sometimes the situation is indeed this simple. In the case of health and riches, it may be that the two effects are independent: that getting rich makes you happier whether you are well or ill, and getting well makes you happier, by the same amount, whether you are poor or rich. The two IVs in this case have what is called an **additive** effect: they act on happiness without interfering with one another, so that the effect on happiness of going from a state of sick poverty to one of healthy prosperity is the sum of the separate effects of health and wealth.

However, the effects need not be additive, as a simple example illustrates. Some years ago the UK was crippled by a national coal miners' strike. The country suffered increasing power cuts and general discomfort, and the question arose of who was to blame? Incidentally, the word used by Aristotle which is usually translated as "cause", αἴτιον or aition, also had the connotation of blame or responsibility for an effect (it is also the root for the word "aetiology", or the study of the causes of disease). It seems to be a human trait to seek out some one person or agency to blame for any negative happening. With the miners' strike, the miners criticised the employers (the National Coal Board) for poor conditions and inadequate pay. They argued that there would have been no strike, and so no misery, but for this. The NCB laid the responsibility for the strike on the miners' militant leadership, without whom it would not have happened. Either the NCB or the miners' leadership could be blamed, and the choice was usually determined by political prejudice.

Suppose we try to analyse this in terms of two IVs: behaviour of the NCB and behaviour of the miners, and one DV, the level of misery caused by the strike.

In reality it makes no sense to blame either party exclusively, since causality here was not additive. In the event that the miners' leadership had been less hardline there would have been no strike, nor would there have been if the NCB had been more conciliatory.[1] Starting with both variables fixed at the levels corresponding to good behaviour by the NCB, and non-militant miners, changing just one of them (to a hard-line stance by either the NCB or the miners but not both) would have had no effect. Adding two null effects is still a null effect, but this was not the result of changing *both* variables at once, because the effect was not in fact additive. Describing causality in this situation requires more than a simple attribution to one independent variable or the other. It needs the concept of an **interaction** between two IVs, in which the cumulative effect is different from that of either causal variable on its own: there is a kind of synergy between them.

---

[1] I cannot prove these statements of course, but I am asking you to suppose for the sake of the argument that they are true, for illustrative purposes.

We need to consider the question in more detail. For many purposes, the main ideas can be understood quite well by dealing with a very basic case: that of two nominal IVs, each with two levels, as was the case above, and a continuous DV. Let us take an example with data that I have made up, but which I hope sounds plausible, that of the effects of drug treatment and music therapy on a sample of stroke patients. The patients are divided into two groups according as whether or not they get the drug treatment or a placebo, and further, into a music therapy treatment group, and a control group which did an alternative activity, possibly conventional physiotherapy, at the times when the treatment group was engaged with music. The DV was the change in mobility before and after a three month period during which the treatments were given, measured on some standard scale.

If this were a single IV, two-group design, allocation of patients could be randomised to treatment and placebo groups. A similar strategy can be taken with this double IV situation: both music and drug therapies can be given at random to patients, so this is a fully experimental design, but there is a further consideration. In an RCT, we will generally want the treatment and control groups to be as nearly as possible of equal size (it can be shown that this maximises the chance of detecting an effect); but here we have two IVs rather than one. How does this change things? We have to decide not just between two alternatives for each patient, but between four. A particular patient, John Smith, could get drug and music therapy treatment, drugs but no music therapy, music therapy but no drugs, or neither. John Smith would get precisely one of these alternatives for the trial period: it is an independent group or between-subjects design.

These four options could each have different effects on mobility. We need to make sure that all four options are given a fair trial by allocating patients so as to explore the effects of each of them. Missing out possible alternatives would be a mistake. For example, if we just give the drug and the music therapy together to half the patients, and nothing at all to the other half, omitting the treatments involving just the drug or just the therapy separately, we might find greater improvement in the treatment group but we

Table 11.1.   Cells in a two factor design.

	Music therapy included in treatment	Music therapy not included
Drug therapy included	Patients receive: drug and music	Patients receive: drug and no music
Drug therapy not included	Patients receive: no drug and music	Patients receive: no drug and no music

would be unable to tell if that had been due to the drug or the therapy. We would say in this situation that the effects of the drug and the music therapy had been subject to **confounding**. The answer is to have not two, but four groups: drug and therapy, drug and no therapy, no drug and therapy, and no drug with no therapy. This can be visualised in Table 11.1.

Depending on whether or not they receive drug treatment, therapy treatment, both, or neither, each patient will be allocated to one **cell** of this table. There are four cells, and the best option is usually to choose a **balanced design**, in which the number of participants in each of the available cells is equal. Mathematical complications arise when this is not the case, and henceforth all designs will be assumed to be balanced (the alternatives are considered in the online material). The essential precaution of random allocation means, in this instance, that patients will be randomly allocated to each of the four cells.

Suppose this has now been done, which I will illustrate with an absurdly small sample below, giving the identities of the individuals selected for each cell (see Table 11.2).

So far this is just an outline for an experiment, but once the work has been done we can substitute actual numbers for each participant, representing the DV, in this case improvement in mobility (see Table 11.3).[2]

The negative number for Felix shows that his mobility actually got worse during the experimental period.

---

[2] This means that the DV is the **gain score** in some measurement of mobility.

Table 11.2. Participants allocated to cells in two factor design.

	Music therapy included in treatment	Music therapy not included
Drug therapy included	Tom, Harriet	Sandra, Bert
Drug therapy not included	Jo, Harry	Felix, Nicola

Table 11.3. DV values in cells of two factor design.

	Music therapy included in treatment	Music therapy not included
Drug therapy included	Tom (3.4), Harriet (5.6)	Sandra (2.8), Bert (1.7)
Drug therapy not included	Jo (2.9), Harry (3.3)	Felix (–0.4), Nicola (0.9)

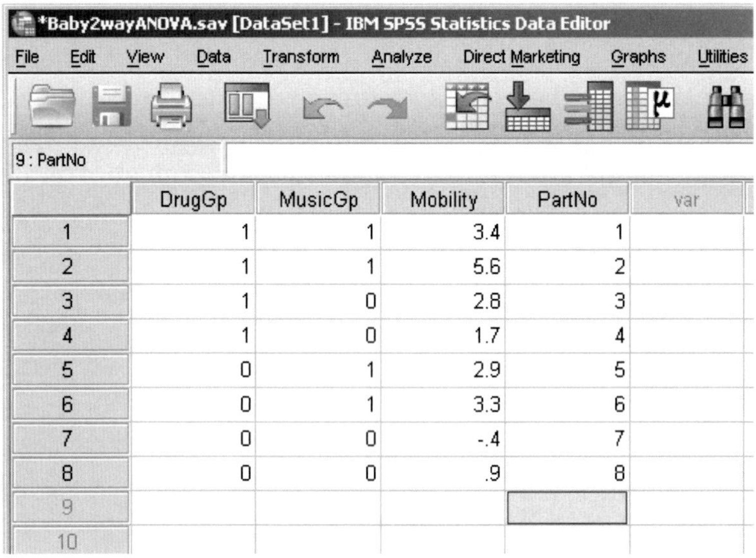

	DrugGp	MusicGp	Mobility	PartNo	var
1	1	1	3.4	1	
2	1	1	5.6	2	
3	1	0	2.8	3	
4	1	0	1.7	4	
5	0	1	2.9	5	
6	0	1	3.3	6	
7	0	0	-.4	7	
8	0	0	.9	8	
9					
10					

Fig. 11.1. SPSS display for two factor dataset.

When this data is input into SPSS, it will appear as in shown in Fig. 11.1 (you can access it direct as Dataset4 in the online material for this chapter).

Ignore "Cheat" for the moment. The two IVs are shown as "DrugGp" and "MusicGp", the DV as "Mobility", where in a

	Music therapy included in treatment	Music therapy not included
Drug therapy included	Tom (3.4), Harriet (5.6)	Sandra (2.8), Bert (1.7)
Drug therapy not included	Jo (2.9), Harry (3.3)	Felix (-0.4), Nicola (0.9)

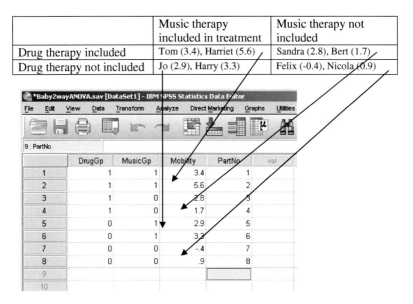

Fig. 11.2.   Details of data entry in two factor dataset.

common convention zero means the patient does not get the active treatment for that variable. So patient 5 receives the music therapy but not the drug, patient 7 gets neither, and patient 2 gets both. I have added a new variable, "PartNo", participant number, to encode the identity of the participants. The data on each row represents all we know about a given participant, and different rows correspond to different participants, so this system gives a method of keeping track of who is who.

There is a link between this dataset and the table above, which I reproduce in Fig. 11.2, along with the dataset.

The numbers for the cells, representing the values of the DV for the participants assigned to those cells of the experimental design, appear not in a 2×2 grid but arranged vertically above one another. First comes the top left cell, represented by the first two numbers in the DV column, then the top right cell, represented by the next two, and so on. They appear in this order because I have ordered the numbers encoding the IVs, in the two left-hand columns, in a systematic way. If you look at the way the zeroes and ones are arranged in the columns for the two IVs, you will notice that they appear in a regular pattern. The two values of the music group variable are given for a fixed value of the drug group variable, which is held constant in the first four rows. This is not essential, but it does help to ensure that you don't lose count of where you have got to when inputting data. It makes sense to have the cell data input in some logical order.

This business of defining cells can be done quite generally for any number of IVs with any number of levels. The key thing to remember is that when the coded IVs are put into SPSS, each cell corresponds to one and only one sequence of numbers, reading across the IVs. For the situation above, the first cell corresponded to coding sequence 1, 1, the second cell to 1, 0, the third one to 0, 1 and the fourth to 0, 0.

With three two-level IVs, there will be three columns in SPSS corresponding to the IVs, and eight rather than four cells. These cells can be represented across the three IV columns as shown in Table 11.4.

Of course, each of these rows will be repeated as many times as there are participants in that cell, and for each participant, that row will record the value of the DV for that participant, in the DV column. In the example above there were just two per cell, but of course realistically you would plan for many more than that.

Table 11.4.   Correspondence between IV column entries and cells in SPSS.

1	1	1
1	1	0
1	0	1
1	0	0
0	1	1
0	1	0
0	0	1
0	0	0

The same device can be used with IVs having more than two levels. The only thing to remember is that each cell is still represented by one and only one combination of values for each IV. With two IVs each having three levels, there would be nine cells, encoded by all possible sequences from [2, 2, 2] to [0, 0, 0].

I have rather laboured this idea of cells firstly because in my experience, it can cause confusion at the outset with multifactorial ANOVA, and secondly because the cells are really the foundation of everything that happens with this method of analysis, as I will proceed to show.

Using all the cell means: the full model

In the one-way ANOVA case, I explained that the omnibus ANOVA test examined whether the IV model was better than the null model, where the null model assigns each participant the mean of the whole set of values of the DV, and the IV model is more granular, and assigns a participant the mean for the group to which the participant belongs.

With multifactorial ANOVA, with more than one IV, the number of cells or subgroups that are defined by the different levels of the various IVs is clearly the product of the levels of the individual IVs. The terminology used to describe an ANOVA in which there are two IVs, each of two levels, as in the example above, is a 2×2 ANOVA. The "2×2" part is significant, as it reminds us that there are four cells. With two IVs, one of 3 and one of 4 levels, it would be a 3×4 ANOVA, and there would be 12 cells, one for each combination of values of the IVs. With a three way ANOVA with IVs of 2, 3 and 5 levels, it would be a $2 \times 3 \times 5$ ANOVA and there would be 30 cells.

A 30-cell ANOVA,[3] can be modelled by taking the means of the values of the DV in each of the 30 cells. This is the obvious way to go in building the best alternative model to the data, since it uses

---

[3] Strictly speaking it is the set of data that has 30 cells rather than the ANOVA, which is a method of analysis rather than a collection of numbers. I am using terms loosely here.

all the information about the participants that the IVs alone give us. This model is termed the **full factorial model**, or the **full model** for short. This suggests that we should start off by comparing the full model with the null model by calculating the F-ratio and testing whether it is significantly greater than one.

Working directly with the data in an Excel spreadsheet, the lofsos for the null model, i.e., the DEVSQ function applied to all the data, is 22.915. The cells consist of consecutive pairs of data, and adding the DEVSQ amounts for each of the four cells to find the lofsos for the full model gives 3.95.

The full model has four parameters, and the null model one parameter, with a difference of 3, so the slope of the first line in the lofsos diagram is $(22.915 - 3.95)/3 = 6.322$. The slope of the second line is $3.95/(8 - 4) = 0.987$, because the saturated model has eight parameters and the full model has four parameters. The ratio is $F(3, 4) = 6.4017$.

To get SPSS to do the calculation for you, requires the Analyze ≫ General Linear Model ≫ Univariate program. NB do not go by mistake to Analyze ≫ Generalised Linear Models, as this is the wrong item altogether.

In the Univariate window put Mobility into the Dependent Variable slot, and the DrugGp and MusicGp IVs into the Fixed Factor(s) slot. Click OK and the box in Table 11.5 will appear.

The output of immediate relevance is on the rows corresponding to the "Source" (i.e., model) for the Corrected Model, the Error, and the Corrected Total rows. I will explain DrugGp, MusicGp and DrugGp * MusicGp later. Do not worry about what a type III sum of squares is; where cell sizes are all equal as here, the type makes no difference anyway.

Just to get some puzzling stuff out of the way first, "Total" refers to the model where all the data is approximated by the value zero. This is technically a zero parameter model (not because it uses zero as an estimate, but because it uses an estimate not taken from the data: no parameters are used up by estimation). This means that its degrees of freedom — the difference between its parameters and the saturated model's parameters — is eight. The sum of squares

Table 11.5.   Output of significance tests in two way ANOVA.

Tests of between-subjects effects

Dependent Variable: Measure of mobility after treatment

Source	Type III sum of squares	df	Mean Square	F	Sig.
Corrected Model	18.965[a]	3	6.322	6.402	0.052
Intercept	51.005	1	51.005	51.651	0.002
DrugGp	5.780	1	5.780	5.853	0.073
MusicGp	13.005	1	13.005	13.170	0.022
DrugGp * MusicGp	0.180	1	0.180	0.182	0.691
Error	3.950	4	0.987		
Total	73.920	8			
Corrected Total	22.915	7			

[a]R-Squared = 0.828 (Adjusted R-Squared = 0.698).

figure for Total is just what you get when you subtract zero from all the data (i.e., leave them unchanged), square the data, and add them. You can check this for yourself if you wish, but the Total model seems pointless to me and I am not sure why SPSS bothers to mention it. I am only explaining it here because I should raise the fact that zero parameter models do exist, and in some cases they can actually be useful (I will introduce an example later where this is the case).

The "Intercept" value, by the way, is the reduction in lofsos between the Total model and the null model. The significance test, in the right hand column, is testing whether the null model fits the data better than the Total model: SPSS does this in case that is of the slightest interest to anybody.

The Corrected Total figure refers to the null model. It has one parameter and therefore seven degrees of freedom. The sum of squares figure is the lofsos value given above for the null model.

The Corrected Model and Error rows are perhaps somewhat confusing. The Corrected Model refers to the full factorial model, but the lofsos for that model is found not on the Corrected Model row, but in the Error row. The error sum of squares is, in the way I have approached models, *identical* to the lofsos for the full model. What SPSS calls the Corrected Model sum of squares is the *difference* between the lofsos for the null model and that for the full models.

The basic calculations are of course identical, but I think the reason SPSS does it this way is that the *F*-ratio for the full model is calculated by taking the ratio of two slopes, and the first slope (of the line joining the full model to the null model) is found by subtracting the full model lofsos from the null model lofsos — this is the vertical "drop" part of the slope — and dividing by the horizontal distance, the difference in degrees of freedom. The only point of the row headed Corrected Model is to present the figures leading to the calculation of this *F*-ratio. The slope of the first line is given in the "Mean Square" column of this row.

The Error row gives rise in the Mean Square column to the slope of the *second* line involved in the *F*-ratio. This is another reason for separating out the full model lofsos and giving it a special name as the Error term. Because it will turn out that just as with the multiple contrasts applied to one-way ANOVA, the distance between the null model and the full model can be sliced up into bite-sized chunks. All the chunks together go to make up the full model, but unlike the full model they can be interpreted in a meaningful fashion. And — this is the really neat thing about ANOVA — they all benefit from the hard work of the full model in reducing the remaining sum of squares to the smallest value possible: the Error sum of squares.

The "chunks" comprise the two main effects and the interaction, which are on the rows listed between the Intercept and Error rows: a DrugGp main effect, a MusicGp main effect, and an interaction which is described as DrugGp * MusicGp. In calculating their *F*-ratios they all use the low slope given by the small Error term as their "noise" component. In combination they sweep up the "good" variance and leave the minimum amount left over of "bad" variance. All benefit from this minimising of the error component.

Two main effects and an interaction: before speaking further about how they work in terms of *F*-ratios, it is high time to try to explain what it is they do, and why it is — generally speaking — so much more useful to think in these terms, rather than in terms of an undifferentiated full model. This is somewhat reminiscent of the situation with one-way ANOVA, when the omnibus test usually told us very little: it was contrasts and pairwise comparisons which were of real interest.

Main effects

If you did not know about multifactorial ANOVA, the obvious way to analyse this data would be by doing a pair of *t*-tests, or equivalently one-way ANOVAs, to find the effects of the drug and music treatments separately. The two main effects correspond to doing exactly this, only better.

To show how this works I want first to do the one-way ANOVAs, as this may help to understand how the two-way ANOVA works. If you go back into the univariate ANOVA menu and remove the MusicGp variable, so that the only IV is DrugGp, the output is as shown in Table 11.6.

The model is now the IV model for the DrugGp variable, and the sum of squares for the model is given as 5.78: just exactly the same as for the DrugGp main effect in the two-way ANOVA. This number measures how much better the IV model fits the data, compared with the null model, and it is the *same* in both analyses. And yet the *F*-ratio for DrugGp is 5.853 in the two-way ANOVA, and only 2.024 in the one-way ANOVA. Why is this?

If you look at the error term sum of squares in the one-way ANOVA, it is 17.135, compared with 3.95 in the two-way ANOVA.

Well that's your problem, right there.

How did the two-way ANOVA manage to chew off (17.135 — 3.95) = 13.185 units of useless error? If you look at the sum of squares for the main effect of MusicGp, which is 13.005, and for the interaction, which is 0.18, you find that these add up exactly to the missing error term.

Table 11.6.   Output when MusicGp variable is removed.

Tests of between-subjects effects

Dependent Variable: Measure of mobility after treatment

Source	Type III Sum of Squares	df	Mean Square	F	Sig.
Corrected Model	5.780[a]	1	5.780	2.024	0.205
Intercept	51.005	1	51.005	17.860	0.006
DrugGp	5.780	1	5.780	2.024	0.205
Error	17.135	6	2.856		
Total	73.920	8			
Corrected Total	22.915	7			

[a]R-Squared = 0.252 (Adjusted R-Squared = 0.128).

The magic of ANOVA is that it turns error into information, by accounting for the error in terms of other, known effects. By giving error a name, we draw its sting. It is similar conceptually to the situation with accumulating contrasts, illustrated in chapter 9 by the circle of four quadrants. The main effect of DrugGp corresponds to quadrant 1, and considered on its own we have no alternative but to treat the remaining variability, quadrants 2, 3 and 4, as error. But if we can sweep up quadrant 2 as the main effect of the other variable, MusicGp, and quadrant 3 as the interaction term (of which more in a moment), then the only error left is in the much smaller quadrant 4.

In this case, where IVs have two levels, main effects can also be viewed in terms of raw effect sizes, just as with a single, two-level IV. The simplest way to find the raw effect size of DrugGp for example, is to carry out a *t*-test with this as the IV and Mobility as the DV. The result is that there is a difference between the drug and no drug treatments of 1.7 units, and the mean for the drug subgroup is higher. Of course, to be able to assert that this difference is real and not just the result of random sampling error, we need to have a significant result for the ANOVA main effect test for DrugGp, which we do not have: the *p*-value is 0.073.

In general, with IVs having more than two levels, significant main effects cannot be interpreted in terms of raw effect sizes in this way. They can, however, be analysed using suitable contrasts, as with the case of one-way ANOVA. Contrasts with multifactorial ANOVA in general requires the ability to write some basic syntax commands in SPSS, using something called *L*-matrices. I will put a short course on contrast syntax with the online material.

However, there is a way to do contrasts using only one-way ANOVA. It may look like cheating, but it seems to work. This is by turning the multifactorial ANOVA into a one-way ANOVA, by creating a new single IV, which has different values for each of the separate cells. I have done this with Dataset4, entering the IV named "cheat". If you use the Analyze >> Compare Means >> One-Way ANOVA menu (it doesn't work with the Univariate ANOVA) you can now test for the main effect of DrugGp by entering the contrast (1, 1, −1, −1), which compares the first two cells (for which drug treatment is present) with the second two (drug absent). You get exactly the same p-value as with the main effect of DrugGp in the two-way ANOVA, and other more complicated contrasts can be done this way too. Note by the way that the IV model with the cheat IV is equivalent to the full model with the two-way ANOVA and both IVs: they both use the cell means as the basis for constructing a model, and only differ in the way they designate the cells.

The last point on main effects is to show how they can be illustrated graphically. This is useful, as it will help to understand what interactions are all about. Use the Univariate program, enter both IVs, and press the Plots button. The box as shown in Fig. 11.3 will appear.

Either move the MusicGp into the Horizontal Axis slot and the DrugGp into the Separate Lines slot (option 1) or vice versa (option 2): the appearance changes but not in an essential way. Then press the Add button (which is greyed out in the screenshot above), press Continue, and OK. If you chose (option 1) the result is shown in Fig. 11.4.

Actually the original plot has solid lines, which is misleading, as it suggests that the Music therapy IV varies continuously

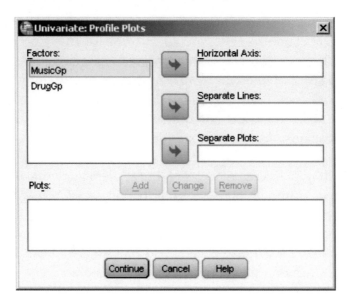

Fig. 11.3.   Profile plots options for two way ANOVA.

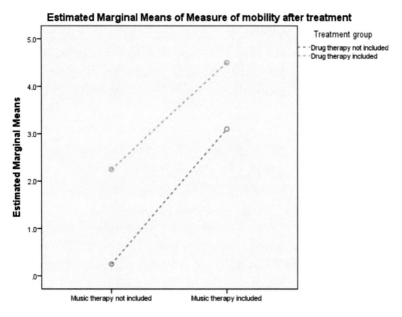

Fig. 11.4. Plot of cell means in two way ANOVA.

between its two values, which is not the case. I have tried to reduce this false impression by making them dotted lines. But the lines serve one purpose: by linking the two endpoints they suggest that the two points have something in common, which they do: they have the same value for the other IV, DrugGp. The left-hand circle on the blue line represents the cell mean for the (no drug, no music) cell, the right-hand circle on that line is the (no drug, with music) cell, and so on. The blue line as a whole represents the no-drug subgroup, composed of these two cells. The green line as a whole represents the with-drug subgroup.

What is the mean for the no-drug subgroup? It is the average of the means of the two cells that comprise it. This average is the vertical measure corresponding to the point half way between the two points on the blue line. The mean for the with-drug subgroup is the corresponding point for the green line. I have indicated these in Fig. 11.5, the solid line showing the with-drug, the dotted line the no-drug mean:

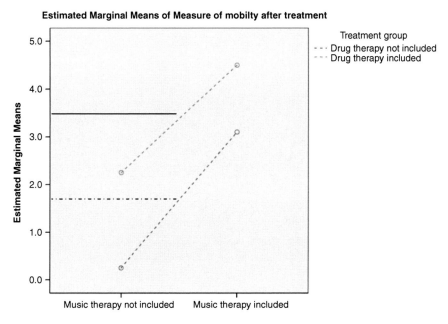

Fig. 11.5. Averages of MusicGp cell means for each value of the DrugGp variable.

The with-drug mean looks to be around 3.4 (actually 3.375) and the no-drug mean around 1.7 (actually, 1.675). The lines were drawn by eye, so the numbers are close enough to provide some assurance that the principle is correct.

We can now find the visual counterpart of the *raw effect size of the drug treatment*: it is the vertical distance between the two points on the vertical axis at the left-hand ends of the two horizontal lines, as these represent the no-drug and with-drug subgroup means.

Since these horizontal lines are parallel, this is the *same* vertical distance as that between the right-hand ends of these lines, which are the mid-points of the blue and green dotted lines. So finally, the raw effect size for the DrugGp IV — the main effect of that IV in other words — is just the length of the *red* vertical line as shown in Fig. 11.6, length 1.7 units:

Visualising the main effect of music therapy on this diagram is a little harder, but the basic idea is the same. The no-music sub-group consists of two cells: no-music no-drug, and no-music with-drug. These cells are represented by the left-hand blue and green

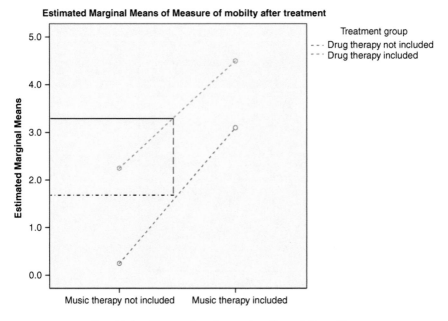

Fig. 11.6.   Illustrating the main effect of DrugGp.

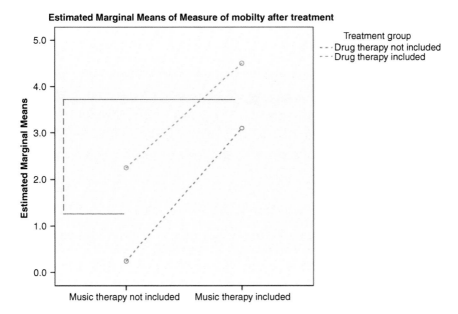

Fig. 11.7. Illustrating the main effect of MusicGp.

dots. The average of the two cell means is given by the point half way between the two. Similarly, the average of the two cell means for the with-music subgroup, are given by the point half way between the right-hand blue and green dots.

The main effect of music is given by the vertical distance between the two subgroup means. The subgroup means, and the vertical red line representing the main effect of music, are shown in Figure 11.7. The subgroup means are 1.25 (no-music) and 3.8 (with-music), so the length of the vertical line, i.e., the raw effect size of music, is 2.55 units (see Fig. 11.7).

The interaction term

The interaction supplies the missing extra piece of the puzzle that we need to move from a knowledge of main effects, to a full knowledge of the configuration of the cell means.

If all we knew was these two main effects and the overall group mean, we could reconstruct most of the information about the cell means, i.e., the information contained in the full model. But not all of it. Knowing the separate effects of music and drugs, we do not know how they combine. This is what the interaction term tells us.

If the effects were purely additive, then the green and blue dotted lines would be parallel. For those who understand geometry, this is because the effect of drug therapy would be the same irrespective of whether music was present as part of the therapy or not, so the vertical sides of the rhombus joining the four cell plots above would be equal in length, making it a parallelogram.

The simple rule is: if the effects in this sample are precisely additive, the blue and green lines are parallel, and conversely any lack of parallelism in the blue and green lines indicates lack of additivity in the sample.[4] Lack of parallelism, and lack of additivity, is the essence of what an interaction term means.

Put another way which may be easier to understand, if there is an interaction term in the analysis, this signifies that **the effect of one variable depends on the level of the other variable**. In the present case, the green and blue lines are almost parallel, and this is reflected in the small sum of squares value for the interaction term, and the fact that it is not significant.

Interpreting the results

The case we have considered is the simplest design possible that still qualifies as a multifactorial ANOVA: a two-factor analysis, each factor having two levels. And yet even in this very basic situation there are subtleties over how to report what is found. Abelson (1995, p. 112, Table 6.2) gives no fewer than six possible combinations of main effects and interactions, together with four different ways of interpreting them. I will attempt to summarise his perceptive analysis in the online material, but to reduce it to its essentials,

---

[4] I stress the words "in the sample". We cannot generalise to the population unless the interaction term is significant.

the advice generally given is to *examine the interaction term first*. If it is significant, report the interaction.

Some say that any main effects should be ignored in the presence of an interaction. Abelson would agree in some cases, disagree in others. It may sound as though I am being evasive, but this probably depends on the research hypothesis, and the effects of likely interest in the context of the experiment. I will deal in a little more detail in the GD section, where simple main effects are explained. To understand the issue properly requires also the concept of qualitative and quantitative interactions, defined below.

If the interaction term is not significant, there is no controversy: report the significant main effect or effects, if any. The absence of interaction means that the two IVs appear to be acting independently of one another. Beware of assuming that the absence of a *significant* interaction means that there is *no* interaction; absence of evidence is not evidence of absence. It may be that the sample size is just too small to detect it. But in the presence of significant main effect(s) and a non-significant interaction, you would be justified in citing the main effect(s) without qualification.

In the present case, subject to one criticism discussed at the start of the GD section, in the absence of an interaction and the presence of a significant effect of the music IV but not the drug IV, you would be justified in reporting that there was evidence that music therapy had an effect on mobility (and a positive one, given the subgroup means), but that there was no strong evidence of an effect of drug treatment. Of course, in reality one would seldom conduct an experiment on such a small sample. If one did — if for example this was a small pilot experiment on a tiny convenience sample — the results might well be written up into a grant application in which mention would be made of the fact that the *p*-value for the drug treatment was as small as 0.073 (*p*-values between 0.05 and 0.10 are sometimes described as indicating a "trend" to significance). The application would probably suggest that an effect was present but the sample size was too small to detect it. But this raises issues of power and sample size calculation which are reserved for the online material.

GOING DEEPER

In Chapter 9, there was mention of the dangers of inflation of FW type I error rates with multiple comparisons. And yet in analysing a two-way ANOVA, where three significance tests are used — two main effects and an interaction — there was no mention of a Bonferroni or any other adjustment being necessary. The textbooks — at least the ones known to me — are mostly silent on this point, though Maxwell and Delaney (p. 259) suggest it does not matter, on the basis of their definition of familywise error rates. In the case of multiple regression, which has features in common with testing multiple main effects in ANOVA, I have seen it suggested that a Bonferroni correction is required.[5] On other sites I have seen the claim that since the main effects and interactions in ANOVA are orthogonal (i.e., the effects are independent of one another: more on this in the online material), Bonferroni corrections are unnecessary.

What follows is my personal suggestion, and feel free to ignore it. But I recommend that rather than using the rather brutal Bonferroni method, there is one quick step which one can take to reduce the FW error rate in ANOVA.[6] This is to inspect the significance test on the "Corrected Model" at the top of the output table. If this is significant, it means that the full model is preferable to the null model in fitting the data. Exploring the main effects and interactions enables one to pinpoint which of the different effects, which together make up the full model, is doing the heavy lifting in making the full model itself superior to the null model. In this case, take the p-values given *without adjustment*. If, on the other hand, the Corrected Model is not significant, I suggest that you should *stop*

---

[5] At: http://www.statsmakemecry.com/smmctheblog/bonferroni-correction-in-regression-fun-to-say-important-to.html.

[6] With ANOVA, one should probably apply the FW criterion to the whole analysis and not just individual factors separately. Hochberg and Tamhane (1987) defined "family" as "any collection of inferences for which it is meaningful to take into account some combined measure of error" and ANOVA, which defines error in terms of the residual variation when all known effects are excluded, certainly seems to fit this definition.

right there: it is unsafe to inspect the main effects and interactions, even those with significant values.

This suggestion will provoke disagreement, but to those who say it is unnecessary I offer the following consideration. (Those uninterested in these details should skip this paragraph.) I have simulated a five-way ANOVA on Excel with random number entries for the DV, so that any effects are by definition type I errors. This design yields 31 varieties of main effects and interactions, so there are certainly a large number of multiple tests being applied. Repeated simulations give, in the majority of cases, at least one significant result out of this array of tests. However, the Corrected Model test gives (as one would expect) no more than the usual one in twenty falsely significant results. Of course, five-way or even four-way ANOVAs are rare in the literature. But I would suggest that some kind of control over total type I error rates is justified even in two-way or three-way analyses, and that the Corrected Model test provides some protection, without ham-stringing the tests of real interest — those of main effects and interactions[7] — by imposing Bonferroni corrections.

Simple main effects

Staying with two-way ANOVA for the moment, it may be appropriate to carry out another form of analysis. Just as a one-way ANOVA could be broken down into orthogonal contrasts or examined using *post hoc* pairwise comparisons of means, with a dataset that is analyzed using two-way ANOVA it sometimes pays to adopt a simple main effects analysis. This is particularly the case where there is a significant interaction term.

A simple main effect is defined as the effect of varying one IV, when the other one is fixed at a certain value. As an illustration of where it might be appropriate, consider the effect of a sleeping pill,

---

[7] This approach has the merit of being applicable also to multiple regression, where the analogue of the full model tested is also provided, helpfully, at the top of the list of outputs by SPSS. Five-way ANOVAs may be as rare as hen's teeth, but regressions with 10 or 20 predictors are rather more common, and pose a similar threat of inflated type I error rates.

Ambien, on men and women. It appears that the genders metabolise Ambien differently, and that the blood levels of the active ingredient can reach levels 45% higher in women than in men. As a result, some women still had sufficient in their system to impair their ability to drive, the morning after taking Ambien.[8]

If one were investigating this effect, one might set up a randomised study of individuals with sleep problems, using a balanced design (that is, equal cell sizes) with two independent group variables: gender, and Ambien use. All participants would be tested on a demanding cognitive task (possibly involving reaction time, if ability to drive was in question) the morning after a night spent either with, or without the use of Ambien.

The following data on cell means is entirely made up, but it illustrates what *might* have been the outcome of such a trial:

- Mean score of males having taken Ambien: 73%,
- Mean score of males not having taken Ambien: 61%,
- Mean score of females having taken Ambien: 48%,
- Mean score of females not having taken Ambien: 65%.

You carry out a conventional two-way ANOVA on these data, and find that there is no main effect of drug, a main effect of gender, and an interaction. The main effect of gender is that men score higher than women. However, it would be really dumb to stop short at reporting a main effect and an interaction in this case. Before reading further, look at the plot of cell means and decide how *you* would interpret the result (Fig. 11.8).

This is an example that is crying out for a simple main effects analysis. The main effect to be dissected here is that of the Ambien drug: it is close to zero, but only because that main effect is *the combination of two simple main effects which cancel out*: the simple main effect of the drug for men (which is positive) and for women (which is negative). An analysis as basic as doing a *t*-test comparing the drug vs. no-drug cells for men, and separately for women, would probably disclose this.

---

[8]This is a real example: see http://drugabuse.com/mars-vs-venus-how-does-gender-affect-prescription-drugs/

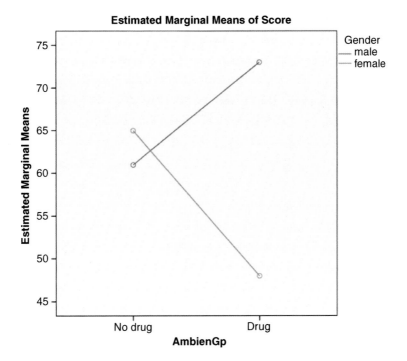

Fig. 11.8.   Plot of cell means for Ambien data.

All analyses are better if you can tell a story explaining the results. Here, the story behind the simple main effects is probably this. Men and women who do not take any drug do roughly the same on the test: the test is gender neutral. But men who take Ambien get a better night's sleep than those who do not, and therefore perform better on the test because they are more alert. Women on the other hand perform worse on the test if they take Ambien, because they are still half asleep the morning after, before the drug has washed out of their systems. This drug effect for women overwhelms the positive impact of getting a better night's sleep.[9] A main effect which turns out to comprise two simple main

---

[9] The end of the story is that the FDA recommended that the standard dose of Ambien for women be halved.

effects working in opposite directions typically creates a significant interaction, as here (can you see why?).[10]

Why is there an apparent main effect of gender? This is an artefact of the presence of the with-drug cells. Without the Ambien, on a level playing field, men and women do practically the same on the test (the two no-drug means are just 4% apart). The main effect is entirely driven by the impact of the with-drug condition, shown by the large gender difference in the two right-hand cell means. Actually, you could have found this by doing a simple main effects analysis on the gender variable: very little effect at one level and a large effect at the other level.

That makes a much more convincing, and interesting, analysis than if you follow a mindless adherence to the main effects and interaction procedure. The take-home lesson is, always look at a visual presentation of your data and use a common-sense check that your interpretation of the analysis is intelligent. In this strategy, the use of simple main effects analysis can be valuable.

Three-way and higher order ANOVAs

If there are three or more IVs, the number of main effects and interactions increases, approximately doubling for each additional IV. With a two-way ANOVA there are just three components to be analysed: two main effects and an interaction. This number increases to seven with three-way ANOVA, fifteen with four-way ANOVA and so on.[11] The most important case is three way ANOVA. If we write the three IVs symbolically as A, B, C, then the seven effects are as follows:

Three main effects: main effect of A, main effect of B, main effect of C.

---

[10] The size of a simple main effect represented by a line as here, is proportional to the slope of the line (why?). Two very different simple main effects have different slopes, meaning that the lines are far from parallel. And non-parallel lines indicate the presence of an interaction.

[11] The general formula is that the number of effects with n-way ANOVA equals $2^n - 1$.

Three two-way interactions: A*B, B*C and A*C.

One three-way interaction: A*B*C.

In broad outline, the logic behind this clutch of effects is similar to the two-way case. The main effects are relatively easy to understand: the main effect of A is its effect, ignoring the effects of the other variables. So with a two-level variable, the raw effect size is the mean of all the cells in which A has one value, minus the mean of all the cells where it has the other value. The two-way interactions are similar to the two-way ANOVA case. The three-way interaction is harder to visualise.

Just as a two-way interaction involves detecting the difference between two simple main effects, so does a three-way interaction involve detecting the difference between two simple interactions.

This can often best be understood by looking at plots. Just as a 2 × 2 interaction really reflects the fact that two lines are not parallel, that is a *change in slope* in moving from one line to another, a 2 × 2 × 2 interaction reflects the fact that two diagrams contain lines which show a *change in degree of parallelism* moving from one diagram to another.

Sex, drugs, and rock 'n' roll

Suppose the earlier example on the effect of drugs and music therapy on post-stroke mobility is expanded by including the variable of gender. Imagine also that the sample size has been increased to a more reasonable level, as an extension of the earlier, pilot study. The dataset is available online as Dataset5.

We can do another two-way ANOVA with just the drug and music therapy variables as the IVs, and if so the line plot delivered by SPSS is as shown in Fig. 11.9.

This suggests two things from the diagram alone. Note by the way that it is important to be able to look at a plot such as this and interpret the likely effects that will be found. One way to get a feel for this kind of thing is to see a series of plots and decide what is happening in each case. I have included a series of two IV plots on

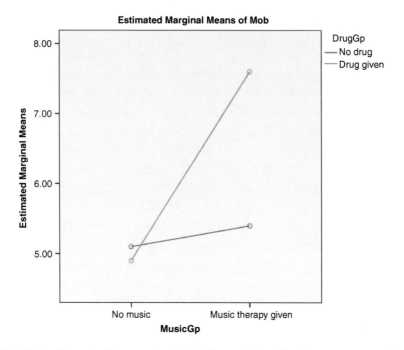

Fig. 11.9.   Plot of cell means for MusicGp and DrugGp, three way example.

the web material that you can use to develop this skill, which is largely a matter of practice.

The diagram suggests that there is probably an interaction between the IVs: the two lines are not parallel.

There may also be a positive main effect of the drug variable: the mid-point of the green line (average of the two with-drug cells) seems to be higher than the midpoint of the blue line (representing the average of the no-drug cells).

Also the point half way between the two right-hand cells looks to be higher than that of the two left-hand cells, suggesting that music therapy also has a positive effect.

If you carry out a two-way ANOVA with these two IVs on the dataset, you will find that both main effects and the interaction are indeed significant, so this interpretation is borne out by the statistical tests.

However, it would be misleading to summarise the outcome as two main effects and an interaction. The most reasonable way to describe this result is probably to state that music therapy and drug therapy on their own had little effect, but in combination, the effect was much stronger.

However persuasive this conclusion might sound based simply on the means plot, given the Ambien example we might not feel much confidence in it without checking whether there was a gender specific effect. This can be found by doing a three-way ANOVA including the gender variable as an IV.

If you do this, you will find that the Corrected Model is significant (a useful preliminary check, as I have argued above), that the main effects of the drug and music IVs are significant but gender is not, and that the three two-way interactions and the three-way drug*music*gender interaction are all significant.

The significance of the highest order interaction suggests that lesser effects cannot be interpreted without great caution, and in particular, the plot diagram given above may be misleading without examining the gender component. We can do this by adding the gender variable in the plot box. To replicate the diagram, go into the Plot box, and place the variables, and then don't forget to press the Add button (see Fig. 11.10).

When this is done, the output will contain two plots, one for the male participants, and one for the females (see Fig. 11.11).

It is now clear how the three-way interaction arises. The two lines are very much not parallel for the male group, but nearly so for the females: there is a *change in parallelism as the level of the gender variable changes*, which is characteristic of a three-way interaction.

It also shows the folly of jumping to premature conclusions as to the effectiveness of music therapy, based on the original analysis. What seems to be happening is that with women, the music therapy is effective, but there is no effect of drug therapy, and no interaction. The two lines are not far apart at the midpoint (no effect of drugs) and almost parallel (no interaction).

With men, the situation is a lot more complicated. What it suggests to me (and this is only my interpretation) is to focus first on the two almost coincident left-hand cell means. These signify that in the no music condition, taking the drug has essentially no effect

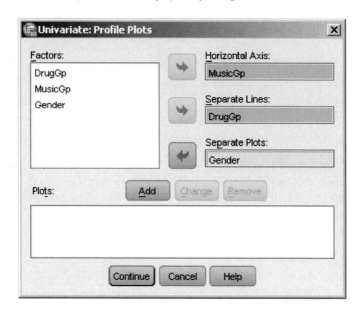

Fig. 11.10. Profile plots command, three way example.

at all (the drug effect in this condition is represented by the vertical distance between the two cell means). Now focus on the lower line, representing the men in the no drug group. For them, the music has if anything a *negative* effect on mobility. But for the men on drugs, music seems to have a marked *positive* effect.

If I was writing this up in a way that was designed to achieve impact, I would probably put it this way: for women, music therapy is effective but drugs are a waste of time. For men, on the other hand, drug therapy can be effective, but only when given in conjunction with music therapy; drug treatment on its own is ineffective and music therapy on its own is possibly even damaging. Note that all these claims are only suggested by the plots. They would need to be backed up by separate, specific tests. As an exercise, I suggest you carry out the analyses that would be needed to support these statements, and check whether all or any of them are indeed valid. I will put my own attempt at this online.

Three things remain to be covered in this chapter, at least briefly: contrasts, models and the qualitative/quantitative

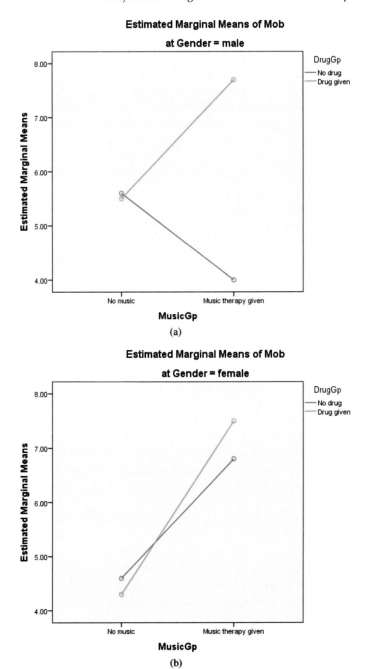

Fig. 11.11.   (a) Means plot for gender = male; (b) for gender = female.

distinction for interactions. The issue of effect sizes in ANOVA is an interesting one. Appendix A goes into this in some detail. An interesting spinoff of the lofsos-parameter plot is that it clearly indicates that the eta-squared measure has a defect (which indeed it has, it is biased) and it also suggests a better measure, which is an effect size named epsilon-squared.

Contrasts

In the simple case where all IVs have only two levels,[12] the main effects and all the interactions of whatever degree can be written explicitly as contrasts. This is because if all the IVs are dichotomous then their degrees of freedom are all one, and if everything has value unity, the degrees of freedom of the higher order effects (found by multiplying the dfs of the lower order components of the effect) are also all one. The general rule is that anything with just one degree of freedom can be written as a contrast. I will do this explicitly in the website for the cases of two-way and three-way ANOVA.

Even when the IVs are not dichotomous, they can still be broken down into orthogonal contrasts as in the one-way ANOVA case, and so in theory, the whole set of effects of any ANOVA can be built up from a succession of mutually orthogonal contrasts. Since the full model can be formed by stacking the main effects and interactions in a sort of tower of Hanoi one on the other, this provides a method of breaking down the full model into a succession of nested models, each supplying one additional parameter until the entire full model is attained.

Models in multifactorial ANOVA

Having laid so much stress on model comparison, I should illustrate at least one example. For the two-way ANOVA case, the full model can be built up as follows, spanning the gap between the null and full models:

---

[12] They are referred to as "dichotomous" in this case.

Null model — one main effect model — both main effects model — main effects plus interaction model = full model. What these actually look like, I will explain verbally here, and illustrate in the online material diagrammatically. It may look confusing in words but is much easier to understand in the line plots. For the benefit of those wishing to use non-balanced designs, I should mention that this situation can only be guaranteed for balanced datasets.

The single main effect model takes one IV (it doesn't matter which one) and approximates all the cells with a given fixed value of that IV, by the mean taken over those cells. For example, in the drugs and music example (ignoring gender), the main effect model would approximate the with-drugs with-music cell and the with-drugs no-music cell by the average of these two cell means, and likewise with the no-drugs cells. Seen as a line plot, the model would look like two horizontal lines, representing the two levels of the drugs variable.

Adding the music IV to the model would give the "both main effects" model. In the line diagram this would be a pair of lines which were no longer horizontal but still parallel. The difference in height between the right- and left-hand sides, would be equal to the raw effect size of the music IV.

Adding the interaction term would tweak the two lines into their final, non-parallel position, where the model values coincide with the cell means given in the full model.

Incidentally, since the three components of the full model are mutually orthogonal, this process could be repeated in any order and still be valid: for example, one could start with an interaction model (two lines of equal and opposite slope, crossing in their centres), an interaction plus drug effect model (lift one of the lines vertically with respect to the other, and the other one down an equal distance, but leave the slopes unchanged) and the interaction plus drug plus music model (take the two right hand ends of the lines, and push then up by some distance, and take the two left hand ends and push them down the same distance).

Turning to the three-way ANOVA example, describing the seven steps from the null to the full model explicitly would probably not be very helpful, but I can illustrate what the whole thing looks like plotted on a lofsos-parameter diagram without too much complexity.

When you do the three-way ANOVA with the online example, you will find that the lofsos for the null model is 99.5: this is the number next to the "corrected total" name, which is how SPSS refers to the null model. This has one parameter. The DrugGp IV model has lofsos which can be found by looking at the sum of squares next to it in the table, which is 10.0, and subtracting it from 99.5. Recall that the 10.0 number is the *improvement* in fit when that IV is included, so the remaining sum of squares for this model is 89.5. Now add successively the two remaining IVs, and the three interaction terms to get another five models; each time subtract the "Type III sum of squares" value for the effect you are adding, to give the running total for that model. The last model is the full model, and the lofsos for that is given by the error sum of squares, which is 26.8.

As a check, the numbers you should get for these 8 models, if you follow the order that the output gives you is as follows: (99.5, 89.5, 67, 66.9, 52.5, 46.1, 31.7, 26.8)

The parameters increase by one at each step, from 1 through 8. The lofsos-parameter diagram then looks as shown in Fig.11.12, where I have labelled only the null model:

The top number in the *F*-ratio for each effect is given by the slope of the line joining the model where it appears, to the model

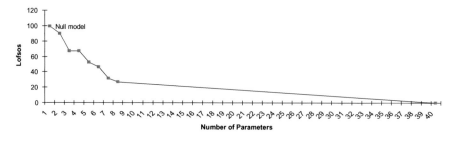

Fig. 11.12.   Graph of set of successive models for three way ANOVA.

above and to the left of it. This slope measures the improvement to the model from adding that term. The bottom number, however, is the same for all the models: it is the slope of the long, very shallow line going off to the right all the way to the saturated model. You can now see the benefit of having a common error term. The line joining the saturated model to, say, the one-IV model, would be a lot steeper than the bottom slope, giving a smaller *F*-ratio than ANOVA gives. And the same goes for the other effects.

You can see that all the effects appear to have, and indeed do have a slope ratio of more than one, except for the third link, which looks pretty flat itself: and this is the additional lofsos that is explained by gender on its own, which is not significant and whose *F*-ratio, if you get SPSS to do the program, works out at 0.119. This may appear paradoxical, as we have seen that gender is important in understanding the result, but the solution is that gender *on its own* does not have an effect: the average of all the cell means for the men, differs very little from the average of all the cell means for the women. It is the interactions that give the useful information, and that is supplied by all the terms which follow it.

Qualitative and quantitative interactions

A full treatment of this issue is given online. All I want to do here is to say what these two definitions mean, and why the difference is important. The definitions apply to a two-way ANOVA with dichotomous variables, and you should imagine that the cell means have been plotted using two lines, as in the two-way ANOVA example above. The presence of an interaction is shown by lines which fail to be parallel, but this can take different forms.

1. The lines may be non-parallel, **non-intersecting**, and with **slopes of the same sign** — i.e., both positive (sloping upward) or negative (sloping downward). This is termed a **quantitative** interaction, or by some people an **ordinal** interaction.

2. The lines may be non-parallel and **intersecting**. This is termed a **qualitative**, or a **disordinal** interaction. The lines may or may not have opposite slopes.
3. The lines may be non-parallel and have slopes of opposite signs: one with positive, one with negative slope. The lines may or may not intersect. This is **also** a qualitative or disordinal interaction.

Most of the sources that mention this idea at all include only category 2 among the qualitative interactions. In one sense it does not matter, because as explained online, if the two lines in a line plot intersect in one diagram, then if you enter the IVs in the opposite order in the plot menu, the lines will come out with opposite slope in the new diagram, and vice versa. The lesson to take home is that if you look at a line plot and the lines don't intersect but do have opposite slope, you are *still* looking at a qualitative or disordinal interaction.

The reason why the distinction is important involves two issues: whether the interaction is real or spurious, and whether or not to interpret the main effect(s) if an interaction is present.

There are three things that can cause interactions to appear in data, where there is really no interaction present in reality, as it were. These are **ceiling effects**, **floor effects** and **scaling effects**, all explained online (and referred to briefly in the glossary at the end of this book). The point is that if such effects are responsible for an interaction, the interaction will be quantitative. Conversely, if you have a qualitative interaction, then you can be fairly reassured that it is genuine, and not the spurious outcome of one of these three effects.

The second point is that whatever some of the textbooks may say about never looking at main effects if an interaction is significant, *if the interaction is quantitative* it often makes sense to include any significant main effects when interpreting the results. Such interactions are quite "weak" in a sense. By the same token of course, qualitative interactions are a more serious proposition, and in such a case the advice of the books should be followed.

Chapter 12

Repeated Measures Designs, and Their ANOVA Counterparts

SUMMARY

Repeated measures or crossover designs defined as those where each participant experiences every combination of IV levels. Carryover effects and counterbalanced designs; Latin square designs. Similarities and differences between RM ANOVA and between-subjects ANOVA. RM and mixed ANOVA in SPSS. Post hoc pairwise comparison of means. Mauchly's test of sphericity. Means plots and contrasts. Designs using blocking. RM ANOVA in a model comparison context.

NEED TO KNOW

So far the only independent variables we have considered have been those which can be represented as two, or a larger number, of groups. The variable might have two values — treatment, and control — and this gives rise to two corresponding groups of separate individuals, the treatment and control groups. We use the independent samples t-test to deal with this, generating a variable in SPSS with two number values (e.g., 0 and 1) corresponding to the groups. Individual participants have one of these two numbers attached to them, depending on their group "membership".

One-way ANOVA enables us to analyse experiments having an IV with more than two levels, but the same correspondence holds between different values of the IV, and separate groups of participants. For each individual — each row in SPSS — there is just one group to which they belong, which is found by reading across to the column of numbers representing the IV. In the same row is found another number, in the column representing the DV, which is the outcome of a measurement process recording the value of that variable. Multifactorial ANOVA includes multiple values, one for each IV, for each participant, but each participant has only one combination of IV values, and there is only one value of the DV for that participant.

However, in testing some experimental hypotheses, it is possible to do things another way. What follows applies only to true experiments, i.e., to RCTs and their multi-level counterparts analysed with one-way ANOVA: it does not apply to group difference studies, for reasons which will soon become obvious. Sometimes you can, as it were, recycle your participants twice over, or many times over, using them on several different occasions with different levels of the IV, and record the value of the DV on each occasion. Clearly you cannot do this if you are comparing, say, men and women or typically developing and autistic children in a group difference study, where the IV is given to you in advance by nature, and not chosen by you as the experimenter.

Imagine that you are comparing some intervention having a short term effect, such as giving participants caffeine, and measuring the effect on some performance task by measuring the reaction times to respond to some stimulus. If Tom, Dick and Harry have been randomly allocated to the control (no caffeine) group, and Fred, Mike and Steve are in the treatment (prior dose of caffeine) group, that would be an RCT. The effect of caffeine on performance would be measured by comparing the mean of the control group with the mean for the treatment group. There would be just three participants in each group, and the signal, if there is any — the difference in the means of the two groups — is likely to be overwhelmed by noise, namely the individual differences between these two very small groups.

But suppose you got Tom to do the task twice, first without caffeine and later with caffeine. The difference between his two scores would also be a measure of the effect of caffeine, and this time there would be no noise element due to individual differences: you would be comparing Tom with himself; as it is sometimes expressed, *Tom is acting as his own control.* You could of course repeat this with Dick, Harry and the rest. You now have a group of not six but effectively 12 participants, since each person is in both the treatment and control groups. Moreover, you can be sure that the two groups are well matched: they consist of the same people!

This is known as a **repeated measures design** (sometimes it is called a crossover design, because participants "cross over" from one treatment level to another during the course of the study). The caffeine example where the effects are short-lived is perhaps an ideal situation to apply such a design, but there are cases where it is just not possible to do so, including those where the IV involves natural groups as mentioned above. Less obviously, a repeated measures study may give misleading results even in a genuinely experimental design, where the IV is entirely under the control of the researcher.

With caffeine, the effect of the stimulant has a half-life of around six hours, so after 48 hours it has essentially gone from the body. A person given caffeine on Tuesday can therefore be tested on Thursday as a member of the control group with the assurance that the effect of the previous "treatment" is no longer present. This sort of design has two major advantages: the number of participants is reduced in proportion to the number of treatment groups, and the "self-controlling" nature of the study means that the noise component of the data will probably be smaller, giving a better chance of detecting a treatment effect if it exists.

However, suppose the "treatment" involves some form of cognitive therapy intended to reduce anxiety in a sample of clinical patients. The aim of such a therapy is presumably to give long term relief, so if it works at all, a person in the treatment group on Tuesday certainly will not be suitable for inclusion in a control group on Thursday. For an IV of this kind, the experimental treatment will have what is known as a **carryover effect**. In this case, it is probably going to be better to have two separate groups of patients, one given the treatment and the other given no treatment (or possibly an alternative treatment, if the aim is to find whether the cognitive therapy is any better than an existing established treatment). Even in the case of the caffeine experiment, where there is no carryover effect of the caffeine, another form of the effect may appear.[1] You may find it helpful to pause here and think what it might be.

It is possible that you may be uncertain at the planning stage of the experiment whether or not a carryover effect will occur. This need not eliminate a repeated measures study, which has great advantages in terms of efficient use of participants; it does, however, mean that you will need to build in an automatic carryover detector into the experimental design. This is achieved by having what is known as a **counterbalanced design**. This is most easily described in the case of a two-level IV. Calling the two levels of the independent variable A and B, a participant can experience them in the order A followed by B, or B followed by A. If half the participants have A then B, and the other half have B then A, it should be possible to detect any carryover effect by examining how, if at all, the set of participants in the first group differ in their responses to those in the second group. This is sometimes known as an AB/BA design.

The exact method of doing this will be explained in GD; for the moment, the important point is that counterbalancing needs to be built in to the experimental design from the outset. Analysis and design cannot be separated from each other: they are mutually supportive. Clever analysis cannot rescue the results of a poor design: it can only process information that is already there in the data, not

---

[1] Mentioned later in this section.

create information that was never there. Counterbalancing is built into the design with a view to ensuring that there is enough information to answer the questions that we need to answer, at the analysis stage.

Counterbalancing when you have an IV with more than two levels becomes, as you would expect, more complicated. With three levels, A, B and C, carryover effects may mean that participants respond differently to treatments in the six possible orders: ABC, ACB, BAC, BCA, CAB, CBA. With four treatment levels there are 24 possible orders. When you consider that participants should be randomly assigned to these 6, or 24, groups, you can see that the number in each group may be too small to be of much use at the analysis stage. Fortunately there is a compromise between this **complete counterbalancing**, as it is called, and no counterbalancing at all. This is to use what is called a **Latin Square** design. For this, the number of separate groups is equal to the number of levels in the IV, meaning that with three or four levels there are three or four subgroups of participants, which is usually manageable.

A Latin Square consists of an array where each row and each column contains each treatment just once. For example with a three level IV, the following is a Latin Square:

$$A\ B\ C$$
$$B\ C\ A$$
$$C\ A\ B$$

This gives rise to three separate groups of participants, to which participants are allocated by randomisation, and the patients in the groups receive the treatments in the orders given in the rows of the square corresponding to their group. This design means that most of the carryover effects can be tested for. It is a compromise and some effects cannot be tested in this way — for example, we cannot tell if having treatment A immediately followed by B has a different effect than B immediately followed by A (though in the second row, we can test for the effect of B followed two steps later by A). We may be able to rule out such an effect for other reasons connected with the specific variables that we are studying. At any event, a compromise design of this kind may be our only option if the study is to be done at all, and it is better than no counterbalancing.

To answer the issue raised above about an additional carryover effect, there are, or may be, effects connected with the sheer length of time that a participant has been involved in a study. These mean that they may respond differently at the second or third time of measuring the DV, than to the first. These effects are commonly known as practice and fatigue effects, and they are particularly likely where tests of performance are concerned.

A repeated measures design where, say, blood pressure is the DV is unlikely to show carryover effects of this nature, though even here, it is possible that initial measurements of blood pressure may be biased upwards by participant anxiety, which may decrease over time. The first encounter with a performance test may be influenced by lack of confidence or failure to fully understand what is required. Repeated exposure will diminish this, and later testing may give much better scores due to acquired skill in doing the task, but this may be replaced still later by boredom or (if the testing is all done in one session) by simple fatigue.

So much for the design of the experiment. We may wish to ask about the similarities and differences between the previous type of factorial design, where all the IVs are between-groups, sometimes called a between-subjects design, and a design which includes one or more RM IVs, a within-subjects design.

Similarities. As with factorial ANOVA, there is a continuous dependent variable and a series of categorical independent variables. The previous experimental questions about the effects, separately and combined, of the IVs on the DV are essentially identical: what are the main effects and the interactions?

The SPSS program breaks down the variance in the DV into contributions from a series of main effects and interactions of the IVs, just as for the between-subjects case. As with between-subjects factorial ANOVA, there are examples where omnibus significance testing is useful, and cases where it is not, and where contrasts or paired comparisons are a better alternative.

Differences. Whilst any RM factorial design could be re-run as a between-subjects factorial design, this does not hold in the reverse direction: some between-subjects designs could *not* be run as RM designs, the most obvious example being group difference studies, where clinical groups represent levels of one IV, or where gender is an IV, for example.

The second difference comes at the analysis stage. Any factorial design which has only between-subjects IVs can be analysed using the univariate ANOVA menu on SPSS (subject to the certain technical conditions involving normality etc.). Any factorial ANOVA which has one or more RM IVs, is analysed using a different menu on SPSS, namely the repeated measures ANOVA. Moreover, the presentation of the output is different: the significance tests for the main effects and interactions which involve *any* of the within-subjects variables are put into one section of the output, whereas those involving *only* the between-subjects variables (if any) are separated into another box of the output.

Another difference concerns the model comparisons that are carried out in RM ANOVA. However, this is somewhat technical, and will be covered in the GD section.

Basic implementation of RM ANOVA in SPSS

The simplest case is that of one repeated measures variable. Suppose the research question involves the effect of happy and sad music on heart rate (HR). The experimental hypothesis might be that happy music raises HR more than sad music, and that both raise HR, compared with a resting state where no music is heard. Although psychology research claims to be hypothesis driven, this type of research is really more exploratory than confirmatory: as with one-way between-subjects ANOVA, we may really be more interested in posing the open-ended question: is there an effect of music on HR, and if so, does it depend on the mood of the music, and — do not forget this — if there is an effect, in which direction does it lie, i.e., to raise or lower HR?

There are basically two options for the design of an experiment to explore this question: the between-subjects and within-subjects alternatives. A between-groups design would require three separate groups of people, who would be exposed to three separate conditions: happy music, sad music and silence, for a specified period of time, say one minute. Their HR at the end of that time could then be measured. HR would be the DV, and the three groups would be the IV. As you know, the data would then be entered into SPSS in the form of two columns: one representing the IV, in which each participant (corresponding to a specific row) would be given a coding indicating their group membership, and the other representing the value of HR found for each participant. If you decided to recruit ten participants per group, which would probably be seen as a bare minimum for this kind of design, you would need a total of thirty people to run through the experiment.

A within-subjects design would have clear attractions in this situation. Because each person is exposed to each of the three levels, to match the between-subjects situation you would need only ten participants. If, as is likely, you recruited more, the power of your experiment to detect an effect would be increased. Admittedly each participant would take longer to test, but this disadvantage is more than offset by the time saved in having to schedule fewer sessions (and reschedule them for participants who miss their appointments). The danger of carryover effects with RM designs is less in this case, because changes in HR caused by music are unlikely to be long lasting. If a control condition such as listening to white noise (or electronic hiss) between sessions is used, then probably carryover effects can be ignored. However, by using a Latin Square design, permuting the order in which the stimuli are presented, this assumption can in any case be tested.

You now collect your data. Each participant will give rise to three separate values of the DV, namely the HR values under silence, happy and sad music. These three values may appear to you to correspond to three separate DVs, but recall that in the between-subjects alternative design they would be regarded as

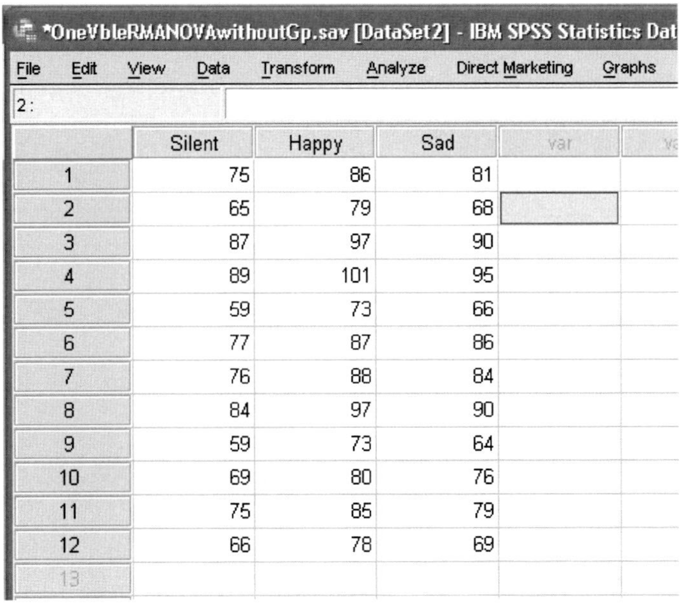

	Silent	Happy	Sad	var	va
1	75	86	81		
2	65	79	68		
3	87	97	90		
4	89	101	95		
5	59	73	66		
6	77	87	86		
7	76	88	84		
8	84	97	90		
9	59	73	64		
10	69	80	76		
11	75	85	79		
12	66	78	69		
13					

Fig. 12.1. SPSS dataset for RM ANOVA.

measuring the same DV over three groups of people. Likewise, with RM ANOVA we regard all measurements as of the same DV, and we think of the three separate measurements for a participant as corresponding to the three separate levels of a single IV.[2]

The first thing to understand about entering the data is that the three levels of the IV are indicated not by a separate column with three numbers in it corresponding to silence, happy music and sad music, as with the between-groups case, but by *three separate columns*, identified as silence, happy and sad music. The coding, in other words, is by column position, not by the number within a single column. It might help to demonstrate what this looks like; remember, we are still at the data entry stage and have not begun the analysis yet (see Fig. 12.1).

So for participant 1, the values of HR measured under the silent, happy and sad conditions were 75, 86 and 81 beats per minute respectively (the data are available online as Dataset6).

---

[2]For completeness, I should add that there is an alternative method of analysis called MANOVA which does treat the three sets of measurements as separate DVs.

This may be an obvious point, but suppose that participant 1 was randomly allocated to group 3, and so received the stimuli in the order C, A, B, or sad music, silence, and happy music. So the actual HR values will have been recorded as the sequence 81, 75 and 86 in time order of measurement. You will of course need to reorder these values to correspond correctly to the columns as I have named them in the SPSS dataset.

In case there is any confusion, it might be helpful to indicate how these data would have been recorded if a between-groups design had been used (see Fig. 12.2).

	*OneVbleRMANOVAasBGANOVA.sav [DataSet2] - IBM SPSS Statist			
File Edit View Data Transform Analyze Direct Marketing Gra				
37 : Group				
	Group	HR	var	var
1	1	75		
2	1	65		
3	1	87		
4	1	89		
5	1	59		
6	1	77		
7	1	76		
8	1	84		
9	1	59		
10	1	69		
11	1	75		
12	1	66		
13	2	86		
14	2	79		
15	2	97		
16	2	101		
17	2	73		
18	2	87		
19	2	88		
20	2	97		
21	2	73		
22	2	80		
23	2	85		
24	2	78		
25	3	81		

Fig. 12.2. Dataset for RM ANOVA, rewritten as one way ANOVA.

This is a partial screenshot of what we would see if exactly the same data had been recorded for three separate groups. What I have done is simply to provide a new column for the DV, named HR, and stacked the three columns for silent, happy and sad under one another, and indicated which is which by a new IV column, Group. Of course in this case I have not 12, but 36 rows, corresponding to the 36 participants I would have needed in the between-groups case to provide this amount of data. Hopefully, the difference in data presentation between the two designs is now clear.

When you start out to analyse your data from a repeated measures or a mixed design, you should have your questions in mind from the beginning. Analysis is not a fishing expedition to find something — anything — that is worth reporting, it is a procedure for answering fairly specific queries. Even in the simple case of a one-way ANOVA, you will recall that there are two possible approaches: using *a priori* contrasts, and *post hoc* pairwise comparisons, depending on whether you have specific, targeted questions from the outset of the study or whether your concern is a broader one, of doing all possible pairwise comparisons of group means with one another.

Similar issues arise with RM or mixed ANOVA analysis. I will illustrate the point by taking you through a (fictitious) example of a clinical drugs trial, firstly with a simple one-way RM ANOVA, involving pairwise comparisons, and then using the same data but incorporating a new, between-groups variable. In each case, the analysis will be linked to the research questions involved. The data are contained in Dataset7.

Suppose then that you have been tasked with testing the efficacy of three commonly used anti-anxiety drugs, A, B and C. There has been some critical reporting that these drugs only achieve their apparent success due to the placebo effect. You therefore decide to include a placebo condition in your study, in which participants are given an inert pill but are not told what it is. You have learned from previous studies that the effects of the drugs are transient, lasting at most for 24 hours. You therefore decide that a repeated measures design will be appropriate, being both more powerful and more economical in participants than a between groups design (and this aspect may be crucial with studies involving clinical groups, where participant numbers may be limited).

Your initial research question is: what if any differences in efficacy are there between the various drugs, and which, if any, of them are better (or worse) than a placebo? Your IV is the type of treatment (A, B, C or placebo) and has four levels. The DV is some measure of the effect of the treatment on anxiety.

The aim of this section is to demonstrate a method of analysis rather than to go in detail into design issues, but I should briefly mention how this study might be carried out in practice. Analysis is best seen as part of an overall process rather than something just learned as a procedure all on its own. You will of course need to choose a means of operationalising the construct of "anxiety". Suppose, to keep things simple, that the measure of current anxiety levels (i.e., "state" anxiety)[3] adopted is resting HR. What is the effect of treatment?

Immediately before the administration of the pill, resting HR is measured. One hour later, resting HR is measured again. The difference in the two readings will be taken to be the effect of that particular treatment. Subsequent treatments might take place at 48 hour intervals. This is admittedly a somewhat arbitrary way of measuring the effects of the drugs. In a more sophisticated study, HR might be monitored over a period of time, and this DV might be supplemented with other, self-report measures of state anxiety.

Even though carryover effects are unlikely to be a problem, for the sake of ruling them out altogether the order of treatments will need to be changed for different participants. This could be done by using a 4 times 4 Latin Square arrangement. Let us suppose that

---

[3] As opposed to "trait" anxiety. I am assuming that the treatments are designed to deal with state rather than trait anxiety. For the difference between state and trait variables (a controversial topic), see any book on the psychology of personality.

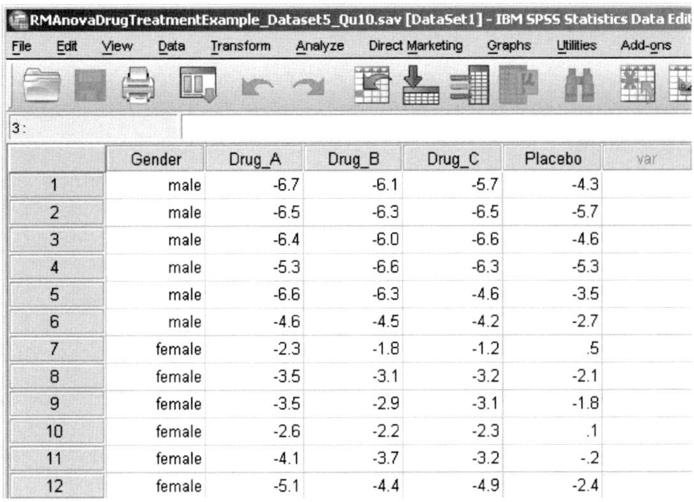

	Gender	Drug_A	Drug_B	Drug_C	Placebo	var
1	male	-6.7	-6.1	-5.7	-4.3	
2	male	-6.5	-6.3	-6.5	-5.7	
3	male	-6.4	-6.0	-6.6	-4.6	
4	male	-5.3	-6.6	-6.3	-5.3	
5	male	-6.6	-6.3	-4.6	-3.5	
6	male	-4.6	-4.5	-4.2	-2.7	
7	female	-2.3	-1.8	-1.2	.5	
8	female	-3.5	-3.1	-3.2	-2.1	
9	female	-3.5	-2.9	-3.1	-1.8	
10	female	-2.6	-2.2	-2.3	.1	
11	female	-4.1	-3.7	-3.2	-.2	
12	female	-5.1	-4.4	-4.9	-2.4	

Fig. 12.3.   Dataset in SPSS for mixed ANOVA analysis.

this has all been done correctly and that we now have a dataset of the effects. In my made-up example it looks as shown in Fig. 12.3.

Note that I have entered an extra column as "Gender". This happens to be showing the labels rather than the numerical coding as I have pressed the "Value Labels" button.

Each participant still has a single row to his or herself, but now there are four values of the DV along that row: one for each level of the treatment IV, since all participants experience all values of the treatment.

In order to carry out a simple RM ANOVA on the treatment IV alone, ignoring Gender at this stage, the basic procedure in SPSS is as follows (see Fig. 12.4).

Click on Analyze ≫ General Linear Model ≫ Repeated measures.

And this window appears as shown in Fig. 12.5.

You can leave the first window at its default setting of "factor 1", though then your outputs will retain this rather uninformative expression and if you wish to copy and paste them into a report, it is better to put in something suitable: here I will substitute "treatment".

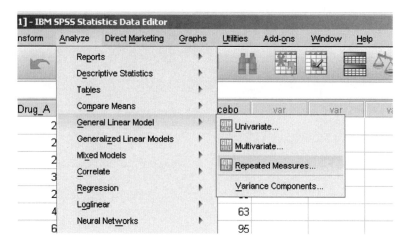

Fig. 12.4. Accessing the RM ANOVA command in SPSS.

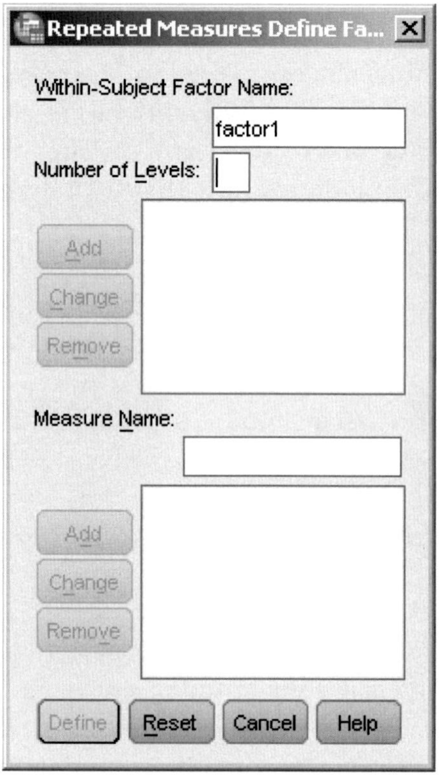

Fig. 12.5. RM ANOVA "Define Factors" box.

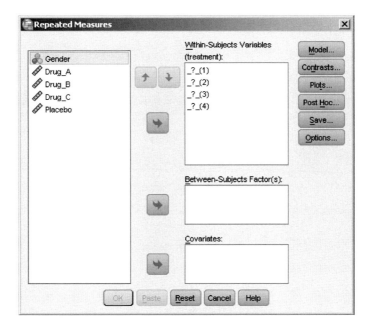

Fig. 12.6.   Designating the within-subjects variables for RM ANOVA.

You absolutely must, however, include a number in the "number of levels" window. The point of this is to tell SPSS how many of the columns of your dataset it must get ready to analyse as the levels of your IV. (Exactly which columns it must analyse, comes at the next step). There are four levels of our IV, so 4 is entered here, and I click on the Add button.

There is no advantage in this case in putting anything in the "Measure Name" window, so the next step is to click on the Define button at bottom left, when the box as shown in Fig. 12.6 appears.

This looks rather worse than it actually is. Telling SPSS that there are four levels of the variable has primed it to produce four blank spaces in the within-subjects variables window, and we now need to move the four relevant variables from the left hand window into these four places, which is done either by left clicking individually on Drug A, etc. and using the blue arrow button or by using the shift key to highlight all four and moving them in one operation. This produces a box as shown in Fig. 12.7.

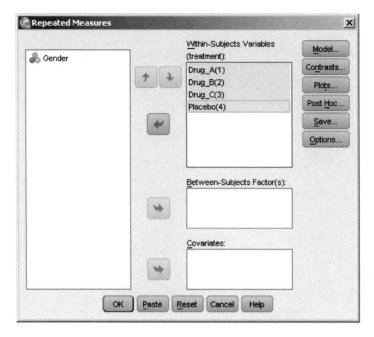

Fig. 12.7. Showing the within-subjects variables designated in RM ANOVA.

At this point you can simply press the OK button and get a result, of sorts. Just as with the between groups case, there is an omnibus *F*-test of significance for one-way RM ANOVA. You need to know how to carry out the omnibus *F*-test, because it is still taught in stats courses and because SPSS puts it centre stage. Orthodox opinion commonly holds that it is necessary as a first step in the analysis, though this view is not shared by the APA committee whose views were reported in the chapter on one-way ANOVA (see Wilkinson *et al.*, 1999).

I will leave the omnibus test to the end of this section, as it is irrelevant to the question at issue, which is pairwise comparisons of the means for the four treatment levels. This is essentially a *post hoc* test, which corresponds to the Tukey HSD test for one-way ANOVA. Unfortunately, there is no statistically slick way of doing post hoc pairwise comparisons with RM ANOVA corresponding to Tukey's test in between-groups ANOVA. What SPSS offers you is the brute force alternative, of carrying out what are basically a

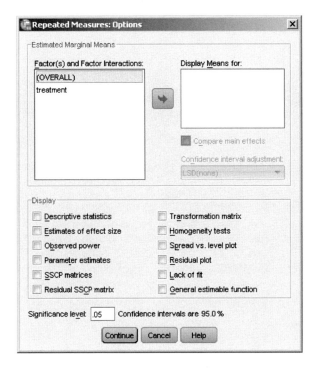

Fig. 12.8.   Post hoc testing in RM ANOVA.

series of *t*-tests on the data, and then guarding against inflation of type I error rates by applying a Bonferroni correction.

This post hoc test might, you would expect, be found by using the Post Hoc button to the right of the box illustrated above. It is not the way of SPSS to do anything so obvious, unfortunately. The Post Hoc button is used only for analysing any between-subjects variables that you may have included, and we have none here. *The post hoc procedure for within-groups variables is accessed via the Options button.* Pressing this produces the windows as shown in Fig. 12.8.

Click on "treatment", move it to the right-hand window, and the "compare main effects" tickbox becomes active. Tick it, and in the drop down menu just below it labelled "confidence interval adjustment", click on the Bonferroni option (see Fig. 12.9).

If you now click on the Continue button at the bottom and then on OK in the repeated measures box, you get some useful output.

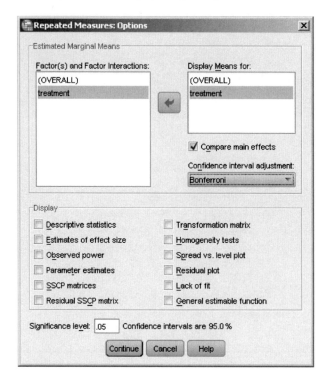

Fig. 12.9.   Applying a Bonferroni correction to post hoc tests in RM ANOVA.

For the purposes of this test, you can ignore the first few boxes in the output, indeed everything up to the two boxes as shown in Table 12.1.

The first box tells you the means of the four levels of the IV. This is similar to the group means in one-way ANOVA. It summarises what the data is telling you about the amounts and directions of the effects. Whether you believe that or not, is determined by the second box, which gives you all the pairwise comparisons between the levels of treatment. The numbers 1–4 refer to the order in which the levels of the IV are listed as columns, in this case drug A, drug B, drug C and placebo. So the first row gives the comparison between drug A and drug B, etc. You do not need to refer back to the dataset to check which is which: in fact the very first box lists the treatment numbers on the left and the names on the right (see Table 12.2).

Table 12.1.   Estimates and pairwise comparisons output in RM ANOVA.

Estimates

Measure: MEASURE_1

Treatment	Mean	Std. error	95% confidence interval	
			Lower bound	Upper bound
1	−4.767	0.457	−5.774	−3.760
2	−4.492	0.503	−5.600	−3.384
3	−4.317	0.508	−5.434	−3.199
4	−2.667	0.604	−3.996	−1.337

Pairwise comparisons

Measure: MEASURE_1

(I) treatment	(J) treatment	Mean difference (I–J)	Std. error	Sig.[a]	95% confidence interval for difference[a]	
					Lower bound	Upper bound
1	2	−0.275	0.151	0.579	−0.760	0.210
	3	−0.450	0.216	0.369	−1.144	0.244
	4	−2.100*	0.307	0.000	−3.084	−1.116
2	1	0.275	0.151	0.579	−0.210	0.760
	3	−0.175	0.178	1.000	−0.746	0.396
	4	−1.825*	0.237	0.000	−2.585	−1.065
3	1	0.450	0.216	0.369	−0.244	1.144
	2	0.175	0.178	1.000	−0.396	0.746
	4	−1.650*	0.198	0.000	−2.286	−1.014
4	1	2.100*	0.307	0.000	1.116	3.084
	2	1.825*	0.237	0.000	1.065	2.585
	3	1.650*	0.198	0.000	1.014	2.286

Based on estimated marginal means
*The mean difference is significant at the 0.05 level.
[a]Adjustment for multiple comparisons: Bonferroni.

Table 12.2.   Output listing the levels of
the repeated measures IV.

Within-subjects factors

Measure: MEASURE_1

Treatment	Dependent Variable
1	Drug_A
2	Drug_B
3	Drug_C
4	Placebo

Now refer back to the pairwise comparison box. You can verify
from this box that the effects of drugs A, B and C do not differ significantly from one another, since the *p*-values of the comparisons
between levels 1 and 2, 1 and 3, and 2 and 3 are all greater than
0.05. However, all differ significantly from the effect of the placebo,
as you can see at the bottom of the box where level 4 (placebo) is
compared with levels 1, 2 and 3. By looking at the table of means
(and this is why it is important) we can see that the effect of the
drugs is in every case to reduce the resting HR by more than placebo (though the placebo on its own does seem to have some effect:
to test its significance you would need to do a one-sample *t*-test on
the placebo readings).

This already answers the research questions which you posed
at the beginning. As promised, I will now deal with the omnibus
F-test, in the event that you wish to carry one out, for whatever
reason. I would argue that it is unnecessary in the case of pairwise
comparisons, and if you wish to use contrasts to answer specific
questions, such as "do the drugs A, B, C together show a significant
effect in comparison with the placebo?". It is also not only unnecessary but may be misleading if you are conducting a trend analysis,
which I will explain later. However, there is a school of thought
which advises that an omnibus test be done at the outset, and only
if that is significant, should one proceed with more specific tests of
hypotheses. You should at least be aware of how this is done.

If you follow the standard minimum procedure on SPSS for getting an output on RM ANOVA, in this case just entering the four levels of the RM variable as in Fig. 12.7, and click OK, the output consists of six separate boxes. The first one lists the separate levels of the RM IV, as in Table 12.2.

You will see that SPSS describes the columns as though they were separate dependent variables, rather than the same DV at four separate levels of the IV. This is confusing, but not wrong: you *can* regard the four columns as four separate DVs, and that is the approach adopted by a method of analysis called MANOVA, or multivariate analysis of variance, which is not covered in this book (and ordinary RM ANOVA is used in practice a great deal more commonly than MANOVA).

The output of RM ANOVA in SPSS happens to carry out a MANOVA by default, and this is continued with the second box of the output, labelled multivariate tests: I suggest you ignore it.

With the third box we come at last to something relevant to the omnibus *F*-test. It is labelled Mauchly's test of sphericity. The technical details are not essential, but it might help to know that sphericity is basically the analogue for RM ANOVA of the homogeneity of variance assumption for between-groups ANOVA. Just as we need HOV to be satisfied for that, we need sphericity to be satisfied for the omnibus *F*-test to be valid as it stands. As with most tests of assumptions,[4] we do *not* want a significant result here. HOV and sphericity are things we wish to hold good for our data, and these tests (Levene's and Mauchly's) essentially treat HOV and sphericity like null hypotheses, and test whether the data allow us to reject them. A significant result here would imply that the sphericity assumption could be rejected, and in that case the standard RM ANOVA calculation of *p*-values would be unsafe.

In this case the test is non-significant, since the *p*-value, found in the Sig column, is greater than 0.05 (see Table 12.3).

---

[4] I only know of one exception to this: exploratory factor analysis and Bartlett's test of sphericity, where a significant result is required. This will be covered in the online chapter on EFA.

Table 12.3.   Mauchly's test of sphericity.

Mauchly's test of sphericity[a]

Measure: MEASURE_1

Within-subjects effect	Mauchly's W	Approx. chi-square	df	Sig.	Epsilon[b]		
					Greenhouse–Geisser	Huynh–Feldt	Lower-bound
treatment	0.407	8.751	5	0.121	0.627	0.752	0.333

Table 12.4.   Significance tests of the within-subjects effects.

Tests of within-subjects effects

Measure: MEASURE_1

Source		Type III sum of squares	df	Mean square	F	Sig.
Treatment	Sphericity assumed	32.316	3	10.772	37.040	0.000
	Greenhouse–Geisser	32.316	1.880	17.187	37.040	0.000
	Huynh–Feldt	32.316	2.255	14.333	37.040	0.000
	Lower-bound	32.316	1.000	32.316	37.040	0.000
Error (treatment)	Sphericity assumed	9.597	33	0.291		
	Greenhouse–Geisser	9.597	20.682	0.464		
	Huynh–Feldt	9.597	24.802	0.387		
	Lower-bound	9.597	11.000	0.872		

We can therefore proceed to the next box, which finally gives the result of the omnibus F-test (see Table 12.4).

The line to read is that which begins "treatment … Sphericity assumed", since our test of assumptions allows us to assume this. We would report this as $F(3, 33) = 37.04$, $p < 0.001$. The 3 and 33 come from the entries in the df column corresponding to the sphericity assumed values for the treatment and error rows.

The fact that a significant result exists tells you nothing directly about how this shows itself in terms of actual treatment effects.

This is the reason for my scepticism of the value of omnibus F-tests, at least for analyses where only one IV is involved.

If, however, you are keen on doing omnibus F-tests, you may now be asking what happens if Mauchly's test is significant. There is no need to give up in despair: no fewer than three alternatives are available with SPSS, as you can see from the box above: the Greenhouse–Geisser, Huynh–Feldt and Lower-bound tests. This is where the whole procedure becomes messy, even by the standards of orthodox statistics. When learning this, I was taught a rule of thumb which I have faithfully repeated to students, which is as follows:

1. If Mauchly's test is significant, examine the part of the Mauchly's test box (Table 12.3) labelled epsilon. (Epsilon, or the Greek letter ε, measures how far the data depart from sphericity, the best possible value for perfect sphericity being 1.)
2. If either the Huynh–Feldt or Greenhouse–Geisser values of epsilon is greater than or equal to 0.75, go to the Huynh–Feldt rows of the test of within-subjects effects box, and read across the values of F, df and significance as before. In this case, if we had found a significant result for Mauchly's test the reported F-value would have been $F(2.26, 24.8) = 37.04$, $p < 0.001$.
3. If both the Huynh–Feldt and Greenhouse–Geisser values of epsilon are less than 0.75, go to the Greenhouse–Geisser rows of the Test of within-subjects effects box, and read across the values of F, df and significance as before.

GOING DEEPER

Mixed ANOVA

First example: examining the gender by treatment interaction.

Before moving on the final area to be covered with RM ANOVA, I should mention two examples where it is appropriate to use a mixed analysis, that is, one which includes both within- and between-subjects IVs. The first is where there is a between-subjects variable that is relevant to your experimental hypothesis. In the previous example, there was a variable — gender — that has appeared without comment in a number of the screenshots. You may wonder why it is has not been drawn on so far. It is a fact that the effects of a number of drugs, whether of use in psychology or otherwise, vary between men and women, perhaps because they interact with hormone levels. In this case, citing the effects of a drugs trial without mentioning gender, even if there are equal numbers of both genders in the study, may be misleading. It is possible, for example, that an exceptionally strong favourable effect of the drug on anxiety in men may be accompanied by a neutral or even a small negative effect on women. Clearly this is something that we would like to check in a study of this kind.

How would we do this? We might carry out separate RM ANOVA analyses on the male and female participants. This would actually be what we described before as a simple main effects analysis: simple, because we are isolating one level of the gender IV at a time, and main effect, because within that group, we are looking at the effect of the drug treatment. However, with this approach, it would not directly test the hypothesis that the drug had different effects on the two genders. The way to achieve this is to include the between-subjects variable of gender in the analysis from the start, by performing a mixed ANOVA.[5]

With mixed ANOVA, the key significance test to answer the "do the genders differ in drug effect?" question, is that of the *interaction* between the between- and within-groups variables. The reason why the interaction is key, is that the interaction is practically defined in terms of how the effect of one IV (on the DV) changes, when the second IV is given different values. In this case we are asking whether the effect of the treatment IV on anxiety varies, when the gender IV is given the values male, and then female.

In my experience, it is always helpful to look at visual aids to help with understanding interactions. To obtain a picture of what

---

[5] This experimental design is sometimes called a "split plot" analysis, for historical reasons connected with the pioneering work at an agricultural research centre.

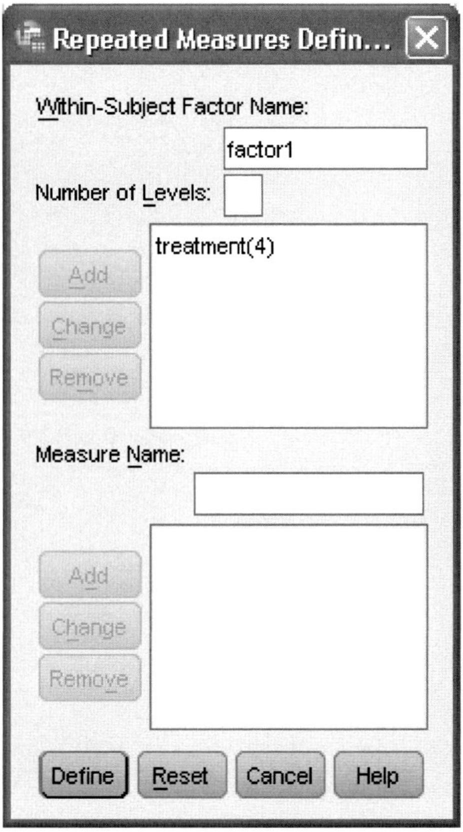

Fig. 12.10. Appearance of box on re-entering RM ANOVA menu.

is going on here, we need to go through the RM ANOVA procedure again, this time adding the gender variable and calling for a line plot. This is relatively simple. One small complication is that when you go back into the RM ANOVA menu that you have just left, SPSS takes you initially into this box, which you don't need to change, and you simply hit the Define button at bottom left (see Fig. 12.10).

Now click on gender and move it using the arrow into the between-subjects factor(s) window as shown in Fig. 12.11.

Click on the Plots button on the right. This produces yet another box (see Fig. 12.12).

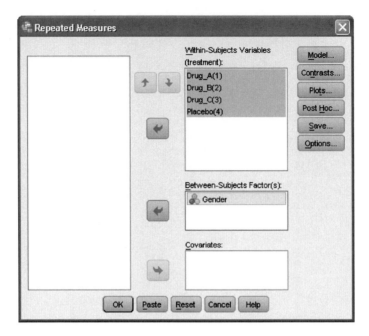

Fig. 12.11.   Appearance on adding gender in between-subjects factors box.

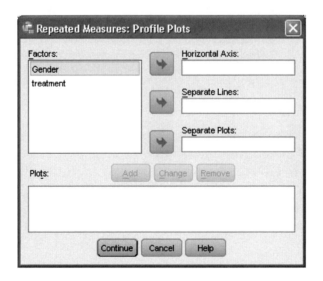

Fig. 12.12.   Appearance of profile plots box.

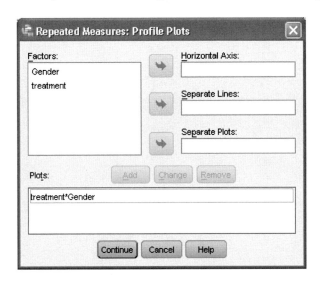

Fig. 12.13.   Profile plots box after both variables have been entered.

One of the two variables needs to go into the Horizontal Axis window, and one into the Separate Lines window. Personally, with a mixed design like this I find it more intuitive to put the within-groups variable into the first window, and the between-groups variable into the second one. Don't forget to click the Add button just above the Plots window, giving you the window as shown in Fig. 12.13.

The variables have gone down into the plots window with an asterisk between them, representing the interaction. Press continue, and finally OK in the original Repeated Measures box to get the results.

The plot looks as shown in Fig. 12.14.

What seems to be happening is that for both men and women, the first three levels (drugs A, B, C) are giving about the same readings, but the placebo, level 4, shows a jump upwards. The two line plots are not quite parallel, but they look quite close to it. This is confirmed by the lack of significance of the gender by treatment interaction, a test which appears with the treatment effect in the test of within-subjects effects part of the output (see Table 12.5).

In the absence of an interaction, the two main effects can be interpreted confidently on their own terms. The lack of interaction

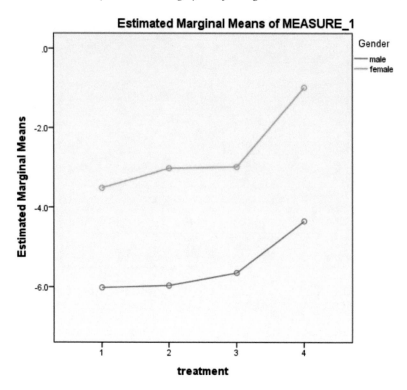

Fig. 12.14.   Means plot for treatment and gender IVs.

signifies that the effects of gender and of treatment operate independently of one another. There is a beneficial effect of the drug, or rather of the three drugs as they don't differ between one another. That effect is independent of gender: so we can now assert that there is no cause for concern, from these data, that an apparent success for the drugs might conceal a potentially dangerous mismatch between their effects on men and women. The effect really does seem to apply across genders. There is also a separate main effect of gender. This can be understood visually from the plot — the male line is everywhere below the female line — and is confirmed by a box which deals with the output relevant to the between-group independent variables (see Table 12.6).

Is this of interest? Not really in the context of investigating the effects of the drugs, though it might be if you were concerned more

Table 12.5.   Output for within-subjects effects when gender is included.

Tests of within-subjects effects

Measure: MEASURE_1

Source		Type III sum of squares	df	Mean square	F	Sig.
Treatment	Sphericity assumed	32.316	3	10.772	38.921	0.000
	Greenhouse–Geisser	32.316	1.843	17.538	38.921	0.000
	Huynh–Feldt	32.316	2.465	13.107	38.921	0.000
	Lower-bound	32.316	1.000	32.316	38.921	0.000
Treatment∗ Gender	Sphericity assumed	1.294	3	0.431	1.558	0.220
	Greenhouse–Geisser	1.294	1.843	0.702	1.558	0.237
	Huynh–Feldt	1.294	2.465	0.525	1.558	0.228
	Lower-bound	1.294	1.000	1.294	1.558	0.240
Error (treatment)	Sphericity assumed	8.303	30	0.277		
	Greenhouse–Geisser	8.303	18.427	0.451		
	Huynh–Feldt	8.303	24.655	0.337		
	Lower-bound	8.303	10.000	0.830		

Table 12.6.   Output for between-subjects effect.

Tests of between-subjects effects

Measure: MEASURE_1

Transformed Variable: Average

Source	Type III sum of squares	df	Mean square	F	Sig.
Intercept	791.375	1	791.375	227.786	0.000
Gender	98.900	1	98.900	28.467	0.000
Error	34.742	10	3.474		

broadly with gender differences. What it means here is that men appear to respond more than women to any intervention, even a dummy one in the form of a placebo pill. Since a placebo effect is present, one assumes, for the genuine drugs as well as for the placebo itself, this tells us simply that the placebo effect is stronger in men than women, but that the effects of the drugs over and above that placebo effect do not differ as between the genders (otherwise there would have been a treatment by gender interaction).

This matter of main effects and interactions, and the ways in which they are interpreted in practice, is quite a subtle one, and the best way to understand them is to look up papers and get into the habit of working out what is going on as between the results and their interpretation.

Second example: are there effects due to treatment order?

This in fact goes back to the previous example of the effects of silence, happy and sad music on heartrate (Dataset6). The particular order in which these are administered may lead to distortion of the results. Recall that the participants were randomly allocated to three groups, representing a different order of administration of silence (A), happy music (B) and sad music (C):

> Group 1, four participants: A, B, C,
> Group 2, four participants: B, C, A,
> Group 3, four participants: C, A, B.

This looks like a case for post hoc pairwise comparisons of the means of the three levels of the within-subjects variable, and if we do this, incorporating a Bonferroni correction, we find that all possible pairwise comparisons are significant; looking at the table of means, it appears that heartrate is highest for happy music, next highest for sad music and lowest of all for the silent condition (see Table 12.7).

But what if the effect depended crucially on the order of presentation? We can gain an idea of whether such an effect exists by including in the dataset a new group variable, recording which group each participant belonged to. This is added to the right of the existing dataset as a "Group" variable, coded as shown in Fig. 12.15.

Table 12.7.   Output showing means for three levels of RM IV.

Estimates

Measure: MEASURE_1

Mood	Mean	Std. error	95% confidence interval	
			Lower bound	Upper bound
1	73.417	2.919	66.991	79.842
2	85.333	2.689	79.414	91.252
3	79.000	3.015	72.364	85.636

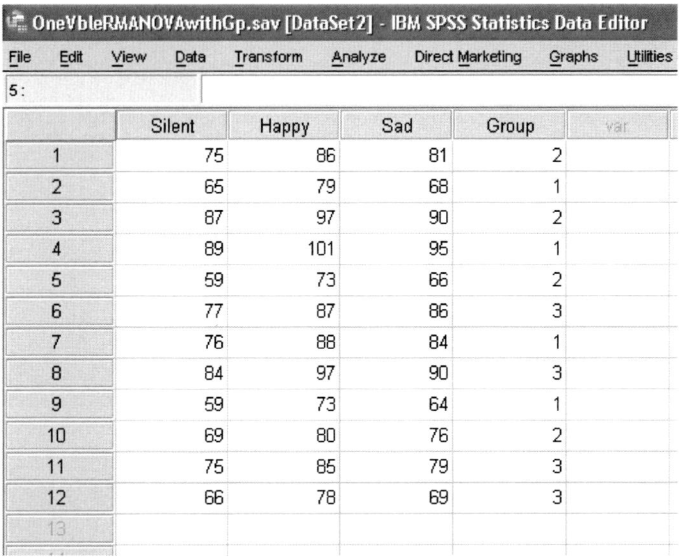

OneVbleRMANOVAwithGp.sav [DataSet2] - IBM SPSS Statistics Data Editor

| File | Edit | View | Data | Transform | Analyze | Direct Marketing | Graphs | Utilities |

5 :

	Silent	Happy	Sad	Group	var
1	75	86	81	2	
2	65	79	68	1	
3	87	97	90	2	
4	89	101	95	1	
5	59	73	66	2	
6	77	87	86	3	
7	76	88	84	1	
8	84	97	90	3	
9	59	73	64	1	
10	69	80	76	2	
11	75	85	79	3	
12	66	78	69	3	
13					

Fig. 12.15.   Addition of group variable to original dataset.

Having added this new information, we can now test whether the order really does have an effect. To get a visual input, I have carried out a plot including group in the separate lines window (see Fig. 12.16).

From this, it looks as though group membership is having little or no effect, as the lines pretty much overlap, and this is confirmed by the output, which shows that neither the group main effect nor the mood by group interaction is significant. This is good news,

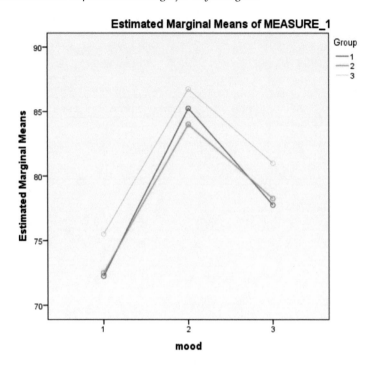

Fig. 12.16.   Means plots for mood, and group variables.

since it means that the effect of musically induced mood on the heartrate DV is not being interfered with by the order in which the stimuli were applied, so that the separate effects do appear to be independent of one another.

Incidentally, there are technical terms for the effects that are seen in this sort of analysis when either the group variable, or its interaction with the repeated measures variable, is significant: order and sequence effects. See the online material for a careful explanation of the difference between these; a summary is included in the glossary under the entries for order effect and sequence effect.

Contrasts in RM ANOVA

As with between-groups ANOVA, it is possible to carry out contrast analyses in RM ANOVA using SPSS. As before, there are two types of contrast: those comparing two sets of means, and those involving trend analysis. Conceptually, there is little real difference in the two cases. Mauchly's test of sphericity is not appropriate when contrasts are being tested. This is because in RM ANOVA, contrasts are equivalent to one-sample *t*-tests, in which variance assumptions are not made.

In the book, I will consider only the first type. Trend analysis using polynomial contrasts goes very similarly to the non-RM ANOVA case. I will provide an example of how it is done in the online material.

Comparing sets of means might be appropriate in a RM design if, for example, participants are treated with two classes of drugs, each of which has several specific drugs in it. You might want to compare the effects of type A drugs combined with the effect of type B drugs, but not be that interested in the differences between two type A drugs, or two type B drugs. Or you may wish to compare the effects of a set of drug treatments combined, with the effect of a placebo.

Such a comparison can sometimes be done in SPSS using the set of contrasts made available using the contrasts button (see Fig. 12.17).

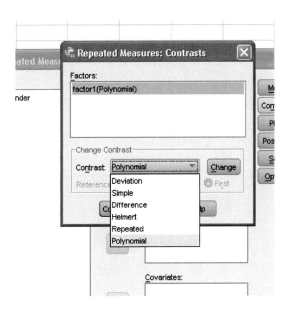

Fig. 12.17.   Accessing non-polynomial contrasts in RM ANOVA.

Definitions of these can be found by clicking on the help button at the bottom of this box, and I also include them on the website. However, unlike with the one-way ANOVA program available via Analyze >> Compare Means, you cannot use this to construct your own tailor made contrast. The most efficient way to do this involves, unfortunately, creating your own syntax command for SPSS using something called an MMATRIX. This is analogous to the LMATRIX command for carrying out general contrasts in between-subjects ANOVA, and details of how to do this are explained on the book website.

However, there is a method available when using RM ANOVA that is quick and easy, though not in general quite so powerful as the MMATRIX method. This involves creating the contrast by simple calculation from the existing data and doing a one-sample t-test on it, to check whether it is significantly different from zero. I will illustrate this for the case of the drug-placebo comparison.

If we wish to compare the means for drugs A, B and C combined with the mean for the placebo, the comparison is between the average of M_A, M_B and M_C, with $M_{placebo}$. By the same logic you are familiar with from the between-participants case, the contrast coefficients, taking the means in this order, are (1, 1, 1, −3). We can actually calculate the value of this contrast for each participant and so create a new column, which can then be tested. Using the compute variable command and naming the variable "contrast", we simply type in the expression corresponding to this set of coefficients (see Fig. 12.18).

And carry out a one sample t-test (there is more on this in the online material) (see Fig. 12.19)

And this gives a significant result (see Table 12.8).

And the negative value of the contrast shows that the result is in favour of the drugs over the placebo (see Table 12.9).

Designs using "matching" or "blocking"

There is a closely related experimental design that is a kind of hybrid between the between subjects and repeated measures designs. It is basically an independent groups experiment in that

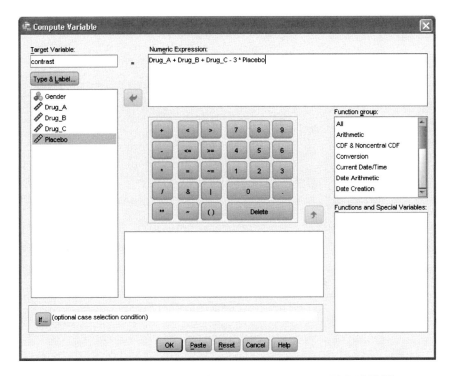

Fig. 12.18. Creating a variable to test a contrast in RM ANOVA.

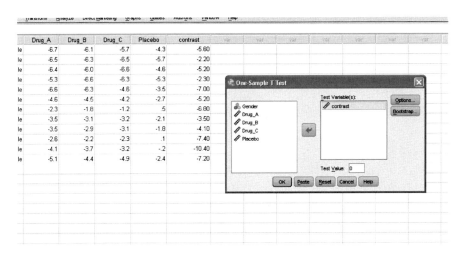

Fig. 12.19. Testing the significance of the contrast variable using the one sample *t*-test.

Table 12.8.   Outcome of one-sample *t*-test for contrast variable.

One-sample test

Test value = 0

	t	df	Sig. (2-tailed)	Mean difference	95% confidence interval of the difference	
					Lower	Upper
contrast	−8.157	11	0.000	−5.57500	−7.0793	−4.0707

Table 12.9.   Statistics for one sample *t*-test of contrast variable.

One-sample statistics				
	N	Mean	Std. deviation	Std. error mean
contrast	12	−5.5750	2.36763	0.68348

each participant only experiences one level of the treatment variable: there is only one measurement per person. But it is like the RM design in another way. The RM design is useful because it effectively uses each participant as their own control, thus removing a source of between-subjects variability in the DV. In blocking, you need some variable that will do the same job of eliminating noise in the DV but which can be measured. Any IV which can be measured in the participants *before* the experiment and which is likely to correlate highly with the DV you are measuring, will do.

It is best illustrated by an example. If you wish to predict the effects of different computerised stats teaching methods on knowledge of statistics (measured, say, by performance in some exam assessment), you would find that a lot of the difference between participants could be attributed to previous experience. So the students who were more knowledgeable at the start of the course would tend to do better no matter which method was used. This would be a source of unwanted noise.

The way to get rid of this noise is as follows. Suppose you have three different teaching methods and 60 participants. You could give them all a *pre-test* in basic stats, and put the results in rank order. The top three participants would then form one 'block' and you would randomly assign them, one each to the three teaching methods. The 4th, 5th and 6th ranking would form a second block, and would be randomly assigned, and so on. By looking at the average effect of the treatments *within blocks,* you would have eliminated much of the variability. You would analyse the results in SPSS using the same statistical method as for RM ANOVA, but this time the rows would represent individual *blocks* rather than individual *people.* The columns would represent the different treatment levels.

So this design uses essentially the between-subjects measurement methodology and the within-subjects statistical analysis, with the important proviso that allocation to treatment groups is still random *but* random within blocks not among participants as a whole. The difference in random allocation doesn't matter as far as drawing causal conclusions is concerned, i.e., internal validity: as long as randomness enters somewhere, the deduction — that the changes in treatment level *cause* any difference in DV means — is still valid. This method has the advantage over a fully within-subjects design, that there is no possibility of any carry over effects.

Model comparison in RM ANOVA

The null and full models in RM ANOVA are somewhat different from those in between-subjects ANOVA. This is because there is additional information in the dataset in RM ANOVA, namely the fact that each item of data belongs to a special subset of the total: namely the subset which consists of *all the measurements belonging to the same participant.* The existence of this subdivision of the dataset provides crucial information, which we need to exploit in order to attempt to replicate the data using a model.

To understand how models work in RM ANOVA, I need to use the idea of effect parameters introduced on page 296. Effect parameters measure the amount by which the group means in one-way

ANOVA depart from the overall mean for the whole set of data. Effect parameters will play a key role in understanding how the IV model works in RM ANOVA.

Open the dataset for the example of the effect of music on heart rate Dataset6. If the experiment had been carried out on three separate groups and was being analysed with one-way ANOVA, the overall mean would be 79.25 and the three group means would be 73.4, 85.3 and 79, as you can confirm by copying the dataset to Excel and finding the means. The effect parameters are then (73.4–79.25) for the first group, (85.3–79.25) for the second and so on, or (–5.8, 6.1, –0.25) for the three groups. These represent the effects that are specific to each group, the effects, that is, that remain once the overall average for the dataset has been subtracted, and ignoring individual variation within the group.

The first step is to find a suitable null model for the dataset. The obvious choice would be to take the overall mean of 79.25 as the model, just as with one-way ANOVA. This would certainly fulfil one condition of a null model — that it should not allow for any effect of the IV — but it loses valuable information. As mentioned above, there is an internal "structure": subgroups of points representing the same participant. Throwing this information away would give a null model which is a less good approximation to the data than we can make it.

A better model, which takes account of the internal structure while still ignoring any effect of the IV, would be to take the average over the three IV levels not of the whole dataset, but of *each individual participant*. So the null model consists not of one single number, but of a whole series of numbers, one per participant.

The first participant has scores of 75, 86 and 81 for the three conditions. The average of this is 80.7, and this is the null model for that participant. And so on for all the participants. The null model attempts to reproduce the data by allocating participant 1 the value 80.7 for each of her three scores, by allocating participant 2 the value 70.7 (the average of 65, 79, 68) for each of his three scores, and so on. This is truly a null model since score is independent of IV

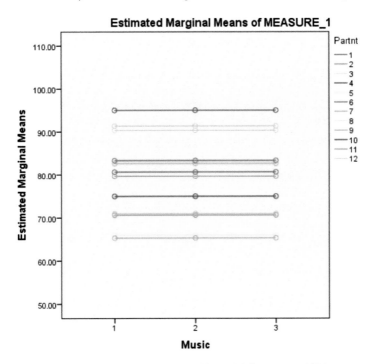

Fig. 12.20.   Illustrating the null model for RM ANOVA.

level, and it is much closer to the dataset than the crude, one size fits all value of 79.25. If you do the calculation on Excel, you will find that the lofsos of the new null model is 903.3, compared with 4132.8 for the crude, single number null model.

To illustrate what the null model looks like, Fig. 12.20 shows a plot of the predictions for each participant according to that model.

The values are constant for each participant over the three levels of the music variable.

For comparison, Fig. 12.21 shows a plot of the actual data; equivalently, it is the predicted values of the saturated model.

How should we construct the IV model? Evidently it must be at least as complex as the null model, so it is no good taking a one size fits all approach to the group means as we did before and approximating all the numbers for a certain level of the IV by a single number, the group mean. The individual differences between the

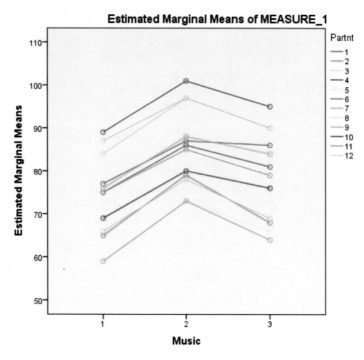

Fig. 12.21.   Plot of actual data for music and participant variables.

participants need to be built in to the model, as we did with the null model. But at the same time, we need to take into account the fact that the levels differ overall: level 2 seems from the plot to be higher than the other two, but the null model does not allow for this.

So let us get down to the level of the individual participant. For participant 1, the null model predicted her DV on all three levels of the IV to be 80.7, so the row of numbers for her entry should be (80.7, 80.7, 80.7). The IV model should incorporate the effects of the different levels of the IV on this set of numbers. What is the natural way to do this? It should use those effects of the IV that depend only on the IV and not the individual person (because we want to be able to generalise over a whole population).

The effects of the IV averaged over the sample have already been found: they are simply the effect parameters listed above. So to obtain the IV model prediction for the values of participant 1, we simply apply the effect parameters (5.8, –6.1, 0.25) to the base-level prediction (80.7, 80.7, 80.7) for participant 1, by adding the numbers consecutively to get (80.7 + 5.8, 80.7 – 6.1, 80.7 + 20.5) or (86.5, 74.6, 80.95). This is the IV model prediction for participant 1. Now proceed to do the same for participant 2, through participant 12, at each stage applying the effect parameters to the baseline average *for that participant* over all three levels.

What do the predicted values for the IV model look like? They are going to include the same effect parameters in all cases, but superimposed on a varying level of baseline for each participant, so we would expect the plots for each person to vary in height but otherwise to be similar in shape, as indeed they are as shown in Fig. 12.22.

This is now looking much more like the plot of the original data, but the plots are all parallel, as they must be because this reflects the fact that the same effect parameters have been used for all participants.

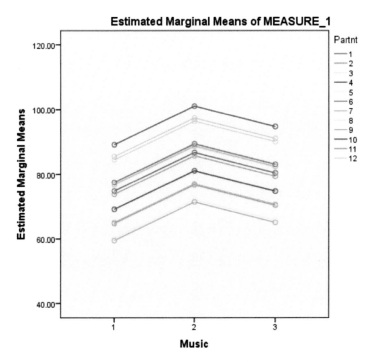

Fig. 12.22.   Illustrating the IV model for RM ANOVA.

The lofsos of the IV model can be calculated and compared with that of the null model, as in every other example in this book. It turns out to be 50.2, compared with the 903.3 for the null model. In order to calculate an *F*-ratio, we need now only work out how many parameters each model has, and how many the saturated model has. The null model required 12 means to be calculated, one per participant, and so it has 12 parameters. The IV model apparently needed three more numbers, namely the three effect parameters. But these three parameters are not independent: they must add to zero, because they represent the deviations from the mean, and the deviations must cancel out when added. Put another way, given any two effect parameters, you can calculate the third. So in fact the IV model adds only *two* parameters, for a total of 14.

The saturated model specifies the exact value of the DV for each point in the dataset, and there are 36 of these, three per participant. So the parameters of these three models are 12 for the null, 14 for the IV model, and 36 for the saturated model, and the lofsos values are 903.3, 50.2 and zero respectively.

The lofsos-parameter plot is as shown in Fig. 12.23.

The slope of the line joining the null and IV models is (903.3– 50.2)/2 because there are two parameters separating the two models, and this works out at 426.5. The slope of the second line, joining the IV model to the saturated model is $50.2/(36 - 14) = 2.28$.

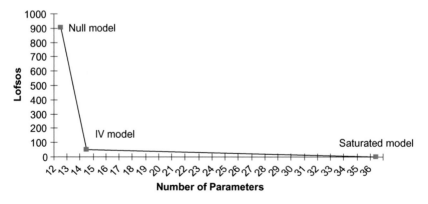

Fig. 12.23.   Graph of models in RM ANOVA.

Table 12.10. Sum of squares for Music variable, and for Error.

Source		Type III sum of squares	df	Mean Square	F	Sig.
Music	Sphericity assumed	853.167	2	426.583	187.073	0.000
Error (Music)	Sphericity assumed	50.167	22	2.280		

The ratio of the slopes is 187.1, so finally the test is whether $F(2, 22) = 187.1$ is significant, which it certainly is.

These calculations are represented in the SPSS output table, from which I have extracted the relevant rows (see Table 12.10).

The "Music" sum of squares here is the difference of lofsos between the null and IV models, and the "Error" sum of squares is the lofsos for the IV model.

Actually, I have glossed over a complication here, a complication which I avoided by using a particular null model. In fact, this approach works fine in practice, which illustrates how the model comparison method pushes through difficulties. However, the conventional explanation of RM ANOVA takes a different path, which I should explain.

The usual explanation of the method is that the null hypothesis test does in fact use the "standard" null model — that the entries are all equal to the grand mean of the whole dataset. But it then uses not one but two IVs to find the effect of the levels of the main IV of interest (in this case, musical moods). What is the other IV? Simply the IV representing the participants. In the dataset, I have numbered the participants by the IV "Partnt" label, from 1 to 12. What is happening in RM ANOVA is that the program is testing the main effects of both the IV of interest and the IV that represents the participants. It is possible to rewrite any RM dataset so that it can be analysed in this way, and the sums of squares come out just as calculated above.

If you try doing this (and I show online how it can be done) you will find that the significance tests come out blank, and this is because the error term is zero. The reason for this, is that a standard ANOVA includes the interaction term in the analysis. But in this case, it is the participant * IV term that is the error term! It is possible to make SPSS still produce the right answer, by going into the Model button, and insisting that the model being tested includes only the main effects, and no interaction.

The reason for this anomaly is that the main effects plus interaction model, what earlier I called the full model, *coincides with the saturated model*. The reason for this, is that the cells defined by the participant variable and the IV level together have just one sample point in each of them. When you know the participant number and the level of IV, you can read across to the unique value measured for that participant at that level.

An explanation as to how the model comparison approach works for the case of mixed ANOVA, is given in the worked examples for this chapter on line. The details are interesting and important, but please remember the value of underlying principles. Model comparison provides a set of ideas that will help you to understand not only how to carry out the right statistical test for the job, but also how to interpret the results constructively. Today, more raw data is available than ever before but this abundance is not always matched by intelligent interpretation. Ignorance, prejudice and greed sometimes shout louder. But I am an optimist and I believe with Carlyle that in the long run, thought is stronger than artillery-parks.

Appendix A
On Finding the Right Effect Size

Figure A.1 shows a typical lofsos-parameter plot. The question arises, what is the most natural way to measure the effect size, that is the improvement of the full model over the null model? We cannot use the F-ratio for this, as the F-ratio will depend on the sample size, whereas effect sizes are a property of populations, and our estimate of them should not depend on the sample size.

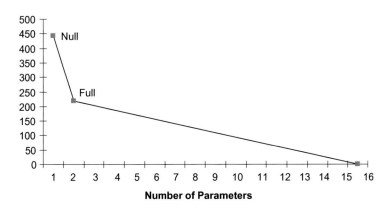

Fig. A.1.   Lofsos diagram comparing full and null models.

First attempt

The question of how much better the full is than the null model has an apparently simple answer: the full model is closer to the actual data, by an amount equal to the vertical drop in lofsos when passing from the null to the full model on this diagram, so that should be the effect size.

But that drop depends on the units used to measure the DV. In this diagram there is an improvement which looks by eye to be around 220 units, from about 440 units to 220 units, taking the full model half way to the bottom. But in another case, the null model might have a lofsos of say 100220 and the full model one of 100000, and the improvement would still be 220 units, but in this case the improvement looks much less impressive.

Second attempt

One obvious answer is to measure the value of the full model not by the *absolute* value of the improvement, but by its *relative* value, relative to the lofsos distance of the null model. In other words, the effect size is the ratio of the lofsos improvement of the full over the null model, to the lofsos of the null model. In the present case, this would give an effect size of around one half.

To discuss the implications of this, it is better to draw a separate figure to represent the situation: see Figure A.2.

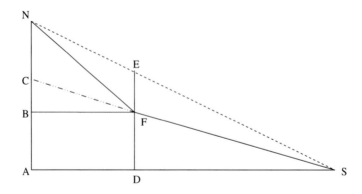

Fig. A.2.   Modified lofsos diagram.

In this diagram the points N, F and S represent the null, full and saturated models on a lofsos-parameter diagram, and the line NS is the Occam line. Note that point A is at the point on the horizontal parameter axis corresponding to the number of parameters for the null model (usually 1, but in the case of an RM ANOVA, it will be greater than 1). The lines AN and ED are vertical, and the line BF is horizontal, and parallel to AS. The line CF is an extension of the line FS, so that CFS is one single straight line.

Incidentally, this diagram illustrates another way of looking at the F-ratio, as the ratio between two lengths, namely NB:CB. This is because NB is the slope of NF times the distance BF, and CB is the slope of SF times the distance BF. In taking the ratio of the slopes, BF cancels out, and F = NB/CB. It may be easier to appreciate the meaning of the F-ratio in terms of two distances, than two slopes.

The lofsos of the null model is the distance AN, and the lofsos of the full model is the distance FD, which is equal to the distance AB. So the improvement in the lofsos given by the full model is given by AN – AB, or a distance BN. The relative improvement is now just BN/AN.

This measure of effect size has a name, or rather two names. In ANOVA-type analyses, it is usually called η^2 or eta-squared. In multiple regression, it is called R^2 or R-squared. But the two symbols refer to exactly the same thing, conceptually.

However, there is still a problem. To understand this, imagine that F was actually situated on the Occam line, vertically above its present position, at point E. Using the previous definition, the full model would still have a positive effect size, because point E has a smaller lofsos than N, even though it is doing no better than would be expected if the null hypothesis were true. In other words, this measure of effect size takes no account of Occam's principle. Surely, we would want any point on the Occam line to have an effect size of zero. In technical terms, eta-squared or R-squared suffers from a **positive bias**.

Third attempt

Looking at the diagram, is there a natural definition of effect size for F which does not have this handicap? Surely the improvement in lofsos for F that we should be measuring is not the improvement relative to the null model, but that relative to the equivalent model *with the same number of parameters* as the full model. This equivalent model is located by definition on the Occam line, at position E. The lofsos for this model is the distance ED. The improvement achieved by F is now not NB, but FE, which is smaller. So the correct measure of effect size is EF/ED. This is in fact the effect size measure used by SPSS in regression calculations, and it is known as **adjusted R-squared**. In ANOVA applications, it is known as **epsilon-squared** (ε^2).

To see how this measure relates to the original measure *R*-squared, extend the line SF, until it hits the line AN at C. At this point, I need a geometrical result about similar triangles, which gives the result that EF/ED = NC/NA. This can be seen intuitively, if you imagine the line EFD being projected by some light source at S onto a vertical screen at AN. All the proportions of distances between points on the line ED will be preserved by this projection, just as the proportions on a film slide are preserved by projection, provided the slide is parallel to the wall on which it is projected.

The correct effect size is NC/NA, compared with the second attempt at an effect size measure, of NB/NA. Since NC is smaller than NB, the real effect size is smaller than the apparent one, confirming that *R*-squared was indeed biased positively.

To find a formula for the new effect size in terms of *R*-squared, proceed as follows. To simplify the calculations, I am going to take NA to be of unit length (this amounts to dividing all original lengths by the length of NA, leaving all ratios and therefore effect sizes unchanged).

If the length of AN is 1, then the length of NB must be *R*-squared (since NB/NA = R^2). So by subtraction, the length of AB is $1 - R^2$, and this is equal to the length of FD since ABFD is a rectangle (the equality of AB and FD is obvious if you look at the diagram).

Since the triangles SDF and SAC are similar, the length of AC is AS/DS times the length of FD. You can see this as before by imagining FD projected from S onto AN. The length of the image is proportional to its distance from S.

But AS represents the difference between the number of parameters of the null model and the parameters of the saturated model, which is the definition of the degrees of freedom of the null model. By a similar argument, DS is the number of degrees of freedom of the full model.

So with the obvious notation, the length of AC is $df_N/df_F \cdot (1 - R^2)$, and the length of NC is $1 - \{df_N/df_F \cdot (1 - R^2)\}$, which is the standard formula for adjusted R^2, sometimes called Wherry's formula 1.

It is possible for adjusted R-squared to turn out to be negative. This is the case if, and only if, the plot for the full model is above the Occam line. In that case, the model is clearly has no merit.

In ANOVA, the formula given for epsilon-squared is:

$$\varepsilon^2 = (SS_b - df_b MS_W)/SS_t,$$

where the first SS is the between sum of squares (corresponding to the distance NB in the diagram), the df is the "between" degrees of freedom, namely the parameter difference AD, the MS term is the mean within sum of squares (which is the slope of the line FS, i.e., the denominator in the F-ratio) and the final SS term is the total sum of squares, which is the distance AN.

This may seem a rather complicated formula with no relevance to what has gone before, but you can see that this is equivalent to the formula for adjusted R-squared as follows. Since MS_W is the gradient of the line CF, and since df_b is the length BF, $df_b MS_W$ is the vertical rise of CF over the distance BF namely BC. So $(SS_b - df_b MS_W)$ is simply the length NB − CB = NC, and the whole expression is NC/NA, which is precisely the same as the previous formula for adjusted R-squared.

For some reason, while the adjusted R-squared is the standard correction for effect size with regression, with ANOVA most people seem to prefer something called omega-squared, which is close to but not identical with epsilon-squared. The main thing to take away from this analysis is that the original measure (R-squared or eta-squared) requires modification to allow for its violation of Occam's principle.

Appendix B

Why Orthogonal Contrasts are Useful

It will require some knowledge of linear algebra to understand this appendix fully, but nothing beyond the level of a first year undergraduate course in mathematics.

In looking at contrasts, I will adopt a different approach to the idea of making models more and more elaborate. Instead of focusing on a dataset and attempting to fit it using increasingly complex models, I will do something more paradoxical: keep the model fixed while making the dataset more and more simple.

All this amounts to in practice is that we will work, not on the original dataset, but on the set of **residuals** at each stage. A residual is the observed value minus the predicted value, so this can be written symbolically as follows:

$$\text{Residuals} = \text{dataset} - \text{modelled values}.$$

The point of this approach is that the aim of each successive step in the modelling process is to make the set of residuals as small as possible. This is a simpler problem than working out how to add to an existing model to make the result as close as possible to the original dataset, though of course logically the two are identical.

In what follows I will in fact work with a simplified version of the dataset, to make things less complicated. Suppose we have some kind of ANOVA, with k cells, and let the means of these cells be M_i, where i runs from 1 to k. This set of means can be represented by a vector with k components, which I will write $\mathbf{M}$. At the first stage, the model will attempt to approximate to the vector **M**, with a vector **E** (where E stands for "effect"), which will typically represent, in sequence, the null model, the first main effect model, the first and second main effects model, and so on.

However, as stated above I will work with the succession of residuals **M** – **E**, which I will write **R**. So at each stage of making the model more complex, I will instead subtract an equivalent vector from **R**, to represent the fact that the residuals are being reduced in an optimum manner.

In what follows, you may wish to assume that cell sizes are equal — the design is balanced — so that all the methods of calculating sums of squares are equivalent. This also means that working with the k-dimensional vector space representing the cell means and cell residuals, the Euclidean distance function is consistent with that in the original N-dimensional vector space representing the dataset.

Now suppose we have arrived at some stage in the construction of the model where the residual vector is **R**, and that we are given a contrast vector **C** and wish to find the closest approximation to **R** that we can obtain using a vector which is a multiple of **C**. (This is effectively how contrasts work in constructing models.) So we want a multiple λ**C** of **C** such that λ**C** has the minimum distance from **R**, as λ varies.

It is known from elementary linear algebra that the solution to this problem is to find the value α such that $(\mathbf{R} - \alpha\mathbf{C})$ is orthogonal to α**C**. This gives the equation:

$$(\mathbf{R} - \alpha\mathbf{C}) \cdot \mathbf{C} = 0,$$

where the dot represents the scalar product in the Euclidean space.

From this, $\alpha = \mathbf{R}\cdot\mathbf{C}/\mathbf{C}^2$, so the new residual after this contrast has been added to the model is

$$\mathbf{R'} = \mathbf{R} - (\mathbf{R}\cdot\mathbf{C}/\mathbf{C}^2)\,\mathbf{C}. \tag{B.1}$$

The map which takes **R** to **R'** is a linear transformation, and can be applied to any vector in the k-dimensional space. Indeed, it can equally be defined as the projection of the vector onto the hyperplane which is the orthogonal space of **C**. It is convenient to have a name for this transformation: call it T_C. So to each contrast there corresponds a linear mapping of the vector space. In what follows I will investigate a basic algebraic property relating these linear mappings.

I can write **R′** as $T_C(\mathbf{R})$.

Suppose now another contrast **D** is proposed for adding to the model (I do not assume anything else about **D** at this stage). If we now apply D to the new residual $T_C(\mathbf{R})$, we get a further residual, $T_D T_C(\mathbf{R})$.

Applying the contrasts in reverse order, we would obtain $T_C T_D(\mathbf{R})$.

It would be convenient if the order in which the contrasts were applied made no difference to the outcome, in other words, if the transformations commuted.

The condition for this can be found by applying the formula in (B.1) for C followed by D, and in the reverse order.

It can easily be calculated that the values are as follows:

$$T_D T_C(\mathbf{R}) = \mathbf{R} - (\mathbf{R} \cdot \mathbf{C}/\mathbf{C}^2)\mathbf{C} - (\mathbf{R} \cdot \mathbf{D}/\mathbf{D}^2)\mathbf{D} + (\mathbf{R} \cdot \mathbf{C}/\mathbf{C}^2)(\mathbf{C} \cdot \mathbf{D}/\mathbf{D}^2)\mathbf{D},$$

$$T_C T_D(\mathbf{R}) = \mathbf{R} - (\mathbf{R} \cdot \mathbf{C}/\mathbf{C}^2)\mathbf{C} - (\mathbf{R} \cdot \mathbf{D}/\mathbf{D}^2)\mathbf{D} + (\mathbf{R} \cdot \mathbf{D}/\mathbf{D}^2)(\mathbf{C} \cdot \mathbf{D}/\mathbf{C}^2)\mathbf{C}.$$

These commute if and only if the difference is zero, i.e., if and only if

$$(\mathbf{C} \cdot \mathbf{D})\{(\mathbf{R} \cdot \mathbf{C}/\mathbf{C}^2\mathbf{D}^2)\mathbf{D} - (\mathbf{R} \cdot \mathbf{D}/\mathbf{D}^2\mathbf{C}^2)\mathbf{C}\} = 0.$$

From this it follows that as maps on the whole vector space, T_C and T_D commute if and only if $\mathbf{C} \cdot \mathbf{D} = 0$ i.e., if and only if the contrasts are orthogonal.

This result can be extended to more general effects, which unlike contrasts may not be one dimensional. For example, a main effect for an IV with b levels can be seen as an approximation of R by a $(b-1)$-dimensional subspace, or equivalently, as a transformation by projection onto the space orthogonal to the effect subspace. Orthogonal effects commute, because the product of two orthogonal effects is the projection onto the intersection of the spaces orthogonal to the effect spaces. Given a set of effects, they commute if and only if they are orthogonal. The fact that orthogonal effects can be applied in any order can be useful when interpreting the results. Main effects and interactions are orthogonal when the design is fully balanced, or when type III sums of squares are used.

Appendix C
Mathematical Justification for the Occam Line

Suppose the dataset is of size N, and designate the lofsos of the null model by lofsos(null). The geometry of the Occam line is such that by well-known principles of similar triangles, the vertical distance of the Occam line above the horizontal axis at the point corresponding to a parameter number of k is

$$\text{lofsos(null)} \cdot \{(N-k)/(N-1)\}.$$

Call this lofsos(k) for short. For $k = 1$, this of course gives a value of lofsos(null), as we would expect since the null model has one parameter, and for the saturated model with $N = k$, it reduces to the correct distance of zero.

This value has been claimed to represent in some sense the value of lofsos for a k-parameter model which is telling us nothing useful about the dataset. This is the meaning of the Occam penalty, which tells us to treat any model which plots on this line in the lofsos-parameter diagram, as equivalent to both the null and the saturated models. I will now justify this statement.

By the definition of lofsos, if the total dataset is represented as $\{x_i : 1 \leq i \leq N\}$,

$$\text{lofsos(null)} = \sum_N (x_i - \underline{x})^2,$$

where $\underline{x}$ is the overall mean, and any text on mathematical statistics shows that this can be simplified to

$$\sum (x_i^2) - \left(\sum x_i\right)^2 / N.$$

Expanding the right-hand term, this in turn reduces to

$$\{(N-1)/N\}\cdot\sum (x_i^2) - \{2/N\}\cdot\sum_{i\neq j} (x_i x_j).$$

Therefore the height of the Occam line for parameter value k is

$$[\{(N-1)/N\}\cdot\sum (x_i^2) - \{2/N\}\cdot\sum_{i\neq j} (x_i x_j)]\cdot\{(N-k)/(N-1)\}$$

$$= \{(N-k)/N\}\cdot\sum (x_j^2) - \{2/N\}.\{(N-k)/(N-1)\}\cdot\sum_{i\neq j} (x_i x_j). \quad \text{(c.1)}$$

Suppose now that I divide the actual dataset of N points into k disjoint subsets, of size $n_1, \ldots, n_k$.

The division into the k subsets can be written as

$\{x_{11}, x_{12}, \ldots\}, \{x_{21}, x_{22}, \ldots\}, \ldots, \{x_{k1}, x_{k2}, \ldots\}$, where the size of the rth subset is n_r.

What is the lofsos value for this particular division?

It is the sum of the values of the form $\sum_n (x_i - \underline{x})^2$, where n runs through the values $n_1, \ldots, n_k$, and the values of x_i for, say, the rth subset runs through the n_r values $\{x_{r1}, x_{r2}, \ldots\}$. I write the summand in the simplified form $\sum_n (x_i - \underline{x})^2$, to prevent a proliferation of subscripts. In this summand, $\underline{x}$ represents the mean of the values of x within that specific group, and what I have called the lofsos for the division is the lofsos of the model which approximates the dataset by the means of the subgroups for that division.

Each such summand can be written, using the same reasoning as above, in the form $\{(n-1)/n\}\cdot\sum(x_i^2) - \{2/n\}\cdot\sum i\neq j(x_i x_j)$, where now the summation is taken over only the values x_{ri} and x_{rj} in the rth subset, omitting the r subscript for simplicity. So the total lofsos can be written in the form

$$\sum \left[\{(n-1)/n\}\cdot\sum (x_i^2) - \{2/n\}\cdot\sum_{i\neq j} (x_i x_j) \right], \quad \text{(c.2)}$$

where the leftmost summation is taken over the subsets numbered from 1 to k, and the interior summations are taken *within* these successive subsets.

I will now show that when these expressions are taken over all the possible combinations into which the original set can be thus divided, the average value of all these expressions lies on the Occam line. By "all the possible combinations" I mean all distinct subdivisions of the original set of size N into subsets of sizes n_1 through n_k.

The result I will need is that the mean of all possible expressions of the form (c.2) must be of the form

$$\alpha \cdot \sum_i (x_i^2) + \beta \cdot \sum_{i \neq j} (x_i x_j). \tag{c.3}$$

The summations in (c.3) are taken over all the values of $\{x_i : 1 \leq i \leq N\}$ in the original dataset.

A heuristic explanation for (c.3) is that when taking the average of the expressions (c.2) over all possible combinations of subsets, each datapoint is treated precisely equally: the symmetry of the situation means that the coefficient of each term x_i^2 must be equal to any other term x_j^2 for any values of i and j. Likewise, any pair (i, j) with $i \neq j$ must have the same coefficient in the final average for the term $(x_i x_j)$, for any other pair (p, q) with $p \neq q$, for the term $(x_p x_q)$.

In more mathematical terms, consider the set of expressions of the form (c.2) over all the $N! / (n_1! n_2! \ldots n_k!)$ possible subdivisions of the original dataset. This set can be operated on by members of the complete group of permutations on N objects, the symmetric group S_N, in the obvious way, with elements of S_N permuting the subscripts in the algebraic expressions. Since the set of expressions corresponds to the whole set of possible subdivisions of the dataset, the set is closed under the effect of S_N. This means that the sum of the algebraic expressions is invariant under the action of any member of S_N: any symmetric group element merely permutes the terms of the sum among themselves, leaving the sum itself unaltered. So the average of the terms, which is merely the sum of the terms divided by a constant, is also invariant. It is immediately obvious that the only expression in the terms x_i^2 and $(x_i x_j)$ with $i \neq j$ that satisfies these criteria is the one where all the terms x_i^2 have the same coefficient as one another, and likewise all the terms $(x_i x_j)$ with $i \neq j$ have the same coefficient, whence the form of (c.3) follows.

It may appear that we are very little further forward. But there is a very useful property of the original expressions of the form (c.2) which we can now exploit.

Consider one of the expressions of this form, corresponding to a particular subdivision of the dataset: it does not matter which one. Suppose we add the coefficients of the terms of the form x_i^2. In the expression

$$\sum \left[\{(n-1)/n\} \cdot \sum (x_i^2) - \{2/n\} \cdot \sum_{i \neq j} (x_i x_j) \right].$$

Consider any particular summand, which can be written

$$\{(n-1)/n\} \cdot \sum (x_i^2) - \{2/n\} \cdot \sum_{i \neq j} (x_i x_j).$$

There are n terms of the form x_i^2, each with coefficient $(n-1)/n$, so the sum of the coefficients is $n-1$. This is the case for each of the k summands, so the overall sum of the coefficients of squared terms is

$$(n_1 - 1) + \cdots + (n_k - 1) = n_1 + \cdots + n_k - k = N - k.$$

This sum of coefficients does not depend on the particular subdivision chosen. Therefore, the sum of these coefficients in the average taken over all possible subdivisions must also be $N - k$.

From (c.3), this sum is $\alpha \cdot N$, so $\alpha \cdot N = N - k$, and finally,

$$\alpha = (N - k)/N.$$

The value of β is found similarly. The sum of the coefficients for $x_i x_j$ in

$$\{(n-1)/n\} \cdot \sum (x_i^2) - \{2/n\} \cdot \sum_{i \neq j} (x_i x_j) \text{ is } -(2/n) \cdot n \cdot (n-1)/2,$$

since there are $n \cdot (n-1)/2$ ways of choosing terms $x_i x_j$ out of n possible terms, and each such term has the same coefficient $-2/n$.

This simplifies to $-(n-1)$. As before, summing this over all values of $n = n_i$ for this particular subdivision gives a total of $-(N-k)$.

The sum of the coefficients in the expression for the average, expression (c.3), must therefore also be $-(N-k)$.

The second term in (c.3), namely $\beta \cdot \Sigma_{i \neq j}(x_i x_j)$, is taken over all such pairs from the set $\{x_i : 1 \leq i \leq N\}$, of which there are $N(N-1)/2$ terms, each with the same coefficient β. These coefficients sum to $\beta \cdot N(N-1)/2$ which by the previous calculation is equal to $-(N-k)$.

Therefore $\beta = -2(N-k)/N(N-1)$.

Substituting these values in (c.3), we have the following : the result of averaging all possible expressions of the form (c.2) must be of the form

$$\{(N-k)/N\} \cdot \sum (x_i^2) - 2\{(N-k)/N(N-1)\} \cdot \sum_{i \neq j} (x_i x_j), \qquad \text{(c.4)}$$

and this expression is seen to be identical to (c.1), which lies on the Occam line.

Therefore this point on the Occam line represents the lofsos that we would expect for a k-parameter model consisting of k groups, if the k groups were chosen entirely at random subject to the first one having n_1 points, the second one having n_2, and so on.

Clearly if this is the case, then any model which plots on the Occam line and which consists of k groups with n_1, etc. points, is doing no better than if the points had been grouped entirely at random. Such a model is certainly not telling us anything useful about the data.

What about the general k-parameter model with k groups? Any such model must specify in advance the size of the subgroups, and therefore can be analyzed as above, with the values of n_1 as given. Since the point on the Occam line depends only on the value of k and not on the sizes of the subgroups, the same analysis applies, and the same conclusion follows: the model must plot below the line in order to have any kind of merit.

Glossary

A priori hypothesis: a research hypothesis that is generated before the collection and analysis of data takes place. It can often be formulated in terms of a contrast or a set of contrasts.

Additive effects: in multivariate ANOVA, the main effects of a pair of IVs are additive if there is no interaction between the IVs. In that case, the difference in the effects on a DV due to the simultaneous change in the two IVs is equal to the sum of the separate differences. For example, if the effect on the DV of fixing IV2 and changing IV1 from level 1 to level 2 is to increase the DV by five units, and if the effect on the DV of fixing IV1 and changing IV2 from level 1 to level 2 is to increase the DV by three units, then the effect of simultaneously changing IV1 and IV2 from level 1 to level 2 will be to increase the DV by eight units, on average.

ANOVA: analysis of variance, a general approach which includes a great variety of methods of statistical analysis. They have in common a mechanism for dividing the variability in a set of data into a group of non-overlapping effects, such as main effects and interactions, and provide a method for testing whether the individual effects differ significantly from null effects. See also RM ANOVA, mixed ANOVA.

Bacon paradigm: a version of the hypothetico-deductive method in which an experiment is designed to distinguish between a number of possible rival hypotheses. It may incorporate an experimental intervention, and involves observation of some effect or effects, with the expectation that it will provide useful information as to which hypothesis is true.

Balanced design: one in which the number of participants (or other experimental units) in each cell are equal. See Cell.

Bar chart: a visual means of displaying the association between a nominal IV and a scale DV, in which different levels of the IV correspond to distinct, non-touching bars on a horizontal axis and the average of the DV for each value of IV is represented by the height of the bar above the horizontal axis. It is possible to display more than one IV using elaboration of the basic idea, for example two IVs can be represented using a clustered bar chart.

Basic model equation: the conceptual link between a dataset and a model represented as data = model + error. The model term attempts to reproduce the original data as closely as possible, by minimising the error term.

Before–after two group design: a variant of the randomised controlled trial in which the value of a DV is measured in participants of both treatment and control groups at a certain time point before treatment, and then again after treatment. It is often analysed by comparing the gain scores in the two groups. See also gain score.

Bell curve: a common name for the normal or Gaussian distribution curve.

Bessel's correction: a correction applied to the usual formula for calculating variance in a population, when estimating the population variance from a random sample. The population variance is found by subtracting the population mean from each measurement, squaring the results, adding them and dividing by the population size N. Bessel's correction consists of subtracting the sample mean from each sample value, squaring the results, adding them and dividing by $N - 1$, where N is the sample size. The purpose of Bessel's correction is to allow for the fact that the sample mean will not in general be the true value of the population mean but only an approximation to it.

Bimodal distribution: this describes the distribution of a scale variable, in a sample or a population, where there are two separate modes, or local maxima for the variable. In a sample, a bimodal distribution suggests that the variable does not have a Gaussian distribution in the population from which the sample was drawn. It may suggest that the population comprises two separate sub-populations with different means, located near the two modes of the sample distribution.

Bins: in a histogram, a simplified visual representation of the distribution of a scale variable, the values of the variable represented on the horizontal axis are divided into segments of equal length known as bins. The height of the bar of the histogram corresponding to a particular bin is the number of units with values between the bin limits, inclusive of the lower value of the bin, and exclusive of the upper value. Bin sizes and limits may be varied, giving different appearances of the histogram. In SPSS, the bin sizes are estimated by default so as to provide a histogram that provides near to the maximum information that a histogram can convey about a distribution.

Blocking: in a variant of repeated measures designs, blocking consists of grouping participants (or other experimental units) into groups which share some characteristic, or which score similar values on some measurement taken prior to the experiment. Members of a given block may be randomly allocated to different treatment conditions, one to each condition. The results may then be analysed using the blocks, rather than the original participants, as the experimental units, with RM ANOVA. Blocking is also known as matching.

Bonferroni correction: a means of negating the threat of inflation of type I error rate, when multiple comparative statistical tests are conducted on a single set of data. The correction is implemented in two different but equivalent ways, depending on whether the correction is applied by the analyst to raw *p*-values, or whether it is applied automatically in some versions of SPSS programs. In the correction implemented by the researcher directly, the alpha level (cut-off criterion for significance) assumed for the study is divided by the number of tests undertaken, and this number used as the new alpha level. In SPSS, when instructed to apply a Bonferroni correction it multiplies the uncorrected *p*-value for each test by the number of tests; the *p*-values can then be judged by comparison with the original alpha level. For example, with an alpha of 0.05 and five tests with raw *p*-values of 0.04, 0.03, 0.02, 0.008 and 0.001, the first method involves dividing 0.05 by 5 to give 0.01 and comparing this with the *p*-values, to determine that only the last two are significant at the 0.05 level. In SPSS, the raw values would be multiplied by 5 to give 0.20, 0.15, 0.10, 0.04, 0.005, and these compared with 0.05, to give the same result.

Carryover effect: in repeated measures designs, the tendency of a participant's undergoing one level of the repeated measures variable, to influence their response to a subsequent level of that variable. It can be reduced by incorporating a counterbalanced design, in which the sequence of the levels is varied for different participants.

Causal hypothesis: a form of research hypothesis in which the IV or IVs are supposed to have a causal impact on the values of the DV.

Causal model: the model which best fits the data representing a possible causal hypothesis.

Ceiling effect: it is sometimes found that varying the level of an IV beyond a certain level no longer has any effect on increasing the level of a scale DV. This may be the case if the range of variation of the DV is limited by some upper bound, such as the maximum score possible on some test of ability or the physical limitations of the human mind or body. For example, two hours a week of cardio-vascular training for a sedentary person may produce a marked improvement in fitness, four hours may produce additional improvement, but after a certain level of training a peak level of fitness will be achieved which cannot be improved upon. Ceiling effects may give rise to quantitative interactions.

Cell: a term applied to a particular combination of levels in a multifactorial design, and the collection of experimental units belonging to this combination. For example, in a three-way ANOVA combining the IVs of gender, age (old vs. young) and musical training (musicians vs. non-musicians) the group of young, female musicians would represent a single cell. The values of the IV for a participant give complete information as to which cell that participant belongs, and vice versa.

Central Limit Theorem: this states that in certain conditions the sum of a large number of independent, identically distributed random variables will tend to a Gaussian distribution as the number of variables increases, regardless of the distribution of the individual variables. It helps to account for the ubiquity of the Gaussian curve in the distribution of scale variables in nature, where multiple, small influences affect the outcome.

Complete counterbalancing: a repeated measures design in which every possible sequence of treatments is included. A completely counterbalanced design with three treatments A, B, C would include six separate groups of participants, receiving conditions in the orders ABC, ACB, BAC, BCA, CAB, CBA. Such a design would require more participants, in general, than more efficient versions such as a Latin square arrangement.

Confidence interval: a range within which a characteristic of a population can be stated to lie, with a specified level of certainty. For example, a 95% CI for a population mean μ may be given as between 13.4 and 19.6. This is sometimes interpreted as stating that there is a 95% probability that μ lies between 13.4 and 19.6. However, it is closer to the spirit of the way in which confidence intervals are calculated to state that there is a 95% probability that the boundaries of the CI estimated from the data, in this case 13.4 and 19.6, happen to include the true value of μ. The probability claim for CIs refers to the distribution of the limits, not the distribution of the population parameter, which is assumed to be fixed.

Confounding variable: a variable which has an influence on the dependent variable of interest, and which is not independent of an IV being tested for its effect on the DV. There is nothing intrinsically evil about confounds: just as a weed is a plant in the wrong place, a confound variable might be a garden variety variable which the experimenter has overlooked.

The most common type occurs in experimental studies where treatment and control groups differ not only on the treatment variable but also in a factor which affects the DV. For example, if participants are recruited from a student body and the first thirty to volunteer in semester 1 are put into the treatment group, and the following thirty who volunteer in semester 2 are put into the control group, the groups may differ systematically in ways which will have an effect on the DV. If the groups then show a significant difference in the DV, it is not safe to deduce that the difference is due to the "official" treatment variable. Confounds of this type are therefore a threat to internal validity, and may give rise to type I errors. A well designed experiment with randomised allocation and double blinding is usually sufficient to prevent this type of confound. See also Construct Confounds.

Construct confound: a type of confounding variable which varies systematically with an IV as a consequence of the way in which the IV has been operationalised, and which has an effect on a DV of interest. The difference between a construct and an ordinary confound is one of degree, and involves the extent to which the link between the confound and the IV is localised and part of poor experimental design, or is general and an intrinsic but unconsidered part of the way the IV has been implemented. In the latter case, the confound may be a threat to construct validity but not internal validity, a less serious fault.

For example, an experiment to detect the effect of vitamin C on cognitive ability in undernourished children may involve feeding the treatment group with orange juice, and the control group with an equivalent volume of clean water. If the treatment group shows a relative improvement, the researcher may conclude that the vitamin C was responsible. However, it might also have been due to the positive action of the sugar content of the drink on calorie-deprived brains. In that case, the sugar content would have been a construct confound, due to the operationalisation of the construct of vitamin C provision via the use of orange juice. If that were the case, then operationalising the same construct using vitamin C tablets would have produced no effect on cognition.

This confound can be seen as a threat to construct validity but not internal validity. Internal validity would still be intact, in the sense that the administration of juice really did lead to the cognitive improvement, but the interpretation would have been false. In that case, a government policy of feeding children orange juice might have a positive impact on child health, but not for the stated reasons.

Construct validity: a form of validity in which an effect of an IV on a DV is claimed, in which the IV and DV are stated be an operationalisation of two specific concepts, and in which the linkage between the two concepts is correctly demonstrated by the experimental outcome. In the example given in the Construct Confound entry, the claim would have construct validity if it were to be claimed that vitamin C improved cognitive ability, if the DV was an accurate measure of cognitive ability, and if the success of the intervention was indeed due to the vitamin C in the juice an not to a construct confound such as the presence of sugar.

If possible construct confounds such as the effects of sugar are taken into account at the planning stage of the experiment, they can be eliminated by good experimental design: in this case, the inclusion of a third group of children fed water with the same sugar content as the juice would allow for the elimination of this potential confound, by showing that the juice-fed children did better than the sugar-solution group. In general, it can be said that a confound is a relevant variable that the researcher has forgotten to plan for.

Contrast: a series of numbers representing a comparison between group means, or cell means in ANOVA. Each number in the contrast, known as a coefficient, refers to a particular group or cell. The coefficients in a contrast always sum to zero. Contrasts represent a means of comparing cell or group means in a statistically meaningful way. For example, in the case of a one-way ANOVA having a single IV with three levels (three groups), a contrast comparing the first two group means with one another could be written (1, −1, 0). A contrast comparing the first two group means jointly with the third group mean could be written (1, 1, −2).

A given contrast can be applied to a specific set of group or cell means by multiplying the successive contrast coefficients and means pairwise and adding the result, to give a single number. For example, the contrast (1, 1, −2) applied to the group means (12, 14, 11) would have the value $1 \times 12 + 1 \times 14 - 2 \times 11$, or 4. For a particular set of group or cell means, a specific contrast can be tested for significance using a *t*-test. Contrasts are of value because they have one degree of freedom, and a significant result can be interpreted unambiguously as a directional effect. They can be used to test complex hypotheses involving comparison between two sets of group means, or to detect linear, quadratic and higher order trends when an IV has the properties of an interval variable. Research hypotheses can often be more efficiently expressed in terms of a small number of well-focused *a priori* contrasts, rather than as general hypotheses involving potentially many pairwise comparisons of group means.

Control group: a set of participants in a randomised controlled trial who do not receive the treatment of interest. The main purpose of having a control group is to enable the researcher to estimate the value of the DV of interest in the population from which the sample was drawn, in the absence of the treatment condition. Another benefit is that it enables the researcher to allow for the fact that the measurement of the DV in laboratory conditions may be influenced by the specific circumstances of the experiment, time of day etc. If the treatment and control groups experience identical environments apart from the treatment variable, any difference can only be due to the treatment. In pretest–posttest designs, the presence of a control group also cancels out the effects of changes that participants may undergo such as maturation, which are unconnected with treatment but may have an effect on the DV.

The control group, whose main function is to safeguard internal validity, may be supplemented by an additional "placebo" group, especially in clinical trials, to protect against the threat to construct validity posed by participant expectations.

Convenience sample: limitations of time and resources sometimes make it impossible or impractical to undertake random sampling from a population of interest. In this case a researcher may choose to recruit participants from the most easily accessible source drawn from that population. This may be from patients in a clinical setting, psychology undergraduates required to obtain credits for participation, or respondents to an internet-based survey. Convenience samples may be used if it is not required to provide empirical proof that the conclusions have population validity: for example, it may be argued on theoretical grounds that common mechanisms within a population will ensure that results from a sample will generalise.

Corrected model: in the SPSS output for the results of an ANOVA, the corrected model refers to the full factorial model. The sum of squares value given in the output for the corrected model is the difference between the lack of fit sum of squares for the null and full factorial models. The significance of this model is found by calculating the F-ratio for the corrected model sum of squares and the error sum of squares.

Counterbalanced design: a repeated measures design in which carryover effects are controlled for by varying the order in which levels of the IV are applied. In the simplest case of two levels, A and B, there will be two groups, receiving the treatments in the order AB, and BA. Analysis of the data using a mixed ANOVA and including the group variable, will show the significance of the group main effect, and the group by RM variable interaction. If both are non-significant, it can be safely concluded that the results were not subject to carryover effects. With more complex RM IVs, complete counterbalancing (see above) may be impractical and more efficient designs using the principle of the Latin square and its variants may be used.

Crossover design: a term sometimes used in clinical applications to denote a type of repeated measures design, in which patients are exposed to different conditions over a period of time, but where any one person will not receive the full range of treatments included in the study. The proper analysis of crossover designs in general involves understanding random effects analysis.

Data dredging: the practice of gathering and investigating data without first laying down clear research hypotheses, and constructing such hypotheses *post hoc* on the basis of statistically significant patterns that are found in the results. If such results are presented as though the hypotheses were *a priori*, the claims will amount to scientific fraud, because they will lead to a high probability of type I errors.

Degrees of freedom: a concept which it is simplest to define in terms of model comparison. The degrees of freedom for a comparison between two models, is the difference in the number of parameters of each. The models must be directly comparable, that is, one must be nested within the other, as in the case of the full and null models in multifactorial ANOVA. Comparisons with one degree of freedom are particularly easy to interpret in terms of a single number or effect size.

Dependent variable: when a researcher wishes to test a possible causal link between a variable X and another variable Y, Y is known as the dependent variable (as Y is dependent on X). The dependent variable is measured by the researcher, and not manipulated directly. The dependent variable is usually claimed to embody a construct of interest, such as cognitive ability or emotional state, a claim which amounts to a claim of construct validity, a concept also applicable to independent variables.

Dichotomous: a type of variable defined on a sample or population which has just two distinct values.

Double blind design: a type of experimental design in which neither the participant, nor the person(s) conducting the experiment and gathering the data, have knowledge of the experimental group to which the individual participant belongs.

Ecological validity: a study has ecological validity if the results obtained will be replicated if the study is repeated in different settings, places and times. This is not the same concept as realism, though it is connected with it. Realism can be defined as freedom of confounds due to the artificial conditions of an experimental setting (such as participant anxiety).

Effect parameters: the difference between means of the groups representing different levels of an IV, and the overall data mean. They give an estimate of the effects on the DV of varying the levels of the IV, compared to a baseline represented by the average of all the groups.

Error term: the expression which represents the difference between a set of data and a model which attempts to model it. The error term is given by a set of numbers but can be given an overall numerical value by squaring the individual items and summing them, a result known as the lack of fit sum of squares or lofsos. The error values are sometimes known as the residuals.

Experimental approach: a type of research design in which the researcher manipulates the IV or IVs under test in the research hypothesis. The opposite alternative is the observational approach.

Experimental hypothesis: an essential precondition to running a hypothesis-driven study, this is a clear statement of the cause–effect or other process which it is the aim of the study to reveal. A common synonym for "research hypothesis".

External validity: the ability of a result to be replicable outside the specific sample, and the specific settings in which was tested. It can be defined as the combination of population validity with ecological validity.

Falsificationism: a theory of the philosophy of science which maintains that science advances not through confirmation of hypotheses, but by falsifying them. Popper argued that a hypothesis could never be proven correct by observation, but only refuted. Falsification of one hypothesis should result, in this view, in a new and better hypothesis which may be falsified in its turn, the net result being hypotheses that have withstood a growing list of attempts to refute them. In one approach to significance testing, the rejection of the null hypothesis at a certain level of significance is seen as an application of the idea behind falsificationism.

Familywise error rate: this is the rate at which type I errors will be introduced if a proposed series of significance tests is applied to a set of data. The FW error rate therefore depends on how the significance tests are conducted. A naïve application of standard statistical testing at a nominal threshold of, say, 0.05 will often lead to a FW error rate of much higher than 0.05. To avoid such inflation of type I error rates, various countermeasures can be adopted, including the Bonferroni correction method. The definitions in the literature of what constitutes a "family" of tests are not all mutually consistent.

Floor effect: the opposite of a "ceiling effect". This may appear if a DV has a lower limit due to physical or other constraints, which make it less sensitive to influence by the IV at the bottom end of the range of variation of the DV. For example, a reaction time is limited at the lower end as it cannot be less than zero, and scores on tests of ability will be limited similarly. The presence of a floor effect may make it appear that an interaction is present, which is in fact an artefact of the lack of responsiveness of the DV at the floor end of its range.

F-ratio: the central concept behind most orthodox statistical significance testing, this is conventionally defined as the ratio of two estimates of variance within a dataset, such that if the null hypothesis is true, the two estimates should give a similar result. A sufficiently large value of the *F*-ratio is therefore taken as evidence that the null hypothesis is false. It can also be defined from the geometry of the lofsos-parameter graph as an indicator that the plot of a model under test lies significantly below the Occam line.

Full model or **full factorial model**: the model derived in multifactorial ANOVA by approximating every data point to the mean of the cell in which it appears. It can be tested for significance using an omnibus *F*-test. One safeguard against type I errors when analysing the subsidiary effects in multifactorial ANOVA is to test the full model for significance and to proceed no further if it is not.

Gain score: in a pretest–posttest design in which the change in score between the two test periods is the variable of real interest, the result is often analysed by creating a new DV, the difference between the posttest and pretest values, known as the gain score. For this method to be valid, the experimental hypothesis should state that the error terms do not vary between groups, i.e., that there is no significant dependence of gain score on pretest score. Otherwise, the data may be better analysed using analysis of covariance.

Galton board: a means of demonstrating the formation of a Gaussian distribution from non-Gaussian random processes, invented by Sir Francis Galton. It consists of a triangular array of pins below which is a horizontal series of bins. Pinballs are poured down the array and segregate themselves into the pins in an approximately Gaussian shape. In effect, the Galton board amounts to a visual proof the Central Limit Theorem.

Games–Howell test: a statistical test which simultaneously compares all pairs of means in one-way ANOVA, detecting significant differences without inflation of type I error rates. Unlike the Tukey test, Games–Howell does not depend on homogeneity of variance for its validity, and so is preferable to Tukey when HOV is violated. When HOV can be assumed, however, the Tukey alternative is preferable since under those circumstances it is more powerful than Games–Howell.

Gaussian distribution: a mathematical abstraction, this is a probability distribution resembling a hat or bell (hence its alternative name of the bell curve) which closely approximates the distribution in populations of many scale variables in nature. Gaussian distributions all have a certain shape in common, but they differ in both mean and variance. In a sense, they are the simplest distribution a continuous variable can have, and their ubiquity is explained by the Central Limit Theorem, which predicts that many different processes will result in a Gaussian distribution (see Galton Board).

One basic assumption of the calculations behind most orthodox statistics, and in particular the calculation of significance tests for the F-ratio, is that the error distributions in models will be approximately Gaussian. This is the fundamental assumption behind all parametric statistical analysis.

Generalisability of models: the degree of confidence we may have in the accuracy to which a model derived from a specific set of data will remain an accurate representation of the whole population from which the data was derived. When comparing models derived from a set of sample data, the model which best fits the sample will not necessarily be the one which best fits the population. In fact there is a tendency for the estimate of fit from a sample to be an overestimate of fit to the population, the discrepancy increasing with the number of model parameters to be estimated from the sample. Significance testing can be seen as one means of ensuring that models with more parameters are only preferred if there is strong evidence that their population accuracy justifies it.

Group difference design: a form of independent groups study in which the separate groups are selected from distinct populations. The research hypothesis is to discover whether the populations differ on certain parameters, usually population mean scores on the value of given DV(s). The populations may be clinical groups based on a diagnosis, or natural groups based on gender or other demographic variables. It is important that all groups receive identical experiences in the research setting, as otherwise the group difference IV may be confounded by other variables. A group difference design is distinct from a non-equivalent groups design: the latter refers to groups which are as similar as possible, in cases where complete random allocation is not possible, and where treatment conditions differ across groups.

Histogram: a way of summarising the distribution of a scale variable visually. It consists of a horizontal series of rectangles whose height is proportional to the frequency of the variable within the limits represented by the bases of the rectangles. It can at a glance give an indication of the presence of outliers, bimodality or other gross departures from a Gaussian distribution.

HOV or **homogeneity of variance**: an assumption of the standard analysis of independent groups designs such as between-subjects multifactorial ANOVA. The assumption is that the variances of the populations from which the groups are drawn are equal. The assumption can be tested using Levene's test, which is carried out automatically in SPSS with independent samples t-tests, but has to be called for explicitly in ANOVA. If the result of the t-test is significance, HOV, which corresponds to the null hypothesis in this test, can be rejected. In that case, results need to be interpreted with caution. Fortunately, in most applications there are alternative tests which do not require this assumption, such as the Welch–Satterthwaite version of the t-test and the Games–Howell variant of the Tukey test.

Hypothesis: a claim concerning the presence of a process or mechanism in the real world, often in the form of a statement that a cause–effect relationship exists between two variables.

Hypothesis-driven research: a study or programme of study that is motivated by the need to test the truth or a specified hypothesis, which should be clearly stated beforehand. This contrasts with exploratory research, in which the research question may be stated in a much less specific way, but for which there is still a requirement to have stated a well-defined area of interest. No work can begin without at least a broad terms of reference.

Hypothetico-deductive method: a process of testing the truth of an explanation of a phenomenon by deducing certain consequences on the supposition that the hypothesis is true, and comparing these consequences with the results of observation. If the results of observation are inconsistent with the deductions from the hypothesis, then the original hypothesis must be incorrect.

Independent variable: in a causal relationship, it is claimed that a change in the value of a variable X will generate a change in the value of another variable Y. In this case X is termed the independent variable, and Y the dependent variable. In true experimental studies, the independent variable of interest will be subject to manipulation by the researcher.

Induction by elimination: an application of the hypothetico-deductive method to the situation where it is believed that the true explanation for some phenomenon is one of a specified set of hypotheses. If the results of an experiment are inconsistent with all but one of the hypotheses, it can be concluded that this is the true one. The method is similar to that of deducing the identity of a criminal by showing that all but one of the possible suspects could not have committed the offence.

Inferential test: a statistical procedure that tests a hypothesis about a population or populations on the basis of data from a sample. A significant value for the test enables a fact about the population(s) to be inferred from the data. For example, an inferential t-test on the difference between two group means may enable the conclusion that the population means are different.

Inflation of type I error rate: an uncontrolled increase of actual over nominal type I error rate, most often caused by carrying out multiple statistical tests of different but related hypotheses on the same set of data. If per-comparison type I error rates are fixed in relation to a standard criterion for each test, the familywise error rate for the set of tests may greatly exceed the criterion. Inflation of type I error rates requires correction, such as the use of a different statistical test designed to control error rates while doing multiple comparisons (such as Tukey's HSD), or a Bonferroni correction.

Interaction: the presence of an interaction between two IVs means that the main effects of the IVs are not independent of one another, so that the effect of one IV at a specific value of the other IV varies as the second IV varies. For example, the effect of eating a candy bar (the first IV) on pleasure (the DV) will be greater if a person has taken no food for 24 hours than if she has just eaten to repletion (second IV).

Intercept: in the SPSS univariate ANOVA output, the intercept refers to the null model, obtained from the overall mean of the data. The sum of squares value for the intercept is the difference in sum of squares fit to data between the null model and the model which approximates every data point by zero. This test is of little or no significance in ANOVA, though the concept of an intercept is important in understanding multiple regression.

Internal validity: the ability of an experimental design to enable the researcher to correctly deduce the presence of a causal relationship between independent and dependent variables from analysis of the data.

Interquartile range: the difference between the value of the 25th percentile and 75th percentile values of a scale variable. It is a measure of dispersion of a variable that is resistant to the introduction of errors due to the presence of outliers, and can be seen as a non-parametric counterpart to the standard deviation, which is sensitive to the presence of outliers and other departures from a Gaussian distribution. The interquartile range is the basis for the calculation of Tukey's box plots, which can be used as a non-parametric method for the detection of outliers.

Interval scale: this refers to a scale variable which does not have a zero point defined in terms which are meaningful for all its applications, but for which there is a well-defined concept of the interval between two points on the scale. The classic example of an interval scale is the Celsius scale of temperature, defined in terms of the triple point of water, which is physically but not thermodynamically well defined. The alternative Kelvin scale is a ratio scale, because the zero point is thermodynamically meaningful. Most psychological scale variables are effectively interval scales.

IV model: in one-way ANOVA, the IV model for a set of data is found by setting the value of a data point equal to the mean of the group to which it belongs.

Kurtosis: a measure of the symmetric departure of a distribution from the Gaussian form (a non-symmetric departure is measured by skewness). There are two versions of the formula for kurtosis: according to one version the Gaussian distribution has a value of 3, according to the other, a value of zero. The second version is more accurately known as excess kurtosis, but SPSS, and Excel, use the second version and refer to it simply as "kurtosis". For most purposes, parametric tests are robust to departures from zero kurtosis, though extreme negative scores may be a cause for concern as indicating bimodality: the minimal possible value for (excess) kurtosis is –2, occurring with a point distribution over two values. A high positive kurtosis may indicate the presence of outliers at high and low values of the variable. However, a better method of detecting outliers is generally to use boxplots.

Latin square design: a method of counterbalancing in repeated measures designs. It is a compromise version of complete counterbalancing, which may require an excessive number of permutations for the sample size. A Latin square design ensures that there will be no systematic tendency for a particular level of the RM IV to be associated with any particular order of administration. For example, a three level IV may be administered to three groups in the orders ABC, CBA, BAC. A treatment level such as A appears equally often in the first, second and third positions. Moreover, the relative position of two treatments is varied. However, not all possible effects can be accounted for: if for example the effect of C followed by A is anomalous, this cannot be detected. The assumption is usually made that such anomalous effects are unlikely.

Levene's test: a statistical test of the assumption that HOV (homogeneity of variance) is satisfied, necessary for the calculation of F-ratios to be justified. Statistical tests are usually robust to small departures from HOV, but if Levene's test is significant, this suggests that HOV may be substantially violated and alternative tests may be preferable which do not make the assumption of HOV.

Lofsos: an abbreviation used in this book for lack of fit sum of squares of a model to a dataset, calculated as the sum of the squared differences between the values of a dataset and the values predicted from the model. Fitting a model to data involves adjusting the model parameters until the lofsos is at a minimum. This process underlies most orthodox parametric statistics, and can be justified mathematically on the basis of the assumption of a Gaussian distribution of the error terms. In multiple regression, it is known as the OLS (ordinary least squares) method.

Lofsos-parameter graph: the diagram produced when models are compared on a diagram with lofsos as vertical axis and parameter number as horizontal axis.

Main effect: in multifactorial ANOVA, this is the effect that variations in one IV have on the DV, averaged over all the other values of the remaining IVs. If the IV has just two values, the main effect has one degree of freedom and can be represented as a single number, but in general the main effect can only be directly expressed as a reduction in sum of squares. In balanced designs, main effects and interactions are orthogonal, and make exclusive (non-overlapping) and exhaustive (they together account for the total) contributions to the difference between the lofsos for the null and full factorial models. A main effect can be reduced to a succession of orthogonal contrasts in different ways, which may provide a more meaningful analysis where the IV is not dichotomous.

Matching: see Blocking.

Mean: a measure of central tendency, synonymous with "average". The mean of a sample randomly selected from a population is an unbiased estimator of the population mean. The sample mean has mathematical advantages as an estimator compared with the main alternative, the sample median, but is more vulnerable to distortion by outliers.

Mean absolute deviation: a measure of dispersion in a sample, found by subtracting the sample mean from each value, converting each to a positive number and taking the mean of the resulting set. It has few if any advantages over the standard deviation as a measure of dispersion, though it may be simpler to understand.

Means plot: a visual representation of the group or cell means of a DV, useful as an indication of the form in which main effects or interactions in ANOVA manifest themselves. It is sometimes possible to make more sense of the presence of significant effects from an ANOVA in terms of the patterns relative slopes and positions of lines in a means plot, than by simply examining the numerical output of the analysis.

Measure of central tendency: a calculation which attempts to summarise the overall structure of a set of numbers, by a single central value. The commonest measures are the mean, median and mode.

Measure of dispersion: a calculation which attempts to summarise the overall tendency of a set of numbers to depart from constancy, by a single number. The commonest measures are the standard deviation, interquartile range and range. The variance, or squared standard deviation, is often used as a measure of dispersion but has the disadvantage that it measures dispersion in squared units of the original variable and is harder to interpret. The sample variance is, however, an unbiased estimator of the variance of a population from which it is randomly drawn, which is not the case for the sample standard deviation and population standard deviation.

Measurement: the process of finding a value for a variable as defined operationally, applied to specific experimental units or participants.

Median: a measure of central tendency, found as the value of the number half way up a set of numbers arranged in numerical order. If there is no single central value, the median is taken to be the average of the two numbers either side of the centre.

Mixed ANOVA: the analysis of a multifactorial dataset in which there is one or more repeated measures IV, and one or more independent groups IV. Also sometimes referred to as "split plot ANOVA".

Mode: a measure of central tendency defined as the value of a scale variable for which the frequency achieves its maximum value. It is of little direct use in analysing datasets, except that it allows for the definition of a bimodal or multimodal distribution, whose presence may indicate that a supposed homogeneous sample has in fact been drawn from distinct populations, making the interpretation of the analysis problematic.

Model: a well-defined construct, whose characteristics are fully known and predictable, which is held to have a meaningful relationship with the real world and which claims to explain or predict aspects of the world that would otherwise not be explained or predicted. A model of a dataset involves the specification of one or more numbers which define the model, known as parameters. A model is often the representative of a hypothesis, which best fits the data available.

Modus tollens: a means of reasoning which holds that if the truth of A implies the truth of B, and that if B is false, then A must also be false. A modified version of this, in which truth is replaced by probability, is used to justify the conclusion of a null hypothesis significance test.

Multifactorial design: an experimental design in which more than one IV is used together with a single DV.

Negatively skewed: a characteristic of the distribution of a population or sample, which involves a lack of symmetry, the left-hand tail of the distribution being more extended than the right-hand tail. Non-zero values of skewness are associated with departures from a Gaussian distribution, and this may make the results of parametric analyses misleading.

New experimentalism: the name of an approach to the philosophy of science which attempts to address criticisms of positivism on the grounds of its unsafe reliance on observational data as the basis for theorising. Critics pointed out that data and observations are themselves often highly dependent on theory, and rely on layers of convention and tacit understanding. The new experimentalists replace observation with an account of the whole experimental process, from which observations may arise only as a final step. In some versions, replicable experimental activity is seen as the basis from which all abstract theorising must be based, and emphasise the importance of the particular apparatus and how it is used. This approach is consistent with the importance placed on providing clear operational definitions in experimental psychology, a tendency it inherits from behaviouralism.

The new experimentalism is seen by some as providing hope that science may regain some measure of credibility for its claims of objectivity, seen has under threat since the views of thinkers such as Thomas Kuhn and Paul Feyerabend became widely accepted.

Nominal variable: a variable which takes one of a (usually small) finite number of values, and which cannot easily be regarded as lying along a single numerical scale. Nominal variables are also known as categorical variables.

Non-equivalent group design: an experimental design sometimes used when it is not possible to have random allocation to treatment and control groups. Typical non-equivalent groups might be two classes in different schools chosen to trial a new teaching method. The groups will be chosen to be as similar to one another as possible, but systematic differences cannot be ruled out so there are threats to internal validity present in this design that are not encountered in a fully randomised trial. Some of these threats can be avoided if pretesting is used as well as posttesting. If the results show a significant interaction between the group variable and the pretest–posttest repeated measures variable, an effect of treatment is indicated. The presence of a qualitative interaction between these two variables suggests a strong degree of internal validity for the conclusion that a treatment effect was found.

Normal distribution: synonymous with a Gaussian distribution, or a bell curve.

Null hypothesis: the claim that there is no effect of a specified IV on a specified DV, in a particular population or populations. The hypothesis usually takes the form of specifying that a given set of population means are all equal, though in the case of contrasts, the null hypothesis may involve a quite complex relationship between the means. The aim of a statistical analysis is usually to show that a particular null hypothesis can be rejected. However, when certain assumptions are required to hold for a statistical analysis to be valid, these assumptions are usually in the form of a null hypothesis. When subjected to a null hypothesis significance test, the best outcome is a non-significant result, in which case the assumptions are taken to be valid.

Null hypothesis significance test: an inferential test in which a significant result at a certain level of significance allows the rejection of the null hypothesis.

Null model: the model which provides the closest fit to data of all the models consistent with the null hypothesis.

Observation: the outcome of a targetted, operationally defined process resulting in a numerical value. An observation was regarded under the positivist philosophy as having an objective value independent of any assumptions, but is now seen to be dependent on a series of conventions and procedures, a viewpoint made explicit in the New Experimentalism.

Observational approach: a method of testing the effect of an IV on a DV in which the change in IV is not imposed by the experimenter, but observed passively when it happens due to other reasons. An example of a field in which the observational approach is important is the science of ethology, in which the behaviour of animals is studied in a natural environment. Observation has the benefit of revealing phenomena that may not have been predicted in advance.

Occam line: a line in a lofsos-parameter graph joining the points representing the null and saturated models. The point on the line above any value for the parameter, gives the expected value of the lofsos for a model with that number of parameters, if the null hypothesis for that model is true. It can be regarded as setting a standard which any model must exceed if it is to be preferred to the null hypothesis, and this enshrines Occam's principle in geometrical form.

Omnibus *F*-test: a test of significance in which the full model for a set of data is compared with the null model. The significance of this test can be used as a criterion for deciding whether to proceed with an examination of main effects and interactions, in order to avoid inflation of type I error rates from multiple comparisons.

One sample *t*-test: a statistical test for the null hypothesis that a given set of numbers has been sampled randomly from a population with a specified mean. This mean is often set at zero, but the SPSS one sample *t*-test allows for the insertion of a different value. The significance test for a two level repeated measures variable is equivalent to a one sample *t*-test on the difference score between the two levels.

One-way ANOVA: a between-subjects ANOVA in which a single IV is involved. If *n* IVs are present, the term used is *n*-way ANOVA.

Operational definition: usually applied to the definition of a dependent variable, but sometimes to an independent variable, this is the set of activities required to measure the variable. If this set of activities results in a measurement that does truly embody the meaning implied in the description of the variable, the definition is said to have construct validity.

Order effect: this is a type of carryover effect that may be seen with repeated measures designs. Carryover effects involve changes in response patterns due to variations in the order of administration of the RM variable. For example, a single RM variable with two levels can be administered to half the participants in the order AB, and to the other half in the order BA. An order effect exists if the performance in condition B *relative* to condition A is different between these two groups. If participants in the AB group score more highly on A than on B, but in the BA group they score more highly on B that on A, there is an order effect: coming first in the order of administration of the levels increases the value of the DV compared with coming second. The presence of an order effect can be found by analysing the counterbalancing group by repeated measures variable interaction. See also Sequence Effect.

Ordinal variable: a variable which has a naturally defined sense of direction, but no natural unit in which one can measure the difference between two levels. Therefore one might determine that the relationship between two levels of such a variable is one of greater or lesser, or positive or negative, but not the absolute magnitude of the difference.

Orthogonal effects: this refers to effects for which the sum of squares distance of the combined effect is the sum of the squares for the individual effects. It means that part of the variability in a dataset is accounted for by non-overlapping sectors due to the separate effects. Variance is most efficiently reduced by using orthogonal effects. In a balanced design, the main effects and interactions found using ANOVA are all orthogonal, and together make up the whole of the reduction in sum of squares from the null model given by the full model.

In a balanced design, two contrasts are orthogonal if their scalar product (sum of products of corresponding coefficients) is zero.

However, if the cell sizes differ, the condition for orthogonality becomes more complex.

Parameters of a model: the numbers specifying a model which are determined from the dataset itself. The parameters can be viewed as numbers which are unspecified in a hypothesis, but which are given definite values in a model. The total model in which all values are set to zero is a zero parameter model, but most models in orthodox statistics have parameters ranging from one in the null model to the number of cells in the full factorial model. This use of the word parameter is not to be confused with the definition of a parameter as a characteristic of a population of interest, such as its mean or variance, which is estimated from a value calculated from a sample, which is known as the sample statistic corresponding to that parameter.

Parametric methods of analysis: this refers to any analytical method which relies on the assumption that the error terms or residuals between the model predictions and the actual data have a Gaussian distribution. Usually there are additional assumptions, such as that the Gaussian distributions have identical mean (of zero) and variance, and that they are independent of one another.

Participants: the experimental units of a study in human psychology, the individuals who take part in the study as part of the experimental process and whose responses are the topic of the research question. The term replaces the older name of subjects, which was felt to have undesirable connotations, though the word still appears in the alternative description of repeated measures designs as within-subjects designs, and of independent group designs as between-subjects designs.

Per-comparison error rate: the alpha value or significance level adopted for an individual statistical test which is part of a series of tests. It could also be termed the nominal type I error rate. In an isolated test, the alpha value is an accurate measure of the type I error rate, but in a family of tests the error rate for the family as a whole is greater than the per-comparison error rate. This can create problems if, out of a family of tests, only a small minority are significant at a given alpha level: there may be a high probability that these are type I errors, much higher than the nominal alpha level. Alternative treatments of familywise testing include setting a lower alpha level, or using the so-called false discovery rate procedure.

Percentile: if the range of values of a scale variable in a population is ordered by value, and the lowest one percent of the population is recorded, the maximum value in this group will be the first percentile of the variable. The highest score in the lowest two percent of the population will be the second percentile, and so on. The fiftieth percentile is half way up, and so is equal to the median. For each percentile corresponds a score on the variable, and conversely each variable score gives rise to a percentile: the percentage of the population scoring at that value or lower than it.

This relationship between the percentile score for a variable and the actual value of the variable takes a mathematically determined form in the case of a standard normal distribution, for which the relation between the value of the variable (the z-score) and the percentile can be found from tables. Using such tables, the proportion of the population falling between two values, say between z-scores of 0.3 and 0.5, can be found by obtaining the percentile score for $z = 0.3$ and subtracting it from the percentile score for $z = 0.5$.

Placebo effect: if a patient in a clinical trial believes that they are receiving treatment, and expects an improvement in their condition, they may experience beneficial effects due solely to their expectations. This is known as the placebo effect. The opposite effect is called the "nocebo" effect. It has been claimed that faith healing and the effectiveness of alternative medicines may largely or wholly be due to the placebo effect. The placebo effect is a threat to the validity of a randomised trial if patients are aware which group they are in: if they are blind to their group, they may still be able to deduce membership of the treatment group from experiencing side effects of the medication. In this case it may be more effective to have two overt drug "treatment" groups, drug

A being the actual medication under trial and drug B, a placebo. The assumption is that any placebo effect will apply equally to groups A and B.

Polynomial contrasts: an expression of polynomial trends expressed in the form of contrasts, which can be applied to group means in ANOVA to generate a trend analysis. They are provided automatically in SPSS. See Trend Analysis.

Population of interest: in planning research based on sampling and inferential statistics, it is important to define in advance the population about which inferences from the sample will be drawn. Inferences from a random sample of university students may be valid for the population of students, but not for the general adult population of a country. It is particularly important to do this when the population of interest is defined in terms of a clinical condition. It is essential in this case to confirm that participants do indeed have the condition in question, either by verification from medical records or by screening using an accepted diagnostic method, such as ADOS for individuals with autism.

Population validity: this is a property of an experimental design which enables the results of inferential tests on a sample to be extended to the specified population as a whole. Random sampling from a population is in general a guarantee of population validity, though most practical studies fall some way short of this ideal.

Positively skewed: a distribution with positive skewness is asymmetric, with the longer, thinner tail extending in the positive direction. All Gaussian distributions have zero skewness, so a positively skewed distribution is by definition not Gaussian; however, most tests are robust to small values. As a rough guide, if the ratio of the skewness to its standard error is less than two, skewness can probably be ignored. In many cases positive skewness can be corrected by a mathematical transformation of the DV. Positive skewness is common in the distribution of certain variables, for example in the case of reaction times.

Post hoc comparison of means: in a one-way ANOVA there may be no specific *a priori* expectations of what the data will show. For example, in a trial of a number of alternative drug therapies, a researcher may have an open mind as to which will turn out to be most effective. In this case it may be appropriate to carry out a statistical procedure which will allow for the testing of all possible pairwise comparisons between group means.

However, as the number of groups increases, the number of comparisons goes up rapidly: with six groups there are already 15 comparisons. Using standard independent sample *t*-tests for each comparison would lead to unacceptably high familywise type I error rates. To correct for this, specific tests have been devised which control type I error rates and which are in general more powerful than multiple *t*-tests combined with a Bonferroni correction to control error rates. Tukey's HSD is appropriate when HOV holds, and Games–Howell is generally suitable when HOV is violated. The use of such methods makes a preliminary omnibus *F*-test redundant.

Posttest only control group design: another term for an RCT in which the DV is measured only at the end of the experimental treatment. It is in general less powerful than the pretest–posttest control group design, but may have compensating advantages, for example if pretesting may lead to changes in participants which interfere with the treatment; posttest only designs are also simpler and cheaper. If testing, for example of animals, involves post mortem examination, then pretesting is clearly impractical.

Powerful design: when two designs are both possible means of testing a hypothesis, it sometimes happens that one of the two will be more likely to give a significant result for a given effect size. The probability that a significant result will be obtained for a given effect size and sample size is known as the power of an experiment. It will depend not only on estimated effect size, but also on sample size as well as experimental design. Certain types of design are, however, nearly always more powerful for given effect and sample sizes: for example, repeated measures designs are generally more powerful than independent group designs. However, other factors such as the presence of serious carryover effects may make the repeated measures alternative impractical.

Pretest–posttest control group design: a type of RCT in which the DV is measured before as well as after the treatment. If certain assumptions are satisfied, this design can be analysed using the gain score (posttest value of DV — pretest value of DV) for each participant as the new dependent variable. This design is generally more powerful than the posttest only control group design.

p-**value**: the *p*-value is a number produced calculated by the application of a specific inferential test to a set of data. For example, suppose the test provides an estimate of a raw effect size, E. Then the *p*-value is the probability that a result at least as extreme as E would be produced, if the null hypothesis happened to be true. If as usually happens the null hypothesis predicts an average value for E of zero, the *p*-value would be the probability, on the assumption of the null hypothesis, that if the experiment were repeated a large number of times, the value found for the effect size would be less than –E, or greater than E.

Knowing the exact *p*-value is in most cases of little use: one merely needs to know whether it is less than the criterion adopted for significance in the test, in which case the null hypothesis can be rejected. For most cases it is more important to know the value of the effect size, and the limits within which the effect size can be confidently assumed to lie (such as the 95% confidence interval).

Qualitative (disordinal) and **quantitative (ordinal) interactions**: the presence of a significant interaction in a 2×2 ANOVA may be of two kinds. If in a line graph of the cell means the two lines either intersect or have slopes of opposite signs (or both), the interaction is qualitative; if neither of these hold, it is quantitative. The presence of a qualitative interaction generally means that attention should be focused on the interaction and not the main effects, if any, when interpreting the result. Quantitative interactions may be caused by artifacts such as floor, ceiling or scale effects.

A quantitative interaction due to a scale effect may disappear under a suitable transformation of the dependent variable.

Random error: this term may be applied in several ways. A measurement process may produce different results when applied to the same individual multiple times, due to the presence of a random error term (in this application, random errors are contrasted with systematic error, or bias, in which the measurement process produces outcomes whose average value differs from the true value of the measurement). A theoretical model of a process may incorporate a term representing a random variable, standing for the effect of additional unknown variables on the process in question. A model devised to fit a given dataset will generally fail to give an exact fit to the data: the difference is usually described as the error term, and model analysis generally assumes that the errors are random and independent.

Randomisation: this is used in experimental design to refer to the random allocation of experimental units to different treatment groups. It has a separate application to certain methods of statistical analysis, in which randomisation is applied to datasets as a means for finding a p-value when the conditions for applying standard parametric tests do not apply.

Randomised controlled trial: an experimental design in which members of a sample are randomly allocated to two or more groups, differing in the values of the independent variable whose effects are under investigation. RCTs may be single blind (participants are ignorant of which group they belong to) or double blind (both participants and the people administering the experiment are ignorant of group membership). A triple blind trial is one in which, in addition, the person analysing the results does not know the nature of the experimental groups. For this purpose, the group variable may for example be given the values 1, 2 and 3, corresponding in some order to treatment group, placebo group and control group, but the analyst will not be informed which is which until after reporting the results of the analysis. This is seen as a safeguard against "torturing the data until they confess": repeatedly applying different statistical methods until one of them gives the desired result.

Range: the difference between the largest and smallest of a set of numbers. It is common to report the range of certain so-called demographic statistics (such as the age of participants) not only as a difference score, but also to give the actual largest and smallest values in the set. It is more useful to know that the age of a sample ranged from 13 to 33 than to know that the range was 20 years.

Ratio scale: a type of interval scale variable in which a zero point is meaningfully defined. In psychology, the property of being an interval scale is sufficient for all practical purposes.

Raw effect size: the effect of an IV on a DV measured in the original units of the DV. The raw effect size is usually estimated from the sample, but the concept applies to the population from which it is drawn. For example, the difference between the group means in an RCT is a sample raw effect size. It provides an estimate for the raw effect size in the population: that is, the average effect if the treatment were applied to the whole population. It is often more meaningful to report a raw effect size together with a 95% confidence interval for its value. A raw effect size of zero for the population corresponds to the null hypothesis, so provided the inferential test was significant, the CI will lie entirely either to the positive side, or to the negative side of zero: zero is within the range of the CI only if the test is non-significant.

Recruitment: the process of identifying suitable participants for a study and obtaining their informed consent to involvement with it. The process of recruitment is important to the validity of any claims that are made about the nature of the population from which the sample was obtained, and about whether the sampling process was truly random. Recruitment may often involve compromising one of these objectives (usually the second) in order to secure the other.

Reliability of a measurement: reliability in this context usually refers to the random error component in the measurement actually produced. A reliable measurement is one with small random error, with reference to some standard, whereas an unreliable measurement has large random error. Reliability does not refer to the accuracy of a measurement: a bathroom scales that consistently under-reads by exactly 20 pounds may be highly reliable but also highly misleading.

This definition of reliability is related to the concept of test–retest reliability, which measures the consistency of scores on a test taken by the same individual at two time points. With psychological measurements, repeated testing of the same individual may introduce other spurious effects, such as test familiarity, so test–retest reliability may differ from reliability as defined above.

Replicability: a characteristic of a reported study, referring to the ability of other researchers to repeat the essential findings of the study on the basis of the details as reported. Since no study can be repeated under identical circumstances, replicability will depend on the extent to which the contextual variables can be altered without changing the results. Different types of experimental validity can be defined in terms of the robustness of the outcome to changes in these variables: for example, construct validity refers to robustness under a change of variables which operationalise the constructs claimed in the reported study.

Researcher manipulated variable: an independent variable such that there is no constraint on the researcher as to which participant may receive which level of the variable. For example, the treatment variable in an RCT is researcher manipulated.

RM ANOVA: the repeated measures version of one-way or multifactorial independent groups ANOVA. It is used to analyse the effects of independent variables in which every participant is exposed to every level of every repeated measures IV.

RM design: an experimental design in which there are a certain number of independent variables, the repeated measures IVs, for which every participant is exposed to every level of these variables. In a mixed RM ANOVA, there are in addition between-subjects variables, such that for each such variable, a participant is in one and only one level of the variable. RM designs are usually more powerful than a fully between-subjects design testing the same hypothesis. RM designs are often described as those in which each participant serves as their own control.

Sampling: the process of identifying and selecting members from a population of interest. Random sampling describes a process by which every member of the population has an equal probability of being selected. Truly random sampling is rare, though a good alternative is to use methods such as cluster sampling or stratified sampling.

Saturated model: a model based on a dataset which replicates the dataset exactly, by representing every point by itself. It has the same number of parameters as the number of points in the dataset. In a sense it is the most complex model which can be fitted to the data, and is therefore ruled out by Occam's principle, but it is of theoretical value in providing an ideal standard against which simpler models may be compared. It also provides an anchoring point in the lofsos-parameter diagram for one end of the Occam line.

Scale variable: a variable that can be treated like a continuous variable between certain limits. Scale variables should be interval or ratio scales, so that there is a well-defined unit which means the same thing at any value of the variable.

It is sometimes claimed that in practice nearly all variables in psychology are ordinal variables rather than scale variables. However, in practice, provided a variable has sufficiently many possible values, it makes little difference whether or not it is strictly an interval variable. The main criterion that a variable needs to satisfy in order to apply parametric statistical tests is not that it be an interval variable, but that the distribution of the error terms or residuals should be Gaussian. This is often ensured in practice when a variable is made up by adding together sufficiently many components. This is the case for example when a scale is created by adding the scores on twenty or thirty Likert scale items, in which responses are graded on a limited score from one to five. The Central Limit Theorem then ensures that the sum will behave like a scale variable with a Gaussian distribution. In a quote from a famous paper (Lord, 1953): "the numbers don't remember where they came from".

Scale effect: the appearance of an interaction in a 2 × 2 ANOVA which disappears under a simple transformation of the DV. Such an interaction is always quantitative, and the removal of the interaction by transformation may suggest that the results are better interpreted using the transformed variable, provided the distribution of the residuals remains Gaussian.

Sequence effect: one of the two main types of possible carryover effect in RM designs, a sequence effect is seen with two levels A, B of the IV if there is a tendency for the mean of the scores at levels A and B to be different for the participants exposed to the sequence AB, than for participants experiencing the levels in the sequence BA. A sequence effect in a counterbalanced design can be tested for by looking at the main effect of the counterbalancing group variable.

Signal-to-noise ratio: the result of dividing a number representing useful information by a number representing interference by a random noise element which is superimposed on the signal. The design aim for a communication channel is to maximise the signal-to-noise ratio, and the design aim for an experimental study is to maximise the ratio of the effect seen due to the IV to the random variation due to variability inherent in the sampling and measurement process. The determination of statistical significance using the *F*-ratio can be seen as the calculation of a signal-to-noise ratio.

Simple main effect: in multifactorial ANOVA, a simple main effect is the main effect seen when one IV is varied and the other IVs are all held constant at a specified value. For any one IV, a complete test of all possible simple main effects involves investigating the effects for each possible combination of the other IVs. In some circumstances it may be easier to interpret an outcome in terms of one or more simple main effects than in terms of the standard division of the variance into main effects, interactions and error.

Single blind design: a type of randomised trial in which participants are not aware to which trial group they belong, with the aim of avoiding effects due to participant expectations, which may threaten construct validity.

Skewness: a measure of how far a sample distribution may depart from being Gaussian, resulting in a non-symmetrical histogram. Skewness may be positive or negative. Skewness may be due to a small number of outliers in one tail of the sample, when removal of the outliers may eliminate the skewness, or it may be due to an inherent asymmetry in the underlying population, in which case a suitable transformation of the DV may provide a solution.

Sphericity: an assumption required for the validity of the standard analysis of RM ANOVA, when the RM IV has three or more levels. It is tested in SPSS by Mauchly's test of sphericity, the null hypothesis being that sphericity holds. In the event that the test is significant, SPSS provides alternative versions of the RM ANOVA analysis which remain valid. Sphericity is the analogue for RM designs of homogeneity of variance for between-subjects designs.

If the purpose of an RM design is simply to carry out a trend analysis, testing for sphericity is not necessary, since all such contrasts are equivalent to one sample t-tests which do not make the assumption of sphericity.

Standard deviation: a measure of dispersion found by taking the square root of the variance. The standard deviation is subject to bias when outliers are present, so tests for outliers based on calculating the sample standard deviation are not reliable; tests based on a non-parametric measure of dispersion such as Tukey's boxplots (which use the interquartile range as a measure of dispersion) are preferable. A standard convention is to use σ to denote the standard deviation of a given population, and s to denote the standard deviation found from a sample drawn from that population.

Standard error of the mean: if a population mean, denoted μ, is estimated by finding the mean M of a sample of size N drawn from it, the distribution of M under repeated sampling will according to the Central Limit Theorem tend to a Gaussian distribution with mean μ and standard deviation $\sigma/\sqrt{N}$. If σ is estimated using the sample standard deviation s, this leads to the conclusion that the true value of the population mean is distributed around the sample mean M in a way that resembles a Gaussian distribution with standard deviation $s/\sqrt{N}$. In fact, orthodox statistics does not allow us to make such a strong claim — it is M that varies randomly, not μ — but in calculating confidence intervals for the true position of μ given M, can be treated as a random variable distributed as $N(M, s^2/N)$, with mean M and variance s^2/N. For example, a 95% CI can be approximated as the interval $M \pm 2s/\sqrt{N}$. The statistic $s/\sqrt{N}$ is known as the standard error of the mean.

Standard normal distribution: the uniquely defined normal or Gaussian distribution with a mean of zero and variance of one, also written $N(0, 1)$.

Student's *t*-test: also known as the independent samples *t*-test, this is a test of significance applied to two sample groups, taken from a population in which neither the mean nor the standard deviation is known. The test can be seen as calculating a signal-to-noise ratio, in which the signal is the difference between the means of the two groups, and the noise is a measure of the random variability of the difference between group means, calculated by pooling the variance of the DV over the two groups. The null hypothesis is that the two population means are equal, and the *t*-test determines whether the sample mean difference is far enough from zero that the null hypothesis can be rejected. The *t*-test can be seen as equivalent to the *F*-ratio test of significance with $F = t^2$.

Sum of squares distance: a measure of the extent to which a model departs from a perfect description of a dataset, found by squaring and adding the differences between the model predictions and the actual values.

Systematic error: a characteristic of a measurement process in which repeated measurement of the same experimental unit would, on average, be different from the true value of the measurement for that unit, whereas random errors would by themselves in the long run average out to zero.

Test of assumptions: parametric tests usually rely on a series of assumptions about the distributions involved, such as a Gaussian distribution of residuals, or homogeneity of variance. Such assumptions should be tested before parametric analysis is uncritically applied to the data, since otherwise spurious type I errors may result. Most tests of assumptions are in the form of significance tests, where usually the null hypothesis consists of the assumption under test. The convention is adopted that if the significance test does not give a positive result, then the null hypothesis is not rejected and the assumption can be assumed to hold. Some regard this convention as controversial.

Test–retest reliability: a measure of how similar the results of a psychometric test will be when taken on the same individual over two periods of time. Any test claiming to measure a long lasting characteristic of a person such as a personality trait should have high test–retest reliability. Reliability is calculated by administering the test to a sample of individuals, and retesting them after a specified period: the correlation between the two sets of data measures the reliability. Test–retest reliability may depend on the period of time separating the tests: in general, the longer the separation, the lower the reliability.

Total model: the term I have used to designate the model which approximates every point in a dataset by zero; the term was suggested by the fact that SPSS gives the lofsos for this model is given in the row headed Total in the univariate ANOVA output.

Treatment group: in an RCT, the group of participants which are exposed to the treatment, whose effect on the DV it is desired to investigate.

Trend analysis: if a nominal IV in an ANOVA analysis has an interpretation as lying on the values of an interval variable, the effect on the DV may be analysed using trend analysis, even if only a small number of values for the IV are used. Trend analysis approximates the values of the sample group means using a set of orthogonal contrasts corresponding to linear, quadratic and sometimes cubic polynomials: contrasts of higher degree are rare. A trend analysis can also be carried out on a RM IV. Trend analysis can answer research questions of interest when investigating dose-response curves, and can help in predicting the response to values of the IV which have not been included in the study. The contrasts comprising the analysis are subject to independent significance testing, and some precaution should be taken against type I error rate inflation if multiple contrasts are used.

Tukey's HSD test: Tukey's "Honestly Significant Difference" test can be applied to a single IV in ANOVA when it is required to explore the full set of relationships between all pairs of group means. It is generally a more powerful test than the alternative of using multiple *t*-tests with a Bonferroni correction.

Type I error rate: if a statistical test or series of tests is proposed, the type I error rate is the proportion of times such tests would give a significant result, if the experiment were to be repeated over and over again, and on the assumption that the null hypothesis was true. In other words, the type I error rate is the rate at which the experimental and testing setup would generate false positives if the null were true. Given that type I errors are generally seen as more damaging than type II errors and therefore should be avoided as a priority, much effort is devoted to minimising type I error rates, and at the very least, keeping the rate below some upper bound considered acceptable.

Unbiased estimator: an estimator is a means of calculating a number derived from a sample of data, known as a statistic, which is considered to be an estimate of an important characteristic of the population, known as a parameter of that population. An estimator is unbiased provided that, if a large number of samples were drawn repeatedly from the same population, the mean value of the statistic derived from the sample would converge to the value of the population parameter.

The sample mean is an unbiased estimator of the population mean, and the sample variance (calculated using Bessel's correction) is an unbiased estimator of the population variance.

Validity of a measurement: validity for a measurement refers to the property that if measurements are repeatedly taken of the same unit, the mean of the set of measurements will converge to the true value of the measured variable. A high degree of validity for a measurement is the same as a low level of systematic bias.

Variance: a measure of dispersion that is more commonly used in the form of its square root, known as the standard deviation.

z-score: a standard measure of the value of a scale variable with a Gaussian distribution, given in terms of the distance of the value above or below the population mean, in units of the standard deviation. For example, the z-score for an IQ score in terms of a population with a mean of 100 and a standard deviation of 15, is found by subtracting 100 from the score, and dividing the result by 15. z-scores are useful among other reasons because every z-score gives a corresponding percentile, consisting of the percentage of the population scoring at or below that level. From this, given two z-scores, the percentage of the population lying between these limits can be found by subtracting the percentile for the lower z-score from the percentile for the higher z-score.

Further Reading

Having made the decision to base this book on model comparison, I looked round for previous coverage of the subject intended for students of the behavioural sciences. I found just two texts of this kind using the model comparison approach to orthodox statistics: "Data analysis: a model comparison approach" by Charles Judd and Gary McClelland, and "Designing experiments and analysing data. A model comparison perspective", by Scott Maxwell and Harold Delaney. The first book is a relatively gentle introduction to the subject; the second is more demanding mathematically, and generally more thorough, with the exception of the important topic of multiple regression to which it makes only a brief reference.

Both books have proved very useful to me in helping to understand the topic and in suggesting ways of explaining it, and I would recommend that anyone wishing to take the subject further should, if not acquire the books for themselves, at least borrow them from a college library and compare how they cover the topics included here.

While in the final stages of preparing this book for publication I became aware of a third book: "Psychologie statistique avec R" by Yvonnick Noël. It apparently covers both orthodox ("Fisherian" as Noël terms it) and Bayesian statistics from a model comparison perspective. I have not read the book, but it may well turn out to be important. This raises the point, worth making for those unfamiliar with it, that all Bayesian inference involves model comparison; Bayesians will wonder what all the fuss is about. The fact is that however familiar it may be to Bayesians, proponents of orthodox statistics have yet to become fully aware of model comparison.

For those whose interest in Bayesian statistics has been piqued, a superb introduction aimed specifically at psychologists is "Understanding psychology as a science", by Zoltán Dienes. The book is far more than simply an introduction to Bayesianism: in a lively and penetrating way it covers the central philosophical aspects of how we acquire knowledge, as well as explaining an interesting modification of Bayesianism based on likelihood. And the book is, by textbook standards, reasonably priced. It is probably a "best buy" out of all these.

For more material on the AIC and BIC (Akaike Information Criterion and Bayesian Information Criterion) I recommend "Model selection and multimodel inference: a practical information-theoretic approach", by Kenneth Burnham. Burnham seems to favour the AIC, which is based on information theory, over the BIC, which is derived from a Bayesian approach, though he suggests that the AIC can also be viewed from a Bayesian perspective. Both the AIC and BIC incorporate Occam's principle into model comparison, though they have different ways of penalising model complexity. The controversy over which approach is "better" continues: at least, if it has been resolved, the news has not filtered down to those of us working at the coal face.

The paper by Lord (1953) referred to in the Glossary, entitled "On the statistical treatment of football numbers", can be found online at:

http://www-stat.wharton.upenn.edu/~hwainer/Readings/
Frederick%20Lord_On%20the%20statistical%20treatment%20
of%20football%20numbers.pdf

The present book has a restricted coverage of the details of experimental design, and of the considerable literature on such things as validity. Maxwell and Delaney have a short but remarkably enlightening section on validity in their chapter 1, but anyone wanting to understand the area in depth could do worse than to go back to the pioneering book on the topic, "Experimental and quasi-experimental designs for research" by Donald Campbell and Julian Stanley, or its successive editions by Cook and Campbell, or by Shadish, Cook and Campbell.

Entering "The New Experimentalism" on a well known search engine produces over 400,000 entries. Out of this mass of information I would suggest that anything by Deborah Mayo is worth reading, and a good introduction to NE can be found in her 1994 paper at:

http://www.phil.vt.edu/dmayo/personal_website/%281994%29%20The%20New%20Experimentalism,%20Topical%20Hypotheses,%20and%20Learning%20from%20Error.pdf

Those interested in going more deeply into the philosophy of Karl Popper from his own writings might start with "Conjectures and refutations: the growth of scientific knowledge". For a contrasting view, it is worth reading Thomas Kuhn's short but brilliant work: "The structure of scientific revolutions".

Few practising researchers of any great distinction have written on the philosophy of scientific method, but Peter Medawar did so with matchless panache. The collection of essays and reviews in "Pluto's Republic" expounds not only his practical grasp of Popper's ideas, but also acknowledges the contribution of those such as Claude Bernard who anticipated Popper.

To this list I can add Sir James Frazer, whose massive work "The Golden Bough" is a classic of Victorian anthropology. Page 62 of the one volume abridgement (of the twelve volume 1922 edition) published in the Wordsworth Reference Series, contains the following passage: "The slow, the never-ending approach to truth consists in perpetually forming and testing hypotheses, accepting those which at the time seem to fit the facts, and rejecting the others". Written twelve years before Popper's first statement of his own views in "The logic of scientific discovery", this is the best concise explanation of falsificationism that I have encountered. Perhaps psychologists should take heart from this demonstration that you do not have to be a physicist or a philosopher to understand how science works.

References

Abelson, R. P. (1995). *Statistics as Principled Argument*. Hillsdale, NJ: Lawrence Erlbaum.

Ashby, W. R. (1964). *An Itroduction to Cybernetics*. London: Methuen.

Burnham, K. (2013). *Model Selection and Multimodel Inference: A Practical Information-Theoretic Approach*. New York: Springer.

Campbell, D. and Stanley, J. (1966). *Experimental and Quasi-experimental Designs for Research*. Boston: Houghton Mifflin.

Chalmers, A. F. (1999). *What is This Thing Called Science?* Maidenhead: Open University Press.

Dienes, Z. (2008). *Understanding Psychology as a Science: An Introduction to Scientific and Statistical Inference*. Basingstoke: Palgrave Macmillan.

Fisher, R. A. (1935). *The Design of Experiments*. Edinburgh: Oliver and Boyd.

Frazer, J. (1993). *The Golden Bough: A Study in Magic and Religion*. Ware: Wordsworth Editions (Original work published 1922).

Gadian, D. G. and Vargha-Khadem, F. (2000). Magnetic resonance and memory function in children with focal brain damage. *Revue De Neuropsychologie* **10**(3), 405–416.

Gibbon, G. (1989). *Explanation in Archaeology*. Oxford: Basil Blackwell.

Gower, B. (1997). *Scientific Method: An Historical and Philosophical Introduction*. London: Routledge.

Harré, R. (1997). An outline of the main methods for social psychology. In N. Hayes (ed.), *Doing Qualitative Analysis in Psychology* (pp. 17–38). Hove: Psychology Press.

Hladký, V. and Havlíček, J. (2013). Was Tinbergen an Aristotelian? Comparison of Tinbergen's four whys and Aristotle's four causes. *Human Ethology Bulletin* **28**(4), 3–11.

Holland, P. W. (1986). Statistics and causal inference. *Journal of the American Statistical Association* **81**(396), 945–960.

Judd, C. and McClelland, G. (2009). *Data Analysis: A Model Comparison Approach*. Oxford: Routledge.

Kirkby, J. A., Blythe, H. I., Drieghe, D. and Liversedge, S. P. (2011). Reading text increases binocular disparity in dyslexic children. *PLoS One*, **6**(11), 7.

Kuhn, T. (1962). *The Structure of Scientific Revolutions*. Chicago: University of Chicago Press.

Maxwell, S. and Delaney, H. (2000). *Designing Experiments and Analyzing Data: A Model Comparison Perspective*. New Jersey: Lawrence Erlbaum Associates.

Medawar, P. (1984). *Pluto's Republic*. Oxford: Oxford University Press.

Mitchell, M. and Jolley, J. M. (2007). *Research Design Explained*. Belmont, CA: Thomson Wadsworth.

Noël, Y. (2013). *Psychologie statistique avec R*. Paris: Springer.

Popper, K. (1963). *Conjectures and Refutations: The Growth of Scientific Knowledge*. Oxford: Routledge and Kegan Paul.

Urbach, P. (1987). *Francis Bacon's Philosophy of Science*. La Salle, Ill: Open Court.

Wilkinson, L., *et al*. (1999). Statistical methods in psychology journals: Guidelines and explanations. *American Psychologist* **54**(8), 594–604.

NOTE

The Hladký paper is available for free download at: http://ishe.org/wp-content/uploads/2015/04/HEB_2013_28_4_3-11.pdf

The Wilkinson paper is available at: http://www.cs.uic.edu/~wilkinson/Publications/apasig.pdf

Index

Made in the USA
Monee, IL
18 September 2020